UNTIL THERE IS JUSTICE

UNTIL THERE IS JUSTICE

The Life of Anna Arnold Hedgeman

Jennifer Scanlon

OXFORD
UNIVERSITY PRESS

Oxford University Press is a department of the University of Oxford. It furthers
the University's objective of excellence in research, scholarship, and education
by publishing worldwide. Oxford is a registered trade mark of Oxford University
Press in the UK and certain other countries.

Published in the United States of America by Oxford University Press
198 Madison Avenue, New York, NY 10016, United States of America.

Cataloging-in-Publication data is on file at the Library of Congress.
ISBN 978-0-19-024859-8

9 8 7 6 5 4 3 2 1
Printed by Edwards Brothers, USA

Frontispiece: Anna Arnold Hedgeman looks out between A. Philip Randolph
and Martin Luther King Jr. The photograph invites us to take her seriously in a movement
in which they all played vital roles.
Courtesy National Afro-American Museum and Cultural Center

We will not rest until there is justice in our beloved country and we know that as justice comes to all Americans, it will come in increasing measure to the people of the world.

ANNA ARNOLD HEDGEMAN, *The Trumpet Sounds*

CONTENTS

UNTIL THERE IS JUSTICE

PROLOGUE

A PURPOSEFUL LIFE

New York City, 1934: In the midst of the Great Depression, widespread unemployment and a near halt in industrial production meant, for all too many urban dwellers, falling wages, fruitless job searches, squalid living conditions, and dire poverty. It was bad all around, yet African American residents of New York City were particularly hard hit compared with their white neighbors. Being white in New York literally doubled one's chances of securing employment.[1] On top of that, discrimination ran rampant in the distribution of essential welfare services for those who, try as they might, remained unemployed through the worst of the nation's deprivation. Anna Arnold Hedgeman, New York City's first consultant on racial problems, was frustrated that no blacks were in decision-making positions with any real power, and she quit her job to try to change things from the outside. She then secured the first 150 civil service appointments given to black Americans in the city of New York.

Washington, DC, 1948: On the eve of the national election, Democratic president Harry Truman faced potential party splits from the left, right, and center, and it seemed clear that, for the first time, the African American vote might well swing the election. Anna Arnold Hedgeman became the Democratic Party's strategist for securing the black vote in key states and gave a series of speeches from her own, race-based, whistle-stop tour, helping to fortify the black vote and keep the incumbent in office.

New York City, 1966: As the black freedom coalition seemed to be unraveling, most of the major civil rights leaders anxiously refuted cries of and for black power, and a generational divide appeared certain between civil rights and black power advocates. Anna Arnold Hedgeman urged the older generation, of which she was, not incidentally, a part, to do more listening than talking, to try and make sense of the nascent but insistent claims for power. She admonished Martin Luther King Jr. that "what love opposes is precisely the misuse and abuse of power, not power itself."[2]

Until There Is Justice is a history of America's black freedom struggles as seen through the life and work of Anna Arnold Hedgeman, a remarkable—and remarkably understudied—twentieth-century civil rights leader, educator, social service worker, policymaker, religious activist, and politician. She played a key role in more than half a century of social justice initiatives, altering the civil rights landscape with her ideas, determination, and accomplishments. She made the choice to make a difference, and to do it with conscience and dignity. Although most Americans have not heard of her, her life story demands a full-scale biography. It also offers readers both a number of surprises and a sense of national pride in a woman we should collectively recognize and claim as our own. In telling the inspiring story of Hedgeman's singular life, *Until There Is Justice* recasts key elements of America's civil rights history, placing an exceptional woman in the central role she earned and deserves.

Anna Arnold Hedgeman played a vital role in more than six decades of racial justice efforts. She worked as a teacher in the Deep South and grappled with a segregated YWCA as an executive in the North during the 1920s; she was an emergency relief worker and supervisor in New York City during the Great Depression, a fair employment practices advocate in Washington during World War II, a national political appointee in health and human services in the postwar period, and an assistant to New York City's Mayor Robert F. Wagner Jr. in the 1950s; and she was a critical advocate for civil rights legislation in the 1960s and 1970s. She ran for political office three times, helped pass major civil rights legislation, and worked as the only female member of the organizing committee that planned the famed 1963 March on Washington.

The events of Hedgeman's life would be reason enough for a biography, but her experiences also provide a window into the ways in which Americans tangled with critical questions about personal, religious, and national identity as they moved through the twentieth century. Born into a family of midwestern pioneers, Hedgeman was often a pioneer herself. She was both proud of and frustrated by her many "firsts": the first black student to attend Hamline University in St. Paul, Minnesota, the first black woman to run for Congress in the Bronx, the first woman and first African American to join a mayoral cabinet in New York City, and the keynote speaker at the first joint African American–African women's conference, in Ghana.

She was raised to seek excellence and showcase her talents, yet Hedgeman had to wonder what her life would have been like had she not felt the need to fight relentlessly for racial justice. One white woman she encountered, she lamented, "was a little taken aback when I told her that I had been forced to spend my whole life discussing the implications of color and that this was to me a waste of time and of whatever talent I had."[3] Her "waste" was clearly the nation's gain. Her lifelong practice of questioning and challenging common assumptions about race, gender, and Christian ethics provides an invaluable lens to explore social change and the cost to those who make it happen.

Hedgeman's life and work transcended many shifts in African American history, and she struggled at times to figure out where she fit in to such a long freedom struggle. She played a key role in politics during the move American blacks made from the party of Lincoln to the Democratic Party. She participated in a community of struggle to achieve interracialism, which most often mirrored her personal, political, and religious needs but which also occasionally conflicted with a desire, born of frustration, for black separatism. She attempted to raise issues of gender in a prefeminist era and then struggled with white feminists as a founding member of the National Organization for Women.

She traveled to Ghana but found the "welcome home" to Africa complicated by how American the trip also made her feel. She struggled to understand how her religious life fit with her political life, how to integrate civil rights and black power philosophies and demands, and, perhaps most important, how to foster lasting social change. She interacted on a close professional and personal level with many of the movement's most well-known male leaders, and she alternately deferred to them and resisted their authority. The March on Washington provides a characteristic example of the significance of Hedgeman's life story. At A. Philip Randolph's invitation, she joined the administrative committee for the march. She also took responsibility, in her job at the National Council of Churches (NCC), for inviting or, better yet, summoning, thirty thousand white Protestants to the march. Drawing on her long-standing relationships in government and in the black, religious, and women's communities she had served, she worked tirelessly to get the message out to white Christians about the hazards of racism, for them as well as for black Americans, and the NCC later estimated that forty thousand people had marched under its banner.[4] Anna Arnold Hedgeman, to put it simply, recruited the majority of white attendees to the March on Washington. She also advocated, with some limited success, for the inclusion of more black women in the planning and implementation of the march, and in the immediate aftermath of the march she played a central role in the passage of related civil rights legislation.

The 1963 March on Washington played a key and then formative role in the nation's history. Its direct results included legislation, most notably the Civil Rights Act of 1964 and the Voting Rights Act of 1965. Over time it provided a model for mass mobilization that would bring life to the women's, antiwar, environmental, LGBTQ, and disability rights movements. Hedgeman and other black women played essential roles in the organizing that led up to the march, as well as in the larger civil rights struggle of which the march was a part. Their styles

of leadership and activism, as well as their own understandings of the intersections of race and class and gender, shaped the movement in important and lasting ways. Yet before and during the march, women were largely ignored by the
male organizational leadership and by the media. Since then, these women have
been, with few exceptions, ignored by historians as well.[5] Hedgeman's contributions to the march, paired with her attempts to get the male leaders to embrace
gender as well as racial justice, provide a critical new lens for understanding the
civil rights movement's limits as well as its legacies.

By all accounts, Hedgeman should have been one of the speakers at the
March on Washington. She was an established leader with a long history of
energizing crowds and moving them to action. She had served on the planning
committee for the march from day one. But the male leaders balked, refusing to
consider women as speakers and remaining unwilling or unable to acknowledge,
own, or eradicate the deep discrimination they practiced. The irony was not lost
on Hedgeman. As proud as she was of the interracial and interfaith effort, she
felt angry listening to Dr. King's speech, wishing he had claimed "We Have a
Dream" rather than "I Have a Dream," acknowledging the far larger collective of
which black women were an essential part.[6]

Given the resistance she encountered in her work on the March on
Washington, and in other civil rights endeavors over her long life, Anna Arnold
Hedgeman felt at times bitter and humiliated. She met resistance from male organizers who dismissed her entreaties for the full involvement of women, activists
who scorned policy initiatives and policymakers who dismissed the potential of
mass movements, and white religious and civic leaders who felt that the march,
or other solitary events, formed ends in themselves. She relied on her faith and
her family as she resolutely carried on. Because she viewed racism and sexism as
religious assaults, and as damaging to perpetrators as they were to victims, and
because she attempted to articulate those concerns to a wide variety of audiences,
her life story uncovers many of the critical complexities of the nation's continuing march toward dignity, equality, and justice for all its citizens.

In "Oughta Be a Woman," the poet June Jordan explores the ways in which
Americans, black and white, have depended so thoroughly on black women but
then also paid them so little mind. "What do you think would be her surprise,"
Jordan writes of the black woman, "if the world was as willing as she's able."[7]
Hedgeman had such a world in her sights, and she drew the nation a bit closer
to it. Her long and fascinating life provides a meditation on some of the most
enormous changes in our nation's last century, as well as on the still unfinished
social justice work ahead of us. Anna Arnold Hedgeman's life story encourages
us, still, to be as willing as she was able.

1 A MIDWESTERN CHILDHOOD

Anoka, Minnesota, 1900. The main street was three blocks long. There was no mail delivery. The jail was so lacking that the only prisoner in recent memory who had been placed there overnight parted the bars and walked out of town before the sun came up. There were trees to climb, frogs to catch, dogs to chase, penny candy to be savored, and drugstore lunch counter stools to swivel on. Children bathed often in summer, in the river, but during the rest of the year they suffered through Saturday night soaks in the tub; the oldest children got the cleanest bath. There was church to attend, of course, and neighbors to visit.

Report cards came home on occasion, and parents looked first at "deportment," because if behavior was not up to their standards, nothing else mattered much. Now and then those same parents would take their children with them on the train, "going below" to the city of Minneapolis, but most of the time children traveled only as far as their own legs could carry them. There were surnames to learn to pronounce, since the candy store owner was Greek, the laundry owner was Chinese, and the mill, shoe factory, logging, and agricultural workers were an eclectic mix of Germans, Poles, Swedes, Norwegians, Finns, and Irish. Only one black family, the Arnolds, lived in town, and as one might imagine, their history of migration and settlement, and some elements of their everyday lives, differed a bit from those of their friends and neighbors.[1]

Anna Arnold, born in 1899 in Marshalltown, Iowa, and raised in Anoka, was the descendant of black migrants who had made their way north and west, looking for the better life that vast expanses of land seemed to promise. Her people, she would explain with pride throughout her life, were pioneers, resourceful men and women who braved poverty, discrimination, and the elements in order to create new lives for themselves and their children. She loved to recount the stories her parents, William and Marie Arnold, told of their families' lives on the frontier, and she did so with reverence, understanding that what had seemed harsh in their approach to life and family was also what had gotten them through.[2]

Anoka got its name from both the Dakota and the Chippewa Indians: in Dakota, it means "on both sides"; in Chippewa, it means "laborer," "labor," or "work." Both meanings are apt for the mill town sitting on both sides of the Rum River. Living in Anoka was a deliberate decision on the part of William Arnold. He had, as his daughter put it, "rejected city streets" and refused to raise his children in his wife's hometown of St. Paul. Instead, the Arnolds lived in a rambling twelve-room house, right in town, with climbing trees and a garden. The children spent a great deal of time outdoors.

Anoka prided itself on the very characteristics William had sought. "Travel where you will, from rocky Maine to variegated California," the town's boosterish 1889 history claimed, "and you will find no more enterprising and thriving farmers than those of Anoka County." Prospective settlers would have "the advantage of good society" while they educated their children in fine public schools, took one or both of the local weekly newspapers, and earned decent money.[3] Another Anoka publication reflecting on life at the turn of the century was perhaps a bit more reliable and a little less self-promoting. People in Anoka worked long and hard, the publication acknowledged, in agriculture, logging, and factory work. Even with their struggles, the availability of fresh food meant that few people would go hungry.[4] Indeed, Anna Arnold Hedgeman would remember Anoka in much this way: "There was no poverty in Anoka as I have come to know it in the slums of our urban centers. I had not realized that a man could need bread and not be able to get it."[5]

Although white people in Anoka, indeed in much of Minnesota, had little contact with black people, and although the Arnolds were somewhat of a curiosity in their small town, African Americans did have a history, and a few distinct communities in the Twin Cities—Minneapolis and St. Paul—and the state had a history of efforts on behalf of racial justice. Before emancipation, Southerners who brought slaves with them when they visited resorts in Minnesota sometimes roused a good deal of anger in the local white citizens. In one instance, a Southern military colonel brought an enslaved woman, Eliza Winston, along on his family vacation. Through the wife of the local black barber, Winston made contact with a group of white citizens who took her case to court; the judge sided with Mrs. Winston, who subsequently headed north to Canada.[6]

Minnesota was a strong supporter of the Union during the Civil War. It was the first state to offer troops to Abraham Lincoln, and eight men from Anoka claimed to have been among the first to sign up. In all, more than twenty thousand Minnesotans served, including more than one hundred African Americans.

Given that the census of 1860 reported only 259 blacks in the state, their contribution to the war effort was significant.[7]

During the war, another group of black pioneers moved from the South to settle in the Twin Cities. By one account they found assistance for their relocation from Union soldiers; by another they towed their boat up the Mississippi River behind a steamer. They called themselves pilgrims and founded Pilgrim Baptist Church in St. Paul.[8] Anna was related, through her mother, Marie, to some of those pilgrims.[9] Marie's father, a porter in charge of railroad magnate James J. Hill's private railway car, was proud to have been born free, and he always carried his papers with him. The family name, Parker, had originally been Parquet in New Orleans, suggesting Cajun ancestry, but the family anglicized the name as they made their way north. Marie's mother died when Marie was only three, but her father lived long enough that her children had the opportunity to know their grandfather.[10]

Members of the Twin Cities pilgrim group founded a black newspaper in 1885 and secured posts in the fire, police, and postal departments in the 1880s.[11] They formed enough of a community to draw Frederick Douglass and Booker T. Washington to town for lectures.[12] But discrimination accompanied integration in the Twin Cities as elsewhere. In 1894, a black railroad porter named John Blair saved the lives of a group of passengers involved in a devastating railway fire. The train's engineer and crewman were feted in a ceremony afterward, but Blair went unrecognized. Black citizens subsequently hosted their own celebration, during which several of the surviving white passengers also expressed their gratitude for Blair's heroism. By the time of Anna Arnold's childhood, black communities in St. Paul and Minneapolis were home to barbers, clerks, carpenters, tailors, lawyers, and government workers. But outside of the Twin Cities, families like the Arnolds remained, in significant ways, pioneers.

Anna's father, William James Arnold II, was born on a farm in Greenville, South Carolina, most likely, according to family lore, the grandson of the farm's owner, as he shared not only the man's name but also his light complexion. The Arnold farm was a busy place, engaged in blacksmithing, horse training, growing flowers, agriculture, and animal husbandry. When emancipation arrived, the farm's owner did not inform William's parents that they were free. His mother later confronted the owner: "Miss Mary," she demanded, "why didn't you tell me I was free?" Mary Arnold begged her not to leave the farm, promising a good life if she were to stay. "My children need education just like your children need education," William's mother informed her, well aware that the promised "good life" included hard manual labor rather than opportunities for advancement for her generation or the next, and the family moved on as soon as they could. All of the Arnold children received an education, and two of William's siblings, Anna's uncles, became teachers.

William attended Atlanta University for part of elementary school and all of high school and college. Although it is surprising now to read of a college that contained within it an elementary and secondary school, black institutions in the South recognized that they had the responsibility to prepare young people to one day be ready for the college education they themselves provided. At Atlanta University, Anna's father studied with William Crogman, a West Indian who had studied at Atlanta, taught there, and become the college's first black president.[13] Every student learned a trade in addition to an academic course of study. William Arnold learned harness making as his trade; through Crogman's influence, he also became a scholar of the classics.[14]

Following his college graduation in 1890, William Arnold left the South for the open spaces of North Dakota, where he became involved in regional land development. An entrepreneurial man, he exercised significant influence, developing what became the North Dakota Chamber of Commerce. When, to their surprise, some of the local people discovered the light-skinned Arnold was African American, they promptly gave him the gift of a watch and sent him on his way. As the story was passed on to the children, William often had this experience, of being thought white for a time. "He was so aggressive," recalled daughter Olive with pride. "Nobody thought a black man would be like that." From North Dakota, Arnold moved to South Dakota, again engaging in land development and also coming up with a plan to bottle and sell mineral water, a venture in which he was about a hundred years ahead of his time.[15]

William Arnold continued to move around the Midwest and, on a trip to Chicago, met Marie Ellen Parker, who was there to study with one of the most famous black actors of the time, Richard B. Harrison. Marie left the theater to marry William, in 1897, and they moved to her hometown of St. Paul. The couple briefly moved to Iowa, where Anna was born, but they soon returned to Minnesota, settling into a life in Anoka, roughly thirty miles from St. Paul.

From his home base in Anoka, William Arnold proposed a program for regional development in the Midwest that caught the attention of industry, clergy, educators, and chambers of commerce in five states. He traveled often, to and through those states, delivering lectures and helping to create policy.

In one Minnesota census William Arnold is listed as a lecturer, in another as a newspaper editor.[16] A talented singer, he was also part of a traveling singing group that presented "Songs and Stories of the Southland." He might have worked for one of the fourteen black newspapers published in the Twin Cities between 1876 and 1930, but given his work, it is more likely that he edited some kind of business publication.[17] At any rate, he made a good living, providing for his family and maintaining ownership of a house and an automobile through the economic ups and downs of the early years of the century. Anna would later say about her father, "The pioneering spirit of the southern Negro and the pioneering experience of the western United States somehow meshed, and a crusading settler was the result."[18]

Anna's formidable father was an enormous, lifelong influence, and she had a great deal more to say about him than she did about her mother, but however quiet and understated a presence, Marie Arnold was influential as well. She softened the rigidity of life with William, without, as Anna explained, "in any way demeaning the efforts he was making and adding to it many, many times in her own way."[19] Each day after school Marie led the children in a study session around the big dining table, and she ran the household during her husband's frequent absences, usually according to his rules.

Occasionally, though, the children turned to their mother to help them side-step their father. When Anna's sister Blanche got fed up and decided to take a turn at dancing, a forbidden activity in their conservative Christian household, Marie found out about it. Not only did Marie not reprimand Blanche, but, more important, she did not tell her husband. Anna thought her mother had "a broader sensibility" than her father. One can imagine that, like many women, Marie had to manage her husband as well as her six children. She certainly had enormous responsibilities. Feeding eight family members was no mean feat: she baked eight loaves of bread a week, sewed the family's clothing, made candy, gardened, and canned potatoes, beets, and other vegetables.[20]

Although Marie had been raised Catholic, the family attended the Methodist church, where William served on the board; in religion, as in most things, William Arnold had his way. Marie was also involved in the church and community, attending meetings and participating in bake sales and other fundraisers.[21] Although she was less stern than William, she expected her children to demonstrate significant self-sufficiency at an early age. Olive, the baby of the family, had to dress herself and put on her own shoes by age three. Because of her asthma, Marie occasionally put Anna in charge of the family for periods of time, but no disability prevented her from living and embracing the role of the pioneer wife: hardworking and purposeful, involved in the community, and mostly in agreement with her domineering spouse.

The culture of the Anoka community both encouraged and inhibited young Anna's national and racial identity. Her neighbors told stories of their homelands, of Poland and Finland, Ireland and Norway. That was clearly part of their identity, but they also stressed their love of their new home, the United States. Likewise, Anna's mother, a proud American, regaled her children with tales of courageous black pioneers, and her father spoke with reverence of the African

American people he had grown up with, stating, simply, that "South Carolina Negroes are superior."[22]

But while Anna heard these stories at home, outside her home, in school and among her neighbors, the Arnold family's African ancestry was never part of the conversation the way their neighbors' European ethnicity was. Later in life, when somebody complained that most white people did not understand the history of American blacks, Anna smiled: as a child, neither had she. In her hometown, she would explain wryly, "we were Norwegian, Swedish, Irish and German."[23] Africa, for the young Anna, as much as for her neighbors, "was a jungle to which we sent our missionary money by way of tiny missionary boxes."[24]

Having had little experience with African Americans, some of the people in Anoka, as had happened before, initially believed William Arnold to be white. He never failed to admit to being African American if it came up, but he found no reason to bring up race when introducing himself. As a result, it might be some time before people realized they were dealing with, perhaps even taking direction from, a black man. Although it had not worked out for him in North Dakota, most of the time William Arnold maintained his standing. "By the time his color was discovered," Anna explained, "he had already been able to communicate any idea with which he was concerned."[25] In an interview decades after her father's death, when she was asked if the townspeople in Anoka accepted him, Anna was blunt. The issue was not whether he was accepted. "He decided," she stated simply. She conceded that her family faced some challenges from neighbors on account of race. "But my father, believe it or not, helped run that town."[26]

From young Anna's point of view, the most significant social difference in Anoka was not race but religion, and she readily absorbed the prejudices that circulated in her Methodist congregation. The wealthy Congregationalists, she believed, would have trouble getting into heaven. The Catholics, who heard from the pope every day, had divided loyalties and might not actually be loyal Americans. When a Catholic friend invited Anna to Sunday Mass, she went, with some trepidation. She found it far less troubling than she had anticipated. Yes, the building was ornate, filled with images of saints, but there was not much else to complain about. But when Anna invited her friend to attend the Methodist church the following Sunday, and the girl's parents refused, Anna was insulted and indignant: "I finished with Catholics that day."[27]

Even though she knew that her own mother had been raised Catholic, Anna embraced the Midwestern distrust of the faith. There were rumors that the local nuns would usher children under their robes into the basement of the convent, from which they might never return, and Anna believed it. When her father took her to the convent for piano lessons, she was terrified. She grew to adore the sister who taught her piano, but ran past the other nuns and tried desperately to avoid any contact with the mother superior.[28] The steeple-lined town did not offer significant religious diversity. There was one Jewish family in Anoka, but they left after a year, tired of having to travel to Minneapolis to find any sense of community.[29]

Protestant values held sway, and if business was William Arnold's vocation, eliminating the "demon rum" from people's lives was surely his avocation. As a local head of the antialcohol league, Arnold, according to his daughters, served on the committee that, seated around the family's dining table, thrashed out a rough draft of the amendment eventually introduced in Congress.[30] It is not clear how many saloons William Arnold succeeded in closing, or how many lives he changed when he was "speechifying all over the place" during the years of Prohibition, but his work would have gained him both friends and enemies.[31] In the early twentieth century, Minnesota's population, largely immigrant, nevertheless had its divisions, and they often related to alcohol. The farmers tended to be Scandinavian, Lutheran, fairly settled, socially conservative, and "dry." The miners and meatpacking workers, from Finland and Ireland and southern Europe, tended to be more transient and far less conservative, and they enjoyed a drink. Towns farther out on the frontier were known for gambling, prostitution, and violence, which often accompanied the whiskey trade, but even the subdued town of Anoka had thirteen saloons for fewer than five thousand residents.[32] Both the "wets" and the "drys" stereotyped the other group, and differences among the various ethnic groups were often described as "racial."[33]

This interethnic divide may have helped provide a space within which the Arnold family existed. They were not, after all, the only ones whose whiteness was contested in Minnesota at this time.[34] William Arnold's ability to speak on behalf of temperance, and to get things done, earned him a solid place among the proponents of Prohibition—earning him and his family, perhaps, at least in part, a right to "whiteness."

2 EDUCATION

THE FIRST MEASURE OF INDEPENDENCE

William Arnold was no less demanding at home than he was out in the world. "The almost fanatical desire for education engendered by former slave parents was part of [Father's] inheritance," Anna remembered. There was no question but that the Arnold children would excel in school. Each child had assigned chores at home, and their work was inspected. They were all expected to play the piano, regardless of interest or talent. "One lived to work, plan, study, discipline one's self, search for truth and pray for God's guidance," Anna remembered later.[1]

Sunday, the Lord's Day, was, for the children, "painful." Play in the Arnold household was "strictly limited" every day, but on Sundays, all activity stopped. They attended church as a family, but afterward and for the rest of the day the children could not read the Sunday comics, listen to music other than hymns, or engage in any active play. The only thing they were allowed to do was to take a walk.[2] They were all quite pleased when William purchased a family car and began taking the whole brood for Sunday drives, with the youngest, Olive, tucked in between her parents in the front seat.[3] William was constantly pointing out "the beauty of the trees, the lakes and plains of wheat,"[4] which, Anna suspected, was out of guilt for doing something as pleasant as taking a drive on the Lord's Day.

As exacting as William and Marie were as parents, they also enjoyed a laugh, and the family often had a good time around the dining table. When William's mother visited and gave the evening prayer, the children joked that the biscuits were always cold by the time they ate because their grandmother prayed for so many people.[5]

Occasionally, the Arnold children even got away with joking about their father. Whenever they had company, William Arnold would dramatically recount the tale of Olive's near-fatal childhood illness. As he was getting toward the end, one of the boys would run to the kitchen and shout, "Put the potatoes on! Dad has Olive at the pearly gates!"[6] They also made fun of their father's driving, which they found intolerably slow. "Should we get out and push?" they would tease.[7]

Before Anna was born, Marie Arnold gave birth to a son, Charles Raymond, but the baby became ill and died in infancy. All of the children, but perhaps Anna more than the rest, had to contend with the specter of Charles Raymond, who would have been not only the eldest but also the firstborn son.[8] William's very high expectations for Anna were raised even higher by the loss of Charles Raymond. By age six, she had learned to read and felt ready for school, but her father did not want her exposed to influences outside of the home yet. One imagines that her mother would have been ready to see her go, given the other children she had to take care of, but William's word was law.[9]

The gender expectations in the Arnold family caused Anna some confusion. Her father had great hopes for Anna in particular, as the oldest and the successor to Charles Raymond—perhaps too great. She took pride in her academic accomplishments, but she also learned that girls were expected to be feminine, to look pretty. Sadly, she believed those qualities fell to her sisters Grayce and Blanche, but not to her. "Mother tried to compensate for this by flattering comments about my disposition, my ability to read and my goodness to my little sister," she wrote later. "But what child wants even these treasured compliments if she senses that other children have the beauty she lacks?"[10] Anna was raised to keep achievement and service at the forefront of her consciousness, but realistically, she knew that beauty would have been an asset.

Anna desperately wanted to please her parents, but she found it especially challenging where her father was concerned. "I was afraid of Father," she remembered later, "because he always seemed to expect more of me than I could do."[11] She tried to meet William's expectations, both stated and unstated. On Sunday nights the family had what they called a "program." The children would review the day's sermon and Sunday school lesson, recite poetry, play the piano, and sing. Once again, Anna was at a disadvantage; two of her sisters could sing beautifully, but she was tone-deaf. She redeemed herself by playing mistress of ceremonies. Anna tried to hide just how much she enjoyed the role, as it allowed her to be what she thought she was naturally, a bossy older sister.[12]

All the Arnold children were careful not to appear overly confident in their own abilities. They also learned early not to expect praise, particularly from William. One day, after having memorized ten pages of a reading, Anna wanted to show off for her father. She proudly announced that she could recite the entire ten pages. William took the text from her, looked it over, and asked her who had written it. She did not know. Shaken, she told him it was a class assignment. He had not asked that, he told her. Who was the author? When she could not answer, he informed her that they should not talk about the piece given that Anna had no information about who had written the work or where the author came from.[13]

When Anna was sixteen, she asked to attend the county fair. Her father was against it. She pleaded, so he listed the myriad reasons he was against her going—and then told her it was up to her. He was famous for that, and she hated the position it put her in. Anna complained bitterly to her mother, but Marie simply attempted to explain William's reasoning.[14] On another occasion, her parents took a trip to Minneapolis for supplies, leaving Anna in charge. She orchestrated a major cleaning of all twelve rooms of the house. The children even cleaned up the barn and cut the grass, and then "each of us slicked up within an inch of our lives." When their parents returned home, Marie sang their praises, but William only pointed out that they had failed to empty the coal scuttle. Anna retreated to her room to sulk. William eventually came in and asked what was wrong. Prompted by his gentle tone, she poured her heart out to him, explaining that he never seemed to see any good in what she and her siblings did. Expecting an apology, she was crushed when he instead told her never to expect praise in life. "You will discover that is your vulnerable spot," he warned. It was a tough charge for a child: serving without praise, always being obedient to God and her father, never expecting anything in return.[15]

William Arnold's sternness was legendary in Anoka, and some parents would use him as a barometer: if Mr. Arnold said an activity was acceptable for his children, it was certainly OK for theirs. One night, Anna attended a church function and was due home at 9:00 p.m., just as the refreshments were served. Feeling it was impolite to leave, and wanting to stay, Anna began to eat. The phone rang, and on the other end her father asked the minister why he was keeping the Arnold children out so late. When the minister had the audacity to tell him they had just started eating, and to ask if they couldn't stay a bit longer, William Arnold was furious. "Please send my children home," he replied curtly. "I shall discuss this with the Board of Trustees on Monday." Needless to say, he did.[16]

William Arnold's formidable presence was stifling at times, but he also encouraged in Anna a strength, particularly where religion was concerned. The family prayed together twice a day and attended services every week, and Anna loved church. She found the minister stern, serious about God like her father was, but also lively and friendly. On top of that, he talked about God in ways that made sense to her.[17] When Anna learned she would have to actively join the church to formalize her relationship to God, she was confident enough in that relationship to tell the minister "there was no need to ask for forgiveness of my sins since I had always obeyed my parents and . . . no need to pray for me especially, since I prayed for myself every day."[18]

However idyllic Anoka, Minnesota, seemed to William, the Arnold family encountered occasional instances of racial prejudice. One of Anna's classmates later recalled that people in Anoka "weren't really used to dealing with black people," but that an elementary school teacher she shared with Anna "tried to do her best."[19] It is not clear what "doing her best" entailed, but the remark suggests that the Arnolds were not always looked upon as simply one of the many ethnic families in town. The most hurtful of Anna's experiences with racial prejudice occurred right in her neighborhood. She was often welcomed on her way home from school by a young neighbor, a child named Isabel, who inevitably greeted her with a kiss on the cheek. One day the girl asked Anna if it was true that she was a "nigger." "Although I had never heard the word before," Anna wrote years later, "I knew from the tone in which the child said it that it was not a good thing."[20]

Anna escorted Isabel home and told the child's mother what she had said. Isabel's mother, clearly embarrassed, insisted that Isabel had not heard the word from her, then gave her daughter a severe spanking to make her point. Horrified by the name-calling and the spanking both, Anna went home and asked her own mother for an explanation. Marie Arnold told her that demeaning names existed for all the people in their neighborhood, the Swedes, the Italians, and the Irish, but that Anna must never use "such un-Christian names," for all races had to be respected. "If anyone calls you a name of this kind," she told her, "you must realize he is not an intelligent person. Ask the Lord to forgive him and then forget about it."[21] That was the end of it, at least for her mother. For Anna the pain lingered, particularly because little Isabel never again met her at the end of the school day.[22]

The white families in Anoka may have found the Arnold family curious, and at times may have treated them with suspicion or disdain, but some also took pride in having such an accomplished family in their midst. The town librarian appreciated Anna's studiousness and always had a book waiting on her desk, specially selected, when Anna went in for a visit. Most of her teachers also treated Anna with respect, perhaps recognizing her talents, but also possibly fearing William Arnold, who would not stand for anything less. And the whole town took pride in Olive, who was well known for her piano playing, distinguished herself in the state high school music competitions, and would go on to become a singer and composer. A classmate bragged about Olive's performances, claiming that "all us Anokans almost 'busted our buttons' with pride."[23]

Nevertheless, Olive never forgot the slights they encountered growing up the only black children in their elementary and high schools. After Anna's death, she wrote, "The sad fact is that racism was carefully choreographed in those days, and even our warmest and closest friends and associates had no real knowledge of the Negro's history and contributions to American life." Without specifically listing the everyday indignities, she continued, "There were many acts of prejudice that we had to combat on a daily basis."[24]

Issues around race would have come to a head for the Arnold children when they reached puberty—that is, if their father had allowed them to date. William, of course, had no use for that. In his opinion, books and romance did not mix, and graduation from college was soon enough for a first date. "We also knew that we must not think of white boys in terms of romance," Anna remembered later. "I didn't understand this because I only knew white boys and they seemed nice enough."[25] It may well be that her father's prohibition, which her mother went along with, was as much to protect Anna from the community's racism as it was to protect her from boys. Regardless of her parents' reasoning, the teenage Anna found it all terribly confusing. When she developed a crush on a boy at school, her parents expressly told her it was not to be pursued. They also let her know that that particular young man was not worthy of her, but one suspects she would have been hard-pressed to come up with somebody who did not elicit the same response.

One Easter, when Anna and her sisters received an invitation to visit their mother's friends and family in St. Paul, their father actually consented to the trip; until that point, William had orchestrated family visits so that they took place in Anoka rather than in the Twin Cities. Anna was elated. She was going to meet and spend time with black people. She had grown up hearing about other black people more than actually interacting with them, outside of her extended family, at least. Her father had told her tales of the distinguished African American men he had gone to school with at Atlanta University, who had gone on to accomplish great things. Her mother had delighted the Arnold children with tales of the black pioneers, those valiant ancestors who left the South to make a better life. All this left Anna with high expectations for St. Paul's African American community.

"They were the fearless ones," she believed. "They were the salt of the earth."[26] She had grown up surrounded by white people and, no doubt, loved many of them. "I loved the Doyles next door as much as any neighbors I will ever have," she wrote later of their Irish neighbors.[27] But black people by and large remained a mystery, one she was finally going to crack.

Anna's excitement increased when she discovered that the trip included not just African American people in general but black teens in particular. For this she had her mother to thank. William was initially opposed to his daughters venturing to St. Paul, and he complained bitterly that he was not trying to raise socialites. But this time, Marie persevered and somehow won out, and Anna found herself on her way, expectations high. "The trip to St. Paul, on Easter

Sunday, was a step then toward a kind of 'promised land.' " It did turn out to be wonderful, but given how high Anna's expectations had been, she was bound to be at least a bit disappointed. She found the families warm and welcoming, or "brown and welcoming," as she put it. She met a group of African American teens, including Edith Ella Adams, whose father was the owner of the respected black newspaper the *Appeal*. Blonde and very "Irish-looking," Edith frightened Anna with her "quiet sophistication" and demonstrated to her that the range of skin tones among black Americans extended well beyond the range within her own family. Then there was Courtney Hillyard, who seemed to the naive Anna a "brown Casanova," and who nearly struck her dumb, "for I had no light conversation at my command." Roy Wilkins, who would become editor of the *Appeal* before becoming famous as editor of the *Crisis*, and then executive director of the National Association for the Advancement of Colored People (NAACP), was there as well.[28] Anna met some of the residents of "Oatmeal Hill," the bluff overlooking downtown that had been settled by the city's black elite, some of whom had first made their way to Minnesota during the Civil War.[29]

Anna returned home ebullient but also a bit disconcerted. The boys seemed to her, more or less, just like the white boys she was friendly with at Anoka High School; they did not impress her as she had hoped and expected. Nevertheless, she had gotten a taste of what it meant to have a social life and looked forward to continuing it. Unfortunately, once William learned just how much socializing they had done, including having teenage boys over to Marie's sister's house, he was incensed: that was the end of social visits to St. Paul for his daughters. They would thereafter be safely staying in Anoka. Anna would have been far more distraught over this development had she not been a senior at Anoka High School. She knew that college, even if it did not involve dating, would inevitably include some relief from her father's impossibly strict dictates. And college, for Anna Arnold, was only a few short months away.

Few of Anna's peers at Anoka High School pursued higher education, even though graduation guaranteed admission to the state university, but there was no question that the "brilliant and popular" Anna Arnold would attend college.[30] And from her father's perspective, there was little question about where she would go. One might expect that William Arnold, a graduate of one of the southern Historically Black Colleges and Universities (HBCUs), most of which were coeducational from the start, would want his oldest child to have a similar experience. But as a Methodist community leader with little tolerance for secularism and a desire to keep his daughter close, William had his eye on Hamline University in St. Paul, just thirty miles away. Not only was Hamline a Methodist school, but William had a personal connection to the college. Hamline's president, Dr. Samuel Fletcher Kerfoot, whom he considered a "gracious Christian gentleman," had worked with William Arnold on the Prohibition amendment.[31]

Named in honor of Methodist bishop Leonidas Lent Hamline, who raised the funds for its construction, Hamline University was academically distinguished and the oldest college in the state, founded when Minnesota was still a territory.[32] It seemed an ideal placement. With Anna safely in the hands of the Methodists, and less than an hour away, William Arnold would see her often enough to remind her of his expectations for her, both academically and socially. Anna, who never even considered that she might select her own college, was equally delighted to venture off to St. Paul and Hamline.[33]

By all accounts, the fall of 1918 was a punishing time for Minnesotans, as it was for the rest of the nation. Newspapers published long lists of local men who lost their lives in the bloody "Great War" in Europe. Fires in the forests of northern Minnesota combined to form the worst natural disaster in the state's history, killing nearly five hundred people, injuring or displacing more than fifty thousand, destroying nearly forty communities, and blackening a quarter of a million acres of land. The influenza pandemic that killed nearly fifty million people across the globe affected seventy-five thousand Minnesotans and claimed the lives of more than ten thousand. Unlike most influenzas, which killed those whose health was in some way compromised, this flu ravaged populations of previously healthy young adults, so panic about its spread triggered the closing of churches, schools, saloons, dance halls, public libraries, and theaters, lessening people's contact with the infected but increasing their isolation. For many, it must have felt like the apocalypse.[34]

Anna Arnold was in many ways a typical young person. Her concerns in the fall of 1918 were more about the particulars of her own life than any national or global calamities. She was, after all, leaving home and entering college, and no one in her immediate family fought in World War I or contracted the flu. With her fellow students at Hamline University, she would march through St. Paul in November to celebrate the end of the war, and to thank those who had served, but her everyday life was largely free of adult concerns. Anna knew that her life would someday be about service to others, but for now, she was focused, intently and selfishly, in the way of the young, on herself and her prospects in the world.[35]

Hamline was among the first coeducational universities in the nation. The college's first students, a group of seventy-two young men and women, initially attended classes on the second floor of the general store in the village of Red Wing, in 1856. The two women in that class, sisters Elizabeth and Emily Sorin, would have been enrolled in the "Lady Baccalaureate of Arts" program, which modified the male curriculum by omitting the study of Greek, abridging

Latin and mathematics, and offering instead French, German, and the fine arts. Ladies, Hamline's founders seemed to think, had an "abridged" intellectual capacity. The St. Paul campus opened in 1880, and by the time Anna arrived at Hamline in September 1918, women and men pursued the same curriculum.[36] They remained fairly segregated socially, however, and most of Anna's college memories involved her fellow coeds rather than any particular young men.

Hamline University did not attract an especially progressive student body, even during the Progressive Era. A class orator in 1891 had explained to the student body that immigrants, because of their "false religious training," lacked "stern Puritan piety" and featured instead a disposition to criminality. The editor of the student newspaper in 1896 submitted that the urban poor had only themselves to blame for their disordered lives. The campus was less blatantly anti-Catholic and anti-immigrant by the time Anna arrived, but as the first black student at Hamline, she found that people, both students and faculty, sometimes stiffened in her presence.[37] Minnesota's African American population at the time was confined by and large to a few neighborhoods in the Twin Cities, and most of Anna's fellow students would have had little if any contact with black Minnesotans. One St. Paul business college specifically advertised that "colored persons" were not welcome as students, but most schools probably felt little need to advertise a prohibition that was unlikely to be challenged.[38]

As much as William Arnold believed he had given Hamline University a gift by enrolling his daughter, he did have to abide by some rules about race that, however unspoken, remained firm. He told Anna he would not allow her to live on campus, but it is more likely that was the school's decision.[39] He secured a room for his daughter in the home of old friends, Methodist minister Frank Doran and his wife, who lived within walking distance of campus. Anna, who lived there throughout her college years, enjoyed Mrs. Doran's company but was sometimes embarrassed by her effusive compliments. "I get a lot more pleasure out of having Anna in my home than I did with my own daughter," Mrs. Doran told visitors. Years later it occurred to Anna that this may have been the white woman's response to criticism for letting Anna reside with her.[40] At the time, however, the confident, self-possessed, and still very young Anna would probably have agreed that the Dorans benefited from the arrangement as much as she did.

Either because of campus unease about her presence, or simply because she was so eager to get on with things, Anna was first in line for course registration in the fall of 1918. Once she had completed her schedule, she stayed back to help Mary Poston, the girl who stood in line behind her. A tall, Irish redhead from the almost completely Norwegian American town of Thief River Falls, in northwest Minnesota, Mary Poston would become Anna's closest friend at Hamline. That first night they discovered that they had been raised with similar, small-town, conservative Christian values, including the idea that dancing was sinful. Arriving at a social gathering in the women's lounge of the main building, Goheen Hall, they were dismayed to find girls dancing around the room with each other. When the dean not only did not intervene but actually seemed to approve of the scandalous behavior, Anna and Mary wondered how this could be tolerated.

Uncomfortable as they were, Anna and Mary made a decision: for fear of being called home for good, they would not tell their parents about what they had witnessed. As time went by, the girls spent many hours together, roaming around the campus and the city, arguing and making up their own minds about sin and salvation, and ultimately enlarging their ideas about the place of religion in their lives.[41] In this way and others, Hamline played a major role in forming the adult Anna would become.[42] She attended every subsequent dance, including the coed ones, but while the other girls had their dance cards signed by young men, Anna introduced a "sit-out card." The men would sign it and take turns sitting out a dance with her, talking about books and ideas "and all the rest."[43]

Dancing aside, Anna Arnold found Hamline to be, in many ways, an extension of home. Instead of gathering with her family twice a day for prayers at the dining table, she attended daily chapel services. As her father had, the college stressed Christian training for service to life, "not money, not position, not power."[44] There was "nothing casual," she remembered, in their love of books and ideas. "One must find a sense of the wholeness of all things," Professor Gregory Dexter Wolcott lectured, "or you won't become whole."[45] Anna had never had male teachers before, but she responded well to the almost all-male faculty, probably because of her experience attempting to meet her father's expectations. She chose English as her major largely because of Professor Thomas Percival Beyer, whom she considered the consummate teacher, scholar, and citizen.[46] Her professors, like her father, wanted her to search for truth. Unlike her father, however, many of the faculty at Hamline had broader definitions of truth seeking and challenged Anna to re-examine her own assumptions, explore new ideas, and express opinions, even controversial ones. She responded well, finding enormous rewards in particular in the study of religion, especially the class "Varieties of Religious Experience," based on William James's controversial book of the same title, which demonstrated to her just how parochial her own training had been.[47]

As enlightened as Anna considered herself to be, a female faculty member at Hamline created a good deal of trauma for her and her friend Mary. The woman and her husband both taught in the sciences, which by itself encouraged a great deal of gossip among the students. But when the professor continued to work and sit on the faculty platform at chapel once she was visibly pregnant, Anna and Mary were appalled. What if she gave birth in the chapel? After a good deal of anguished deliberation, they decided again that it was no time for letters home. Instead, in a letter to Mary's sister, a social worker in New York City, they shared their dismay and embarrassment. The sister's reply was not what they had expected: "Since when has pregnancy become shameful and hidden?" she admonished. She sent them some literature about pregnancy, and they quieted down. Nevertheless, the two young women were relieved when the baby was born in a hospital and not in the chapel.[48]

Anna spent her days at Hamline studying, attending concerts and plays, going to the gymnasium for activities, attending chapel, and reading, always reading. She felt engaged, independent, and happy. Bigotry occasionally invaded her relatively comfortable college life, though. Her parents would have counseled her to simply ignore the ignorant, but the idea that deeds accompanied truths had come to mean more and more to the young scholar, and she began to engage in provocation as well as submission in the face of discrimination. One English teacher, for example, let it be known that he did not approve of Anna's presence on campus. She subsequently made it a point to visit all of his classes.[49]

In another instance, when Anna and Mary enrolled in the same public speaking class, the professor put them in separate divisions, explaining to Mary's division, clearly for her benefit, that while it was all right for blacks to attend college, it was unnecessary for whites to befriend them. In response, Anna took him on, subtly. For the class presentation, she read aloud Wendell Phillip's eulogy to famed black revolutionary Toussaint L'Ouverture. She opened the oration with a flair, exclaiming to the thirty blue-eyed students, "Now, blue-eyed Saxon, proud of your race, go back with me to the commencement of the century, and select what statesman you please." She continued, revealing the majesty of L'Ouverture and concluding with the eulogy's argument that his story overshadowed that of any statesmen her audience could put forward and claim as their own.[50]

Anna received a standing ovation from the class, "for I had put the passion engendered by the teacher's rejection into it," but the professor merely bowed his head, mumbled, "Very good; next," and moved on. Her victory tempered, Anna drew next on her parents' counsel to meet such ignorance by ignoring it. For the rest of her time at Hamline, she determined, "He did not exist for me."[51]

Anna Arnold continually found it confounding as well as challenging that white Christians could behave in such a manner, but she also learned that she would have to pick and choose when and how to respond to prejudice. She would also have to count on her white allies. Anna and Mary both suspected at the time that Mary's older sister, whom they had relied on as their mentor during and after her years at Hamline, was rejected by the college literary society because of their friendship. Resisting or giving in to racism—both had their costs, for the white girls as well as the black.[52]

During her sophomore year, Anna had an experience that, significant as it seemed then, grew even more in importance over time. Her Spanish professor invited the students to a lecture by a famous black leader none of them had heard of. Because black leaders never visited campus, and few visited the Midwest at all, Anna was intrigued, but she was downright astonished by the palpable enthusiasm of the crowd at the fully packed St. Paul church. Then, in stepped W. E. B. Du Bois, who offered her the thrill of celebrity, the dazzle of erudition, the manifestation of dignity. He spoke about his recent time in Paris, and to Anna, who had never considered traveling any farther than Chicago, he might as well have been speaking about another planet. He went on, lecturing eloquently about black people, colonialism, and freedom, and Anna felt that she understood; she instinctively and immediately embraced his explanation of the realities of the global color line.

Du Bois spoke favorably of a classical education, which her father and her college mentors had promoted, and his notion of double consciousness put into words the experience she had been having at Hamline, of coming to see herself through the eyes of resistant, even racist whites. Anna rushed home from Du Bois's lecture to read *Souls of Black Folk*, and for some time she carried with her the two things she was left with after reading it: the ache of recognition and the fulfillment of feeling part of a collective far larger and far greater than Hamline University.[53]

Hamline challenged Anna's ideas about faith and about family. It provided her a means to achieve some independence, and it helped her find her voice. In a number of ways, it prepared her for the world, but still, she knew something was lacking. When she returned to campus twenty-five years later, and then again after another twenty years, she was able to articulate with considerable clarity what it had been—a more progressive study of the workings of religion and race. In 1947, the class of 1922, Anna Arnold Hedgeman's graduating class, recommended her for an honorary degree. Because she had been away from the college for some time, and was the first woman to be considered for such an honor, the committee invited her to campus to give a talk, so it would have a chance to evaluate her first.

For Hedgeman, the honor of the invitation was accompanied by a dilemma: Should she be honest about her experiences at Hamline, which in retrospect were less than satisfying, particularly where race was concerned? Or should she, instead, "butter the boys a bit to receive the honorary doctorate"? If she spoke the truth, would she accomplish anything more than embarrassing those who nominated her? There was always that risk when one spoke about racial injustice. Did white people really want to hear about black people's experiences, or did they want to consider their invitation to speak justice enough? In the end, she decided, "I had to say it as I saw it."[54]

Sitting in the audience during her remarks, Professor Thomas Beyer, who had inspired her all those years earlier, found Anna Arnold Hedgeman's rebuke both warranted and humbling. "I was a very tired liberal when you were on campus," he contritely told her afterward. Beyer invited her to meet with the college's curriculum committee, which had begun the formidable task of transforming their curriculum to prepare students for the "real" world.[55] Hedgeman readily offered her services. A year later, in June 1948, Hamline University awarded Anna Arnold Hedgeman an honorary doctor of humane letters, the first of four she would receive in her lifetime. She would later joke about her honorary degrees that yes, they were honorary but, still, she *had* earned them. Indeed, she had.

Anna Arnold Hedgeman was a woman of many firsts. She appreciated the personal growth and the accolades that came with it, but she felt the loneliness as well. As the years went by, she discovered that other black women had had experiences that mirrored hers, and she would share with them the relief as well as the anger that such solidarity afforded. One friend, Muriel Sutherland Snowden, a social worker and settlement house founder, had attended Radcliffe College, where she, too, was prohibited from living in the residence hall. When Snowden returned to the campus forty years later and spoke about her time there, she discovered that the students found it hard to believe that things could have been like that, particularly in their elite northern environment.[56] For Snowden, and for Hedgeman, young people's lack of awareness of these histories and their legacies was almost as troubling as their own experiences had been.

Anna Arnold Hedgeman came to believe that many social and racial problems could be solved through studied attention to religion. When she was invited to speak on the Hamline campus again in 1960, almost forty years after her graduation, she emphasized the responsibility of educational institutions, which could rework their curricula to make the study of religion the study, also, of social change. At a school much like Hamline, she said, she had asked a group of students what they would like her to address during her time with them. Anything but religion, this group of otherwise thoughtful young people told her. In response, she very deliberately chose as the text for her remarks "The Lord's Prayer," Anna Arnold Hedgeman style. "Our Father, which art in heaven," she recited, "hallowed be thy name." But, as always, she modified the next phrase, concluding with "thy kingdom come, thy will be done, on earth," leaving off the bit about heaven.

In truth, Hedgeman had been, since her days at Hamline, developing her own theology, one that started with the critical questions posed at Hamline but that went a great deal further, a theology that chose earth over heaven, action over contemplation, and Jesus not as an otherworldly savior but rather as "the tough courageous son of God who studied, worked, dreamed, planned, and lived to produce change in his turbulent world."[57] She believed in reconciliation but believed it had to be informed, fully, by recognition of race. Her critiques of her experiences of race and religion at Hamline University grew more incisive as the years passed, but even while she was there, her firm sense of self, expectations of excellence from her faculty and peers, belief in a just God, and refusal to give way to racial prejudice, all furthered by that single lecture by W. E. B. Du Bois, meant that she was well along the path to living a life she could be proud of.

During her senior year of college, Anna Arnold increasingly looked forward to graduation and a career. She had never worked for pay, and she recognized it as a critical next step in her path to independence.[58] She was to graduate from Hamline in 1922, a time when women, even those with bachelor's degrees, found limited opportunities for employment. Most of the women in her class either became teachers or got married after graduation. She had no intention of entering marriage. There was no pressure from her family to get married, and because Minnesota was home to a good number of women who stayed single their entire lives, she may have grown up among women for whom marriage was neither a goal nor an option.[59] By now, she also knew that she did not want to return to Anoka, a town that, with the distance of four years and an expanded racial consciousness, appeared too provincial for a young black woman coming into her own.

Anna Arnold prepared, as a result, to become a teacher, as much by default as through deliberation. She had asked her father if she could attend graduate school, but he had three other children in college by then. Even if he could have afforded it, he would not have sent her. "You don't know enough about life," he told her, "to know what you really want to use your talent for."[60] As a result, she pursued Hamline's teacher training program, which customarily placed student teachers in the St. Paul public schools. She thought that her placement in a first-year English class on the Hamline campus came as an honor, a tribute to her hard work and excellence. It was some time before she realized that she secured the assignment only because St. Paul would not allow her to teach in its public schools.

Anna Arnold remained similarly uninformed about the limits of her job prospects after her college graduation, and no one seemed inclined to tell her that as a black woman she was unlikely to find employment in the public school system in the Twin Cities. Instead, Dr. Doran, with whom she boarded, helped her identify potential teaching placements outside the region through the Board of Education of the Methodist Church. She received four offers, one each in Missouri, North Carolina, South Carolina, and Mississippi. She chose Rust College, in Mississippi, precisely because it was the farthest south. "For me, going south meant an opportunity to find the unique culture which my father had always praised." She did not realize that Dr. Doran's urging her south was not so much a result of his devotion to southern culture as of his inability to help her secure a teaching post in the North.[61] "I've since put together all sorts of things that happened to me during that time," she would recall years later.[62] But then, in the summer of 1922, Anna Arnold left Hamline University a proud graduate, "equipped with my B.A. degree, a sense of adventure, and a deep conviction that the world was waiting for me to serve it as best I could."[63]

3 TEACHING IN THE SEGREGATED SOUTH

In September 1922, an eager but naive twenty-three-year-old Anna Arnold left her home in Anoka, Minnesota, to begin her teaching career at Rust College in Holly Springs, Mississippi.[1] Her father, strict even by the standards of their proper Christian community, granted her permission to stop in Chicago to visit with cousins on her way south. While Anna daydreamed about the sights she would see in the Windy City, William was more concerned with the timing of her trip; he did not want his daughter to commit the impropriety of arriving on a Christian campus in the South on a Sunday. They planned a careful itinerary, with her scheduled to leave home on a Wednesday, spend Thursday in Chicago, re-embark on Friday, and arrive in Holly Springs on Saturday, just a couple of days in advance of the opening of the school year.

The Chicago relatives had other plans. They had taught in the South themselves, and they convinced their cousin to stay in Chicago a couple of extra days. The cotton crop schedule always trumped the school schedule, they explained, and few students or faculty would arrive on campus as early as that Saturday; in fact, students would continue trickling in over the coming weeks and even months. Anna Arnold did not think too much about any of that; she just made the most of her time in Chicago making new friends, visiting the Loop, seeing a show at the Tivoli Theater, shopping at Marshall Field's, driving along Lake Michigan, and riding the elevated train.[2]

As much as she enjoyed the city, Arnold looked forward to the train ride south, particularly since she had discovered on the first leg, from St. Paul to Chicago, how exciting it was to sit and eat in the dining car. With their white table linens, polished silverware, and fresh-cut flowers, railway dining cars offered food that equaled most any restaurant's, with several meticulously served courses at every meal. On top of that, she would get another opportunity to wear her new traveling clothes.[3] But Anna Arnold was in for a rude awakening, one she might not have been prepared for, even if she had been warned.

Arnold had grown up in the only black family in Anoka, a particularly respectable, middle-class family at that, and she had just graduated from college.[4] Racism was always present, of course, but Anoka was a tolerant town, and her father had been a particularly respected man. Likewise, Hamline University, for all the occasional slights and insults she had had to endure there, was a Christian institution of higher learning, and if it was not what we would consider enlightened about race, it was at least operating on principles that pointed it in the right direction. In neither setting had she felt compelled to believe that the world would not see her as she had been taught to see herself: smart, capable, proper, educated, and clearly destined to make her mark. She had no way of anticipating Jim Crow.

Jim Crow, however impossible to understand, had to be experienced to be believed, and Anna Arnold was wholly unprepared. Growing up in Anoka, she listened to William Arnold paint a glowing picture of life in the South. The stories he had told of his early days in South Carolina had always focused on the dignity of African Americans, the formality of southern dress and relationships, and the culture he considered superior to what he had encountered in the Midwest.

But his daughter was headed to Mississippi, home to some of the most egregious manifestations of Jim Crow in the nation. In the immediate post–Civil War period, African Americans had attained political rights in their state, as did blacks throughout the South. In 1867, more than sixty thousand blacks had placed themselves on the voting rolls. But the enormity of the retreat from justice cannot be overstated. Reconstruction—the extension of rights to freed slaves in the South, enforced through federal occupation—ended by 1875 in Mississippi, and by 1892, only eighty-five hundred black citizens remained on the voting rolls. Between literacy requirements and poll taxes, not to mention threats of violence and economic reprisals, more than 90 percent of blacks were disenfranchised and driven into abject poverty. Though it was never submitted to the voters for ratification, Mississippi even drafted a new state constitution that codified these practices.[5]

Complicated dynamics led the South to implement such an inhumane system. In part, the forces that kept extremism at bay had eroded in the region by the late nineteenth century.[6] The belief that whites and blacks were almost two different species of human prevailed over any more moderate approaches to the economic and social changes that followed the Civil War. The *New York Age*, a popular black newspaper, noted the resulting contradiction, pointing out that the white South "lays down the declaration that the Negro is incapable of rising, then it adopts every possible precaution to keep him from rising." The editorial concluded, quite sensibly, "It would seem needless to take precautions to keep down a people incapable of rising."[7] In Mississippi, white residents surely must have gone through their own bizarre set of psychological twists and turns to make the transition from Reconstruction to Jim Crow.

One wonders, for example, what those whites who knew James D. Lynch, who had been Mississippi's secretary of state during Reconstruction, thought when his body was disinterred and moved to a black cemetery because Jim Crow thinking dictated that his presence would be disturbing to the whites among whom he had been buried. What of the white colleagues of J. C. Crittenden, a black member of the Board of Supervisors of Bolivar County, who, during Reconstruction, helped to build the courthouse but who could only find work in the building as a porter when Reconstruction came to an end?[8]

For many people, Mississippi continues to serve as a metaphor for all that was wrong with the post-Reconstruction South. One historian, James Cobb, called it "the most southern place on earth"; another, Steven Lawson, talks about the racism behind the state's "Magnolia Curtain." One of singer Nina Simone's most famous civil rights anthems is titled "Mississippi Goddam." Journalist Robert Sherrill maintains that Mississippi was the center of the "super South"; Lawson and others have considered it, in a more contemporary rendering, the South on steroids.[9] Anna Arnold was heading, in 1922, into a very oppressive environment.

The means of transportation that Arnold used to get to Mississippi has been just as infamous in historical memory and the national imagination. Some people equated the train's movement with the civil rights movement. As one African American rider put it, "It's dynamic, it's forceful, it always has a certain destination. It always reaches a certain point."[10] The train certainly did transport millions of southern blacks who sought opportunity in northern cities before and after the First World War. But for many others, the rail system, even as it carried masses of people north, epitomized the worst aspects of Jim Crow.[11] And of course, when Anna Arnold boarded the train at Chicago's Central Station, she headed south, not north. Among other lessons, she would soon understand what black writer and social critic W. E. B. Du Bois meant when he asked what the point of fighting to get service on a train was, if you didn't want to go where it was headed.[12]

Although each hour on the Illinois Central brought her closer to a career and a new, independent life, the passage was marked by a series of indignities. The white conductor in Chicago instructed Arnold in a rude voice that she could sit where she liked until they reached Cairo, Illinois, and then move to the "colored" car, or she could start out in the "colored" car and not have to move later. She opted to stay where she was, in the mixed car. Several hours later they arrived in Cairo, the southernmost city in Illinois, situated both at the confluence of the Mississippi and Ohio Rivers and at the boundary between North and South.

Ongoing racial strife in the city, including a lynching a decade before her arrival there, provides evidence of how porous that boundary remained well into the twentieth century.[13]

At Cairo, a black porter escorted Arnold to the car that sat directly behind the engine, where she immediately felt upset but also strangely fearful. The control she had sought over her own life, she realized, had been stripped away from her at a single station stop. The train car was dirty and soot-filled, with worn, uncomfortable seats and incessant noise. "How could the railroad company permit such disgraceful service to any American?" she wondered, identifying her fellow passengers as she identified herself, not first as black but as American. For the first time among many in the two years she would spend in the Jim Crow South, Anna Arnold found herself being humiliated and enraged at the experience of other people, white people, exercising the power to define the fundamentals of who and what she was.[14]

The train trip south provided Arnold hard-learned lessons not only about segregation but also about how little she understood the real, seemingly intractable link between race and poverty in the South. Once the train left Cairo, a few of her fellow segregated sojourners tried to strike up a conversation with the young woman, but she turned away. She had not been raised to speak with strangers, especially men. The contrast between her fine traveling clothes and their threadbare attire was as striking as the contrast between the first coach she sat in and the second, and it all made her uncomfortable. Her coach-mates' continuous conversation, eating, and laughter prevented her from sleeping, and they seemed to her "noisy and uncouth." Some entered the train with their farm animals, and many crowded several children into seats meant for one. Initially Arnold felt little more than disdain for her fellow travelers; only later would she realize she "had no way of knowing the warmth and heartache beneath those rough exteriors."[15]

Like other privileged black women of her generation, Anna Arnold had been raised to believe that her personal conduct and not the behavior of others would both open and close doors in her life. No one was superior to her, she had learned; that is, no one except those whose conduct surpassed her own.[16] So when she met with such disrespect, she might well have taken a moment to look herself over, to make certain that her actions had not precipitated or heightened the gravity of the situation.

Some years earlier, Mary Church Terrell, the first African American woman in the United States to earn a college degree, and who would become one of Anna Arnold's most important mentors, experienced something similar on a train. Her father, with whom she had been traveling, left the first-class car they had been riding in to have a smoke. While he was gone, the conductor attempted to move the girl to the "colored" car. When she told her mother about it afterward, she tried to deflect the blame she anticipated. "I assured her I had been careful to do everything she told me to do. For instance, my hands were clean and so was my face. I hadn't mussed my hair. . . . I hadn't soiled my dress a single bit. I was sitting up 'straight and proper.' Neither was I looking out of the window, resting on my knees with my feet on the seat (as I dearly loved to do). I wasn't talking loud. . . . I was behaving 'like a little lady' as she told me to do."[17]

Like Terrell before her, Arnold had to contend with a mix of emotions and responses as she encountered a situation that challenged not only her worldview but also her innermost sensibilities. Like many of her contemporaries, she had been raised with what one historian calls an ethos of "socially responsible individualism."[18] Even though their parents or grandparents had been slaves, members of this generation knew they were meant to be leaders. They had had advantages, and they understood they were to put those advantages to good use on behalf of their communities. They all had to learn to contend with racism, and some were unprepared, as was Anna Arnold.

Over the years she would come to learn, sometimes painfully, how her particular class, gender, and religious identity simultaneously drew her close to and set her apart from the African American communities she would encounter.[19] Having grown up in a household where her comportment and achievements were considered the decisive factors in her relationships and her future, Arnold would struggle against the realities of racism, which dictated that what mattered about her was what she "was," not who she was, or how she behaved. And what she "was" was black first, always black first, and American later.[20] It did not take Anna Arnold long to understand that in the eyes of southern whites on this train, she and her traveling companions were more alike than different, no matter what she wore, or where she had gone to school, or who she thought herself to be.

After a night of watching the men, women, and children in her car pull out lunchboxes and share their food, Arnold was eager to make her way to the dining car for a proper meal. When she asked for directions that next morning, the conductor briskly informed her, "Niggers better not go in there." A man seated nearby offered her a sandwich, but Arnold was afraid he would get the wrong idea about her. She had not yet learned, she realized later, "the sense of responsibility which the 'segregated' feel for each other." Instead, she bought coffee and a sandwich from a butcher boy who entered the train at a station stop, but the coffee was bitter, the bread stale.[21]

Anna Arnold grew increasingly despondent as the train rattled on. Staring out the window at the landscape provided no respite from the dismal state of her immediate surroundings, as she was greeted at every station, and even when the train passed railroad worker toilets along the tracks, with the omnipresent "colored" and "white" signs. They signaled, she began to realize, the divide she had largely been able to ignore if not transcend until this point in her life.[22]

Finally, she arrived in Holly Springs, a small town in north-central Mississippi, and although her expectations might have been tempered along the way, she remained eager to discover what Rust College had in store for her. But first she had to actually get there from the station. She did not know that Mississippi had recently passed a law forbidding black and white passengers riding together in the same taxi.[23] But her problem was getting a ride at all, never mind a shared ride. The first taxicab she saw looked comfortable enough, but the white driver quickly let her know what was what. "You must be from up North," he said. "I don't ride niggers."[24]

Anna Arnold was learning what it meant to be black in the South, and it was only through this new understanding that she would come to realize what it meant to be black in America. But these were necessary lessons, things she had to experience, in order to become somebody who would do something to change it.

Her immediate task, after such an eye-opening train ride, was to rise above the depravity she had witnessed aboard the Illinois Central.[25]

Rust College sat on the northwest side of Holly Springs, the seat of Marshall County and the "Antebellum Capital of the Mid-South." The landscape featured rolling hills, hayfields, pine and oak trees, and in the bottoms, endless expanses of cotton. Much of the uncultivated land was overrun with kudzu, a weedy vine that can grow as much as a foot per day. Even though Holly Springs was a short drive from Memphis, and outside the boundaries of the infamous Mississippi Delta to its west, most of the town's black residents' lives closely resembled those of their neighbors across the Delta divide. The Delta, with its enormously fertile, river-flooded soil, was purported to have the richest cotton-farming land in the United States, and cotton was king in the soil-rich Holly Springs as well. The sharecropping system defined black life in Holly Springs as it did in the Delta, meaning that it was nearly impossible for black people to earn a living.[26]

Had African Americans secured their "forty acres and a mule" as reparation for the unpaid work they performed in the South before the Civil War, sharecropping would not have become the region's dominant agricultural and economic system. The War Department's Freedmen's Bureau proposed reparations, but Congress failed to provide the funding, and the result was a black population almost as beholden to white landowners as they had been under slavery.[27] Black tenants farmed and lived on the white owner's land, giving him from one-quarter to one-half of the year's crop in exchange for a shack, the use of mules, and the seeds and tools they needed to raise a crop. They had to purchase the remaining provisions they needed for their families from a plantation commissary, and they had to survive the months between crops without any income at all.

The landowner bought the whole of the cotton crop, but he was also the one to set the price. If the cash earned on the cotton proved greater than the "furnish," sharecroppers would end up with some cash at the end of the season. But deflated cotton prices, combined with inflated prices in the commissary, ensured it was more likely that tenants ended up in debt at the end of the year. Honest transactions were uncommon, and tenants had few rights even when they could name or calculate the injustices they faced.[28]

Illiteracy among sharecroppers made them especially vulnerable to the landowners, who generally kept the accounts. As one sharecropper explained, owners would try to make it seem as though they were all in the cotton project together. "Deep down inside, you didn't believe that," he explained, "but in the surface of your mind, maybe as a way of not facing reality, you'd want to believe whatever he'd told you."[29] The consequences were devastating. One Mississippi sharecropper cleared money only six times in thirty-six years of farming.[30] Another estimated that, taking into account all of the crops and labor they had provided, her family had paid for their house, which they still did not own, three times over.[31]

Parents knew that their children's education held the greatest promise for escaping these slave-like conditions. But the cotton season, from early March through November, wreaked havoc with the school year. In order to survive, the entire family had to work from 5:00 to 11:00 each morning, eat and rest for an hour, then return to the fields until dark; as one farmer described it, they were in the fields from "can see to can't see."[32] By age thirteen, when they ought to have been preparing to enter high school, children were considered adult workers, and few families could do without their earnings. Even with the children in the fields instead of school, they were all terribly vulnerable. When cotton prices dropped significantly in the 1920s, during Anna Arnold's time in Mississippi, sharecroppers' overall pay declined, and many barely survived.[33]

When blacks tried to resist the abysmal conditions, whites responded by firing them, which in the sharecropping economy essentially amounted to starving them. The most established plantations made their own laws, or operated with the support of the local authorities, and most sharecroppers lived in rough wooden houses with poor insulation, leaky roofs and walls, and no electricity. Until the Great Migration drew them north, before and after the First World War, there was really no place else for them to go. Working-class whites often lived under conditions that were little better, but they went along with the system, taking comfort in the few crumbs of privilege that occasionally came their way. For Holly Springs' black population, survival required subservient behavior in the face of economic injustice. As progressive white southern journalist

Hodding Carter noted about the town, "There was no need to kill here, only to deprive."[34]

A cotton-rich railroad town, Holly Springs had served as a supply depot and personal headquarters for General Ulysses S. Grant during the Civil War. It changed hands almost sixty times during the war.[35] It was also one of many sites of southern anti-Semitism. In response to a rumor that Jewish merchants were smuggling cotton out of Holly Springs to avoid Grant's control, the general attempted to force all the Jews out of town. Following an intense lobbying effort by Jewish leaders nationally, President Lincoln eventually rescinded the order. There was still a small Jewish community in town when Anna Arnold arrived, and Jewish merchants in Holly Springs as elsewhere, despite local custom, often catered specifically to black clientele. Anna Arnold would remember Levy's Department Store as the lone Holly Springs establishment that welcomed students and faculty from Rust College and treated them with respect.[36]

Holly Springs was also the birthplace of Ida B. Wells, who did more than any other American to expose and challenge lynching in the South. Wells grew up in Holly Springs and attended Rust College before Anna Arnold's time there. She had to leave school to care for her younger siblings after her parents died in the 1878 yellow fever epidemic, which killed more than five hundred residents of this one small town.[37] Rust granted Wells an honorary degree in 1892.[38] And in a discovery that links the Civil War era with more recent times, scholars have identified a mid-1800s diary from a homestead in Holly Springs as the source for significant aspects of William Faulkner's depictions of his fictionalized Yoknapatawpha County, Mississippi.[39]

Holly Springs had a reputation throughout the nineteenth century for its progressive approach to the education of girls, but specifically white girls. Mississippi in fact founded the first state-supported college for women in the United States, the Industrial Institute and College for the Education of White Girls, in 1884, and Holly Springs was home to the Holly Springs Collegiate Institution for young women, which granted the mistress of polite literature degree. In the years before and after the Civil War, education furthered racial divides, rather than healed them, and public education for black Mississippians lagged so far behind that it barely existed.

The United Daughters of the Confederacy played a significant role in public education, with an approach unmarred by subtlety. The inherent racial superiority of whites was a given. The classroom texts they persuaded school systems to purchase, for blacks as well as whites, featured chivalrous white men protecting women and children from predatory black men, and images of Confederate president Jefferson Davis hung on the walls of most classrooms. The efforts of white women to weave their version of southern history through public education and public monuments contributed to both the potency and the longevity of segregation in Mississippi.[40]

Rust College was among the best educational possibilities for blacks in Mississippi, which, well into the twentieth century, ranked near or at the bottom for black literacy rates nationally, and for the length of the school year for black children.[41] In 1866, under the auspices of the Freedman's Aid Society of the Methodist Episcopal Church, the Reverend A. C. McDonald founded the college to teach former slaves to read and write. With emancipation, McDonald wrote, the newly freed found themselves "utterly unequipped to compete in white society."[42] Under the leadership of Methodist abolitionists, the Freedman's Aid Society attempted to remedy this situation throughout the South, opening and maintaining twenty-two schools, ten of them colleges or professional schools, by 1890.[43] By one account, Rust College sat on property that had formerly been a slave auction site.[44] By another, it housed a bell tower that had once rung for slaves to go to work but later signaled them to go to school.[45]

The college had no prohibition against whites, but none attended.[46] As with many other schools aimed at newly freed blacks, support came not just from white missionaries but also from the dirt-poor residents of the communities finally provided with educational opportunities. "The colored people take a lively interest in the institution," the Freedman's Aid Society reported in 1868, noting that African Americans in Mississippi had contributed $2,000 toward Rust College's construction.[47] As was true of Anna Arnold's grandparents, who paid tuition for her father to attend elementary and secondary school as well as college, many freed people's commitment to education was as acute as it was hard to achieve.

Regardless of—or perhaps in part because of—its long-standing commitment to the education of whites, Holly Springs offered its black citizens meager elementary education and no high schooling at all; in fact, only three communities in the entire state of Mississippi offered high school to black students.[48] After all, high school prepared young people for college, for citizenship and leadership, and for employment—in short, to play roles that their white neighbors did not want them to play.[49] As a result, in Marshall County, Rust College and black families would assume that responsibility, for children of all ages, for a good number of years. The college did not eliminate its grade school program until 1938, and not until 1952 could it declare itself exclusively a college.[50] Colleges that served students of all ages were not unique to Mississippi—after all, William Arnold had attended Atlanta University from grade school through high school—but the practice was most pronounced there. Even Tougaloo College, the best private black institution in the state of Mississippi, provided elementary and secondary education for many years after its founding in 1869.[51]

When Anna Arnold arrived at Rust, its primary commitment was to elementary and high school students. Not understanding the history of education in the state, and having attended public schools herself, she wondered why parents, most of whom had little money, would pay tuition at Rust instead of sending their children to public school at no cost. A visit to the local elementary school for black children proved instructive. Crowded into a building in the yard of the Holly Springs jail, overseen by a teacher who had, after forty years, given up on teaching, the students often had little more to do than talk with the prisoners through the bars of the jail.[52] Given that Mississippi paid the lowest teacher salaries in the nation, it is little wonder that so many children lacked prepared and enthusiastic instructors.[53]

Whites in southern states used the tax monies provided by black citizens to build up their own schools, while condemning the children of those same taxpaying citizens to unconscionable educational prospects. Once again, things southern were amplified in Mississippi, the only southern state that allotted no funds for school buses for black children.[54] Those fortunate enough to receive any education at all would have to walk to school, watching the white children on the passing buses with a combination, one imagines, of puzzlement, resignation, and anger. Their parents would have been hard-pressed to explain the situation. In a staggering injustice, African American parents, who were miserably underpaid for their work, paid not once but twice for their children's education: first in taxes, which subsidized white education, and then again in tuition.[55] But those parents would not be deterred. The superintendent of education for the Freedmen's Bureau, John W. Alvord, predicted that whites "would find it harder fighting the alphabet and spelling books than they did Grant and Sherman,"[56] and black parents were determined to see that day come.

But even Rust College, which was relatively sound financially, had few facilities. It did not have a library, science building, gymnasium, or adequate classroom space. The dining hall, auditorium, student dorms, and classrooms all shared one building, McDonald Hall, which also housed the president's office. Expansion proved challenging, as the college was entirely dependent on missionary aid and the local African American community. And even though the state failed to provide anywhere near adequate funding for black education, Rust could not apply for federal educational funding because it was a private institution.[57] It would be another forty years before the college would have a real library, at which point Anna Arnold Hedgeman, along with famed opera singer Leontyne Price, whose mother was a Rust alum, would be invited back to break ground for its construction.[58]

Families struggled enormously to pay the tuition, and they often had no choice but to pay in goods rather than cash. Parents used various forms of payment to keep their children at private institutions in Mississippi: gallon tins of molasses, flocks of geese, wagonloads of corn. One young man went off to school with an aggregate contribution to his tuition: "Aunt Hester Robinson gave a pound of butter and a dime, Grandma Willis a chicken, Aunt Lucy McConnell 'four bits' [fifty cents], Sarah Pernell a chicken, Effie McCoy a cake and five cents, Sam McCoy five cents, Bessie Harvey one of her dresses, Washington Lincoln Johnson two pecks of meal, Mandy Willis a dozen eggs."[59]

Anna Arnold encountered the consequences of poverty at Rust; she also encountered southern culture in its most strict religious manifestations. She would have been unlikely to embrace the well-known practices of the Roaring Twenties had she stayed in the North during these years, but she might at least have chanced upon them. James Farmer, the son of a Rust College faculty member, later recalled that the Roaring Twenties "didn't roar very much" at the college; "they just purred, and rather demurely at that."[60] The strict codes of behavior at schools like Rust were often attributed to the puritanical values of white teachers and administrators, but many of the parents shared those values.[61] "This was, after all," Farmer observed, "the Bible belt for blacks as well as whites. It was also a citadel of moralistic Methodism."[62]

The main building, McDonald Hall, featured separate entrances for women and men, faculty included, and each faculty member lived on a corridor alongside students to supplement the supervision by the residence hall matron. The religious leanings of the school also dictated that the administration defined "teaching" broadly. Teachers provided considerable mentoring, if not actual monitoring, in many aspects of daily life; their duties included supervising study halls from seven to nine each evening, and chaperoning students to town for doctors' appointments and shopping. The teachers served as guidance counselors and informal gym teachers, taking the students hiking to promote physical fitness.[63]

Arnold's considerable teaching load included logic, mythology, and modern and ancient history in addition to her own field, English. Her students might have been undereducated, but they hungered for learning, and she often had to work to stay a few steps ahead of them.[64] Neither teachers nor students, however, could ignore the ways poverty intruded on daily life. Most teachers used a portion of each paycheck to subsidize the school or the students: they regularly bought books and magazines to share with students or made direct gifts of money to the worst off. Like many of her fellow teachers, Anna Arnold also maintained some financial responsibility for her family back home. One day, she received a letter from her father asking her to send money so that her sister Grayce, then in college, could buy a new spring coat. Grayce never forgot the gesture, describing it decades later: "That was one of the prettiest coats I ever had—black velvet with red fur cuffs. I wore it on a date with Jimmy Hensley and he said I looked very 'katash'—some complimentary word I never really knew the meaning of."[65]

In her first year on campus, Anna Arnold found that her northern ways did not always mesh well with southern sensibilities. On her way to town one afternoon, she encountered a woman with a heavy basket of clothes on her head. When she heard the woman say, "Good evening," she looked around, wondering whom the woman was addressing. When the young teacher failed to respond, the woman stopped and demanded to know what had happened to her manners. Arnold apologized and explained that she did not remember meeting her before, and the woman again scolded her. "You don't have to know me to be polite." Again, the younger woman tried to explain away her rudeness: she simply had not been raised to speak to strangers. "Never you mind, honey," the woman said a bit more gently, "down here we speak to everybody."[66] But as with much of life in the Jim Crow South, speaking to strangers had strict racial dimensions. Anna Arnold was certainly not to greet white people with a "good evening" on her walks to and from town.

Another day, she overheard a group of students talking about her because she had gone off to Holly Springs without her hat and gloves. At Hamline, Louise Young, a dean who always dressed formally, had instructed students that "a lady always wears her hat and gloves when leaving the campus for the city."[67] In Mississippi, Arnold learned, that same dress code had a different rationale. As a faculty member later explained to her, white men always posed a potential danger, and black women had to dress as formally as possible so as not to encounter "unpleasant experiences." She soon witnessed the danger herself, as she found that a white lawyer deliberately stood at his window and winked at her every time she walked past his Holly Springs law practice.[68]

Black faculty at Rust College worked hard to maintain self-respect in the face of such indignities. One practice they passed on to Arnold was to never give her first name to a store merchant. If she introduced herself as "Anna Arnold," it was guaranteed that the proprietor would always call her "Anna" thereafter, and never "Miss Arnold," a familiarity they would not have assumed with a white customer. Teachers had learned to introduce themselves using their initials, avoiding the disrespectful use of their first names. Sure enough, when the young teacher entered the bank to cash her first check, the teller called her by her first name. She bit her tongue, remembering her mother's advice about keeping quiet in the face of bigotry.[69]

Anna Arnold's own educational process continued at Rust College, as she got to know her students and learn about their lives. One day, walking across campus, she encountered a girl who pressed her thumb against her nostril and blew her nose. Horrified by such coarse behavior, Arnold immediately reprimanded the girl. When she realized that she had humiliated the girl, she sat on a tree stump with her to talk. From Judy Mae, she learned a lesson as valuable as the one she delivered.

Judy Mae's father, a sharecropper, had saved up over the years to buy a small parcel of land, but he died young. Her mother decided that her daughter's education was more important than the land; she sold it, but the sale didn't provide nearly enough for tuition. Judy Mae stayed on at the school, struggling financially, and in other ways, as well. For one thing, Arnold came to recognize, "it took great courage for a tall and sturdily built girl to sit in a third grade classroom." For another, Judy Mae was keenly aware of how out of place she was, how unprepared she was, socially and academically, in this new, utterly unfamiliar environment. Finally, Judy Mae suffered in the classroom because she urgently needed glasses but couldn't afford them. Arnold used part of her paycheck to help the young girl purchase glasses, but she came to realize that neither she nor her equally generous colleagues could adequately help their students meet their most basic needs.[70]

Methodist congregations around the country met many of the school's expenses through their missionary donations, and as she came to understand how critical those donations were, Anna Arnold also gained her first awareness of the vast distance and difference between the northern donors and the southern recipients of such charity. "I remembered how casually I had placed my own missionary collection in the plate at home," she recalled later, "and I knew I would never again be unaware of the importance of the missionary gift."[71]

The school provided some scholarship money and on-campus employment, but many of the costs were borne by parents. Members of the faculty were privy to letters parents wrote, explaining in what had to be humiliating detail both the sacrifices they made and how much they came up short anyway. Most of the students at Rust College succeeded not simply because they worked hard but rather thanks to the "untiring efforts of the folks at home, who held that education was the strongest weapon against the inhumanity of the South."[72]

Anna Arnold's experience of college had been very different. William and Marie Arnold had always assumed their daughter and the five siblings who followed her would attend college. They sacrificed to make that happen, but they did not confront anything like the financial and social obstacles black citizens of Mississippi's cotton lands faced. Attending her first graduation ceremony at Rust in 1923, only a year after her own college graduation, the young teacher could not help but be struck by the contrasts. As important as the graduation ceremony was in the lives of so many families, a good number of parents did not attend. Often, they had to choose between providing graduation clothes for their children or making the trip themselves.[73]

But seeing poverty and unlearning ingrained prejudices against the poor were not the same thing, a lesson Anna Arnold would have to learn again and again, despite her religious training to love her neighbor and to serve those less fortunate. As she made her way across campus to that first graduation ceremony, an elderly woman approached her and asked to be directed to the college president. Arnold looked the woman over and, deciding that a college president should not be bothered by a poorly dressed, clearly uneducated woman on such a ceremonious occasion, she told the woman the president was unavailable. The woman refused to give up. Was she a teacher at Rust?, the woman asked. When Arnold admitted that she was, the woman told her that if she could not deliver the message herself, Arnold would have to do it for her. She reached into the pocket of her work shirt, pulled out a knotted handkerchief, and opened it. Piece by piece, her gnarled brown hands delivered nickels, dimes, and quarters, about two dollars in total. "I wants you to give dis money to de president," the woman told her. "Take good keer of it. I washed and ironed and scrubbed for it; I want some kid ter have a chance I ain't never had."[74] Humility set in again, but for Arnold it was humility paired with anger and with a determination to address such appalling injustices head-on, rather than just be embarrassed and paralyzed by them.

After a year of teaching, Anna Arnold felt she had to return to school herself. She wanted to spend some time in an environment where people addressed the big questions about what she witnessed around her. How, she wondered, could a nation's economic system include sharecropping, an absolutely unjust, untenable arrangement? She imagined that other people, black and white, must have been asking such questions, and she wanted to learn about what they thought, what they had read, what they had written.[75] She was reminded of her college reading of *Souls of Black Folk*, in which W. E. B. Du Bois recalled his experiences teaching in a school in rural Tennessee for two summers. Du Bois's instruction, provided in a log crib used during the rest of the year to store corn, formed the full extent of formal schooling the local children received. When he returned to the community ten years later, he found that his favorite student had died and that most of the families he had come to know lived in poverty, pain, and violence. "I came to a region where the world was split into white and black halves," he wrote, "and where the darker half was held back by race prejudice and legal bonds as well as by deep ignorance and dire poverty."[76]

Du Bois relied on the intellectual community he developed at Fisk University to help him process and come to terms with what he saw. "A new loyalty and allegiance replaced my Americanism," he wrote. "Hence-forward I was a Negro."[77] Anna Arnold experienced something similar at Rust College. The college's first black president, M. S. Davage, had been appointed in 1920, just two years prior to her arrival. And Leonard J. Farmer, who had been the first black PhD in Texas, and may have been the first black PhD in Mississippi as well, served as dean, campus minister, and professor of religion and philosophy. As Farmer's son, the noted civil rights worker James Farmer, recalled later, even local white people could not help but be dazzled by him.[78] They allowed themselves to call him "Dr.," ironically enough, since they would have refused to call him "Mr." Living among these black leaders had a significant impact on Arnold. She began to identify more and more as black, a decision due as much to the positive influence of these intellectual mentors as to the negative influence of southern whites.

Arnold applied for summer school admission at the University of Minnesota but could not manage the tuition on her meager salary, which she repeatedly dipped into to support the students and the academic program at Rust. She decided to visit her family's banker in Anoka and apply for a loan—without telling her father. In another measured but important step in her growing independence, she secured the loan and attended graduate classes. She felt proud that the banker, who agreed not to inform her father, loaned her money based on her signature alone. She probably did not realize just how remarkable a feat it actually was for a single woman of her generation to secure a loan on her own. It would be another fifty years before American women could readily access credit on their own, without a father's or a husband's signature. It certainly suggests the level of respect that Arnold, not to mention her family generally and her father specifically, attained in their small town in Minnesota.[79]

Returning to Rust College for a second year, Arnold was immediately grateful for the kind attentions of Dean Farmer, who took her under his wing. He was concerned that the depths of racist deprivation she witnessed would lead her to see blacks as wholly acquiescent. Under his tutelage she undertook study in black history and, at his insistence, black resistance. Farmer helped her formulate an approach to race relations that included anger tempered by knowledge and activism bolstered by the understanding that others had paved the way, paying with their lives if they had to.[80] The second year at Rust passed much like the first, and by the time she had been in the state for two years, Anna Arnold had more than learned the meaning of the words of a native Mississippian, surgeon and civil rights leader Theodore Roosevelt Mason Howard: "You have got to be a black man in Mississippi at least 24 hours to understand what it means to be a Negro." She had learned, and she was ready to leave.[81]

Many others of Anna Arnold's generation would feel the same. James Farmer, whose father had played such a key role at Rust College, believed his father paid a significant price for staying in the South. As one of the most highly educated men of his generation, black or white, Dr. Farmer was reduced to regularly negotiating "the complexity and absurdity of southern caste" in Holly Springs. James

Farmer believed the system made his father "less than a man" and vowed, "I'll never do that when I grow up. They have to kill me."[82]

In fact, the younger Farmer's response to racism was to cofound the Congress of Racial Equality (CORE) and initiate the Freedom Rides, which would help bring an end to segregated public transportation in the South. Perhaps his father had not been able to fully live out the resistance he encouraged others to explore, but he managed to convey some of it to his son. As difficult as this racist southern environment was, it also inspired a dedication to social change. Many leaders of the later civil rights movement, including James Weldon Johnson, Walter White, Mary Frances Berry, Martin Luther King Jr., and Stokely Carmichael, graduated from historically black institutions in the South.[83]

To Anna Arnold's way of thinking, though, too many of her charges, whether or not they made it through Rust College, had few substantial opportunities because of the South's Jim Crow system. In Holly Springs, she had "met the ugliness of segregation head on," and, calculating that opportunities to resist racism increased across the miles, she encouraged her students and their families to relocate in the North.[84]

As well intentioned as she was, this northern transplant missed a few things. For one, some black Mississippians wanted to make their lives better in the South, which was their home, rather than leave. A significant number were determined to stay and fight. In 1918, blacks had appealed to the state legislature, demanding justice through education. "We cannot understand by what process of reasoning that you can conclude," they petitioned, "to take the common funds of all and use it to the glory of your children, and leave ours in ignorance, squalor, and shame." The time for silence, for obedience, had ended: "The Negro has been silent, gentlemen, but not asleep to these gross neglects, for these facts are too patent, even to the most obtuse."[85]

Even the white newspaper in the state capital, Jackson, acknowledged the realities: "In the past we actually have not maintained a dual system of schools, financially. We have maintained a white system and left the negro schools to go with meager attention."[86] Anna Arnold would not be alone in considering efforts to alter the state of things in Mississippi futile, but there is no doubt that such early attempts to foster change set the stage for later, more effective means of resistance to intolerable conditions across the region.

There is no doubt, either, that Arnold was simply not privy to many instances of resistance that took place around her. She was not there, after all, when Juanita Scott's mother, who, when asked by the white farmer where her children were, told him that her children were the same place as his children, at school. She was not there when D. L. Dorsey, determined that nothing would get in the way of his children's education, carried a gun as he walked them to school each day. And she was not there when Alverrine Parker asked the woman she babysat for why she cleaned the already-clean bathroom after Alverrine used it.[87] Anna Arnold was an outsider, and it is likely that much of the resistance that took place in black Holly Springs would have remained invisible to her.[88]

White people, however, knew, anticipated, or imagined that African American resistance existed just below the surface, and they tried to forestall the inevitable. A 1921 state law made it illegal to "print or publish or circulate" literature favoring social equality, thereby attempting to limit black Mississippians' access to northern black newspapers.[89] E. R. Franklin received a fine and a jail sentence for selling the NAACP newspaper, the *Crisis*, because an editorial demanded "too many rights for the negroes and would only serve to swell their heads."[90] Still, communication networks survived and thrived. Pullman porters carried the newspapers south on their train runs from Chicago, and people read, heard, and shared the collective sounds of resistance at their beauty parlors and barbershops, church gatherings, pool halls, and other meeting places.[91]

World War I had ushered in some change in race relations in the South, but only a fraction of what was needed. In Mississippi some argued that things had improved during the war, when blacks managed to obtain better wages, but when the postwar economy reduced labor shortages, employers resumed their most discriminatory practices.[92] Whites seemed to suffer at the very notion of blacks attaining even the most minor improvements in their financial straits. When one black woman quit her job as a cook for a white family when her husband began to earn more money, she was visited by the police, who informed her that she would be arrested for vagrancy if she did not return to work. In another case, two black women were tarred and feathered for leaving their jobs.[93]

Black newspapers told stories of black heroism and loyalty during the war, for which many soldiers expected to be rewarded, but it was not to be. "You niggers are wondering how you are going to be treated after the war," one southern newspaper informed them. "Well, I'll tell you. You are going to be treated exactly like you were before the war; this is a white man's country and we expect to rule it."[94] Mississippi's governor, the infamous Theodore Bilbo, warned black servicemen not to return at all if they expected equal treatment. "We have all the room in the world for what we know as N-i-g-g-e-r-s," he stated, "but none whatsoever for 'colored ladies and gentlemen.'"[95]

Anna Arnold might not have been aware of what came to be called the Great Migration when she stopped over in Chicago on her way to Mississippi, but she witnessed it directly once she arrived. "I saw some of the first trainloads of Afro-Americans leaving for Detroit and the automobile industry," she wrote later, "for Chicago and the stockyards, for Harlem and the larger freedom of that national mecca." In fact, the Great Migration was already well underway when she arrived in 1922. Between 1910 and 1920, some 7 percent of the black population of the South moved north; in Mississippi the figure was 15 percent. In one county in the Delta, fully 60 percent of the black labor force moved away, leaving behind a cotton crop with few to pick it.[96] The long list of incentives for relocation, topped of course by jobs paying a reasonable wage, included the 1920s reorganization of the Ku Klux Klan in the southern states and the brutality of working-class whites who, regardless of the degree to which they too suffered under that economic system, inflicted tremendous violence against their black neighbors. Mississippi held the first-place position with regard to lynchings;[97] it also held the first place in the numbers of African Americans who left the state to head north.[98]

Regardless of black resistance, the gap in black and white education widened in the years between the two world wars. By 1940 nearly half of all black children enrolled in school in Mississippi were in the first and second grades, and the funding disparities had actually grown wider. At the turn of the century, black children constituted 60 percent of all school-age children in the state and received 19 percent of the funding. By World War II, they constituted 57 percent of school-age children but received only 14 percent of the annual school appropriation.[99]

Private foundations, including the Rosenwald Foundation, established by the founder of Sears Roebuck, had played a large role in getting schools built for black children. By 1932, when the Rosenwald fund ended its school construction program in Mississippi, it had been in involved in building more than six hundred schools.[100] Even with the Rosenwald support, however, communities had to raise matching funds. Black parents invested a veritable fortune to support schooling for their children and their communities. But for increasing numbers of blacks, getting their children an education seemed to necessitate leaving home and heading north.

After two years amid the staggering poverty and discrimination of Mississippi, Anna Arnold came to believe in the exodus, and she eagerly counseled those who would listen to leave. She wished for them what she had experienced in the North. "In my naiveté I saw these trainloads of people as representative of all people who search for freedom and for a little while, I was hopeful." It did not occur to her that the northern cities "had no experience with which to evaluate these newcomers in their midst," she wrote later.[101] As a privileged northerner, black though she was, she herself lacked the capacity to recognize the strengths of many of the southern blacks she encountered. Only later did she realize that if she had failed to judge them fairly, the white North would hardly do better.

In her time at Rust College, Anna Arnold had grown to hate three things: the land, which produced cotton; the spring, which took her students away from

her; and white people, who appeared terrifically callous at best, simply heart-
less at worst. She found little to recommend living in her father's beloved South.
During the time she spent in Holly Springs, no hospital in the state would allow
black physicians to treat patients.[102] Lynchings remained common, and Arnold
held the state's clergy partly to blame. She was not alone in believing that lynchings would not have been so common in Mississippi had clergy and their congregations condemned the practice, but she felt as if she were.[103]

Arnold prepared to leave Mississippi, just as she counseled her students and
their families to do. She had discovered that her critiques of the South did not
meet with uniform welcome, either by her students, their parents, or her fellow
Rust College faculty. She admired the other black faculty at Rust, many of them
southerners who had gone north for their educations and deliberately returned
home to teach. Arnold first saw such decisions as self-sacrificing, only later realizing that her trust in the North actually resembled their aching love for the
South. As Preston Holmes would say about his home state, "Mississippi, it's hell,
but it's home."[104]

At the time, however, Arnold felt that just as her peers' obligations had drawn
them south, her obligation was pushing her in the opposite direction. She tempered her verbal assaults on southern ways so as not offend her colleagues, but
her opinion did not change, and she began to plan her exit. She would return to
the North to stir things up, to find allies and a way to change what she had seen
in Holly Springs. As she imagined, confidently, "Courageous southern Negroes
had to be rescued from the kind of white people I had seen in the South."[105]

Two elements characterized Anna Arnold's youthful ambition: the notion
that she could do the rescuing, and the idea that the North would embrace her
ideas for change.[106] Later on, with a great deal more experience and more than
a little bitterness, she would revise her thinking about her time in Mississippi.
"I did not yet know that the basic difference between the North and the South
is the difference between an ax and a stiletto."[107] She would come to learn what
scores of civil rights activists and civil rights historians would have to learn as
well: the North was no citadel of democracy for American blacks. But in 1924,
with spirited determination, Anna Arnold headed north, to save the South from
itself.

4 HEADING NORTH TO SPREAD THE WORD

THE YWCA YEARS

When Anna Arnold left Mississippi, she was, as she remembered later, "bitter as W. E. B. Du Bois, James Farmer, and Malcolm X rolled into one."[1] It was a bitterness tempered by high expectations, though, for herself and for the North, where she had been raised and educated, and where she had meaningful relationships with white people. Back in the North, she believed, she would readily find support for her attack on southern racism.

With two years of teaching behind her, Arnold assumed she would find another teaching position upon her return north in 1924, and she could settle in somewhere to educate young people and identify ways to advocate for meaningful social change in the South. As soon as she started making inquiries among her white college friends about job openings, she began to realize how foolish her belief in the unqualified distinction between North and South had been. Her friends, "blushing and stammering," admitted what none of them, including Anna, had fully faced or articulated before: the schools they taught in would not find her a suitable candidate for employment.[2] Discouraged, Arnold moved back home with her family and began to search for other suitable work, while struggling to fit her new experience into the racial worldview she had developed while in Mississippi.

Because she had entered the teaching profession more by default than by desire, leaving teaching was no great hardship, but few other professions readily opened their doors to women, fewer still to black women. A white friend suggested she write to one of the two black executives in the Young Women's Christian Association (YWCA). Given that it was both northern and Christian, Arnold was dismayed to discover that the YWCA was a segregated organization. Worse, she would learn, in cities where the YWCA had both a black and a white affiliate, the white branch had much more extensive resources.

When she received an offer of the executive directorship of the black YWCA branch in Springfield, Ohio, Arnold accepted, mindful of her obligation to use her education for good purposes, but her enthusiasm was tempered by her growing understanding of the pervasive workings of race. Perhaps she hoped to challenge the organization's limits as she embraced the opportunities it offered: the YWCA, after all, deliberately and purposefully provided executive-level opportunities to black women. It is hard to imagine she was not also quite aware that professional employment was a necessary component of sustaining and furthering her independence.[3]

William Arnold approved of this next phase in his daughter's professional life. Like his home, like Hamline University, and like Rust College, the YWCA was Christian and, more specifically, Protestant. Founded with the mission of "bringing about the kingdom of God among young women," the YWCA provided a space for black and white women to come together "through a bond of dedication to Christian service."[4] Regardless of William Arnold's approval or Anna's ambitions, the organization proved itself far less able to live up to that sisterhood than its mission statement promised. True, it was the only large national women's organization in the United States to have significant participation of black and white women, but they existed in separate, segregated branches, even in the North.[5] Black women certainly tried to change things. Once employed, Anna Arnold joined myriad other YWCA women who used the language of Christianity to convince their white sisters that a commitment to Jesus and a commitment to racial justice were one and the same.[6]

Founded in the mid-nineteenth century to assist and uplift poor and working-class white women while indoctrinating them into evangelical Protestantism, the YWCA provided young women with an alternative to the street, to bars, and to dance halls.[7] The organization provided lunchtime prayer meetings for factory workers, Bible study as a means of teaching literacy, lecture and exercise programs, and industrial training classes.[8] In addition to delivering assistance to young women challenged by poverty, poor educational opportunities, difficult home lives, and abuse, the organization deliberately provided leadership opportunities for middle-class white and, later, black women. "We believe that it is important for women to work with men, but not until they have learned to work with women," one member explained. "In the churches, women have usually held subsidiary positions. They have prepared the food and washed the dishes, while men have made the decisions." In the YWCA, women would experience both the rewards and the burdens of responsibility.

Although the YWCA made room for African American women and provided them with those same opportunities, until the mid-twentieth century most cities had separate black and white branches. The white branch would generally be named after the city, and the black branch after the street it was on. This permitted the organization to segregate black and white women without advertising it: rather than calling them a white branch and a black branch, there was a Springfield branch and a West Clark Street branch, a Jersey City branch and an Ege Avenue branch, a Brooklyn branch and an Ashland Place branch.[9] This form of segregation provided the opportunity for black women to live out "the advantages of the disadvantages."[10] Had the YWCA started out as an integrated organization, it is unlikely that African American women would have found opportunities to serve in leadership positions, particularly top management positions like the executive director's slot.

But many of the black women who seized those opportunities would recognize, as Anna Arnold did in short order, that leadership without autonomy was not true leadership. Branch activities were subject to central—that is, white—approval. White women from the central governing organization sat on the governing boards of the black branches, while black women were appointed to the white boards primarily as tokens, one at a time, and slowly. The advantage of leadership, then, was compromised not only by segregation but also by the oversight by white women of black women's work. African American women were not happy about it, but they also understood that their choice at that time was not between segregation and integration, or between autonomy and subordination, but between segregation and outright exclusion.[11] Black YWCA workers developed a variety of strategies to influence their branches and the larger organization. These ranged widely, with some black women making the best of things, others directly confronting the organizational hierarchy, and still others finding ways to do the work they deemed vital without drawing attention to it.[12]

Anna Arnold learned a great deal at the Springfield YWCA about organizational culture and the workings of racism. And since the YWCA's work encouraged an active and ongoing consideration of the ways in which women's spiritual, material, personal, and political well-being were intertwined, she also honed her understanding of the ways in which black women's multiple identities, as workers, as Christians, as women, and as African American citizens, influenced their everyday lives.[13]

In Springfield, a city in southwestern Ohio, the naive distinction Arnold had made between North and South was finally and firmly broken. "Here," she wrote, "I met the sugar-coated segregated pattern of social work and housing in the North."[14] Although the white women did not call what they practiced "segregation," and instead maintained an illusion that black and white women worked together within a mutually beneficial structure of Christian social service, no other name could be applied to the practices the YWCA had put into place. Blatant "colored" and "white" signs, so pervasive in Mississippi, might have been absent, but it was because they were unnecessary, which was in some ways worse. Segregation was not spelled out, but everyone in Springfield, like Anna Arnold's friends from Hamline, understood how it worked.

In the Springfield YWCA, black staff members could not eat in the cafeteria of the central association, and members of the black branch could not enter the central building, which offered its members a pool and a gymnasium. Arnold found little of the peaceful coexistence between blacks and whites that she had experienced in what increasingly seemed to be the rare—and rarefied—environments of her hometown of Anoka, or of Hamline University. Just as she had in Mississippi, she found herself expending a great deal of energy trying to encourage confidence in youth, in the face of the commonplace racist indignities that marked their daily lives.[15] Many black women withdrew from interracial work based on such occurrences, but for now Arnold tried her best to maintain some faith in white people and to execute change through Christian channels.[16] She did not want to believe, as one African American member of the YWCA did, that the organization was a "spiritual farce" rather than a "spiritual force."[17]

Her faith would be sorely tested. In addition to trying to ameliorate the effects of racism in the lives of the young women who joined the organization, she found she was also assigned the task of "race relations" in the YWCA and in the larger community. What that entailed, she discovered, was finding ways to explain white Christian hypocrisy to white people. Anna Arnold would assume this responsibility for the rest of her life, while simultaneously admonishing white people for not taking on this most basic Christian task of self-evaluation. With a mixture of rage and resignation, she concluded that in Springfield, "there WERE no relations" between black and white people generally, or black and white Christians in particular. She gave many talks and grew weary of following to the podium people who quoted Jesus but never put his dictates into practice. When she and others doggedly insisted that improved race relations meant eliminating segregation in the organization, white YWCA leaders balked. She felt the weight of history, in the North as in the South, bury the possibility of real Christian fellowship or female solidarity.[18]

In truth, changes had begun to take place in the racial dynamics of the YWCA: in 1924, Elizabeth Ross Hayes became the first black woman elected to the national board, and by 1930 some twenty-five cities, including Springfield, had placed black women on their general boards.[19] Truly significant changes, however, would take decades to implement.[20] The words of older African American women she met, who had been involved in early-twentieth-century civil rights work, began to make more and more sense to the young and generally optimistic Arnold. Mrs. Oscar Harris, who served as the black representative to Springfield's central board, warned her not to get her hopes up: "You know as well as I do," she told her, "that white Christians are not yet Christians."[21] Arnold increasingly understood, to a degree she could not have appreciated before, that the YWCA's policy could never mean separate but equal; for black women, separate always meant "inferior, despised and unequal."[22] In 1925, at the helm of a beleaguered black branch, she would likely have found the changes in the YWCA nominal, rather than material. Even though she knew little if anything of national civil rights struggles at that time, she began to understand that change had to come, in the North as well as in the South, and to be meaningful it had to be substantial.

After Arnold had spent more than a year in Springfield, the national YWCA offered her the opportunity to travel to New York City for leadership training. Perhaps this was part of the protracted national effort to move toward integration. Whether it was a conscious move or not, Anna Arnold was the only black woman in the group, and she found the intensive training, which addressed issues of race, excellent not just for her but for all of her peers. One woman confided in her that she did not know how she could return home after the experience and remain "reasonable and honorable and decent." After all, her father was an officer in the Ku Klux Klan.[23] After spending several thought-provoking weeks getting to know New York City, visiting Harlem for the first time, and recognizing that since she had come to view not only the South but now also the Midwest with "hate and fear," Arnold realized that it might be time, again, for her to move on.[24]

Using the contacts she had developed, Arnold secured a position as executive director of the Ege Street YWCA, in Jersey City, New Jersey, just across the Hudson River from New York City. She hoped for greater success in her appeals to white Christian women on the East Coast than she had had in Ohio. She felt terrifically guilty for leaving behind all those young women in Springfield, as they clearly needed her or someone like her, but they and their families saw great promise in their executive director and understood that she had to move on. She tendered her resignation with their support and blessing.

Once in New Jersey, Arnold again encountered the separate that was not equal. As executive director of a segregated, black YWCA branch, even in the Northeast, she found her influence limited and her resources paltry. The building was inferior to the white branch in every way. She raised the question of merging the two sites, believing integration was the most basic answer to inequality and injustice, but white leadership in New Jersey proved no more interested in integration than white leadership in Ohio.[25] Passionately committed to the survival and betterment of working-class white girls, they raised funds for a new building, filled it with amenities, and then allowed only the white affiliate to move in. They offered the most tired of excuses: the community was not "ready" for a "drastic" move, and young black people were probably happier among their own kind. Arnold called them on their racism in a meeting. "How could any intelligent young Negro be happy?" she demanded. No one responded.[26]

Enormously frustrated, but recognizing the limits of her influence, the new executive director tried instead to focus on her constituents, the young black women who gathered at the YWCA for fellowship and support. A large number of laundry workers had joined the ranks of the membership, and they provided her first lessons in the politics and economics of industrial labor. The women participated in some of the educational and cultural programs she designed to foster "uplift" as well as leadership development, but she found them less engaged than she would have wished. Arnold mistook their lack of focus for a lack of seriousness, their exhaustion for laziness. She had some lessons to learn. When she complained about the girls to one of the program leaders, the woman turned it around on her. How much experience, she asked, did the executive director have toiling in a laundry? She challenged Arnold to spend her upcoming vacation working in a laundry and see how she felt at the end of the workday.

Arnold agreed that it would be helpful to have a better understanding of the lives of her charges, and she secured a position in a laundry the following Monday morning. She found the work physically draining and emotionally traumatic. Tuberculosis ran rampant through the black female workforce, and the daily break for lunch was so brief that the women ate at their machines. The most exhausted of the group, young nursing mothers, trudged home at the end of the day to feed their babies their "hot, tired milk."[27]

At the end of a week, Arnold felt as weary as any of her charges and found herself positively limp when she attempted to participate in YWCA-scheduled activities, regardless of how entertaining or edifying they promised to be.[28] As she had been reminded again and again in Holly Springs, Mississippi, she realized that she had lived a life of significant privilege, and there was much about the lives of others she simply could not see. She would have to keep that in mind to work respectfully and effectively with those whose lives she hoped to better. Although it was a lesson Arnold would have to learn repeatedly, she was beginning to understand the words of E. T. Ware, the president of her father's alma mater: "You cannot expect to have much influence over one whom you look down upon. If you are by your work of the brains to help make life worth living you must heartily respect and honor the workers with the arms who make life possible."[29]

The brief episode of working in the laundry proved formative as more than just a lesson in humility; it provided Arnold's first foray into the politics of labor. Raised a Republican and inclined toward individual rather than collective responses to social problems, she had been antiunion without understanding what it was that unions afforded or what workers lacked. She had had little incentive to think about unions in the largely agricultural settings of small-town Minnesota or rural Mississippi. Even in the more industrial Springfield, Ohio, racism in the automobile and related industries had prevented young YWCA members from securing employment at all, never mind unionization opportunities in manufacturing. But in Jersey City, Arnold broadened her thinking about black women's work. She witnessed the realities of work for undereducated, underpaid women in underdeveloped urban communities and then struggled, as did other African American women in the YWCA, to reframe the organization so that it could more effectively acknowledge racial disparities, empower the disempowered, and work toward substantive changes in the communities she served.[30]

Many of the laundry workers had participated in the Great Migration, the movement north that Arnold had naively and unequivocally supported a few years earlier when she witnessed the misery of life in Mississippi. Here in New Jersey, she learned a bit more about what the trip entailed and the life it led to. Many of these women had been recruited by employment agencies, some of which were notorious for their abuses. The women paid exorbitant fees for their passage and work contacts, receiving in the end poor housing, dismal wages, and abysmal working conditions. Some of the women recruited to domestic service lived in conditions close to slavery, earning only room and board. Were she alive today, Arnold would be shocked to learn that domestic service servitude continues in the United States, entrapping, most of the time, undocumented immigrant women from a wide range of countries around the world.

Once she understood the situation, Arnold longed to remedy it. Although a coworker had begun to instruct her in the complicated nature of unionization efforts, particularly for laundry and domestic service workers, she still felt compelled to raise the issue of unionizing with her board. The YWCA "must act," she concluded, presenting the matter to the industrial committee and then to the board as a whole.[31] She found the resistance from the leadership both troubling and instructive. Only one or two women seemed inclined to pursue the issue by raising it with employers. As Arnold discovered, social service organizations generally shied away from union organizing efforts. More important, she learned that the YWCA's major donors, some of whom held an interest in the very industries that employed the membership, would not have appreciated such intercessions.

Not one to back down easily, and increasingly passionate about the work lives of the women she served, Arnold began to visit churches and deliver lectures, hoping that even if the decision-makers in the YWCA would not side with her,

Christians, her natural constituency, would respond to injustice with action. She studied the Bible, taking comfort in the stories of Jesus, whose concern for the multitudes provided her with inspiration as well as apt quotes for her lectures.[32] But, she found, white Christians in New Jersey were not unlike those in the Midwest: several came up to speak with her after her talks, but their commitment usually went no farther than the church door. She found it increasingly difficult to live out her parents' mandate to use her education not only to secure her future but also to live in righteous community with those less fortunate. Religion and race, as she had discovered during her college years, were intertwined in confusing, complex ways.

Now in her midtwenties, Arnold hungered for more of a social life than that available to a young, black, single professional woman in Jersey City. With Maude Green, her assistant at work, she regularly traveled to Harlem on her days off.[33] They loved the energy they found in Harlem's six square miles of brick and asphalt.[34] Bitter about the racism that seemed to entrap Jersey City's YWCA members, the two young women loved Harlem's audacious street life, finding solace, for example, in hearing black men laugh as they recounted racial indignities they faced. It was the time of the New Negro Renaissance, and Harlem was, in the words of philosopher Alain Locke, "the Mecca of the New Negro."[35] Harlem was the place to be.

The neighborhood was home to active National Urban League and NAACP offices; myriad civic, religious, and fraternal organizations; and black-owned restaurants, florists, funeral parlors, and employment agencies. In 1926, Arturo Schomburg, an immigrant from Puerto Rico who had amassed a huge collection of books on black history and culture, added his collection to that of the fledgling black history collection at the public library branch on 135th Street, only a block from where Anna Arnold would live for decades.[36] A street corner one block farther, at 135th Street and Seventh Avenue, became known as "The Campus"; it was filled with soapbox orators proclaiming every possible political, religious, and social position. Marcus Garvey and A. Philip Randolph carried on the London tradition of getting up on a box or a stepladder and delivering lectures, but many other speakers, women as well as men, were equally renowned at the time.[37]

It was a heady atmosphere for Arnold. She had lived primarily among whites in Minnesota, and primarily among blacks in Mississippi, but this form of segregation felt altogether different. By 1920, some sections of Harlem were 90 percent black, and to Anna Arnold it felt right rather than oppressive.[38] A character in a Rudolph Fisher short story expresses the sort of enthusiasm she felt when he exits the subway at Lenox Avenue and 130th Street and sees Harlem for the first time: "Negroes at every turn . . . big, lanky Negroes, short, squat Negroes; black ones, brown ones, yellow ones, men . . . women . . . children . . . Negroes predominantly, overwhelmingly everywhere."[39] This was just what Arnold craved, a break from white people and an immersion in a more empowered black life.[40]

Anna Arnold had by now served as the executive director of two YWCA branches, one in the Midwest and one in the East, and in each case she had worked fairly closely with white people. Sadly, this experience had done nothing to ease the antipathy she had developed for whites during her time in the South. So, when the executive secretary of Harlem's black YWCA branch, Cecelia Holloway Cabaniss Saunders, offered her a position as membership secretary, she was elated. As membership secretary she would deal primarily with the members, not with white people, and by relocating to Harlem, she would no longer have to live with or travel among them. As she explained, "I was completely free of and through with white people."[41] White people were exhausting and exasperating: "Why should I take an hour to say I'm a human being and another hour to say I'm an American citizen and another hour to say I am proud of being a Negro and another hour to say that all I want out of life is what any American should have? They weren't worth it. I had finished with them."[42]

Arnold moved to Harlem, and to the Harlem YWCA, with a specific agenda: self-segregation. "I could see only one way to freedom, 'nationalism,'" she reflected later. "Although the word 'nationalism' was not in my vocabulary, I knew that somehow the great talent and spirit of Negroes must be developed into a unified voice to demand not alms, but its birthright."[43] She was beginning to develop the political perspective she would hone as the years passed. It was marked by a move to the left politically, a demand that Christianity follow rather than deny Christ, and an increasing awareness of the need for black autonomy in an American, and then a global, context.

Before she started her new position, the twenty-eight-year-old Anna Arnold traveled home to visit with her family and share both her good news and her evolving political perspective. She found herself looking at her neighbors, her pastor, and her home congregation differently. They were white, and she was black; did they ever really, *could* they ever really, respect her? She tallied things up: to date, she figured, she had known only six white people who "lived as though they respected all mankind."[44] Such thoughts seemed treasonous in her hometown, and she found herself an outsider even within her own family. Communication was a struggle. Anna told her siblings about the wonders of New York City, its theaters and concert halls, but she could not find the words to describe the racism that also pervaded American life without, she feared, making them wary of going out into the world themselves. She was more frank with her parents, frightening her mother and provoking her father, who found her discussions of race overblown. She had no more success explaining herself to her beloved white neighbors next door or to the church family that invited her to speak at Sunday service, and she ended her visit feeling embittered and misunderstood.

Arnold returned east, having relinquished her executive position in New Jersey as readily as she now seemed to abandon the interracial legacy her parents had tried to pass along. She would eventually return to it, but only after experiencing the affirming, edifying, and therapeutic effects of living in Harlem. Ironically, she would realize later, she needed to live among black people to restore her faith first in humanity, and then in the potential of whites.

New York City's first black YWCA branch, founded in 1905, had been housed on West 63rd Street. When that building was sold, the branch reopened on West 54th Street, in a predominantly black neighborhood. In 1913, the black New York City branch moved to Harlem, joining the many black people and institutions that were moving there in the second decade of the twentieth century.[45] Local white women attempted to prevent its relocation to what they still considered "their" Harlem, but with the support of Grace Dodge, a white woman who had served as the first president of the YWCA, black women secured the funds to purchase two houses on West 132nd Street.[46] Eventually, the branch settled on West 137th Street, its location when Anna Arnold was hired. Cecelia Cabaniss Saunders, a Fisk University graduate, a member of the YWCA's national board, and the woman who would both hire and inspire Arnold, became its general secretary in 1914 and then stayed with the YWCA for more than thirty years.[47]

Saunders ran a formidable organization. In 1905, the black branch of the YWCA had a budget of less than $500 and no full-time general secretary. Its minutes of March 1908 reveal that the board worried about how it would pay the rent, a $25 phone bill, and a $6.90 coal bill, with only $97 in the treasury. Fundraising efforts consisted of appointing two members, Mrs. H. Jackson and Miss L. Robinson, "to visit all rich ladies who might aid us, and tell them of our necessities."[48] Under Saunders's brilliant leadership, the organization saw tremendous expansion; when it celebrated its twenty-fifth anniversary, in 1930, it occupied a half-million-dollar building, employed a staff of nearly one hundred, had a budget just shy of $2 million, and offered classes on more than fifty subjects to a thousand girls and women a year.[49]

The 137th Street YWCA initially offered boarding opportunities to a dozen women, but by 1930 the Emma Ransom House, named after one of the board chairs, provided housing for 165 women.[50] By the 1930s the facility also included a four-hundred-seat auditorium, rooms for club activities, and new facilities for the trade school.[51] By the time Saunders retired, the membership had climbed from two hundred to six thousand, and the YWCA trade school provided instruction for up to three thousand women a year. Saunders's more sophisticated fundraising techniques included soliciting help from the Rockefellers and the Rosenwald Fund in addition to soliciting aid from the "rich ladies" of New York City.[52] Under her leadership, the YWCA became the largest social service agency in Harlem.[53]

Arnold's world expanded tremendously at the 137th Street YWCA. She worked among hundreds of people who furthered a mission she believed in, blossomed in the vibrant black and actively Christian environment, and took advantage of the bustling literary and artistic programs on offer. Poets Langston Hughes and Countee Cullen regularly dropped in to give or listen to impromptu poetry readings. Other Harlem luminaries mingled in the lobby, attended talks, and listened to performances of Negro spirituals. Indeed, if Harlem was the center of black America, its YWCA was, for some, the cultural center of Harlem.[54] Its cafeteria served a hundred people a day, and one never knew who might drop in for a meal. As Jean Blackwell Huston, director of the Schomburg Library, recalled, diners "who could have eaten almost any place would come and have Sunday dinner there."[55]

The YWCA's Emma Ransom House provided comfortable lodgings for working women and for travelers passing through; like the cafeteria, it provided a space in which people from a wide variety of social and economic circles would be around each other if not in conversation with each other. It also provided maid service, elevator service until midnight, message and laundry services, a sewing room, a piano, a beauty parlor, and a dressmaking, mending, and pressing shop. In 1930, perhaps with some trepidation, Cecelia Saunders had to pen a letter of regret to W. E. B. Du Bois, who had tried to secure housing for his cousin while she was visiting New York. The Emma Ransom House was "booked solid," she told Du Bois, promising to see to it that his cousin was "comfortably placed in an investigated home."[56]

During her years at the 137th Street YWCA, Anna Arnold developed no white friendships and wanted none.[57] She spent a good deal of time with her family, sharing an apartment with the sister and two brothers who followed her to New York City.[58] She also developed meaningful and lasting relationships with African American women, many of them fellow YWCA employees. Cecelia Cabaniss Saunders was her most powerful inspiration; she more than anyone shaped the organization's staff and its culture, finding her own ways to resist the racist structure still in place nationally in the YWCA. Most important among them, perhaps, was Saunders's practice of hiring her own people without checking in with higher-ups. Once she knew that Arnold was interested in the membership secretary position, she made the offer without going through any further channels. A few years later, when Saunders interviewed Dorothy Height for the position of assistant director of the Emma Ransom House, Height, who already knew the workings of the YWCA, expressed surprise that the larger board would not be consulted in her hiring. "In this branch, we look out for our own. We select our own people," Saunders told her.[59]

In fostering a climate of excellence for black women, Saunders created a space in which they could work together and develop the networks they would rely on, personally and professionally, for many years to come. White women had one clear means of demonstrating their suitability for professional employment: their race. African American women had to call on a wider range of criteria to establish their credibility, including their education, activism, religious commitment, and dedication to a cause. In each of these areas, which certainly overlapped, they developed invaluable networks.[60] One of Arnold's closest YWCA relationships was with Pauli Murray, who later became a scholar, civil and women's rights activist, poet, lawyer, and Episcopal priest. Murray and Arnold worked together on a range of issues, provided mutual support in the face of everyday indignities of racism and sexism, furthered and celebrated each other's professional accomplishments, and would one day commemorate fifty years of friendship.[61]

Arnold became friendly with Mable Keaton Staupers, who worked to open the field of nursing to black women, and Dorothy Height, who would later become president of the National Council of Negro Women, a post she would hold for forty years. She also got to know sisters Cordella Winn and Eva Bowles, both employees of the YWCA national board in New York who played significant roles in expanding the organization's services for black women. As Cordella Winn later recalled, "Practically every Negro woman worker in Negro social institutions or agencies had at one time or another been a Y.W.C.A. worker."[62] Given that more than a hundred organizations held their meetings in the many meeting rooms at the YWCA, women working there met and interacted with an extremely wide range of professionals providing one kind of service or another to their Harlem community.[63] (How telling it is, given the depth of her influence, that Cecelia Cabaniss Saunders is almost completely absent from historical explorations of Harlem life during the New Negro Renaissance of the 1920s or the Great Depression of the 1930s.)

Since it was her job to invite guests to the YWCA to provide members with educational, literary, and cultural programs, Arnold met and developed relationships with a wide range of accomplished African American women, many of whom became part of her network. She was particularly passionate about the lecture program, which brought professional women to speak with the YWCA members about their lives and work. Because black students got short shrift from both public school and college guidance counselors, who tended to "limit the perspective of the Negro student," as Arnold explained, these lectures proved formative, introducing young black women to the possibilities of improved lives through nursing, teaching, entrepreneurship, social work, and other career paths.[64]

While even some members of the Harlem community felt it best to limit black women's aspirations, couching discouragement in notions of "realistic opportunities," Cecelia Saunders and Anna Arnold presented every dream as possible, every career path as attainable. "There isn't the freedom here that they expect," Saunders instructed Arnold about the many young women seeking opportunities in New York City. "But we are going to prepare them to go after the things which are their due."[65] The list of speakers formed a who's who of African American women of the day, including bank president Maggie Walker, soon-to-be presidential adviser Mary McLeod Bethune, religious leader and businesswoman Nannie Helen Burroughs, and cosmetics entrepreneur Annie Turbo Malone. Anna Arnold's favorite lecturer, activist Mary Church Terrell, who had been one of the first black graduates of Oberlin College and who inspired others also to pursue a college education, instructed the YWCA members that excellence, above all else, must mark all of their endeavors.

Because of racial restrictions at white hotels in New York City, visitors from all over the black diaspora stayed in Harlem, and they inevitably stopped in and signed the guest book at the YWCA. Most of the nation's black intellectual and political leaders spoke there at one point or another, generally without charging a fee. Because the white press rarely reported on these black notables, such events at the YWCA felt at once monumental and intimate.[66] They also allowed for significant contact between people at different rungs of the black social ladder. "The college president, the distinguished professor, the professional worker, the domestic servant, the foreign Negro, the Pullman porter, the laundry worker, the housewife, father and husband shared the identical agony," Arnold lamented, "the commonality of rejection." That did not mean that the mood was low, however, for the determination to change things was acute. As she explained, "They talked of this rejection but did not moan about it. Their concern centered around plans and strategies which would bring the Negro his rightful and creative relationship to the total American scene."[67]

Given the centrality of the YWCA to the life of Harlem, Cecelia Cabaniss Saunders expected the women who worked at the information desk in the lobby to assist anyone who happened along. The "all-knowing guardian" of the desk, she explained, "must be prepared to furnish names and addresses of all social welfare agencies and workers, hospitals and sanitariums, Negro newspapers, summer boarding places, music schools, express companies, taxicab companies, theaters and moving picture houses, public stenographers, churches, and addresses of prominent colored New Yorkers."[68] Sometimes she and her husband would stop by the front desk to test the woman on staff, asking her an obscure question they imagined a guest from abroad might pose. The front desk staff read the *New York Times* every morning in anticipation of questions about current events, serving, in a way, like research librarians for greater Harlem. It was important to Saunders that "there was recognition of neither race nor age, sex nor creed, in giving information to applicants in distress."[69]

The bustling YWCA lobby of the 1920s was also known as an environment in which young professionals could relax a bit and make new acquaintances. Perhaps they met there before they went off to the nearby Lafayette Theater for live drama, to a fraternity or sorority social, to Connie's Inn for a nightclub act, to A'Lelia Walker's Dark Tower salon for a lecture, or to church for a rousing social gospel sermon. It was a lively and friendly place, and Anna Arnold was not the only one to meet her future husband in the lobby of the YWCA.[70]

Merritt Hedgeman's mother served as a volunteer for Arnold's "Thursday nighters," a support and advocacy group for domestic workers. One day she saw Arnold writing invitations for a rooftop dance party and asked her to consider inviting her son. Thinking that the diminutive and young-looking Mrs. Hedgeman had only small children, Arnold told her the dance was for grown-ups. Mrs. Hedgeman laughed and described Merritt, a six-foot-tall Fisk University graduate. Hearing this, the membership secretary readily included him on the guest list.[71]

Once they had met, Anna was intrigued by Merritt, but since she was dating someone else, she began to call him her "Secret Passion." Whenever he would stop in, one of her colleagues would let her know that "S.P." was in the building. Anna would grab a notepad and pencil and "happen to appear" on the scene. One day she heard music through the door of her office, and when she peeked into an adjoining room, there he was, singing in his strong, clear tenor voice. She had a tin ear, but her father was also a tenor and, as it turned out, had a musical orientation similar to Merritt's, so they found a lot to talk about. The friendship developed slowly into a romance, and Merritt introduced Anna to another side of Harlem, the world of Negro spirituals. A former soloist in the Fisk Jubilee Singers, Merritt had by now developed a reputation as one of the finest young tenors in New York.

As the couple got to know one another, they discovered that they shared, among other things, a commitment to a Christianity that gave full and unequivocal support to the wholeness of the black experience.[72] Neither could extricate religion from race, race from religion. Such an understanding always informed their work lives, prompting Merritt's dedication to Negro spirituals and Anna's approach to politics and society. It would also provide the foundation for a long and loving relationship.

Regardless of her intentions, Anna Arnold could not completely avoid dealing with white people while she worked at the YWCA. One of her duties was to deliver a talk to tourists, many of them white, who concluded their tour of Harlem with a stop in the building. She experienced this limited degree of contact as somewhat gratifying, as she was able to craft the way in which her beloved Harlem would be defined for these visitors before they left town. Ultimately, though, she found the experience frustrating, feeling once again that white people simply could not escape their narrow worldviews. Invariably, after her presentation, a few of the white visitors would insult her, Harlem, and all black people with the same two questions. What did Negroes want, they wondered, and wasn't intermarriage taking things too far? Black people wanted no more and no less than what white people wanted, she would explain, trying to contain her irritation, and the truly tragic chapter of American history concerned not intermarriage but rape, the generations-long practice of sexual violence forced by white men on black women.[73]

Arnold did not always contain her sarcasm. "I tried to soften the blow by saying that it was entirely possible that there might be some white people whose breadth of experience could make them worthy mates of Negroes, but this was not so easy to predict, since white people suffered so deeply from the worship of their whiteness."[74] As a Christian, she later wondered about the efficacy of these interactions: Did these verbal attacks on white people push them along in their understandings of race, or did her open expressions of anger simply provide a means for them to believe they had heard and understood black complaints, and for her to vent her rage, with the result that nothing actually changed?

Anna Arnold felt proud of her community, proud of her race, and excited about the positive work accomplished at the YWCA in the late 1920s. The cultural and work milieus she revolved in, however, did not keep her fully apprised of the dire challenges many of the residents of her community faced. True, the First World War brought with it sufficient economic prosperity that a new black middle class was able to thrive in Harlem.[75] Arnold had many peers, other young African American professional women and men for whom Harlem seemed to offer everything. In 1920, Arthur Q. Hart had launched the first black-owned five-and-ten store on 138th Street, attracting a thousand people a day.[76] Also in 1920, the Blumstein family, owners of a local department store, despite their infamously discriminatory hiring practices, spent more than a million dollars on a new building on 125th Street, the "uptown Saks Fifth Avenue."[77] By 1929, more than a hundred black-owned businesses in Harlem organized into the Colored Merchants Association in order to buy merchandise cooperatively and sell competitively.[78] It was relatively easy to read Harlem on the surface and view the 1920s as a "roaring" decade for the community.

The mood was high, but the complications of race and inequality in urban New York City in the 1920s resulted in larger and larger swaths of Harlem designated as slum areas.[79] Progress in the neighborhood may have appeared "as regular as the running of the subway," but in truth, continued white control of the community's resources kept the neighborhood from developing to its potential, if at all.[80] Whites, many of them absentee landlords of the most negligent sort, owned more than 80 percent of the wealth in the community.[81] Harlem saw a 66 percent increase in its black population from 1910 to 1920, and buildings were increasingly overcrowded. Conditions continued to worsen rather than improve through the decade.[82] Black immigrants and migrants from the South may have wanted to settle down, but they often lived transient lives, driven from one overpriced tenement to another. Underemployment also plagued black New Yorkers. As sociologist E. Franklin Frazier explained, there were only two types of businesses in New York, those that employed "Negroes in menial positions," and those that employed "no Negroes at all."[83] Even before the Great Depression, blacks were already seriously underemployed.[84]

Still, Anna Arnold and others who worked, lived, or socialized at the YWCA could easily have gotten the impression that things were better than they actually were, as black newspapers advertised the Horatio Alger stories of ordinary men and women who had gotten rich. But the public health issues that accompanied starvation wages and poor housing existed in Harlem in the 1920s just as they did in rural Mississippi. The leading causes of death in 1925 in Harlem included pneumonia, infant mortality, and tuberculosis, which served as fairly reliable barometers of a community's economic well-being.[85] At the same time that prestigious colleges like Fisk, Howard, and Lincoln held annual alumni galas in Harlem, nearby residents held rent parties to come up with their monthly payments. Blacks spent more than twice as much of their income on rent as white New Yorkers did, and twice as many blacks as whites had to take in boarders to meet their expenses.[86] Harlem experienced depression well before the Great Depression provided a name for the experience.[87]

Black residents of New York City needed increased access to lucrative jobs, but the employment situation was extremely slow to change. Black journalist George Schuyler put it this way: "Turn a machine gun on a crowd of red caps, and you would slaughter a score of Bachelors of Arts, Doctors of Law, Doctors of Medicine, Doctors of Dental Surgery."[88] Redcaps would all have been men, but a similar point could be made about black women: among those who were lucky enough to secure domestic employment in the North were many women who had worked as teachers in the South.[89]

Cecelia Cabaniss Saunders tried to keep her eye on the big picture, and she taught Anna Arnold a great deal through her relentless advocacy for their members. While the educational center developed training programs in nursing, domestic service, secretarial work, bookkeeping, dressmaking, design, and power machine operation, Saunders met with private and public sector employers and union representatives to advocate for the removal of the color line in employment. As the brochure for the YWCA trade school described it, the goal was "to prepare Negro women to successfully invade the industrial and business world."[90] Arnold was enormously proud to be hosting the invasion. But as the decade progressed, troubling signs were in place, not just on the horizon.

Anna Arnold had headed north in 1922 to spread the word, but life took her in directions she had not anticipated. She left Mississippi with the firm belief that whites would be her allies in bringing change to a racist South. None of her experiences in the northern, Christian YWCA supported that belief, and instead of fellowship with white Christians, she found herself living in a state of active antagonism. Given her faith, she found this painful, and repeated experiences prevented her from seeing it as temporary. It would take her experience of the Great Depression for her to revisit her Christian commitment to all of God's people, to re-engage with the idea that the salvation of her people, and by that she came to mean all people, depended on keeping race simultaneously at the forefront and far in the background of the national conscience.

5 HARLEM AND BROOKLYN IN THE GREAT DEPRESSION

The 1920s were good years for Anna Arnold. She attended and graduated from college, made advances in her professional life, moved to the mecca of black America, and developed community with other young and progressive black women and men. She recruited hundreds of young women to join the Harlem YWCA, including those who could readily afford the membership fee and those who struggled to pay their dues. Like her, so many of these young people seemed on the cusp of changing their lives for the better. With Cecelia Cabaniss Saunders at the helm, the organization had begun to push open the doors of professional fields previously closed to black women. Between the optimism of the YWCA's leadership and the determination of its constituents, the future appeared bright and certain.

Once the stock market crashed, in 1929, ushering in the Great Depression, the YWCA, as Arnold later remembered, "discovered the rest of the community."[1]

So many African American residents of Harlem already lived from paycheck to paycheck that they did not have far to fall into outright destitution, and fall they did.[2] The damage was rapid and unprecedented: unemployment among black New Yorkers reached 25 percent during the first year of the Depression, and in less than three years, median black family income decreased by almost half.[3]

Statistically, the heaviest toll of the Depression on African Americans occurred in the South, but in New York City the financial disaster seemed to crush the spiritual as well as the material advances of the previous decade. As the National Urban League put it at the start of 1931, black Americans were "hanging on by the barest thread."[4] Lack of access to the basic necessities led to mounting feelings of desperation. In the South, poor people, black and white, might at least supplement their diets by fishing or hunting, but in the urban North they had no such options. Many faced starvation. Writer James Baldwin, a child in Harlem during the Great Depression, recalled both how little his family had to eat and the numbing repetition of a canned-meat diet. "My mother fried corned beef, she boiled [it], she baked it, she put potatoes in it, she disguised it in corn bread, she boiled it in soup, she wrapped it in cloth, she beat it with a hammer, she banged it against the wall, she threw it on the ceiling."[5]

As the community's largest social service agency, and the only agency in the city serving women over twenty-one years of age, the YWCA was immersed in people's everyday struggles and took on an instrumental role in the community's survival. The mood in the lobby changed from gaiety to gloom. The high-spirited women and men who had lined up to get into the cafeteria for a convivial meal were replaced by somber lines of the unemployed, snaking their way to the offices to sign up for any and all sources of support.[6] Anna Arnold later remembered the despair: "A large mass of Negroes was faced with the reality of starvation and they turned sadly to public relief. A few chanted optimistically, 'Jesus will lead me and Welfare will feed me,'" but "men, women and children searched in garbage cans for food, foraging with cats and dogs."[7]

The Harlem YWCA served as a relief registration center, putting Arnold and her coworkers in a position to garner insights into the depths of the Depression. She was charged with the harrowing task of visiting families to determine who most needed relief and who would be turned away. It did not take her long to realize just how arbitrary any such decision-making would be. She settled on one quantifiable measure for determining degrees of privation: the number of children present who needed milk.[8]

Through these early years of the Depression, YWCA workers doggedly attempted to develop and implement useful programs, some well planned and others piecemeal. Arnold continued as membership director, but job titles meant little in the face of such desperate need. She worked directly with any women who came into the building, members or not, screening them for training, helping to maintain an employment referral service, and recruiting nurses' aides for hospitals; she also assisted at soup kitchens, learned to fight evictions, and coordinated people selling apples on the street so that they were not competing for the meager earnings available.

Sitting in her office interviewing people experiencing such hardship was challenging enough, but when she visited local residents at home, Anna Arnold found the conditions so grim that it was hard to comprehend. Too many of her neighbors, she discovered, lived in vermin-ridden tenements with shared baths, toilets that overflowed to the floors below, and gaping holes in the skylights that let already inadequate heat escape. She discovered an entire world below ground. Thousands of families lived in dank basement rooms with tin pails in the corner for toilets and slits in the walls providing the only light.[9] Families rented out their own beds during the day to those who worked night shifts; if they had a bathtub, they often placed a board over it and rented that out as well.[10] Her job was to differentiate the needy from the more needy; needless to say, she found every day exhausting.[11] Too many people, she concluded, lived "packed in damp, rat-ridden dungeons," in conditions that reminded her of the squalid environments endured by sharecroppers in the deepest South.[12]

Regardless of their living conditions, what African Americans wanted above all else was to provide for themselves, and they looked to the YWCA to help find the jobs that would allow them to do so. Cecelia Saunders saw "girl after girl [come] into this branch of the YWCA asking for work, saying that she did not want relief."[13] The YWCA acted first as an unofficial clearinghouse, directing young women to job openings, to training, and to relief services. As months of Depression led to years, the determined YWCA staff developed approaches that increased the organization's clout with employers and its effectiveness with clients.

Employment agencies operated with openly racist policies, and they had little incentive to change when there were more people competing for fewer job openings. In 1926, there were more than a thousand employment agencies in New York City, but nine out of ten refused to take on black clients.[14] Those that did segregated job seekers by race rather than by skill or aptitude. Skilled black women were pushed into domestic work, and some agencies refused to send them out for any other jobs, no matter what their education or employment histories. Being white in New York City literally doubled one's chances of obtaining work during the Great Depression.[15]

Private agencies were the worst offenders, but state agencies were often little better. A YWCA investigation revealed that the state-run agencies were simply "no good," as "white girls got all the good jobs." They found that discrimination was both systematized and blatant. At the employment agency the telephone company used, workers coded the intake forms to eliminate all black women from consideration.[16] When Cecelia Saunders followed up, the telephone company not only admitted it but argued that customers did not want to hear the voices of black women when they called an operator. "Those girls were reared in New York," Saunders observed. "No one would know whether they were colored or white."[17]

The YWCA advocated for black women from a wide variety of backgrounds. While some, like the women who sought employment as telephone operators, were native New Yorkers, others were West Indian immigrants or migrants from the South. As bad as the employment prospects were overall, the southern migrants faced the most extreme exploitation by employment agencies. Agents traveled to the South, luring young women north with promises of opportunity but placing them in situations of near slavery; they were, literally, trafficked into domestic servitude.[18] In one case, a woman from the South paid a two-dollar fee to obtain a position as a domestic with a family in New York City. Once the agency took out money for her bus fare and other fees, only eight dollars remained of her first month's salary of twenty-five dollars.[19] Other women ended up working for room and board only. The best that could be said about the situation these women found in New York was that sharecropping had prepared them for it.

Another YWCA response to the flagrant practices of employment agencies was to set up its own agency, using its training expertise as well as its clout to place black women in a wider variety of positions. Saunders and her staff identified jobs they hoped to open up for black women, including stock clerk, elevator operator, and sewing machine operator. Unlike established employment agencies, the YWCA's primary commitment was to the employee rather than the employer. It took on quite a charge, attempting to reshape employment practices at a time when workers' rights seemed daily to shrink rather than expand. Anticipating that discrimination would not end once their clients secured employment, the YWCA kept track of the women they placed, following up and providing conflict resolution services as needed.[20]

The YWCA employment agency faced its own financial straits as the Depression continued, and it began to charge women for services at the same time their placements were falling. Grappling with the Sisyphean work of securing her clients and her community even small, practical advances, Anna Arnold was reminded of her time in Mississippi, when daily preoccupations prevented her from thinking more broadly about solutions to the problems black Americans faced as they tried to live their lives with dignity.

Arnold and her colleagues may have lacked the sociological terms to describe black women's particular oppression, but they understood the triple jeopardy that discrimination based on race, gender, and social class imposed. How painful, given the history of black women's exploitation in the homes of white women, for the YWCA employment bureau to have to place more and more women in domestic service.[21] In addition to onerous work, humiliating personal treatment, and abysmally low wages, women in domestic service lived with the fear of sexual assault. Some addressed this by attempting to accept only jobs that ended by early evening, before the men in the household returned from work.[22] One of the elevator operators at the YWCA had been raped by the husband of a woman she worked for; she hid the resulting pregnancy for as long as possible, fearing she would lose her job.[23]

As time went on, even women with professional training sought out employment in domestic service. The YWCA took every opportunity to make it clear that this choice was both unusual and temporary, at least as far as educated black women were concerned. As Cecelia Cabaniss Saunders pointedly explained, "contrary to the accepted American stereotype" this work was new to these women.[24] The YWCA also continued pushing for expanded job opportunities and developing training programs for better positions. At the same time, the staff attempted to shore up the dignity of all women workers by professionalizing domestic service and treating it as a serious occupation rather than the lowliest of positions. The YWCA School of Household Work, a well-regarded program, offered young women flexible schedules, evening as well as day classes in domestic work, and a certification program. Anna Arnold and her colleagues maintained and demonstrated, consistently and somewhat successfully, that the home was also a workplace.

At the same time, employing Christian notions of social justice, the YWCA attempted to turn domestic workers into activists. Arnold hosted the "Thursday nighters," a support group that kept domestic workers informed about legislative efforts that might work in their favor. She readily admitted later that this nonunion approach, what is sometimes called the "YWCA model," had limited success. It did not reach most domestic workers, nor did it adequately challenge the notion of the home as a private space rather than a workplace. However well meant, it could never provide the clout that a union might have, but given the lack of interest organized labor took in domestic workers, it was far from a wasted effort.[25] The YWCA managed to institute some basic regulations for the women they placed, including one afternoon and every other Sunday off, private rooms for live-in workers, and follow-up visits by YWCA personnel to make sure the women were being well treated in their employers' homes.[26]

As bad as domestic service work was, it had at least provided some job security for black women through the 1920s. Economic prosperity among whites before the Great Depression had allowed many immigrant women to leave domestic service at marriage, and even permitted their daughters to forgo it altogether in favor of clerical positions in the burgeoning corporate economy. As disempowered as domestic workers generally were, black women had been somewhat successful in improving conditions; for one thing, their refusal to live in, so that they could care for their own children, changed the dynamic between employer and employee for the better. But as with so many other labor issues, the Great Depression quickly depleted the gains of the previous decade.

As the Depression took away white women's options, they began to reconsider domestic service. As a result, some employment agencies began to send black women out for domestic positions only when employers specifically requested them.[27] Saunders described the response of professional black women, who had already been reduced to applying for domestic service jobs: "Imagine her surprise when told that this opportunity was largely preempted by unemployed office workers, many of them white girls who had entered this field . . . working largely for room and board until the work horizon cleared."[28] The work horizon would not clear for a long, long time.

Sometimes the employment agencies hindered black women's access to employers; other times, employers put race-based policies into place. And as long as white women's racism stood in the way of gender-based solidarity, the result was a race to the bottom for poor women, black and white. In one laundry, an employee explained, "They started taking on colored girls but this is the way they did it: a colored girl would come in and the boss said, 'We can't take you on. The white girls don't want to work with you.' The colored girl would start to go and he'd say, 'I'll take you, but you got to work for less money than the white girls.'"[29] Once the employer had a sufficient number of black women employed at the lowest possible wages, he fired the white women. Sometimes these forms of competition meant black women obtained employment; other times it meant white women did. In all cases, wages and working conditions worsened in the jobs at the bottom, the ones that drew the least attention from politicians and policymakers. Marginalization and invisibility marked the work lives of the most needy women, regardless of the efforts of the YWCA.

A few years later, when Anna Arnold worked as a consultant on racial problems for the City of New York, Mayor Fiorello La Guardia asked her to investigate what was widely known as the Bronx slave market. It had become common for black domestic workers to stand on specific street corners, waiting for the white women who would drive by and offer them day work. The employers continually increased the workload and decreased the pay, until the black women were toiling in slave-like conditions. The mayor's concern was not particularly about black women's struggles; his problem was that the work had become so inhumane that black women were demanding relief instead. White taxpayers insisted that no one had the right to refuse paid employment. The mayor asked Arnold to discover the facts. Donning a housedress and carrying a small purse, she made her way to a variety of street corners in the Bronx. Over several days of speaking with employees and employers alike, she amassed a good deal of material on dozens of slave markets.

Arnold's investigation and the subsequent hearings brought attention to the issue, as did an article in the NAACP journal, the *Crisis*, written by two women in her circle, Ella Baker and Marvel Cooke. They described the Bronx slave market's "paperbag brigade," explaining how the Great Depression had ushered in a new, exploitative employer class, the white, lower-middle-class housewife;[30] Arnold's work revealed that these markets operated not just in the Bronx, but across the city. "I had also seen the exploiter at close range," she reported. "Often she had lived in squalor behind a store in some immigrant neighborhood and had saved, sacrificed and planned for a home. Now there was a large house to be cared for, though she was overtired from long hours in the store. Payments on the new home and college tuition had to be made. What better place to cut than the wages of the dayworker?"[31] In response to Arnold's investigation and a series of hearings, the mayor stationed black policewomen at the most problematic street corners, and the city opened a hiring hall so that hour and price controls could be enforced.

Improvements in black women's working conditions would be painfully slow. One of the New Deal's most successful programs, the Social Security Act of 1935, was designed to provide financial support for the elderly, people with disabilities, and the unemployed. As monumental as the legislation was, it left out agricultural and domestic service workers, who were deemed to work in private rather than public occupations, thereby excluding 65 percent of black workers.[32] One YWCA response was to offer summer camps designed to provide workers with the skills to advocate for improved working conditions. At one camp, black women learned the lyrics to a song demanding Social Security justice: "No more mistress, no more maid, No more work that's underpaid . . . Social Security we need, Social Security indeed!"[33] They found little actual justice. In the end, the new federal policies that mandated minimum wages, maximum hours, unemployment compensation, and Social Security benefits reached no more than 10 percent of the nation's black women workers.[34] Only during the Second World War did the conditions for these workers change significantly, and then only because so many women were able to leave domestic service behind.[35]

Harlem residents who could not find work during the Great Depression, as well as those who earned only starvation wages, had no choice but to seek aid. Black New Yorkers were, just as much as whites, reluctant applicants: a full three-fourths of black families seeking relief during the Depression had never sought any type of assistance before.[36] Once they did, they soon discovered that needing relief and actually getting it were different things. Tens of thousands turned to private and public agencies for food, clothing, and temporary shelter, and, for the very fortunate, employment. Private relief agencies practiced racial discrimination egregiously; some refused to serve Harlem at all.[37] As a result, thousands of Harlem residents turned to the state. The Emergency Relief Bureau, later the Department of Welfare, officially followed a "color-blind" approach to aid, but that was rarely the reality.[38] Jobs were the most desirable but hardest "relief" for black citizens to obtain. By 1934, almost half of all Harlem families needed employment, but only 9 percent of them were given government relief jobs.[39]

Most of the help black women received during the Great Depression came from within their own communities.[40] Churches and grassroots organizations played a key role in keeping families alive. All the major black churches had moved from downtown to Harlem by the early 1920s, and as the most secure community institution, and one with some degree of wealth, the church played an enormously influential role in defining Harlem first as a specific and distinct community, and then as a community in need.[41] A group of ministers from seventeen churches organized the Harlem Cooperating Committee on Relief and Unemployment, feeding twenty-four hundred people a day and helping some twenty thousand with food, clothing, rent, and other assistance, just from January through July 1930.[42] Adam Clayton Powell Sr.'s Abyssinian Baptist Church, two blocks from the YWCA, asked its congregants to pledge part of their weekly income to aid the needy, and it provided assistance to more than forty thousand individuals in 1930 and 1931 alone.[43]

"The response from churches in creating jobs, [and] distributing food and clothing, indicates the dawning of a new day in the Negro church," claimed James Hubert of the New York Urban League, which partnered with the churches to develop relief services.[44] Anna Arnold also worked closely with the churches, including her own St. Mark's Methodist Church, just blocks from the YWCA. Many religious leaders encouraged activism among their congregants and practiced it themselves, pioneering new forms of Christian resistance as they tackled the racially discriminatory practices of the city's relief and social work establishments. One of Arnold's mentors, the Reverend John H. Johnson of St. Martin's Episcopal Church, demanded jobs, spearheading an integration effort among businesses on 125th Street, Harlem's primary shopping district and the Main Street of black American culture.[45] Clergy also challenged each other to step up. Adam Clayton Powell Sr. railed against clerical conservatism; his peers, he proclaimed, should "either aid the unemployed or else resign as unfit to lead their congregations."[46] This was a version of Christianity that Arnold could embrace.

But not surprisingly, by the fall of 1931 Anna Arnold, at age thirty-one, found herself feeling overwhelmed and depleted. She was exhausted. "I loved Harlem, but I was tired of the problems of the multitude—to use the ancient Biblical word which had come to have new meaning for me. I needed rest desperately."[47] When fellow Minnesotan Marion Cuthbert, then a graduate student in psychology at Columbia University and one of the many black women in Arnold's circle, invited her to attend an international conference of students at Mount Holyoke College, she could not resist. "It occurred to me," she later remembered, "that the campus of Mt. Holyoke would be comfortable, the food good, and the expense carried by someone else." Every spare penny she had, she noted, "had long since been spent on bread or milk for someone." Arnold gave herself permission to speak candidly when she accepted the invitation from her friend. "I recall telling Dr. Cuthbert that I could even bear living around white people for the ten days that would be involved."[48]

At Mount Holyoke, Arnold found the conference's international focus refreshing and some of the white people more than tolerable. One person in particular, a German student activist named Fritz Beck, moved her with his description of Hitler's early and rapid ascension to power. Beck demanded that all students, black and white, critique their own uses of power as they stood up for democracy. She also developed a friendship with Galib Ali Rifat, a Turkish student delegate on a debating tour across the United States. She arranged for him to visit with her family in Minnesota and was embarrassed when her mother wrote her afterward about how amazed she was "to find so much culture in a Turk."[49] Rifat, on the other hand, was underwhelmed by what he saw of the United States, particularly when he traveled on a Jim Crow train.

Anna Arnold found herself in a peculiar position, one she would find herself in again and again in the coming years. She wanted to defend her country, but she lacked the evidence to support her claims for democracy, and her own personal experiences made it hard to do so sincerely. If she were to justify any national pride she felt, regardless of all she had seen, heard, and lived, she would have to find ways to renew her own faith first. Perhaps it was time to re-engage with white America and build relationships that went beyond the limitations of race.

When Arnold returned to Harlem following the Mount Holyoke conference, she was swept up in the demands of everyday life and had little time to dwell on larger questions of national pride or her relationship to white Americans. She had gotten engaged to Merritt Hedgeman, and they were starting to think about their future together. But Marion Cuthbert was not the only professional to have noticed Arnold. Soon after, in 1933, when leaders of the NAACP were planning a conference in Amenia, New York, to reinvigorate their organization, they invited her to be one of the "young representatives of the colored race." She was both flattered and disturbed; she was being cast as a Negro intellectual, and she feared it was a distinction that separated leaders from the masses of black people barely surviving the Great Depression. Nevertheless, she attended the Amenia conference. Nearly half the attendees were women, and Arnold took an active role in the discussions and a key role in drafting the report that followed.[50]

National black leaders James Weldon Johnson, Walter White, and W. E. B. Du Bois spoke at this conference, but the focus remained, as promised, on the young people and their ideas. They responded eagerly, pushing for a national agenda that included economic as well as political and legal efforts for justice, and they demanded immediate action. "We had ideas of our own," Arnold explained later, "and insisted, as youth always does, that the progress of the Negro had

been too slow."[51] Unlike some of her peers, she would always remain apprecia-
tive and tolerant of youthful impatience. Four decades later, when the leadership of her generation was being supplanted by a younger generation demanding
black power, Anna Arnold Hedgeman would insist that her peers pay attention.
Although wisdom was a quality that comes with age, she maintained, youth had
to be heard.

At Amenia, after days of sleeping in tents, walking in the woods, and talking,
talking, talking, Anna Arnold began to see herself as others saw her: as a young
black leader with greater potential than she had realized.

Accepting the leadership challenges of the Amenia conference meant giving
up the comfort that living and working in Harlem had allowed. Her work had
been taxing, and the challenges many, but none of it was beyond her natural com-
pass, and it kept her in a circumscribed and parochial world. In taking herself
more seriously as an activist, she had to respond to what she was feeling, which
was a pull back to the interracial vision she had been raised with. Ultimately,
a fully Christian relationship to social change required letting go of race as a
category, no matter how painful her experiences with white people had been.
"I could no longer merely talk at white people," she realized. "I would need to
work with them."[52] When she received an invitation to become executive director of the Catherine Street YWCA branch in Philadelphia, Arnold accepted.
She knew that as executive director her professional contacts would widen considerably, even though this was yet another black YWCA branch. She felt it was
again time to attempt to forge "basic communication, if not sisterhood, with
white women."[53] It meant postponing her marriage, but Merritt agreed that this
was the right move, for the moment. He borrowed his mother's Cadillac, drove
Anna to Philadelphia to begin her new job, and returned to New York.[54]

And indeed, within a year of taking up her leadership position in Philadelphia,
Arnold concluded that she had learned, again, "to speak honestly and without
rancor" with white women. She had also made some changes in the branch,
hiring an entire staff of "brown women" in a city in which only "fair people"
generally got jobs.[55] But Merritt Hedgeman, initially supportive of the idea of a
long-distance relationship, grew tired of the arrangement and was determined to
move forward with his life, one way or another. In October 1933 he issued Anna
an ultimatum, telling her she "must either agree to consummate our friendship
through marriage or separate our lives."[56] She chose marriage, and on November
1 the couple married in a quiet ceremony in the Harlem home of a YWCA board
executive. Merritt's mother, with whom Anna had grown close, was their only
guest.[57]

Perhaps hoping not to complicate her professional life in Philadelphia, Anna
and Merritt kept their marriage secret for the next several months, but eventually

they found living apart too difficult. More than once, they had even spoiled their precious weekends together by attempting to surprise each other: Merritt would be sitting in the train heading south to Philadelphia at the same time Anna boarded a train heading north to New York.

In the end, it just made the most sense for the couple to settle in New York City. Merritt, a lifelong New Yorker, supplemented his performing career with jobs in a bank and in the music program of the New Deal's Federal Music Project. His parents and siblings lived there, and by now most of Anna's siblings had moved to New York. Anna and Merritt invited her parents to relocate from Minnesota and live with them in one side of the two-family house Merritt's parents had purchased in the Bronx, and they accepted. It was, Anna and Merritt figured, an ideal arrangement: they could be near their families but remain free to pursue their careers.[58] Anna had no intention of ending her professional life just because she had married.

Anna and Merritt's marriage lasted fifty-four years, until his death in 1988. Merritt, Anna wrote, "has never permitted the fact that I am a woman to color his judgment of me or his support of my work."[59] She took on Merritt's name at marriage but not to the exclusion of her maiden name, and always signed using both. She was Anna for herself, she explained, Arnold for her father, and Hedgeman for her husband; she liked the combination.[60] Their trust and security in each other, and Merritt's support for her career, unusual for their day, extended even to encouraging her to take on opportunities that required her to travel a great deal, or live apart from him for long periods. They had few if any role models, but figured out on their own how to balance their need for independence with their desire for a partnership. Anna often acknowledged Merritt's support in her speeches and correspondence, proud that they produced, as she described it, their own "special symphony."[61]

Anna described them as being "alike in principle but not in its manifestation."[62] Although Merritt was a performer, at ease on the concert stage, he most often preferred to remain behind the scenes where politics was concerned. They had both grown up in and loved the church, but Anna had always responded to the minister's words, Merritt to the music, and that seemed to characterize their orientation in the world as well.[63] Merritt advocated for social change through an internal process by which African Americans would develop and further respectful and passionate relationships with their music, specifically Negro spirituals. Anna advocated for social change through more secular and outward means, although her Christian faith always supplied much of the motivation for her work, as it did for Merritt. Through their differences, they were well matched. As adults and as a married couple, Anna explained, they both fought hard, but never with each other.[64]

Over the years, Anna saved every greeting card and letter Merritt sent her, each one filled with tender messages and endearing nicknames. He sent her lavish Valentine's Day and anniversary cards and wrote her letters almost daily when they were apart. She also wrote to him regularly, and their letters demonstrate that their relationship was loving, and primary for both of them. They even sent each other Mother's Day and Father's Day cards, although they had no children. Anna never spoke or wrote about their family planning decisions or experiences. Members of her family believe that she might once have suffered a miscarriage, but they also believe Anna and Merritt were happy on their own, without children.

Keeping their family limited to just the two of them may well have been a deliberate decision. As supportive as Merritt was of Anna's career, it is difficult to imagine that she could have done as much as she did if they had had children. Many of the professional women of her generation who combined work and family could afford help with their homes and children, but Anna and Merritt never had enough money for that. "It has never been easy," she wrote of their life together, "the Depression, the uncertainty, no saving on either side, no certainty of economic opportunity." They lived, by and large, from paycheck to paycheck, and neither pursued a career that even provided those with a comfortable degree of regularity.[65] Anna spoke repeatedly, and proudly, of the one pressure she did feel, to uphold the four dominant ideals of the Arnold family name: religion, character, education, and service.[66]

When Anna returned to New York City—now Anna Arnold Hedgeman—she found employment in New York City's public relief agency, the Emergency Relief Bureau, which would soon become the Department of Welfare. The bureau had decided to launch a trial program hiring black supervisors, and she was part of its "experiment." For the next two years, Hedgeman supervised forty staff members, many of them formerly on the relief rolls themselves, in Brownsville, Brooklyn, where people lived in such dire poverty that it made what she had witnessed in Harlem pale. She and her coworkers worked with clients by day and organized them at night, putting pressure on the city to increase their meager welfare budget. She drew the notice of the agency's director, Charlotte Carr, who appointed Hedgeman to a new municipal position, consultant on racial problems. She may well have had Hedgeman in mind when she created the job. "It's tough enough to be a woman," Carr confided to her. "How you have stood being both a woman and a Negro I'll never know."[67]

Anna Arnold Hedgeman knew what she wanted for her community, even more than relief: jobs. The distribution of other forms of relief was valuable in the short term but was not a long-term solution to community needs. It was no secret that city, state, and federal government jobs were the best bet for permanent, decently paid employment, but black New Yorkers continued to be underrepresented in civil service. So while in Brooklyn, she revisited an issue she had advanced at the Harlem YWCA: equity in civil service employment. As a member of the city's Advisory Committee on Negro Problems, she had already pushed Mayor La Guardia to put an end to one particularly egregious practice. The Civil Service Commission tested all applicants but appointed only one of every three candidates on any given list of those who had passed. In this way, the workforce could be kept white while the commission seemed to obey the dictates of fair employment. With the new policy in place, they were no longer able to do that, and Hedgeman pushed on.

During her time as a supervisor in Brooklyn, Hedgeman so successfully integrated the relief bureau that her title changed from consultant on racial problems to, simply, assistant to Charlotte Carr.[68] Now, as second-in-command, she could further usher in changes to enable African Americans to rise to the ranks of the middle class. Dorothy Height, another black woman from Hedgeman's YWCA circle who also went on to be a leader in welfare services, remembered how central Hedgeman was to black attempts to obtain government jobs during the Depression. "More than once," she wrote, recalling the struggles she had to launch on behalf of clients, "I thanked God for Anna Hedgeman." Having two black women in positions of power was unusual, and Hedgeman and Height found themselves victims of racist and sexist office politics. Coworkers tried to divide the two women so as to dilute their effectiveness, but they wouldn't have it. "It didn't work," Height explained simply. Instead, the two women developed an effective working relationship and became "treasured friends."[69]

Hedgeman made several other important interventions during her years in Brooklyn. She was one of the first city administrators to draw attention to the Puerto Rican community, which had remained largely invisible politically, despite its growth. The decline of the Puerto Rican sugar and tobacco industries during the Depression initiated an economic exodus, and more than half of all Puerto Ricans who came to the United States lived in New York City.[70] East Harlem, where they began to form communities, did not become known as Spanish Harlem until after World War II. Before that, Puerto Ricans as a group, although numerous, had not claimed a political space in New York City.

External as well as internal pressures complicated the notion of what it was to be Puerto Rican in the city. Even before the exodus from the island, lighter skin, associated as it was with higher social class, conferred clear benefits. Once in the city, politically savvy Puerto Ricans figured out that being labeled black, as they often were, meant that the citizenship benefits they hoped to capitalize on were immediately placed in jeopardy.[71] Political solidarity was a hard sell within this growing community, as well as within Harlem as a whole, which was less and less white, increasingly black and Puerto Rican. Hedgeman understood that Puerto Ricans had to gain recognition as a minority group on their own terms, but she knew too that solidarity between blacks and Puerto Ricans would be advantageous if not critical to progress for both groups. She visited Puerto Rican neighborhoods in Brooklyn and upper Manhattan, interviewed potential candidates, and put forward the names of the first Puerto Ricans to be given positions as welfare workers in the Emergency Relief Bureau.[72]

Having helped black New Yorkers get jobs at the bureau, Hedgeman next helped them push through the glass ceiling. For all the gains she witnessed and facilitated, she remained frustrated that so few blacks had obtained supervisory positions. It seemed to her as if black employees at the agency had to be more qualified and work harder than white workers just to stay afloat. Without someone in an oversight position to insist on fairness in promotions, she feared black workers would lose traction as the grave economic situation persisted. Equity in the distribution of welfare benefits depended on the presence of black welfare workers; the continued presence and fair promotion of those workers depended on the presence of black supervisors. Hedgeman recommended that the city appoint a black deputy commissioner, to send a clear message from the top. Her idea found almost no support.

The situation became critical when the Emergency Relief Bureau became the Department of Welfare and added five hundred new, provisional appointments. Without a black deputy in place, Hedgeman justifiably assumed that few black applicants would be appointed to these positions. These would have been highly coveted jobs under any circumstances; in the middle of the Great Depression, it would be hard to overstate their significance to the community.

Hedgeman continued to advocate but realized she was getting nowhere. Instead of giving up, she made a move that might have seemed foolhardy at the time but was in retrospect bold and politically savvy: she quit her job so that she could work for change from the outside. "The community was the next resort," she reasoned, "and someone was needed to mobilize it."[73] She left her position in the Emergency Relief Bureau to take on the directorship of the black branch of the Brooklyn YWCA, on Ashland Place. If anyone wondered about Hedgeman's motivation, it did not take long to see what she had in mind. She immediately organized the Citizens' Coordinating Committee with the sole purpose of demanding some of the new appointments at the Department of Welfare. She considered the young people who visited the Ashland Place YWCA her staff, the building her base. In nightly meetings during the next several weeks, she turned a hundred young women and men into activists who bombarded the commissioner with letters and postcards, cultivated attention from the press, and met with community leaders. When the young people proved more militant and impatient than the community leaders, she urged them on.

Black leaders in the city were not, as Anna Hedgeman lamented, "as aggressive as we wished," so the citizens' committee assembled a five-person delegation for a carefully orchestrated meeting with the welfare commissioner. The first speaker, a "charming girl who . . . had a radiant smile," praised the commissioner for all he had done for the community. The second speaker, big, dark, and with a booming voice, spelled out their concerns with a purposeful display of "controlled indignation—almost anger." The third, when it seemed the commissioner would explode under what he surely saw as an attack by the second speaker, jumped in to explain that the group understood the previous speaker's anger but wished to proceed in a cooperative rather than combative manner, as they were sure of the commissioner's noble intentions.

The fourth speaker laid out what might appear to have been a somewhat adjusted set of demands, and the fifth presented a written document along with signatures from representatives of the many organizations that had been consulted in the plan's development. The group left the meeting feeling things had gone fairly well; the commissioner had initially, and reluctantly, allotted them ten minutes but actually let them go on for an hour. Familiar with the stubbornness of bureaucracies, Hedgeman pushed for continued advocacy afterward, with positive results. "It was no accident," she asserted, "that we secured the first 150 provisional appointments the city had ever given the Negro community."[74]

Back within the YWCA, Hedgeman again had the opportunity to try out her notions of Christian sisterhood between black and white women, this time with some success. When the local five-and-ten refused to hire young black women as clerks, she helped form a daily picket line, but older YWCA board members, black as well as white, disapproved of such militancy. By now accustomed to older people simply dismissing the young without actually listening to them, she devised a new plan. She invited three young African American women to give a presentation to the large and largely white Race Relations Committee of the Federation of Protestant Churches. When they finished describing the employment discrimination they faced, there was not a dry eye in the house. "They are so young and so poised," one woman told Anna, "and I found myself thinking of my own children who are about their ages."

To follow up, Hedgeman sent delegations of young black and older white women to visit store managers and ask them to change their employment policies. When that did not produce the results she wanted, she came up with yet another plan: the white women, many of them holders of large charge accounts, began to write notes on their monthly bills. "We expect to see Negro clerks among the other clerks in our stores," they wrote. "As Christians we must patronize those stores which respect all human beings." Versions of this kind of economic pressure, including many "Don't Buy Where You Can't Work" campaigns, were taking place around the city, as the YWCA was joining forces with a number of other organizations. As a result, black women began to secure clerk positions in the city's five-and-ten and department stores. Hedgeman was particularly proud that Christianity served as the driving force in recruiting white women to the struggle.[75]

Anna Arnold Hedgeman's interest in young people drew her back to the YWCA again and again, but it also proved, in this case, to be her undoing. With her encouragement, young black women in the Ashland Place YWCA began to see themselves as potential leaders, not just outside in the community but within the ranks of the YWCA itself. With her support, they began to push for their own slate of officers, rather than simply follow the dictates of the largely white board, as had been the practice. When it seemed likely that the young members would elect a new branch chair and replace the board's choice, she was reprimanded. The president of the General Board, she was told, "does not wish a change in Negro branch leadership this year." Nonetheless, the election went forward, the young people prevailed, and the establishment candidate was ousted. Anna went home and told Merritt that she had written her resignation. "You mean you wrote it?" he asked her, incredulously. She assured him that yes, as soon as she went forward with the election she had, essentially, written her resignation, or ensured her dismissal, whichever came first.

Merritt was deeply concerned. The economy had not yet begun to improve, his bank position paid little, and he regularly encountered the discrimination that most black entertainers faced, even in New York City.[76] Although Anna served as an executive in the YWCA, she was underpaid. They had no savings. On top of that, the president of Merritt's bank and the president of the Brooklyn YWCA were friendly with each other. There was a chance, they realized, that both of them might lose their jobs over this incident. Anna had nothing else lined up, and if Merritt lost his job they would have to apply for relief themselves. After what Anna described as a "big caucus," the couple decided to follow their principles. They sent for a welfare application and hung a welfare budget on their curtain, referring to it as their "declaration of independence." Even if it meant they had to join the ranks of the unemployed, they would operate with dignity in the world.

Once Anna and Merritt were clear with each other, they both felt liberated. After all, it was not just Anna who had grown weary of the racism that pervaded professional life. Merritt had grown tired of playing for white audiences who viewed black performers as "natural" talents rather than artists who worked to hone their craft. He decided to limit how much of this he would put up with.[77]

One night Anna returned home from work to find a note from Merritt announcing that he had quit his job at the Cotton Club, the famed, whites-only Harlem nightclub that featured top black performers and that had provided him with some reliable income. "I quit the Cotton Club tonight," he wrote. "I couldn't sing my songs in a strange land."[78] Anna officially resigned from the YWCA, which had, after all, let her know that her leadership extended only so far. She interpreted the Y's resistance to her ideas and advocacy as a personal, professional, and spiritual betrayal. "If the Christian Association in a large Eastern urban city could not practice its avowed purpose to build a fellowship of women and girls committed to the ideals of Jesus Christ," she lamented, "where could I go?"[79]

Anna Hedgeman might have stayed, lived with compromise, and worked her way up through the leadership of the YWCA, within the limits imposed by race. But she was impatient with what she considered at best stupidity, at worst a rejection of the very simple demands of Christianity: to embrace all people as whole people. If she could not find that in the YWCA, she would look elsewhere, in secular as well as in religious contexts, for as long as it took. When she heard after the fact that she would have been fired from the YWCA had she not resigned, Hedgeman took great pleasure in not having given them the "privilege" of releasing her.

It did not take her at all long to secure her next professional position. It was 1942, and the United States had entered the Second World War. Wartime production had begun to create new opportunities for workers at all levels, and the female network that started at the top with First Lady Eleanor Roosevelt and Secretary of Labor Frances Perkins also included a number of black women, among them Crystal Bird Fauset, sister-in-law of Harlem Renaissance writer Jessie Fauset and assistant director and director of race relations at the Office of Civilian Defense. Another professional woman who had come up through the YWCA, Fauset had also become the first black female state legislator, as well as a member of President Franklin Roosevelt's "Black Cabinet" of influential advisers. She had known Anna Hedgeman for many years.[80] Now, appointed to the civilian defense post in large part because of her relationship with Eleanor Roosevelt, an associate in the program, Fauset attended a Brooklyn rally where she heard Hedgeman speak, just days after her resignation from the Ashland Place YWCA. Hedgeman had urged everyone attending the rally to do two things: volunteer whatever hours they could for civilian defense in support of the war, and volunteer whatever hours they had left to picket defense plants that refused to hire black workers. Fauset was impressed.

Within days, Anna received an invitation to interview for a position with the Office of Civilian Defense. She traveled to Washington eager to impress but also bolstered by the declaration of independence she and Merritt had adopted. Frank in delivering her assessment of the nation's discriminatory wartime practices, she was more than a bit surprised when, in spite of her candor, Crystal Bird Fauset offered her the position of assistant in race relations for New York, New Jersey, and Delaware. Hedgeman accepted the post and found no incompatibility in supporting and working for her country while publicly demanding racial justice, seeing those as simultaneous rather than consecutive mandates for a democratic nation at war.[81]

6 WORLD WAR II

A TIME FOR RACIAL JUSTICE

Air-raid drills, bomb shelters, supervised blackouts, nerve gas anti-dotes: all of these were the stuff of civilian defense. But what about child care, playgrounds, racial justice, and the empowerment of women? As an assistant in the civilian defense program during the Second World War, First Lady Eleanor Roosevelt made these, too, the stuff of civilian defense. Roosevelt was the most prominent fig-ure in an increasingly powerful network of enormously accomplished women, black and white, Crystal Bird Fauset and Anna Arnold Hedgeman among them. Through their hard work, civilian defense became not just protecting the nation's roads and homes and ports but also defending the nation by actively living, embracing, and strengthening the practice of democracy in everyday life.[1]

The Office of Civilian Defense (OCD) was established by presi-dential executive order in 1941 and headed by Republican New York City mayor Fiorello La Guardia. Though a New Deal supporter who also helped advance the political and professional careers of a number of black women,[2] La Guardia was nobody's idea of a feminist, and in fact considered the female-driven, nonmilitary elements of the pro-gram "sissy stuff."[3] Hedgeman had benefited from a good working relationship with La Guardia, but her appointment to the Office of Civilian Defense came through the First Lady's female network.

La Guardia left the OCD by the end of the year, and Eleanor Roosevelt's vision won out; what she called not "sissy stuff" but "pro-gressive social legislation" played a significant role in the nation's civilian defense program.[4] And because of her commitment to an inte-grated federal government, the program opened up new employment opportunities for professional black women, including Hedgeman. Although it is not clear when Anna Arnold Hedgeman and Eleanor Roosevelt first met, it was at Roosevelt's suggestion that Hedgeman was hired, and they would come to know each other well as their paths crossed again and again in the coming years.[5]

Because of Eleanor Roosevelt's influence, as it became increasingly clear that a post–Pearl Harbor attack on the US mainland was unlikely, the Office of Civilian Defense concentrated less on air-raid shelters and blackout preparation and more on nonmilitary efforts. Agency personnel recruited volunteers, supported improvements in community and public health, and perhaps most important, attempted to elevate and maintain the nation's morale. Though far less dramatic than what GIs were going through, those left on the home front also experienced significant hardships during the war. Shortages of foods, including sugar, meat, coffee, and canned goods, were accompanied by shortages of fuel, paper, and rubber. As US involvement in the war stepped up, those shortages worsened, and pleas for recycling turned into rationing.

Rationing was a way for civilians to do their "fair share," but it was far from popular. Despite widespread feelings of patriotism, many people felt put upon in a variety of ways. In some cases, wartime shortages exacerbated racial tensions. Gas rationing in the southern states drove more people to public transportation, and strict racial segregation became, to some degree, physically impossible.[6] Tensions grew high. It was no easier to convince already beleaguered white citizens of the importance of racial justice in wartime than it was to persuade black citizens that racial justice had to be sacrificed in the national interest.

Hedgeman's job was to intervene in these kinds of situations, to forge solidarity among all the nation's citizens. Wartime rhetoric trumpeted this solidarity and shared commitment, but not many white citizens understood that realizing it would require them to change the way they behaved. Too many Americans either actively wanted to see the long-established practices of discrimination and segregation continue, or simply assumed that they would, and they found the bitter responses of some African Americans not only confusing but unpatriotic.

Given her mutual commitments to the nation and racial justice, Hedgeman found herself in a challenging position. She had to listen to the complaints of black citizens and attempt to change the behavior of whites. She supported the war but hoped that this war, unlike the last one, would usher in equal opportunity both under the law and in everyday life. Her situation was made no easier by the "declaration of independence" to which she and Merritt had agreed, a move that required, essentially, that she speak truth to power in her professional life.

Hedgeman traveled to cities and towns in New York, New Jersey, and Delaware, trying to promote a sense of community through shared sacrifice over the war's duration. Inevitably and repeatedly, she encountered racial prejudice and discrimination. In meeting after meeting she discovered that racial divisions threatened the feelings of solidarity she believed in personally and promoted professionally. Even well-meaning white liberals tended to live in segregated environments, and they had met few black people and knew little about them. Worse, they unconsciously reflected a culture that told them that their whiteness granted them a certain authority on all matters, including race.

In preparation for one meeting in upstate New York, Hedgeman worked hard to ensure that both blacks and whites would attend, and talk, together, about what it meant to engage in civilian defense in a time of war. As people rose to speak, she noted the community's determination to pay attention to its social welfare—to acknowledge that the economic recovery the war ushered in had not affected all of its residents in the same way. But when a prominent white physician stated that "our little pickaninnies are being taken care of," Hedgeman felt the need to say something.

She immediately took the floor, both to correct the man and to prevent the situation from deteriorating. "We don't call our babies pickaninnies," she explained, but babies, "little American babies." Some whites in the audience protested, and after the meeting she was criticized even by some of the black people who had attended. For one thing, they explained, there were so few white people who cared at all about African American babies or African American lives; this physician, they believed, was their ally, regardless of his limitations. Further, they told Hedgeman, she would return home after the meeting, but they had to stay and work with the white people in their community. Their tolerance level was higher than hers.[7] This proved hard for her to swallow, since she saw the discrimination of African Americans as "a haunting thing," particularly during wartime.[8]

Everywhere she went, Hedgeman encountered black citizens who had to decide, again and again, how to counter such injustice. Their responses were complicated by a number of factors, including, of course, the war. A sense of resignation, a belief in the greater good, or a self-awareness that transcended ignorant white understanding and behavior caused many to err on the side of tolerance. Others became fed up, wondering how they could be expected to support the lofty ideals of democracy when those ideals were so seldom present in their hometowns, their home states, *their* country.

In southern New Jersey, where she spent a good deal of time talking about the solidarity the war effort required, Hedgeman encountered a level of distrust and distress among black citizens that she could not explain away or promise to ameliorate. One community leader found her entreaties unpersuasive. "I don't know why we should be involved in this white man's war," he told her, describing his experience of moving into a white neighborhood and a cross-burning on his lawn. "This is the United States," he said, noting the irony that had begun to enrage even the most tolerant black Americans, "and this is a war for democracy."[9] A newsboy she encountered in Harlem hawked his papers, shouting, "Buy a paper! Buy a paper! Read all about it. You're all gonna be in uniform soon. You're gonna have a chance to fight for the democracy you ain't never had. Buy a paper!"[10]

The vast amount of national publicity about the defense program increased African Americans' recognition of the limits placed on them.[11] Wartime propaganda also had the unintended consequence of focusing black attention on the distance between the nation's rhetoric and its practices. It is not hard to imagine the frustration of black Americans listening to their radios, hearing President Roosevelt claim during one of his fireside chats, "There will be no divisions of party or section or race or nationality or religion. There is not one among us who does not have a stake in the outcome of the effort in which we are now engaged."[12]

Despite the discouragement, Anna Hedgeman continued to seek out opportunities for black and white Americans to interact with each other on behalf of larger ideals. She encouraged blood donation as a nearly effortless way for citizens to contribute to the war effort, but even something that simple was corrupted by racism.

In Wilmington, Delaware, a group of African American women informed Hedgeman that they had no intention of giving blood because they had heard that the Red Cross would just throw away any blood they donated. When, at her urging, the group met with the local head of the Red Cross, they were told that the Red Cross did not throw black blood away "anymore." Needless to say, as Hedgeman explained, "the program among Negroes in that city never got off the ground."[13]

The experience prompted Hedgeman to explore the issue of blood donation further, and while she did not find blood being thrown away, she did encounter a practice that was almost as egregious: segregating it. Blood, it turned out, was no simple matter. Black blood and white blood were deemed, in a stunning conflation of science with racism, incompatible, and they were kept separate at the request of the military. Even in New York State, the Red Cross segregated blood donated for the war effort, designating "white blood" for white soldiers and "black blood" for black soldiers.[14]

Ironically, it was an African American physician, Charles Drew, who had developed the technology to store and ship plasma; he also founded the world's two largest blood banks, initiated the use of bloodmobiles, and served as director of the American Red Cross's blood bank in New York City. When Dr. Drew attempted to explain the absence of science in the Red Cross policy, he was asked to resign from the organization.[15]

Hedgeman found the policy in place everywhere that she visited blood dona-tion centers, and she also encountered the bitterness African Americans felt when they attempted to do what they considered their patriotic duty but repeat-edly confronted these attitudes and practices. At one of the Civilian Defense meetings, where labor leaders were asked to encourage union members to donate blood, Laundry Workers Union founder Charlotte Adelmond, a black woman, declared that she would "give no blood to the war effort, and will not appeal to my workers to give until the practice of the segregation of Negro blood is stopped." After a moment of silence, a union member asked Adelmond what would happen if her own brother died as a result of her refusal to give blood. "If that happens, at least I will know that he died for democracy," she responded. "The meeting ended on that note," Hedgeman later said with pride and anger. "What could anyone say?"[16]

When the issue made its way into New York City's elementary schools, Hedgeman found a way to participate in the resistance. African American par-ents were refusing to donate blood as long as the segregation policy remained in effect, and white children were taunting black children, accusing them of being unpatriotic. Hedgeman teamed up with a white social worker who had founded a youth development program in the city. They had multiracial groups of school-children perform a laboratory experiment. The children gave blood and then analyzed it, learning enough about blood types to recognize the baselessness of using race as a factor in blood analysis.

Involving the children turned them into not only budding scientists but also budding activists. One boy made a poster showing a test tube of blood feeding two arms, one black and one white, with the caption "All blood is the same. Our dying soldier needs it that he may live." Once the children had made presenta-tions in their own schools to spread the word, they decided to take it to the Red Cross itself. "At that time the directors were intelligent," Hedgeman reported, "but very conservative." The meeting was, in her words, "a classic," with children explaining the difference between real and sham science to a group of adults. In 1950, five years after the war ended, and the year that blood plasma innovator Dr. Charles Drew died, the Red Cross finally changed its policy. Those involved in the children's crusade, Hedgeman reported proudly, "like to believe that the candid and graphic presentation made by New York school youngsters represent-ing thirty-nine nationalities of all colors and creeds had some part to play in that change."[17]

As the war continued to rage in Europe and the Pacific, it seemed less and less likely that the nation would experience an attack on its shores. Nevertheless, pre-paring people for this possibility remained an element of civilian defense work. The United States was particularly concerned about the possibility of chemical weapons attacks, since the United States, Germany, and Japan had all developed nerve gas and other chemical agents. Hedgeman was drawn into the issue tangentially when a black man from Brooklyn requested a meeting with her. A chemist, the young man wanted a job with a firm working on chemical weapons. When he attempted to secure employment on his own, he was informed that the company had no vacancies. His father suspected his son was being lied to and encouraged him to seek help from the Office of Civilian Defense.

When Hedgeman called the firm, she was not surprised to learn that it had a number of appropriate openings. After she hung up the phone, she drafted a letter on official stationery, listing the man's name and credentials, and referencing the telephone conversation. She told the young man to hand deliver the letter, and sure enough, he was offered a position. It was a victory, but she still felt discouraged. Her intervention should not have been necessary.

Discrimination in wartime industries ran rampant, and part of Hedgeman's frustration was that she could address it only in individual cases, while the problem continued to be both systemic and intractable. Millions of people, she lamented, "were turned away only because of prejudice against people of certain races, creeds, or origins. Their willing and eager hands were denied the opportunity to contribute to the war effort, while jobs they could fill remained vacant."[18] In a 1941 Bureau of Employment Security study of a group of defense plants, managers reported that they would not consider black applicants for more than half of their anticipated openings. The response of Los Angeles–based North American Aviation Inc. was indicative of the most widely held sentiments and practices: "We do not believe it advisable to include colored people in our regular working force," it reported. "We may at a later date be in a position to add some colored people in minor capacities such as porters and cleaners. . . . Regardless of their training as aircraft workers, we will not employ them."[19]

At the Brooklyn Navy Yard, a supervisor ordered that all workers wear badges labeled "W" for white or "C" for colored.[20] Some people could not help wondering just how different their nation was from the countries they were fighting. One black college student told his professor that he hoped Hitler won the war, as it seemed things could hardly be worse for blacks than they already were. "The Army jim-crows us," he explained. "The Navy lets us serve only as messmen. The Red Cross refused our blood. Employers and labor unions shut us out. Lynchings continue. We are disenfranchised, jim-crowed, spat upon. What more could Hitler do than that?"[21]

At the same time that Anna Hedgeman was grappling with discriminatory civilian defense practices in New York, New Jersey, and Delaware, discrimination in the armed forces hit her hard, even closer to home.[22] In 1943, her husband, Merritt, enlisted in the Army Air Force and was assigned to a large but segregated base in Greensboro, North Carolina. (The US Air Force did not become a separate branch of the military until 1947; until then, it operated as a division of the US Army.) He served as a chaplain's assistant and entertainment specialist for nearly three years, providing spiritual support and planning entertainment for black troops. He organized and directed a soldiers' glee club; arranged musical events for the base, and with local organizations and colleges; and participated in a Special Services unit by preparing war information for troops.[23]

Merritt received special commendation for his work; the official document cited his distinct role in "depicting the achievements of the U.S. Forces and particularly of the African American Servicemen." He understood that black troops needed to feel they were a vital part of the war effort, regardless of the limitations imposed on their service, so every time he went on leave he visited a friend in the Office of War Information in Washington, DC. Using information he obtained there, he created news bulletins, maps, and displays outlining the critical support role of the black Army Air Force.[24] He was proud of all of his service work, but he was particularly pleased when he was released from duty to sing at a meeting at which the First Lady, Eleanor Roosevelt, was the guest of honor.[25]

As Anna had learned in her years in the YWCA, segregation provided black members of organizations with leadership opportunities, but it was never an unalloyed blessing. Black Americans, no matter how able, ending up poorer in resources, respect, and responsibilities. This was the situation Merritt faced on the base in Greensboro: whatever recognition he received was always linked to and thus limited by race. At least he could take pride that the Army Air Force had begun to train black pilots, most notably those at Tuskegee, Alabama, who would go on to serve with distinction. More than half a century later, the story of the Tuskegee Airmen remains one of the few things about African Americans in World War II to hold a place in the popular consciousness.[26]

The many African American women who wanted to contribute to the war effort through military service encountered similar discriminatory policies. Black nurses faced both a quota limiting their numbers and regulations that allowed them to treat only German prisoners—even when an acute shortage of nurses threatened the care of US troops overseas.[27]

In important ways, Anna's war work mirrored her husband's: each participated in and promoted the war effort, and each attempted to bring African American citizens full recognition for their contributions. The parallels extended, unfortunately, to the anguish of repeatedly encountering discrimination, individually and together. When Anna visited Merritt at his camp in Greensboro, she was working for the federal government and he was in the nation's military, but no hotel in Greensboro would let them have a room; no restaurant would serve them a meal. They had to rely on a black community that, as in many other cases, provided unacknowledged wartime service by assisting black Americans when discriminatory practices held them hostage. A black couple in Greensboro gave up their home so that Anna and Merritt could spend an occasional weekend together. They persevered, but sometimes it all felt like too much for Anna: it was, without a doubt, "just horrible to bear."[28]

In the midst of her civilian defense work, Anna Hedgeman had the opportunity to attend a training program at Amherst College, and she looked forward to a break from the routine. It had been about ten years since she attended another training program nearby, at Mount Holyoke College, and she was excited about returning to the beautiful Pioneer Valley. She was the first on her staff to register, but her eagerness diminished when an employee of the Lord Jeffrey Inn, nestled into a corner of the Amherst campus, told her, when she purposefully inquired, that the inn did not accept black guests. Hedgeman was quick to point out that she was traveling as an employee of the US government and expected to be housed at the same facility as everyone else in the group. After some back and forth, she was notified that things had been cleared up, but she remained understandably wary, wondering what kind of a welcome she would actually encounter.

After Hedgeman checked in, the bellhop took her suitcase and escorted her across the street to a private residence. Immediately recognizing that she was being refused service at the inn, she called on one of her colleagues, a Jewish woman who might well have been refused service herself. It turned out Hedgeman's colleague had successfully checked in, and she had no intention of joining Anna in a challenge to the inn or to the conference organizers. She was not, clearly, one of the many Jews who would serve as staunch allies over the years. Instead, this coworker suggested Hedgeman consider her separate housing a sacrifice for the war effort. Hedgeman had her own ideas about that.

As it turned out, as happy as she was to provide her guest with a room, the white homeowner did not relish her part in the maneuver. The two women dined together, and she told Hedgeman that she had worked in the Lord Jeffrey for a number of years, and the management had previously taken measures to exclude Jews as well. After dinner, Hedgeman, feeling she could not stay, boarded a train for New York. Sadly, when her colleagues returned from Amherst after the conference, they treated her like a "red-hot potato," avoiding any discussion of the incident.[29] At times like this the ironies of race and citizenship felt overwhelming: How was she to believe in and promote democratic values at the same time that even her colleagues in the Office of Civilian Defense refused to demand or practice them?

Hedgeman shared such ignominious experiences with other African American women, some of whom also played key roles in supporting the war effort. Maida Springer, a well-known labor leader and the first black woman to represent union interests abroad, traveled to England in 1945 on a trip sponsored by the US Office of War Information. Before the ship left the country, the delegates stopped in Washington, DC, for three days of meetings with members of Congress, officials of various government agencies, and representatives of labor groups. Springer's white colleagues stayed at the Statler Hotel, but even Secretary of Labor Frances Perkins could not secure Springer a room at the Statler or at any other hotel in the capital. Perkins helped put her up at Council House, Mary McLeod Bethune's home and the headquarters of the National Council of Negro Women (NCNW). "Under ordinary circumstances," Springer said later, "to have been invited to be the guest of Dr. Bethune was a great honor. [But if] I had known about the segregation I would never have gone to D.C. to be treated like that when I was going on an overseas trip for the Office of War Information!"[30]

Similarly, Edith Sampson, the first African American alternate delegate to the US mission to the United Nations, returned to the States following a world tour only to be refused a meal at a hotel in Washington. "If I stopped eating every time something like this happened," she scoffed, "I'd be thin as a rail."[31] Hedgeman, Springer, Sampson, and other women found such injustices both too numerous to count and too difficult to explain to whites. After all, as Sampson noted, their white colleagues were simply unaccustomed to thinking twice about things like meals, housing, or transportation. These seemed trivial items, elements of daily life that white professionals did not think about in any serious way.

Because she believed that institutions would not change without pressure from outside as well as from inside, Hedgeman continued to complement her workplace activities with activism. She became involved in a lawsuit when the State Federation of Business and Professional Women's Clubs refused to allow New York City's Midtown chapter admission because Hedgeman and another African American woman were members. Their victory, she commented, was a measure of "the reality of American democracy."[32] She served on the board of directors of the Workers Defense League, a left-leaning group founded during the Great Depression, concerned with the rights of all workers, black as well as white. She interacted with a wide variety of people, particularly in Harlem, but she seemed to find her way, again and again, to A. Philip Randolph, president of the Brotherhood of Sleeping Car Porters (BSCP), with whom she would work on a variety of civil rights projects in the coming years.[33]

Back in her YWCA days, Hedgeman had escorted groups of foreign visitors, eastern college students, and local elementary and secondary school students to visit Harlem notables, and the BSCP office became a favorite stop, and A. Philip Randolph a favorite host. Tall, with an imposing bearing and a booming voice polished by years as a Shakespearean actor and sidewalk orator, Randolph was a real presence. For visitors, he would describe the life of the Pullman porter: the long hours, humiliating treatment, payment only in tips, and the lack of opportunity for advancement. For the children from Harlem, he took a different approach, encouraging them to study their own history.[34] The two activists developed a working relationship that lasted for five decades. Hedgeman would find herself alternately inspired and exasperated by A. Philip Randolph as they worked, separately and together, to put an end to the racist practices in employment that so limited black Americans' opportunities for advancement. Through differences in personalities and politics, Randolph and Hedgeman remained steadfast on one issue: jobs, jobs, jobs.

In 1925, in a Harlem meeting that the *Amsterdam News* called "the greatest mass meeting ever held of, for, and by Negro working men,"[35] Randolph had launched the Brotherhood of Sleeping Car Porters, the nation's first all-black labor union. Through the BSCP, railroad porters, largely invisible to the white railroad passengers who addressed them only as "George," forged "their own brand of civil rights" decades before the civil rights movement.[36] The BSCP played a key role in increasing African Americans' determination to be represented by unions.[37] By the time of World War II, the BSCP headquarters, on 125th Street in Harlem, was considered the political headquarters of black America.[38] Wartime discrimination amplified black Americans' racial consciousness and their willingness to address injustices, and the BSCP both modeled and benefited from that deepened militancy. With the union at the peak of its power during the war, Randolph was widely considered a national black leader, not just a labor leader. The BSCP nonetheless remained frustrated with the continuing discrimination African American workers faced in obtaining defense-related employment and with its own limited ability to change the situation.[39] On top of that, a second critical demand—a desegregated military—received little support outside the black community.

African Americans were patriotic, but their frustration was reflected in a statement popularized during the war: "Write on my tombstone—Here lies a black man, killed fighting a yellow man, for the protection of a white man."[40] They did more than just complain, or share gallows humor about racism, though, issuing a number of challenges to Jim Crow employment and the Jim Crow military. One of them, the all-black March on Washington Movement (MOWM), would draw Hedgeman deeper into A. Philip Randolph's circle.

There are a few different creation stories for the MOWM, but whether or not A. Philip Randolph launched the idea, he quickly emerged as its leader and put forward its simple demands: "We loyal Negro American citizens demand the right to work and fight for our country."[41] Most specifically, the organization promised, or threatened, that if President Roosevelt continued to simply talk about change rather than introducing legislation mandating it, the group would host a massive protest in the nation's capital. As Randolph saw it, the FDR administration "will never give the Negro justice until they see masses—ten, twenty, fifty thousand Negroes on the White House lawn."[42] The *Baltimore Afro-American* concurred: "One individual marching up and down Pennsylvania Avenue in front of the White House denouncing race prejudice is arrested as a crank," the newspaper reported. "Ten thousand persons get respectful attention."[43] They began, seriously, to plan for a mass march on the capital. Anna Arnold Hedgeman readily signed on.

The MOWM gained a great deal of attention in the black press, not all of it favorable. The truth is, support for the war was so strong among African Americans that many were wary of even the far less radical "Double V for Victory" campaign that called for victory against fascism abroad, victory against racism at home; there was little chance they would join a group that refused white people membership.[44] How, many wondered, could a purposefully segregated organization take up the mantle of ending segregation? Randolph had his reasons. A socialist and virulent anticommunist, he believed that keeping whites out was the only way to keep the organization free of communists. He also argued that the organization would promote black self-determination, or "create faith by Negroes in Negroes," as he put it. He maintained that this form of segregation differed significantly in that it hurt no one it excluded. Segregation in wartime employment undoubtedly hurt black workers, but preventing white people from joining the MOWM posed them no real harm. Finally, he reasoned, "If a white person was allowed to join the MOWM he would gain no right he did not already possess before he joined."[45]

In the long term, black Americans would not side with Randolph. Instead of segregation and mass demonstrations, they would, even with the injustices they faced, choose integration and legal redress—but not before the March on Washington Movement secured a key victory for black Americans.[46]

Hedgeman joined the MOWM not for its policy of segregation—she had by now largely abandoned her determination to avoid white people—but because she was drawn to Randolph's developing ideology of nonviolent direct action. An avowed atheist until later in life, when he felt that faith-based militancy finally matched his own, Randolph nonetheless embraced a form of civil disobedience that he defined as "applied Christianity." As he explained, "It is Christianity and democracy brought out of gilded churches and solemn legislative halls and made to work as a dynamic force in our day-to-day life."[47] His approach dovetailed with Hedgeman's philosophy of active Christianity in the name of racial justice. She was eager to participate in a civil rights program that included, at its core, a way to make Christianity manifest.

It is likely that Hedgeman helped advance some of the more religious elements of the March on Washington Movement, including prayer protests and the link between social gospel themes and African American lives. These religious strategies, which would become such a prominent aspect of the civil rights era, formed the core of the MOWM decades earlier.[48] Merritt Hedgeman joined in when the opportunity to infuse the movement with music presented itself, leading a YWCA choir through patriotic and spiritual songs at a rally at New York's City Hall.[49]

Regardless of the resistance some felt to its policy of segregation, because the war had brought more women into the workplace and suggested the potential for far greater justice, the MOWM attracted significant numbers of African American women. Hedgeman served her volunteer hours in New York City, planning among other things a mass rally at Madison Square Garden that attracted twenty thousand black New Yorkers.[50] Layle Lane, a New York City schoolteacher, union leader, and MOWM supporter, penned a regular column in the *New York Age*, pointing to discrimination on the job and in the military, and peppering her articles with compelling stories she gleaned from letters that former students and service members sent her.[51] Hedgeman's friend Pauli Murray, who was now gaining a national profile as a proponent of civil rights, saw the MOWM as the most promising opportunity to make demands for change. "I want to be a loyal citizen," Murray wrote, despite the multiple sources of pain the war produced. "I want something to believe in."[52] For her, that something was the MOWM. Many other black women joined the thirty-six MOWM chapters and raised money, hosted rallies, and recruited and trained young people.[53]

African American women had a tremendous amount to gain from employment-based racial justice efforts. When factories opened their doors to them for war production, black women experienced decent working conditions for the first time in their lives: cash wages instead of credit or scrip for some; workdays with set start and end times for others; and for many, working for the first time with, rather than for, white women.[54] Still, black women, like black men, faced a number of efforts to thwart their progress. In the South, laundry owners and white housewives demanded that black women be kept out of defense work; if not, who would work in the least remunerative, least desirable jobs?[55] Who would take on the jobs that provided white women with a limited degree of freedom from household tasks?

A New Jersey defense firm, Isolantite Incorporated, employed 745 workers, 80 percent of them white women. When a company ad attracted black women, about 600 white women threatened to leave their jobs. Company ads from then on specified its racial preferences.[56] Because situations like this abounded, the MOWM symbolized the possibility of improvements in daily life, which African American women desperately wanted. So many black women supported the movement, in fact, that a colleague of Randolph grumbled, "There are too many women mixed up in this thing, anyhow."[57]

President Roosevelt tried to ignore the fledgling movement, but when it appeared it would not go away on its own, he tried to put an end to it. A wartime march through the nation's capital, exposing the sins of the nation that both preached and allegedly served as a model of democracy, would have proved Roosevelt's greatest embarrassment as president, worse than the Supreme Court's ruling unconstitutional some key provisions of his New Deal plan, worse than the Congress's preventing him from packing the Court so that it would rule in his favor. The president sent Fiorello La Guardia, who was a friend of Randolph, and Eleanor Roosevelt, perhaps his most skilled civil rights emissary, to try and talk some sense into Randolph and his allies in the MOWM—Walter White of the NAACP and Lester Granger of the National Urban League—but to no avail.

Eleanor Roosevelt, who approved of the march's purpose but worried about the numbers and the timing, tried to suggest the potential disaster of a hundred thousand African Americans descending on a segregated capital city. Where would they stay? Where would they eat?[58] They would register at hotels and eat at restaurants, Randolph replied, not letting on that he knew full well the logistical nightmare ahead. Acutely aware of the workings of power, Randolph knew that white leaders, even sympathetic ones, would change their practices only if forced to. He also recognized the advantage he held at that point. Although many people doubted Randolph's ability to actually pull off the march, at this point he knew that he simply had to keep the president thinking he might.[59]

Randolph moved to firm up plans, giving the march both a name and a date. The March on Washington for Jobs and Equal Participation in National Defense was scheduled for July 1, 1941, with a walk down Pennsylvania Avenue followed by an assembly at the Lincoln Memorial.[60] By June 1941, the MOWM had hired buses and chartered trains, and FDR began to realize that Randolph was not going to cancel the event, despite all his efforts. The president's anxiety rose to a new level when he learned that the National Council of Negro Women, the nation's largest black women's organization, was also pushing for the march. The president of the council, Mary McLeod Bethune, one of FDR's trusted "Black Cabinet" advisers and a friend of both Roosevelts, astutely arranged for a Washington meeting of the NCNW on the day before the march, ensuring that large numbers of black women would be on hand on July 1. Men were the public face of this march, but Mary McLeod Bethune and other black women loomed large in the background. This pattern would be repeated twenty years later, during the 1963 March on Washington.[61]

The March on Washington Movement was a significant turning point in the black approach to civil rights. It ushered in a new level of militancy, one that many black women embraced. Speaking for many others, Mary Bethune explained her position: African Americans would no longer be turning the other cheek, as both cheeks were already too blistered. There would be no more begging, either; instead, black Americans would insist on "full freedom, justice, respect, and opportunity."[62]

With only days left until the march and just after the Nazis invaded the Soviet Union, FDR relented. He gave up his attempts to get the movement leaders to compromise and agreed to issue an executive order on fair employment. Randolph helped draft what became Executive Order 8802, establishing the wartime Fair Employment Practice Committee (FEPC), an agency assigned the task of ensuring that companies holding federal contacts hire Americans without regard "to race, creed, color, or national origin." On July 1, 1941, Randolph called off the March on Washington.

Some members of the movement were furious, but Randolph felt they had achieved a substantial victory and could back off temporarily.[63] He maintained that the march had been postponed, not canceled, and vowed to keep the MOWM alive to serve as a watchdog for the FEPC. As he and other MOWM leaders well knew, the executive order failed to address either segregation or discrimination in the military. It exempted much of private industry and largely disabled the fair employment committee by giving it, instead of regulatory powers, only one real tool: "moral suasion."[64] But even with these limitations, members of the committee hoped to have an impact and immediately began to take complaints and hold hearings. For Hedgeman and others involved in the MOWM, the creation of the FEPC was an important step in what they realized would have to be an ongoing process of change. Pauli Murray was elated, viewing the FEPC as "the first national wedge in discrimination in employment."[65]

To no one's surprise, the Fair Employment Practice Committee hearings soon discovered widespread race-based employment violations. In response, some companies changed their practices rather than try to explain them to an investigatory committee, but others simply continued to flaunt their disregard for fair employment. The FEPC made some headway and served as a model for a number of the state commissions that followed, but it suffered—from a lack of resources, from being moved from office to office within the administration, from tremendous opposition from southern Democrats, and above all, from its limited ability to take any legal action against those who persisted in treating African Americans as less than American citizens.

Whatever inroads FEPC officials managed to make during the war, they rightfully feared that most of the gains black workers had made during the war would be lost in the transition to a peacetime economy.[66] Anna Hedgeman worried too that African American women, who had gained a voice in the MOWM and in other efforts for racial justice during wartime, would lose that voice at war's end. She viewed the commitment to black women more as a matter of justice than a matter of national integrity. In "The Role of the Negro Woman," published in 1944, Hedgeman explained that because they held a "particular burden" during the war, black women would have a crucial role to play at war's end, helping the nation "practice what she preaches" and "assume an honest role in the world struggle" to help "people of color all over the world." Black women, she claimed, viewed a permanent FEPC as part of that struggle.[67]

But there was no clear consensus on strategy. When A. Philip Randolph attempted to revive the idea of a march on Washington, in protest of congressional inaction on strengthening or extending the FEPC, black trade unionist George L. P. Weaver captured the sentiments of many when he called for "marching on the polls" rather than marching on the capital.[68] Indeed, black public sentiment seemed to move away from mass agitation as the war wound down. Membership in the NAACP, which favored a legislative over an activist approach, skyrocketed, and interest in the MOWM declined precipitously. A. Philip Randolph would eventually let go of the MOWM, but not of the FEPC. Nor, apparently, was he interested in letting go of Anna Arnold Hedgeman. As the postwar choices seemed to narrow down to extending and strengthening the FEPC or attempting to make it a permanent body,[69] Randolph moved quickly toward the latter, and he soon solicited Hedgeman's help in making fair employment not a wartime practice but a fundamentally American one.[70]

7 FIGHTING FOR FAIR EMPLOYMENT, FIGHTING FOR TRUMAN

Still employed at the Office of Civilian Defense, Anna Arnold Hedgeman was sitting at her desk in the Empire State Building one snowy day in 1944 when A. Philip Randolph telephoned and asked to stop in to see her. He had come up with a strategy for making the Fair Employment Practice Committee permanent, he told her, and he wanted her to lead the effort. Randolph envisioned a national push for equal opportunity in employment, equal wages for the same work, and a right to promotion without regard to race, creed, color, or origin. There would be an educational campaign and a drive for legislation granting far greater powers of enforcement to the FEPC than it had during wartime. The plan was in place, but he needed someone to implement it, and he hoped it would be Hedgeman. Believing in the cause, and in Randolph, she did not hesitate to sign on. The black press took note, referring to Hedgeman as the "young feminist" taking the helm.[1]

After securing permission to leave civilian defense, she held a kick-off rally in Manhattan where she announced that three members of Congress had agreed to sponsor a bill banning employment discrimination and implementing a permanent FEPC. Then she headed off to the nation's capital, where she would serve as the executive director of the National Council for a Permanent FEPC, a paid staff of one.[2]

The National Council was a coalition of minority, religious, civic, and fraternal organizations, along with some labor unions, and would serve as a clearinghouse and center of advocacy for the legislative effort. The membership of the National Council was a who's who of African American leadership and included, in addition to Randolph and his co-chair, the Reverend Allan Knight Chalmers, Walter White, Lester Granger, and others. But the day-to-day implementation of strategy would belong to Hedgeman, who was "green enough," as she remembered later, to believe they could get the bill passed in quick order.[3]

Like many white liberals and many black Americans of various political stripes, Hedgeman believed that only permanent federal legislation would bring justice to the American workplace. The stakes were high. Fair employment meant decent wages, and decent wages bought improved housing, education, medical care, and social opportunities for working people. But it was clear that anything short of federal mandates gave states and municipalities too many opportunities to ignore, collude with, or even participate in discriminatory labor practices. In her civilian defense work, Hedgeman had helped secure positions for a number of people who faced racism in the job market, but she knew that even those meager gains had depended on the wartime FEPC, however inadequate it had proved to be. How frightening it was that the legislation might expire, but how exciting to be playing a vital role in securing permanent, strengthened legislation.

With a permanent FEPC, the end of the war might actually be part of a double victory, a win for democracy within the country in addition to the victory Over There. Black people would be hired and promoted based on their personal merits, not the color of their skin. Fair employment, Hedgeman thought, would become the American "common denominator."[4]

As much as she loved New York City, and Harlem in particular, a move to Washington, DC, held strong professional and personal appeal for Anna Hedgeman. She had gotten a taste of working on a federal level with her civilian defense appointment; living and working in the nation's capital, she would undoubtedly expand an already significant circle of contacts and improve her professional prospects. And while she had embraced the all-black March on Washington Movement, like many other black Americans, she believed that an interracial effort was ultimately both right and necessary. Her theological framework was developing, and she no longer viewed whites merely as obstructionist or racist but instead as incomplete, trapped, in need of help. "White people who cared," she reasoned, "were caught in the structures which had been established without concern for the 'whole' society." It was not only black Americans who needed racial justice; as she was coming to understand, white people, too, suffered from its absence. Perhaps fair employment legislation could serve as "a unifying force," and Hedgeman as a facilitator of that unity.[5]

Washington pulled in another way, of course: with the war still on, Merritt remained in North Carolina, and Anna would have many more opportunities to visit him from a post in DC. Now in their midforties, it was easy for the couple to envision Merritt completing his military service with the end of the war, and the two of them starting a new chapter in their lives in the nation's capital. If that chapter began with Merritt having helped secure democracy abroad and Anna at home, all the better. It looked like their "declaration of independence" was paying off.

Before Hedgeman could actually get to work, she had to lease office space for the National Council, a formidable task for a black woman representing an interracial organization in Washington. She was turned down for every available rental space near the Capitol or in the center of the city. As a former board member of the Workers Defense League, she consulted its national secretary, Morris Milgram, a supporter of FEPC who would later become known for successfully promoting integrated housing. Milgram offered to share the league's small DC office on Fourteenth Street. Anxious to get started, Hedgeman moved in.

Before she had a chance to do much in the way of outreach, Hedgeman learned of a campaign underway to have her evicted because her presence was stirring up other blacks in the building. Elevator operators and janitors, who had previously walked several blocks to use public restrooms, had begun to use the building's facilities.[6] She was witnessing one of the open secrets of segregation: black employees were present, plentiful in fact, in the nation's capital. The smooth workings of government depended on them but also counted on their invisibility. Hedgeman, however, had no intention of being invisible herself, or encouraging anyone else to remain so.

The first step was to fight the eviction. A Jewish member of the National Council suggested they enlist Jewish tenants in the building. When it was pointed out that tolerating practices that discriminated against others might lead to becoming victims themselves, the petition seeking Hedgeman's removal from the building died a quiet death,[7] helped along, no doubt, by recent events abroad.

As Hedgeman set to work and began to understand the magnitude of the legislative effort ahead of her, she realized the inadequacy of a one-woman effort. She convinced the council's leadership to let her hire an executive assistant and two legislative assistants. At the suggestion of National Council members, she hired Sidney Wilkinson, a young, white Protestant woman, as her assistant, and Ida Fox and Beatrice Shalet, two young Jewish women, as legislative aides. Fox, an active socialist and interracial organizer, was assigned to monitor activities in the House, and Shalet, an organizer in the Interracial Consumers' Cooperative Movement, to monitor the Senate.[8] She also tried to lure Pauli Murray to the council, but in the end decided she did not have enough money to offer her friend to make it worth her while.[9]

Hedgeman grew fond of her staff, but she found the working conditions exasperating. The nine-by-fifteen-foot space was so cramped that they could not all work there at the same time, particularly when Workers Defense League employees were also in the office. Because Union Station was the only location in the capital where an interracial staff could eat together, their prospects for meeting outside the office were limited. Even meeting at Union Station proved difficult, as the taxi company that served the station would not pick up black passengers either at the station or on the streets of the city.[10]

Hedgeman certainly was not new to dealing with discrimination, but she nonetheless found segregation in the nation's capital troubling in ways both pedestrian and profound. Certainly, not being able to get a cab was an inconvenience, but seeking justice for African Americans from elected officials who tolerated such practices was a challenge on an altogether different scale. If Anna Hedgeman could not eat in the Senate dining room with legislators, how could she conduct the most basic and productive type of lobbying?[11] If the nation's capital was "the great seal of the United States set down in granite," as a national group studying segregation pointed out, and it was racially segregated, could the leaders who worked in that physical space envision, let alone implement, justice?[12] Was the passage of permanent fair employment legislation even imaginable in such an ignoble environment?

The impending conclusion of World War II did not signal the death of Jim Crow in the capital, but segregation in Washington did draw widespread attention internationally. Racial injustice continued to mar the nation's reputation, and little would actually change during wartime or the early postwar years under the Truman administration.

While transportation in Washington was not segregated, the best transportation jobs, the motorman and conductor positions, remained closed to black workers. Most restaurants, including the airport restaurant, refused service to blacks; in a few, black customers would be served if standing up but not if sitting down, unless they could prove foreign citizenship. Foreign visitors, who regularly reported on such indignities after they returned home, were repeatedly subjected to these arbitrary, enigmatic restrictions when they went out in Washington. In one of many similar cases, four black students from the West Indies were told to leave a restaurant. When they produced British diplomatic passes, the waitress apologized, telling them she did not realize they were "not niggers."[13]

Diplomats from more than sixty countries periodically lived in the capital, but diplomats of color sometimes had to be put up at people's houses because no hotel would provide them rooms. Even churches sometimes refused darkskinned congregants. One visitor from Panama, black, Catholic, and devout, was approached during Mass by a priest who suggested he worship at a black church instead.[14]

Few people in Washington seemed inclined to discuss the problem, and fewer still attempted to remedy it. Some, of course, saw segregation in the nation's capital as a good thing, and profoundly symbolic. Theodore S. Bilbo, the white supremacist from Mississippi who was appointed chair of the Senate District Committee in 1944, was blunt about his motivation in seeking out the appointment: "I wanted this position so I could keep Washington a segregated city."[15] Southern Democrats certainly seemed to exercise undue influence where race was concerned. As the *Washington Evening Star* put it, "It must be viewed as one of the ironies of history that the Confederacy, which was never able to capture Washington during the course of that war, now holds it as a helpless pawn."[16]

Regardless of the challenges—and in part because of them—Hedgeman began to articulate and carry out a sophisticated plan for pushing forward the fair employment bill, which had been drawn up by a team of black lawyers she assembled, all volunteering their time and services.[17] African American attorneys would have been acutely aware of the ongoing restrictions on black employment, as well as the need for large-scale change—it was not until 1950 that the American Bar Association admitted its first black member. Hedgeman relied on the attorneys and National Council members to advocate in their own circles, but she relied nearly as heavily on her own networks. She would be the first to acknowledge she was a novice at Washington politics, but she was also a quick study, and she analyzed and mimicked established practices for getting bills through Congress. Although the white press seemed to care little about her work, the black press, as usual, took dutiful note.[18]

The federal government looked at the country in terms of regions, so Hedgeman would do the same. She initially traveled a great deal, organizing regional councils, then leaving regional leaders in charge of mobilizing the local electorate, and encouraging them to approach their members of Congress. This allowed the always cash-strapped National Council to keep its staff to a minimum, hiring only nine regional representatives but still reaching a good part of the nation, and Hedgeman gained widespread recognition for her skills in organization and advocacy.[19]

She traveled a great deal, speaking to audiences in religious and civic organizations, trying to galvanize support for the legislation. Whenever there was a regional or national meeting, she delivered the major address, "The Right to Work Is the Right to Live." She tried to convey the importance of the legislation in terms anyone could understand: it would help the millions who were turned away from war work "only because of ancient prejudice against people of certain races, creeds, or origins," those "whose willing and eager hands were denied the opportunity to contribute to the war effort, while jobs they could fill remained vacant." The legislation did not mandate that "you hire this person or do not hire that person," she explained, but it did require that "your choice should be only on the basis of merit or ability."[20]

Over and over Hedgeman heard the argument that people's emotions dictated who they wanted to work with, and that the government could not legislate emotion, but she had a ready response: "We explained that we were not legislating emotion, that we were preventing evil emotions from functioning against people. We reminded our hearers of laws against murder and some of us classified the denial of work to any man on the basis of his race, religion or color as a special kind of murder."[21]

As she traveled through cities and towns, some more receptive to a black woman than others, Hedgeman relied on the Brotherhood of Sleeping Car Porters to find places for her to sleep and eat; the union also recruited people to attend her talks and raised money for the cause.[22] She had her first interactions with southern civil rights leaders on these trips, and she laid the groundwork with people like Arkansas newspaper publisher Daisy Bates and Alabama businessman A. G. Gaston that would enable her to call on them again, not only years but decades later.[23] In the end, state-level attempts at fair employment proved more successful than the push for federal legislation, and the grassroots work she did in her travels for the National Council contributed to those regional successes.

Hedgeman was relentless in identifying supporters she could turn into advocates. She reached out specifically to the churches, and fair employment work politicized many religious leaders, priming them for involvement in the civil rights movement to come.[24] She advised her fieldworkers to "lean on the women" and linked her efforts with the women who, fearing that African American women would be the first to be pushed out of their jobs at war's end, ran the "Hold Your Job" campaign of the National Council of Negro Women.[25] She worked with the National Association of Colored Women, helping them celebrate their golden jubilee by hosting a forum on African American club women's roles in legislation, and then organize a silent march of two hundred women to the White House and the Senate in support of the legislation.[26]

Hedgeman looked for ways to develop networks across lines of gender, race, class, and religion, and to combine lobbying with a grassroots movement. In one Indiana city, she recruited a white senator, his white wife, and his black cook to the cause, all of them with specific responsibilities.[27] She also put together a special strategy committee of influential citizens from a range of fraternal, religious, political, labor, consumer, and service organizations; most of them were women.

One of the challenges of her new position was managing A. Philip Randolph. She found it difficult to say no to Randolph, but he was not easy to work with. Hedgeman had trouble keeping him focused on what needed to be done, and she often ended up taking on responsibilities that should have been his, or should have been handled by other members of the National Council. Reluctant to let go of prior responsibilities when he took on new ones, Randolph maintained leadership of the Brotherhood of Sleeping Car Porters, the March on Washington Movement, and the Committee to Organize Colored Locomotive Firemen. He edited *Black Worker* and worked to organize a third political party and to deseg-regate the armed forces. He traveled a great deal and was often unavailable.[28] This was most apparent where fundraising was concerned, but Randolph was also absent at key moments in the campaign. "I discover that people generally seem convinced that you are not as interested in this project as you ought to be," Hedgeman wrote him at one point. "One important individual came right out and said, 'Is Mr. R. really behind this legislation?'"[29]

Still, Hedgeman kept at it, cultivating support in Congress and with the public. William L. Dawson, the third black member of Congress elected in the twentieth century, played a vital role in the effort. An Illinois Democrat, Dawson spoke of himself as a "Congressman first and a Negro second," but he had a strong civil rights agenda.[30] Other key supporters included Representative Charles La Follette, an Indiana Republican; Senator Denis Chavez, a New Mexico Democrat; Senator Robert Wagner, a New York Democrat; and Senator Arthur Capper, a Kansas Republican.[31] After much obstruction, and little prog-ress in the House, Senate hearings on the bill finally began in March 1945, and Hedgeman recruited representatives from dozens of religious, civic, and politi-cal organizations to testify on behalf of permanent fair employment. At her request, Eleanor Roosevelt held an FEPC conference at the White House, and the National Council sponsored the first national interracial dinner ever held at the Mayflower Hotel in Washington, DC. Hedgeman also gathered together representatives of thirty black organizations to urge the president to "resist any and all trickery to kill or emasculate" the FEPC and to warn Congress that sup-port for fair employment legislation "will be one of the chief determinants of our support in future elections."[32]

But the National Council overestimated its support and underestimated the opposition. Despite many events, extensive lobbying, and educational outreach campaigns, legislative efforts would eventually be thwarted in both the House and the Senate; as one observer noted, the FEPC was "postponed to death."[33] Hedgeman responded to the repeated delays on the national level by pushing local councils to advocate for state and local fair employment bills. Such laws were introduced in nearly every state in the North but adopted in only three. Still, she refused to give up. "V-J Day has come," Hedgeman wrote on August 14, 1945, when the surrender of Japan brought the war to an end. "It is impera-tive, therefore, that the bill for a permanent FEPC be passed as soon as Congress reconvenes as possible." Still, Congress did not act.[34]

There was no one culprit in the legislative failure. Some historians have blamed Randolph, suggesting he was stretched too thin to give the effort what it needed. Others point to conflicts within the National Council, exacerbated by conflicts in the broader civil rights coalition. The Reverend Dr. Allan Knight

Chalmers's appointment as cochair was a poor choice, as Chalmers was too conservative a character to push for such radical change.[35] Republican support was sporadic, and southern Democrats were well organized, maintaining a stranglehold over both houses of Congress; their opposition was influential well beyond their borders. The business community's opposition played a role in the bill's defeat, as did "vermin opposition," the race-baiters who warned of the slippery slope from fair employment to interracial marriage and "little brown bastards."[36] Then, as now, some whites were convinced that minority-focused civil rights legislation would "communize" the nation, and that minority groups were attempting to manipulate the marketplace, rather than level the playing field. As always, some insisted the federal government had no business trying to legislate human behavior.[37]

Finally, some have found Anna Hedgeman to blame, arguing that she was difficult to work with, that she was too loyal to Randolph, or that she focused too much on problems of black workers and not enough on people of other racial, ethnic, or religious groups.[38]

Indeed, there were some complaints that Hedgeman was testy, but as a female administrator, she was in a difficult position: she was responsible for making things happen, but at the same time expected to defer to men. Like many other women in key roles, she was expected to be more selfless than the men involved, but no less invested. She frequently clashed with Randolph not just about running the office but also about policy. While some men on the council felt she lacked sufficient experience to be voicing her opinions, it is safe to assume others bristled at her ideas simply because she was a woman. It was a common story. Ella Baker, another influential woman in the civil rights movement, often met with hostility from men. As her biographer, Barbara Ransby, explains, male colleagues often interpreted Baker's straightforward manner as abrasive or annoying, referring to her repeatedly as "difficult."[39] It seems likely that the more Hedgeman attempted to assert herself in the council, the more "difficult" she became. As we might imagine, women in the postwar period faced significant gender discrimination and a double standard in the workplace. Even now, exhibiting the same behaviors, men are considered assertive or direct, and women aggressive or strident.

Interestingly, and perhaps not coincidentally, Anna Hedgeman resigned from the National Council in the same year that Ella Baker resigned from the national staff of the NAACP, both frustrated not just by day-to-day business but by fundamental questions of politics and policy. Another of the likely contributing factors to the failure of the FEPC, then, was, pure and simple sexism. When Hedgeman moved to Washington to set up shop, she relied heavily on the National Council of Negro Women, the only black civil rights organization headquartered in the nation's capital. But the NCNW, like Hedgeman, was most visible to the men when "workers" were needed but least visible when leadership was in demand. Had their collective efforts been taken more seriously, the FEPC would have had a stronger core effort in the capital.

One of the few male leaders of the National Council to support Anna Hedgeman when she eventually submitted her resignation, in July 1946, was the American Federation of Labor representative to the council, Boris Shishkin, who noted that Hedgeman, performing her "extremely arduous task with a degree of brilliance, has earned far more lasting recognition from all those concerned with furthering equality of opportunity in America than you saw fit to give her."[40] And the black press remained eager to acknowledge her work and contributions. "The world is indebted to Anna Hedgeman," wrote prominent black journalist Harry McAlpin, one of her many admirers, about her FEPC work.[41] Regardless of what she managed in the end to achieve, there is no question that Hedgeman regularly faced gender discrimination in her career. But in a prefeminist era, even she had trouble identifying it as problematic. "I didn't know it then at all," she said later, "because I had not really faced the straight-out woman problem, as clearly, then. But it was clear later."[42]

The charge that Hedgeman was less attentive to the needs of minority groups other than blacks certainly merits consideration. Her writings, as well as her hard-earned religious determination to see all people as one, suggest that she would have attempted to be inclusive. At a National Council strategy session where reviving the march was discussed, she was adamant that this time it had to be an "inter-racial, inter-faith, trade-union march."[43] In one of the many documents she wrote, "Is Your Community Interested in a Permanent FEPC?" she specifically sought support for the National Council that was "interracial, interfaith, and truly representative of the community." The council was anxious, she wrote further, "that it be perfectly clear that we want this bill to be for the protection of all minorities and not just for the Negro."[44] Hedgeman instructed her field staff to "pull the whole community together, Japanese, Jews, Negroes, Catholics, Mexicans, etc."[45]

It was true, however, that Hedgeman's extensive networking, hence her most significant contacts, happened in black and progressive white communities.[46] Her journalistic contacts were mainly in the black press, and as a result, white newspapers dismissed the legislative effort as a "Negro issue" rather than an American issue.[47] Hedgeman had made valuable inroads into the Puerto Rican community in New York City, but her contact with other Latino communities, and with Native or Asian communities, was limited. It would have been a significant challenge to further those connections in any circumstances, let alone in the midst of a legislative battle with so few resources.

There were also real problems with the council, starting with the level of commitment at the top. Randolph envisioned a short-term lobbying effort, and Hedgeman turned it, by necessity, into a long-term, national campaign.[48] Her extensive outreach efforts, particularly among women, helped her sustain the effort despite the lack of support she got from the men on the National Council, or their contacts in labor and civil rights organizations. The bulk of funding came from local councils, where women played a key role, not from established civil rights groups, where men held the purse strings.

Funding for the National Council was an ongoing struggle. Randolph had promised Hedgeman a $25,000 budget, but she saw little of that.[49] Responsibility for fundraising should not have fallen to her to the degree that it did, and it could be confusing. She had no experience with the quid pro quo relationships members of Congress expected: in return for their support for her legislation, she was expected to provide financial support when they sought re-election.[50] She had little to give.

When she finally confronted Randolph about the matter, he agreed to take over fundraising but failed to follow through. Uncertain about the council's finances, unable to accurately or effectively communicate to their constituencies what was needed, Hedgeman eventually found she could not meet the payroll. When the situation became public, the black press was wholly sympathetic to her situation. An article in the *Pittsburgh Courier* praised her "fine staff" but noted that without an adequate budget she was forced to hire young, inexperienced activists rather than seasoned lobbyists.[51] An article in the *Atlanta Daily World* reported that Hedgeman "sat at her desk and cried" when seven field workers offered to forgo their salaries and continue working for free. Some members of the staff donated their savings to the council, an act the newspaper described as "typical of the following that the leadership of Mrs. Hedgeman has inspired in her fight for a permanent FEPC."[52] Anna herself donated Merritt's last military bonus to the cause, but the National Council still found its coffers empty. She informed Randolph that his "total disregard" for finances had made her job impossible. He did not respond. Instead, he turned the problem over to another council member.

Hedgeman's difficulties were compounded by basic organizational problems. The regional councils were meant to oversee and assume direct responsibility for the work of the hundred or so local councils, but this never actually happened. The Washington office composed and sent out almost all of the fair employment literature used during the campaign, organized regional meetings, and took charge of group visits to the capital. Many of the regional representatives had good intentions but insufficient experience, and while Hedgeman did her best to maintain enthusiasm and activity in the field, it grew more challenging as the legislative battles dragged on. On top of that, she and her staff were simply and constantly overworked. At times, it would be months before they could respond to letters that came in from local and regional representatives.[53]

Finally, no longer willing to ask her staff to stay on when they were paid irregularly if at all, and frustrated by organizational impediments to doing her job, Anna Hedgeman tendered her resignation in July 1946. She composed a statement charging that the National Council leadership, guilty of more than financial neglect, had failed to forge "the established political connections necessary" to enact permanent legislation.[54]

National Council members asked Hedgeman to excise her criticism from her resignation so as not to "impair the future welfare of the FEPC movement," but she refused. As it turned out, her resignation was the beginning of the end of the council. The following year saw little communication between Washington and the regional offices, with most people associating the National Council more with the now-absent Anna Arnold Hedgeman than with A. Philip Randolph or the board.[55] A contemporary assessment of Hedgeman's role and impact still seems apt. As an observer wrote in 1948, "The successes of the National Council were due in large measure to her leadership, the failures, to factors of finance and top leadership difficulties largely beyond her control."[56]

The wartime fair employment legislation expired in 1946, and some state but no federal policies were enacted to replace it. The robust economy of the postwar period would not provide the same benefits to black Americans as to whites. However, the "tireless crusading Anne Hedgeman," as the *Chicago Defender* called her at the time, did not let go of the dream. She would return twenty years later to play a key role in the passage of the 1964 Civil Rights Act, which established the Equal Employment Opportunity Commission (EEOC), a federal agency whose sole charge was to enforce fair employment practices in the workplace.[57]

A year after they left the National Council, Hedgeman and the staff learned that the group had hired two new employees, both men and both at better salaries than any of the women who had long done "the back-breaking ground work," as Hedgeman's assistant Sidney Wilkinson put it. The council still owed the old staff back pay and the money they had personally extended to keep the effort afloat. The irony of such behavior from a group working to promote fair employment practices was not lost on them. In the end, the staff viewed A. Philip Randolph as the most culpable in what they had experienced, and they threatened to picket him at an upcoming rally in Washington, DC. "I can promise you," Wilkinson wrote, "that the wording on the placards will not be helpful to him or to the Council."[58]

Hedgeman and her staff were clearly victims of Randolph's neglect and his reluctance to give women their due. As one of his biographers points out,

Randolph had a pattern of appointing women to significant positions because they would accept lower salaries than men, never giving them the professional respect they deserved, and dismissing them when his funding sources ran low.[59] In this case, had the female staff of the FEPC had greater autonomy, they might also have had healthier financial reserves. There is no doubt that women played key roles in this early civil rights work, or that men often took them and their contributions for granted.

The women on the National Council staff also found themselves victims of internecine fighting among the male leaders of the movement. A number of them, particularly Roy Wilkins of the NAACP, wanted to marginalize "certain elements" of the fair employment movement, specifically Randolph. They were troubled by Randolph's all-black tactics and his socialism, and because they equated the FEPC effort so fully with Randolph, the NAACP and other organizations gave the council less than their full support.[60] Local, left-leaning branches opposed Randolph's anticommunism and argued that, to gain equity, blacks had to remain unequivocally in support of the war effort. Wilkins eventually succeeded in getting the National Council office moved to the NAACP headquarters in New York, diminishing Randolph's influence.

A few years later, in 1950, the fair employment effort was shifted away from the National Council altogether, toward what became the Leadership Council on Civil Rights (LCCR), where there was even less room for women. A "top-down affair," as one historian describes it, the LCCR was "less concerned with numbers than with the leadership qualities of those who will attend."[61] This greater focus on professionalism and standing was a catch-22 for women, as they were not seen as leaders nor given the opportunity to lead, and their involvement in the fair employment fight dropped off, precipitously.

Hedgeman often remained silent about the discrimination she grew to believe was "always with us."[62] Sometimes she spoke out, telling other women that men had made a "sorry mess of things."[63] Still, she remained loyal, by and large, to A. Philip Randolph. In part it was because she shared his fundamental philosophy in this battle, which was to emphasize jobs and economic justice. Acknowledging and then fighting against the racist practices that unions historically exercised, Randolph helped shift the black middle class to a pro-union position. Hedgeman, who had made this shift herself when she worked at the YWCA, had become a powerful advocate for unionization among African Americans. And for her, when it came to women, Randolph was ultimately little better but hardly worse than other black male leaders.[64]

Over the span of five decades, Hedgeman would alternately praise and decry Randolph's efforts and his treatment of women. Regardless of his shortcomings, he had regularly enlisted women in his work, assigning them real responsibility when so many other men neglected women altogether. In a public tribute in celebration of his eighty-seventh birthday, she pointed out that though she was one of only two women invited to speak, many women owed him a great deal.

In 1945, while Anna was still deeply involved in the National Council for a Permanent FEPC, the war ended and Merritt left the service. Marshall Shepard, recorder of deeds for the city of Washington, invited him to join his staff. The Recorder of Deeds office was well known for employing African Americans, starting with the appointment of Frederick Douglass as recorder in 1881, and the job came with a certain amount of prestige. The Hedgemans were enormously pleased, although they wondered what life would be like for them in the nation's capital. Anna had not yet attempted to secure housing there on her own, and they were wary about the limited options in a segregated city. While Merritt was in the Army Air Force, and Anna at the National Council for a Permanent FEPC, she had relied on the hospitality of friends, living for a time with Helen Noble Curtis, the widow of a US ambassador to Liberia, whom she knew from her YWCA days. Fortunately, Anna and Merritt found pleasant accommodations in the new Mayfair Apartments in northeast Washington and settled in.[65]

The next few years were good for Anna and Merritt: the war was over, they were living in the same city, and Washington was slowly opening its doors to African Americans. When Anna first left the National Council, Merritt insisted she take a year off to rest.[66] She was not opposed to the idea, but with an increasing awareness of gender issues and an interest in young people's commitment to social justice, she found it impossible to resist a temporary appointment as assistant dean of women at Howard University. Among other projects, she worked with the students on a women's day event, inviting Judge Justine Wise Polier, the first woman justice in New York, and Ellen Venice Spraggs, a top reporter at the *Chicago Defender*, to campus. The event was memorable: the young women in attendance, as Hedgeman explained, "saw two people of accomplishment, white and Negro, in the same setting, both of them giving their special talents to their day."[67]

In 1948, Anna caught the attention of another group of dealmakers, those who hoped to get Harry S. Truman into the White House for a second term. Truman had become president at Franklin Roosevelt's death, so this would be his first time facing election, and it was far from a sure thing. In fact, things did not look good for the president, who faced challenges from the right and the left, and from within the party. Popular New York governor Thomas Dewey ran as the Republican challenger, Progressive Party candidate Henry Wallace was mounting a third-party challenge, and southern Democrats were up in arms because they believed northern Democrats had moved away from a long-standing tendency to allow the southern wing of the party to dictate matters of policy on race. Republican candidate Dewey's impressive civil rights record in New York had won endorsements from several leading black newspapers, and many people feared Henry Wallace might split the liberal vote, giving Dewey the election.[68]

This was a period of political transition for African Americans. In 1940, 67 percent of black voters had pulled the lever for Roosevelt, but only 42 percent considered themselves Democrats. They were loyal to FDR, but there was a chance they might move back to the GOP, the party of Lincoln, after his death.[69] Truman had failed, after all, to get permanent fair employment legislation enacted, and the racial politics of southern Democrats always loomed in the background. One of the president's key advisers, Clifford Clark, predicted the worst. "Unless there are new and real efforts," he argued, "the Negro bloc ... will go Republican."[70]

Truman signaled his continued support for the New Deal and upped the ante, calling for, among other things, permanent fair employment legislation, national health insurance, a massive housing program, increased support for education, and an increase in the minimum wage. He outlined a stronger civil rights agenda than a president had ever proposed. "Not all groups are free to live and work where they please or to improve their conditions of life by their own efforts," Truman noted. "Not all groups enjoy the full privilege of citizenship."[71] He called on the Republican-controlled Congress to ensure that the federal government moved forward on civil rights. He even asked Congress to pursue reparations for the Japanese Americans held in internment camps during the war. But Truman had a record of inconsistency in matters of racial justice, which put his sincerity in doubt: Was he promoting a strong civil rights agenda only because he knew Congress would never pass it?[72]

Even with well-publicized civil rights efforts, the black vote was still a challenge for Truman. The New Deal had provided African Americans with much-needed economic support, but their loyalty was not a given. As Henry Lee Moon explained in his election-year book, *The Balance of Power: The Negro Vote* (1948), the black vote was "in the vest pocket of no party" and would have to be earned.[73] Indeed, the black vote had become as diverse as the black population. Those higher up on the economic ladder supported the Republican candidate, while some who had seen the New Deal's limits when it came to race were in the Wallace camp. Three of the four parties—excluding, of course, the States' Rights Party, which grew out of southern Democrats' rebellion on racial issues—promised to advance civil rights. The Republican Party formed the National Council of Negro Republicans, and the Progressive Party hosted events with purposefully integrated audiences.[74] How was the Democratic candidate going to distinguish himself as racially progressive and still hold on to enough southern members of his party? How was he to improve his dismal 36 percent approval rating in the middle of the campaign season?[75]

With no black consensus on the election, Anna Arnold Hedgeman found herself in an interesting position. Many of her friends in Harlem supported the Republican candidate, hoping Dewey could bring his support for civil rights in New York State into a national context. "You have earned the right to be on the winning side," one friend told her, hoping to lure the erstwhile Republican back into the fold.[76] Others might have expected her to support the progressive candidate, Wallace, whom she knew from her work with the FEPC.[77] Indeed, anyone who took a good look at the delegates for the Republican, Democratic, and Progressive Party conventions might well have expected Hedgeman to side with Wallace, whose national convention was peopled by significant numbers of young delegates, female delegates, and delegates of color. The press morphed the differences in race, gender, and age into differences in weight, claiming that the average Progressive at their convention was twenty pounds lighter than a Democratic or Republican counterpart.[78]

But while the diversity, youth, and idealism of Wallace's supporters was appealing, the absence of smoke-filled rooms at the convention also signaled a lack of political experience. Hedgeman was not alone in believing that Truman's experience, coupled with what seemed a sincere commitment to racial and economic justice, would prevail.[79] She also likely understood that Wallace's refusal to purge the Progressive Party of Communists, along with the Communist Party endorsement of his candidacy, virtually guaranteed its failure. As critical as she would later be of the pervasive anticommunism in the national government, she was herself liberal rather than a leftist.

As far as Dewey was concerned, it seemed unlikely that he could translate the New York Republican model into a national context. The dilemma for Dewey was that the more he pointed to his local civil rights victories, the more he inadvertently highlighted what Congress had failed to do on a national level.[80] In fact, the Republican-led Eightieth Congress, dubbed the "Do-Nothing Congress" by Truman, had set out to dismantle the New Deal, and Dewey would have faced nearly as much of a challenge with it as Truman did.[81]

Anna Hedgeman was not the only black female voice speaking out for Truman. Sadie Tanner Alexander, the first African American woman to pursue a PhD in economics in the United States, and a member of Truman's President's Committee on Civil Rights (PCCR), believed that he would desegregate the military and make it "a living symbol of democracy."[82] Dorothy Height, Anna's longtime friend, also supported Truman; she believed his willingness to support fair employment in federal jobs had begun to spread to the private sector.[83] Likewise, Mary McLeod Bethune believed Truman presented the greatest chance for racial justice. At its annual convention, the National Council of Negro Women unanimously passed a resolution Hedgeman introduced to support the president. And the NCNW launched a voter registration drive in the northern and Midwestern states and helped to ensure a Truman victory.[84]

In her first foray into partisan politics, Hedgeman played a formative, though largely forgotten, role in Truman's re-election campaign. Congressman William L. Dawson of Illinois, a strong supporter of permanent fair employment practices legislation, had been appointed vice chair of the party, the highest Democratic position yet attained by an African American politician.[85] He seemed to be one of the few people in Washington who believed Truman could win the election. Dawson saw the black vote as critical, and he sought help from other African American leaders. Among other things, he arranged a speaking tour by William Hastie, the first black circuit court judge, who had been a dean of the Howard University Law School and one of the drafters of the permanent fair employment legislation. Hastie campaigned for Truman right up to the day before the election, when he hosted a climactic rally in Madison Square Garden.[86]

Dawson understood the caution that African Americans felt as they confronted the American political system; after all, he too had recently switched his allegiance from the Republican Party. Like Hedgeman, once he switched, he became an ardent Democrat. Until his death in 1970, Dawson served in the House, and he considered it his duty to encourage other black Americans to move away from the party of Lincoln.[87] For those Republicans who felt that the Democrats were irrevocably tainted by their segregationist southern membership, Dawson had an answer: purge the party of the Dixiecrats. "If the South doesn't want Negroes in the Democratic Party, let them get out, for we are here to stay—If the Republicans want them, they can take them."[88]

Dawson enlisted Hedgeman, naming her director of the National Citizens Committee for the Reelection of President Truman (NCCRPT), the first organized effort to have black Americans influence a presidential race through their financial contributions.[89] Founded by Dawson and *Chicago Defender* editor John H. Sengstacke, the group was determined to raise a million dollars.[90] Hedgeman settled in at the National Democratic Committee headquarters in the Biltmore Hotel in Washington, where she laid out a plan of action and helped Dawson demonstrate the viability of black Americans as a financial substitute for the departing southern segregationists.[91] "I was almost a 'joke' in New York City," she wrote, "where even strong Democratic leadership poked fun at Congressman William L. Dawson for his insistence that Truman could and would win."[92] But Dawson and Sengstacke's belief that it was time for the black electorate to make itself heard resonated with Hedgeman, who had learned from Cecelia Cabaniss Saunders in her YWCA days that African Americans had to invest, literally, to feel invested in a process.

"Mr. Truman planned his whistle-stop campaign," Anna Hedgeman wrote afterward, "and we planned ours."[93] With Dawson and his aides, she developed fundraising targets for the black electorate. She solicited speaking engagements through her black, women's, and Christian networks. Daisy Bates, who would soon become celebrated for her work on school desegregation, invited Hedgeman to Little Rock and introduced her to J. M. Robinson, a black physician; he gave the campaign its first check, for $1,000, and offered to solicit funding from his extensive medical practice.[94] Hedgeman also organized a gathering of the editors of twenty black newspapers, counting on their reach to more than a million readers.[95]

The NCCRPT worked tirelessly, particularly in Illinois and Ohio, states that were critical to the election. Occasionally, their whistle-stop tour and that of the president would cross paths, and they would check in with each other. The organization hosted election rallies, which proved lively and exciting, but nowhere along the way did things look particularly good for Truman. Every one of the nation's fifty leading newspaper publishers, according to a *Newsweek* poll published in October, predicted that Dewey, who had the support of Wall Street and big business, would win the election. Hedgeman and Dawson ignored the pundits and the polls and pushed on.[96]

Four days before the election, Truman spoke to an audience of sixty-five thousand at Dorrance Brooks Square in Harlem, making national news as the first American president to speak in the capital of black America.[97] "Our determination to attain the goal of equal rights," he told the crowd, "must be resolute and unwavering. For my part, I intend to keep moving toward this goal with every ounce of strength and determination that I have."[98] The significance of the location might have escaped the notice of white Americans, but many Harlem residents would have known that Dorrance Brooks was a soldier decorated during World War I, and that Dorrance Square was New York's first public space to be named after an African American soldier. During the event, the Greater New York Committee of Protestant Negro Ministers awarded Truman its Franklin Roosevelt Award, with Eleanor Roosevelt in attendance.

It is not clear that Anna organized this specific event, but it had all the markers of religion and race that she would have included. Some described the meeting as a spiritual experience. Bess Truman, the First Lady, remembered it as "the greatest and most dignified meeting" she had ever attended.[99] One thing is clear: the speech galvanized black support around the incumbent. New York State, not surprisingly, swung for its governor, Dewey, but in Harlem Truman garnered ninety thousand votes to Dewey's twenty-five thousand. The sense that the incumbent remained committed to racial justice carried across state lines, and Truman secured an unprecedented percentage of the black vote in key industrial states.[100]

It was a close race overall, and historians differ over whether it was labor, farmers, or African Americans who cinched the race for Truman.[101] There is no doubt, though, that black Americans contributed to Truman's margins in the key states of Ohio and Illinois, and they may well have played the main role in securing his victory.[102] One black journalist had this to say: "The Negro vote holding the balance of power has returned President Harry S. Truman to the White House. Ignored by all of the nation-wide polls as an 'insignificant minority' whose opinion needed no consideration, this minority has again demonstrated that 15 million Negroes can swing any national ticket."[103] The black press recognized the role of the NCCRPT, with the *Chicago Defender* placing Dawson on its honor roll for "raising more funds for the President's campaign than any other single individual."[104] Anna Hedgeman took great pride, both publicly and in her writing, in having helped return to office the president she thought most likely to support fair employment and full and complete desegregation of the military, among other civil rights agendas.

With the exception of Christopher Manning, in his book on Dawson's political career, not a single scholar has mentioned Hedgeman's role in this critical work.[105] Few even mention Dawson, the NCCRPT, or the role of African Americans in the election. It may be that Hedgeman's role was less significant than she made it out to be, but it is more likely that her efforts, recognized at the time, have been pushed into obscurity since. Like Ella Baker, Anna Hedgeman played a pivotal role but functioned as an "outsider within," close to the centers of power, working on the outside of the inner circle, part of a powerful but largely unseen network of black women who played key roles in the ongoing African American freedom struggle.[106]

Whatever the case, with President Truman securely in office, Hedgeman began to look for a new job, and this time her national profile produced national results. Just two weeks after Harry S. Truman took his oath of office, she took her own, joining the federal government as special assistant to the director of the Federal Security Administration. Anna and Merritt would be staying in the nation's capital for some time to come.

In one of her many firsts, Anna Arnold was the first African American graduate of Hamline University in Minnesota.

Courtesy Hamline University Archives

In 1933, Anna Arnold (front row, fifth from right) was one of the promising young activists invited to attend the NAACP's Amenia Conference in upstate New York and to help define the direction of civil rights nationally.

Courtesy Library of Congress, Lot 13077

Anna Arnold and Merritt Hedgeman enjoyed a marriage that lasted fifty-four years, until his death in 1988. Anna often acknowledged how unconventional their marriage was for their generation. Merritt, she wrote tellingly, "has never permitted the fact that I am a woman to color his judgment of me or his support of my work."

Courtesy Carol Anderson Holmes and National Afro-American Museum and Cultural Center

Anna Hedgeman supported Robert F. Wagner Jr. in his bid for mayor of New York City, forming a fundraising committee and recruiting former First Lady Eleanor Roosevelt (seated, second from right, next to Hedgeman), to chair it.

Courtesy National Afro-American Museum and Cultural Center

Hedgeman was appointed to Mayor Wagner's cabinet, the first woman and first African American to serve in this capacity in the city's history. The photograph captures her swearing-in ceremony in 1954.

Courtesy National Afro-American Museum and Cultural Center

New York City's mayoral cabinet meets former president Harry S. Truman (center), whom Hedgeman had helped win the 1948 election by organizing African Americans on his behalf.

Courtesy National Afro-American Museum and Cultural Center

Hedgeman (center, back) gave the keynote address at the first Conference of the Women of Africa and of African Descent in the newly independent Ghana in 1960.

Courtesy National Afro-American Museum and Cultural Center

In 1962, in one of their many collaborations, A. Philip Randolph and Anna Arnold Hedgeman invited Malcolm X to speak on behalf of predominantly black and Puerto Rican hospital workers in New York City. The photograph has often been printed with Hedgeman cropped out, erasing her from this history.

Local 1199 Files, courtesy Kheel Center, Cornell University

Anna Arnold Hedgeman honors A. Philip Randolph at the 50th anniversary of the Brotherhood of Sleeping Car Porters.

Courtesy National Afro-American Museum and Cultural Center

Hedgeman often marched for justice or faced marchers with very different messages. In the bottom photograph, she is flanked by her white coworkers as they enter an Atlanta restaurant.

Photographs by Ken Thompson, courtesy General Board of Global Ministries, United Methodist Church

An early practitioner of black history, Hedgeman led schoolchildren and adults through her curricula, which she believed to be empowering for black and white citizens alike.

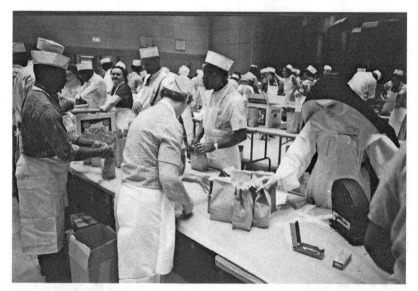

The day before the 1963 March on Washington, Operation Sandwich, organized by Hedgeman, brought together hundreds of volunteers, many of them clergy, to make thousands of sandwiches for the marchers.

Photograph by Ken Thompson, courtesy General Board of Global Ministries, United Methodist Church

Hedgeman participated in the blessing of the sandwiches before refrigerated trucks transported them from New York City to Washington, DC.

Photograph by Ken Thompson, courtesy General Board of Global Ministries, United Methodist Church

Through her position on the National Council of Churches' Commission on Religion and Race, Hedgeman worked tirelessly to recruit white marchers for the March on Washington. The interracial character of the march was due in significant part to her efforts.

Photographs by Ken Thompson, courtesy General Board of Global Ministries, United Methodist Church

Hedgeman encouraged her colleagues on the March on Washington planning committee to address both voting rights and economic justice in the day's program.

Photographs by Ken Thompson, courtesy General Board of Global Ministries, United Methodist Church

Anna Hedgeman sits on the steps of the Lincoln Memorial during the March on Washington. Immediately behind her are three Democratic members of the US Senate, Phillip Hart of Michigan, Wayne Morse of Oregon, and William Proxmire of Wisconsin. After the march, she would call on them to help push through the 1964 Civil Rights Act.

Courtesy AP Photo

The Sixteenth Street Baptist Church in Birmingham, Alabama, in the aftermath of the tragic September 1963 bombing that left four young girls dead. For Anna Arnold Hedgeman and her coworkers in the National Council of Churches' Commission on Religion and Race, the symbolism of the disfigurement of the stained-glass Jesus was profound.

Photograph by Ken Thompson, courtesy General Board of Global Ministries, United Methodist Church

During the funeral service for three of the four girls killed in the September 1963 bombing of the Sixteenth Street Baptist Church in Birmingham, mourners lined the sidewalks. Above, right, Hedgeman confers with Martin Luther King Jr. before the service.

Photographs by Ken Thompson, courtesy General Board of Global Ministries, United Methodist Church

Anna Arnold Hedgeman ran
for office three times, unsuc-
cessfully. In her first bid,
for a congressional seat, she
pledged that "ours is a movement of all neglected people
in the district" and relied on
the support of the Reform
Democrats, including former
Senator Herbert Lehman
(seated, left) and former
First Lady Eleanor Roosevelt
(seated, right).

Hedgeman urged white Christians
to demand that their legislators support the 1964 Civil Rights Act. Here
she talks with President Lyndon
Johnson at the White House celebration of the bill's passage.

Courtesy National Afro-American
Museum and Cultural Center

Hedgeman ran for New York City Council president on the Democratic ticket of William Fitz Ryan in 1965. Her candidacy gave Ryan a stronger foothold in the city's black communities, but neither candidate won the election.

Photos courtesy National Afro-American Museum and Cultural Center

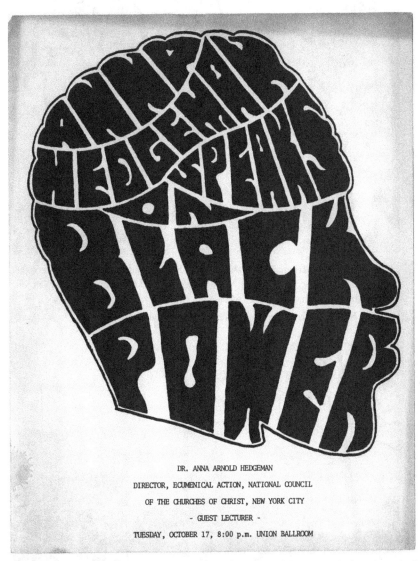

ANNA HEDGEMAN SPEAKS ON BLACK POWER

DR. ANNA ARNOLD HEDGEMAN

DIRECTOR, ECUMENICAL ACTION, NATIONAL COUNCIL

OF THE CHURCHES OF CHRIST, NEW YORK CITY

- GUEST LECTURER -

TUESDAY, OCTOBER 17, 8:00 p.m. UNION BALLROOM

Hedgeman believed that African Americans, like many ethnic groups before them, had to assume power to be fully American.

Courtesy National Afro-American Museum and Cultural Center

Hedgeman and her friend Inez Casiano flank Betty Friedan during a press conference announcing the founding of NOW, the National Organization for Women.
Hedgeman would serve as its vice president.

Courtesy National Afro-American Museum and Cultural Center

Hedgeman was the only woman and the only layperson to sign the various public statements of the National Committee of Negro Churchmen. An organizer of
NCNC events, including a march to the Statue of Liberty in 1966, she played an
important but unacknowledged role in the development of black theology.

Photograph by Ken Thompson, courtesy General Board of Global Ministries, United
Methodist Church

8 "NEW WORLD CITIZEN"

DEVELOPING A NATIONAL PORTFOLIO,
AN INTERNATIONAL CONSCIOUSNESS,
AND AN FBI FILE

On February 12, 1949, forty-eight-year-old Anna Arnold Hedgeman was sworn in as special assistant to the director of the Federal Security Agency (FSA), soon to become the Department of Health, Education, and Welfare (HEW). The appointment would secure her reputation as a national black leader, offer opportunities to implement progressive policies, and lead her to begin thinking of herself as a global citizen. In these postwar, Cold War years, when the world seemed both larger and smaller, more enlightened and more menacing, Hedgeman believed the United States could lead through example by bettering the lives of its citizens.

The appointment also encouraged Hedgeman to think more deeply about the role of black women, nationally and internationally. As she saw it, African American women had already played a central role in advancing "democracy in practice" in America—surely they could play a role on a global scale as well.[1]

With this appointment, Hedgeman became one of the few African Americans at her level of service. President Truman's support for civil rights had so far not translated into fair employment in government work.[2] Systematic racism, combined with bureaucratic inertia, proved formidable obstacles. Some of the resistance to change was subtle, some blatant. Liberal government officials remained largely oblivious to the many ways in which conscious and unconscious bias precluded African Americans' adequate consideration for employment, and southern Democratic committee chairs deliberately went after agencies that tried to address the situation.[3]

Following his success as Democratic Party vice chair, Congressman William Dawson decided to use his now considerable power within the party to personally challenge this resistance. "It's time to stop getting mad," he claimed, "and start getting smart."[4] Patronage in government appointments is sometimes considered suspect, but it is a common method by which governors, mayors, and other politicians influence the direction of politics. In Congressman Dawson's hands, it served as a pragmatic civil rights tool. If black Americans were repeatedly passed over for promotion to significant positions, they would never be in a position to end the cycle that kept them out of power. "I have tried to fight for civil rights where it is most effective," Dawson explained. He targeted federal appointments and claimed later, "Many of the big posts we hold in government today were obtained through this technique."[5]

Evaluating potential candidates on, above all, merit and party loyalty, Dawson attempted to place into government positions black Americans who would serve more than symbolic roles. Franklin Roosevelt's "Black Cabinet," an informal group of forty-five African Americans whom the president appointed to official positions in the federal government, stood as the best example of black influence at the highest ranks of government, but Dawson wanted more than influence, more than token representation, or isolated, occasional influence.[6] He hoped, instead, to weave black appointees into the very fabric of governmental power. A few of the dozen or so most significant appointments he secured were women, Anna Arnold Hedgeman among them, making her one of the first African American beneficiaries of this secondary level of patronage within the federal government.

Given Hedgeman's extensive social work experience, Depression-era welfare work, and service in civilian defense, it is no wonder that Dawson selected her for the FSA, which included in its oversight Social Security, health, welfare, education, and international services. It may also have helped that the agency's director, Oscar Ewing, was a Democratic Party and Truman administration insider. As Ewing's assistant, Hedgeman served as facilitator between the FSA and numerous labor, professional, and social services groups, including the AFL-CIO, the National Education Association, the American Medical Association, and Catholic Charities.[7] She was pleased that she was not there to "represent" her race or advocate solely on issues of race. "Mrs. Hedgeman's position," noted the *Baltimore Afro-American* with discernible pride, "will not confine her work to racial matters. She will be given the same assignments as those given to Mr. Ewing's three other special assistants."[8] The *New York Amsterdam News* considered her appointment one of the highlights of 1949.[9]

Hedgeman now had to figure out how to become part of the system without becoming part of "the system." Given the history of racism within the government, and the recent defeat of permanent fair employment legislation, not all African Americans, and not even all the African American women in Anna's circles, saw party politics as a viable means for racial advancement. She herself had been wary of the complacency and loss of purpose that being an insider could bring, and had always complemented work inside the system with outside activism. What would it mean now to immerse herself even more deeply in a structure that had so clearly rejected efforts to reform it?

The Democratic Party had too often proved a weak ally, and the president had been far less forceful on civil rights than many had hoped. Some of Hedgeman's colleagues wondered if black women should pool their resources not to join the Democrats but rather to critique and challenge them. Harlem journalist and radical Claudia Jones, for example, viewed Hedgeman's entry into government as assimilation rather than integration. She criticized this FSA position as nothing more than a token appointment, an attempt "to whittle down the militancy of Negro women."[10]

Others believed that the US government was simply too corrupt for them to participate in it. But Hedgeman, like Dawson, believed that complaining about political corruption merely continued the isolation of African Americans and hurt them in the long run. Insinuation into the halls of power, on the other hand, offered some promise. "Next to religion itself," Dawson told a crowd of black women, "there is no better device through which we can make progress than through politics. It is the root of all civic benefits, better jobs, and better living."[11]

It was a time of firsts for African Americans in and out of politics. Just two years earlier, in 1947, Jackie Robinson walked out to first base for the Brooklyn Dodgers and became the first black player in Major League Baseball. Just one year earlier, in 1948, high jumper Alice Coachman became the first black woman to win a gold medal for the United States in the Olympics. And a year later, in 1950, poet Gwendolyn Brooks would become the first black American to win a Pulitzer Prize. Anna Hedgeman had far less celebrity, but both the federal government and the nation's capital had such a dearth of black leadership in general, and black female leadership in particular, that her arrival produced what she described as "much excitement in official Washington."[12]

Hedgeman found herself both a token and a player, but what she wanted above all was to have her appointment, and her ideas, taken seriously. On her first day on the job, an elevator operator, excited to welcome the first black person in an administrative position at the FSA, took her aside. "Any time you don't want to ride up with these white folks," she told the new appointee conspiratorially, "just let me know and I'll take you up by yourself, express." Enormously frustrated that she had to spoil the woman's opportunity to feel "superior" for once, Hedgeman nevertheless told the woman she wanted to be treated the same as everyone else who rode the elevator.[13]

Hedgeman had to make another decision that day before she could get to work. She took a phone call from the personnel director, who asked, "Um, do you want, um, a Negro secretary?" She did want a black secretary, because she knew they were not getting the positions they deserved, but she also wanted to be fair. Her experience led her to believe that if she requested files of the best secretaries due for promotion, there would be African American women among them, and she could make a fair and unbiased hire from a diverse pool of candidates. With the help of a white colleague, she concluded that of five stenographers, the two black women had both the best records and the most obvious lack of opportunity. Their files demonstrated, in a microcosm, the fate of even the best black workers nationwide. Now she faced a different color problem: Would she hire the dark-skinned woman or the light-skinned woman? Given her own light skin, Hedgeman feared that if she chose the light-skinned woman, black observers would accuse her of having internalized the "white gaze" that caused so many employers, black as well as white, to favor African Americans who could pass for white.

Before she could act, the darker-skinned woman got a promotion in her own department, most likely because Hedgeman's interest made her supervisor fearful of losing her. Hedgeman hired the other woman; feeling accountable to the darker-skinned people in the building, she asked a black employee on her floor to spread the word that both women were promoted as a result of her interest. She also made a point of following up with the personnel director, letting her know that as qualified as the two African American women were, they ought to have been promoted long before.[14]

Turning to her work, she contacted people in social welfare and government agencies, in labor unions, and in educational institutions to determine national needs and set national priorities. In some of her most exciting work, she was engaged in the very early research that would lead to the *Brown v. Board of Education* (1954) decision outlawing segregation in the schools. Hedgeman did not develop a particular area of expertise; instead, she enjoyed being used "across the board," as she noted, "because I wanted to know as much as I could about the whole picture."[15] She was the first woman to address a national conference of the United Auto Workers and played a key role in her agency's outreach to foreign visitors, helping to develop an international center where visitors could learn about American culture and ask some of the hard questions that staying in a segregated city raised for them. She again found herself having to balance her loyalty to her country with acknowledging its shortcomings.

Even though Hedgeman's position was not about, or focused on, race, she had to address it—too often. In one international gathering, a German visitor claimed that Americans could not know what it was like to fear, every day, "that justice may not come to you." Hedgeman took the podium and corrected him, explaining the costs of racial injustice in the United States. Sometimes people in the agency appreciated her frankness; other times they grew weary of her race talk. Once again, she realized, white people were demonstrating their priv-ilege: they *could* grow bored with a conversation that remained vital to black Americans. Still, she remained hopeful for her nation and always said so.[16] Was her own appointment not a sign of the changing tide?

Anna Hedgeman worked in the FSA for more than four years, accumulat-ing a wealth of experience. In addition to becoming far more expert in assessing the needs of her country's most vulnerable citizens, she developed more of an international consciousness. She purposefully began to place her own identity as a black woman, and a black American, in a global framework, coining the phrase "New World citizen" to describe herself.[17]

Two FSA experiences in particular stood out for her, both of them further informing her sense of herself as a woman, a national leader, and a global citizen. The first was the Midcentury White House Conference on Children and Youth, sponsored by the Children's Bureau, for which she served as the FSA liaison. The Children's Bureau was directed, staffed, and managed almost entirely by women, some of them Hedgeman's close friends. She took pride in the organi-zation of the conference. No top-down federal initiative, it drew on the exper-tise of ordinary citizens and working professionals across the country, bringing together more than six thousand people, including five hundred young adults, to discuss, debate, and formulate child welfare policy. Two hundred foreign del-egates from thirty nations attended as observers, and Hedgeman began to think seriously about what she later called "the international potential of our domestic programs."

Conference attendees worked on developing print materials on young peo-ple's relationships to housing, poverty, health, education, and social problems, making special note of socioeconomic disparities, and recommended the imple-mentation of free school lunch programs and the construction of affordable, community-based public housing. They also focused attention on the needs of migrant workers, the education of children with mental and physical handicaps, and the necessity of abolishing racial segregation in educational environments. Some might have considered it too broad an agenda, but Hedgeman envisioned an approach that would allow a range of hardworking people who cared about children to influence not just the Children's Bureau or the FSA but agencies throughout the federal government. Not surprisingly, the black press noted that, thanks to her, the conference included significant black representation.[18] Again, although Hedgeman's portfolio did not specifically emphasize race, she took spe-cial care to ensure that race would not be overlooked when those deemed "in the know" received their invitations. In the case of the White House conference, to the extent that minority groups appeared in the population, they also appeared at the conference.

Although Hedgeman's fingerprints were all over the conference, she herself was absent, having been hospitalized across town. By now in her early fifties, she was, literally, exhausted. If black people had to work twice as hard as whites to prove their value, and women had to work twice as hard as men to prove theirs, Hedgeman, by necessity as much as by design, did little else but work. "Her present convalescence," one newspaper noted, "is to regain strength which, as her close friends know, has been lost over a long period of time from the strain of overwork."[19] Characteristically, on top of the consuming work she performed at the FSA, Hedgeman had also been engaged in activism on her off-hours, spending evenings and weekends supporting Mary Church Terrell's efforts to desegregate the capital; securing the appointment of Frank Jones, a prominent black physician, as president of the board of the Washington Urban League; running for the unsalaried post of president of the National Council of Negro Women; and organizing meetings to help energize the moribund Washington branch of the NAACP.[20]

Hedgeman's second significant experience in the FSA was a three-month trip to India at the invitation of Chester Bowles, the US ambassador there. As the Cold War heated up, the United States feared that Soviet and Chinese interest in the newly independent nation threatened global stability. The State Department considered it in the national interest to send Americans to India, to travel, meet with leaders and ordinary citizens, and serve as ambassadors of democracy. African Americans were deemed a particularly valuable weapon in the Cold War arsenal, to counter Soviet propaganda about American racism.[21] An international conference on social work seemed an opportune moment for a US presence. As Ambassador Bowles envisioned it, the conference called for quick studies—a group of Americans who could adroitly assess the Indian situation but also "handle successfully whatever tough situations may be thrown at them by Communist delegates."[22]

Bowles had heard about Hedgeman and judged her a good representative of what he wanted. "It is most important that we have at least one or possibly two Negroes as members of our official group," he wrote to the State Department. "I understand that Anna Hedgeman, assistant to Oscar Ewing, would ... be a good selection."[23] He pressed the point in a second letter. "Do not ... know personally Mrs. Anna Hedgeman," he wrote, "but everyone who does says she would be a sensational success in India, and every effort should be made to enable her husband, a talented singer, to accompany her." As Bowles saw it, "Personal contacts with peoples such as these represent our greatest single public relations opportunity in India."[24] In the end, Merritt could not leave either his concert work or his position in the Recorder of Deeds office, but Anna got ready to go. By now she had considerable experience in standing up for America at the same time she critiqued it, and she had no problem with that approach.

Before she could join the group, which included the National Urban League's executive director, Lester Granger, Hedgeman had to obtain a passport, and she fell victim to the same Cold War paranoia her India visit was designed to quell.[25] She applied and waited, but no passport arrived. She did not know what caused the delay and worried that her outspokenness on matters of race might prevent her from leaving the country. Like so many political activists, liberal and leftist, Hedgeman had begun to attract the attention of the House Un-American Activities Committee (HUAC). She had been issued a loyalty questionnaire and wondered if her responses invited increased scrutiny.[26] "I knew that my frank discussion of the race problem would not sit well among those people who were convinced that Communism and criticism of the government were spelled the same way," she recalled later on. When they asked if she were a Communist, Anna fired back in a way she later realized was a bit brash. "I'd had so much difficulty trying to secure my part of American democracy," she'd told them, "that I had no time to study Communism."[27] Perhaps her response to HUAC was coming back to haunt her, something many others had experienced.

Though she knew about the loyalty questionnaire, Hedgeman never learned about the extent of the two loyalty investigations and two follow-up investigations she would be subject to over the next twenty-five years. Unbeknownst to her, the FBI ultimately developed three hundred pages of material on her allegedly suspect activities. A number of agents were assigned to her case; over the years, they interviewed Hedgeman as well as her friends, neighbors, and coworkers, and spent a significant amount of money to discover, again and again, that she was a loyal if occasionally obstreperous American.[28]

Hedgeman may initially have been subject to investigation because of her appointment in the Federal Security Agency, or it may have been because when the FBI interviewed her about other people's loyalty, she let them have it. She told the first agent who interviewed her about a colleague that the whole idea of the loyalty program was "very distasteful to her," refused to answer some of his questions, and exhibited, as he put it, "a very uncooperative attitude and aversion to the investigations of government employees conducted by the Federal Bureau of Investigation." She told him that she had reviewed the loyalty questionnaires that fourteen post office employees had been instructed to fill out. Her frankness, as well as her well-founded suspicion that black postal employees were routinely targeted, probably caused them concern.

Investigating Hedgeman, the FBI over the years searched police records and spoke with people ranging from the housekeeper at Harlem's Theresa Hotel, where she and Merritt often stayed and would later live, to directors of major civil rights organizations. The first investigation took so long that FBI director J. Edgar Hoover complained that hers was "among the most delinquent loyalty investigations being handled by the Bureau as a whole."[29]

Cleared in 1949, but unaware that her belligerence, however patriotic, kept her in the FBI's sights, Hedgeman reported for questioning about a coworker in January 1952. Again, she let them have it. She told the agent that questions about people's associations worried her a great deal "in the undemocratic city of Washington," and demanded to know why the agent was spending his time on this and not on solving racial crimes. Later that year, she told another agent that she had no use for the Communist Party but understood why other members of her race would be drawn to the party's pledges of racial equality.

The FBI reports, which date from 1949, 1952, 1963, and 1964, demonstrate the level of paranoia that permeated the federal government. Today, they seem almost comical, with one agent noting that Hedgeman had been observed driving around Harlem in a small foreign car. When she told another agent he would be more productive investigating racial violence in the South, he noted, perhaps looking for some brownie points, "However, J. EDGAR HOOVER of the Federal Bureau of Investigation continually refers to convictions well over ninety percent throughout the rest of the country." The many interviews the FBI conducted with coworkers reveal tidbits about Hedgeman's character. Every secretary interviewed talked about what a terrific boss she was. Her doctor told of how she "needled" him into doing community work. One person she worked with in the mayor's office called her a "nasty character," but otherwise colleagues unanimously offered their highest praises. None doubted her loyalty.[30]

The use of confidential informants, a common practice, reveals just how distorted the loyalty program was. The only people interviewed who questioned Hedgeman's devotion to her country were the confidential informants, one noting that she attended meetings at which Communists were present, another that, whether she realized it or not, the Communist Party supported her candidacy for public office. Yet another confidential informant, "New York T-1," had had no contact with Anna for twenty years but suspected her of being a Communist or Communist sympathizer. He could recall no specific evidence to back up his suspicions. New York T-1's report concludes in the same way the other confidential informant reports conclude, stating that he "would not furnish a signed statement or appear before a hearing board."[31]

Meanwhile, as she planned her trip to India, Hedgeman had no way to know what was delaying her passport, and she worried more with each passing day that she would miss the flight. The problem might be large, repressive, anticommunist forces, but as an African American woman in Washington, DC, she had to wonder if the delay might not be personal rather than political. She wondered if Ellen Woodward, director of international affairs for the FSA, a white native of Mississippi, might have conveniently lost the paperwork. Her anxiety must have become apparent to Woodward, because she stopped by one day to tell Hedgeman she was doing everything she could to facilitate the process. Hedgeman now felt even worse, guilty as well as anxious: "My needless distrust is another heart-breaking illustration of the additional uncertainty a Negro faces in his relationship with most white people and certainly most Southerners."[32] Four days before the flight, she finally secured a passport.

It was a momentous trip for Anna Hedgeman, who had never before left the country. She and Merritt headed to New York, where she would catch her flight, and on the morning of November 27, 1952, after breakfast in the dining room of the Hotel Theresa, Anna made calls to her siblings, visited with her father-in-law, and then headed to the airport, where she was served champagne and canapés in the Pan Am terminal before boarding. She enjoyed the flight, and when they flew low over Ireland, she wished she could make a quick stop for postcards to send her Irish neighbors back home.[33] An extended delay in London was frustrating, but she was delighted by all the British accents. Air travel was such an exciting, novel experience that she saved everything from the flight, including the air sickness bag. (While in India, she accumulated so many books and pamphlets about the country and its social work practices that she had to enlist the help of a sea captain to take some of her materials back by boat, so that she could meet the airline weight restrictions.)[34]

Once in India, even an inveterate New Yorker like Anna Hedgeman felt overwhelmed by the sights and smells on the streets, where, in addition to countless people, were oxcarts, monkeys, sheep, donkeys, cows. She visited villages, slums, children's institutions, hospitals, universities, trade unions, factories, and farms. She saw the Taj Mahal by moonlight, met Prime Minister Jawaharlal Nehru, and sampled vegetarian cuisine for the first time. The terrible poverty she witnessed brought her back to the Mississippi of the 1920s. "The odor of burning wood and burning fat had gripped my nostrils and in that second I was back in Mississippi thirty years before," she wrote. "I knew then that I would have some basic understanding of this India, for burning wood and burning fat had long since been the symbols of poverty and eroded soil, of hunger and exploitation and the resultant human misery."[35] She took up this theme in letters home. "The variety of brown faces," Anna explained to Merritt, "the complexes about color and caste are all here and sometimes I have to pinch myself to know that I'm not in the deep South."[36] She also felt the weight of colonialism as she reflected on the statue of Queen Victoria "standing in pristine elegance over such fantastic poverty."[37]

Hedgeman attended three major conferences, gave talks to more than a dozen groups in ten cities, and met with leaders in government, education, chambers of commerce, social service organizations, and prisons. She realized that she ought to have had far more training in advance of the trip and suggested that the State Department mandate more cultural education for future program participants. Nevertheless, she concluded that the members of the US delegation had a great deal to offer their counterparts in India, where professional social work was a nascent, inexpert practice. Paid social workers were in the minority, and the volunteers, who exercised the most control, were largely, as she saw it, "of the Lady Bountiful variety," significantly distanced from those they purported to help.[38] It became clear that many privileged Indian women, with few other avenues, anchored their identity in volunteer work. As much as they wanted to help others, their resistance to professionalization hindered development of the field.

Hedgeman's advice included advocacy for more schools of social work, more professional training, and, in response to the tremendous depth and variety of needs, more flexibility in services. As much as she wanted to see attention to best practices, she also recalled the Great Depression and the many times she and others had to ignore "the best professional standards" in the interest of meeting basic needs. Still, she maintained, only professionals could make those kinds of judgments. Hedgeman found much of the discussion at the international conference more theoretical than practical and, given the depths of poverty in India, problematic. The particular focus on children with disabilities seemed misplaced, she reflected, given that almost every child she met seemed handicapped by one obstacle or another.

Hedgeman's dismay grew when she witnessed how many white visitors and residents failed to appreciate the Indian context or adapt to it in any way. And she learned that many Indians preferred the British, their former colonizers, to the Americans. When she gathered the courage to ask how that could be, an Indian colleague answered candidly. The British were reserved but sincere, and the two peoples had a shared history. Americans, on the other hand, were "effervescent at first meeting but may not even recall having met you later," the woman explained. "It is as though the cocktail saves them from the obligation to know me or even listen to me."[39] People asked Hedgeman hard questions about America and Americans, including a basic question that often felt charged with hostility. "Why," she was asked again and again, "are you here?"[40]

As expected, a good number of the questions Hedgeman faced addressed Cold War concerns and global realities, and like many African Americans, she found herself in a strange position. "I was amused that I, who had always been forced to be critical of the United States, suffered now as significant leadership of the world was also critical of us."[41] It was not only national leaders who voiced criticism; many civilians wanted answers to the same questions. "Your *Congressional Record*," one man stated in the most practical terms, "suggests that you owe us aid because you hope it will prevent us from becoming Communists. If your democracy is functioning so well, why are you so fearful of Communists?"[42] Others asked her to explain the US position on colonialism, describe its commitment to world peace, or account for its practices of racial discrimination. She was not alone. Ambassador Bowles reported that the number-one question he faced during his years in India was "What about America's treatment of the Negro?"[43]

Hedgeman, Lester Granger, and other black Americans on the trip had reviewed the US Information Service (USIS) materials about "the Negro in America," but Hedgeman did not refer to what she considered government propaganda when she spoke with Indians. Instead, she spoke the truth as she saw it. She had, after all, gone to India not just as a social worker, not just as an American, but as an African American. This meant that she had, as she put it, "an added responsibility, to speak of the Negro in the United States in honest terms."[44]

In a pamphlet titled "What Are the Facts about Negroes in the United States?," the USIS assembled a series of questions and answers for "our friends in India." The photograph that accompanied the rather upbeat analysis of contemporary race relations pictured an interracial medical team performing surgery in a hospital in Arizona. In an era of Jim Crow health care in the North as well as in the South, they must have done a good deal of digging to come up with that photograph. But the USIS could no more contain the flow of news from the United States to India than it could contain Anna Hedgeman. A *Time* magazine piece published just a few months prior to her trip described the experiences of an Indian labor leader on a State Department–sponsored visit to the United States. After being refused service at three different eating establishments, he revealed his discomfort and his bemusement at being labeled "colored." "After all, isn't white a color?" he asked in the interview. "You people talk democracy, and you must be careful to practice what you preach."[45]

Hedgeman's straightforward analyses of race relations in the United States gained her some detractors among her white American peers in India, but Ambassador Bowles found her delightful. "We have all been quite taken by Anna Hedgeman, who is just as grand a person as you said she was,"[46] he wrote to Donald Montgomery and Mary Taylor, the Washington insider couple who had first suggested her for the trip. In a second letter, he said it was "impossible to exaggerate the contribution which she has made."[47] Bowles and Hedgeman shared a liberal politics and a commitment to racial justice. As the grandson of one of the founders of the National Urban League, he carried forward a family tradition of progressive politics. Before his appointment to India, Bowles had advocated on behalf of black employment in the Office of Price Administration, fought for a strong civil rights plank at the Democratic National Convention of 1948, and as governor of Connecticut had outlawed segregation in the state's National Guard.[48]

Chester Bowles argued repeatedly that the best strategy for good relations with India—not to mention the best way to convince Indians to emulate the United States rather than China or the Soviet Union—was a serious civil rights program at home. In a letter he had written the previous summer to Walter White at the NAACP, Bowles explained: "As you know from our talks, the status of the Negro in the United States is a subject of constantly recurring interest and comment here in India."[49] Anticipating the upcoming national election, he implored White not to let up: "I do hope you will keep up all the pressure you can to see that neither the Democrats nor the Republicans try to ignore or water down the civil rights issue this year." When Republican Dwight D. Eisenhower won the national election during her time in India, Anna wrote to Merritt warning him of the tension the new administration might usher in, not just at home but globally. She especially worried that the influential and respected Bowles would be replaced. Communists in India had already spread the word that the United States was "completely reactionary" on matters of race, she reported, and would have "a field day" if Chester Bowles's tenure ended when Dwight D. Eisenhower took office.[50] Her keen awareness of racial matters had now reached a global level.

The India trip was as enervating as it was exciting and instructive, in part because Hedgeman developed food poisoning but felt compelled to push on before she had fully recovered. "I seldom have worked so hard and attempted to pack so much into so short a time," she wrote afterward, explaining why she practically slept her way through Paris and Istanbul on her way home.[51] Anna also suffered from being away from Merritt for so long. They had been apart from each other in the past, sometimes for considerable periods of time, but this felt altogether different. She longed for someone she could speak with more openly about her experiences. She made a good number of acquaintances and a few new friendships, but she felt significant cultural differences with Indian women. Lester Granger, with whom people assumed she would be friendly, was a Republican, and she felt both the political distance between them and frustration that everyone assumed race would trump politics when it came to their relationship. "I'll never leave you again for so long," Anna wrote to Merritt, who felt wildly out of sorts without her himself. At one point he wrote her six letters in a week's time. Even so, she complained that he didn't tell her enough about his life at home. She wanted to know everything, she instructed, "what time you get up—how long you stay in the bath room, how much hair you cut off while I'm away, where you eat, what wrong things you eat, etc. etc." They prayed for each other regularly and teased each other regularly. When Anna repeatedly addressed him as "Dearest Dog" or as "kutta," which she understood as an Indian translation for dog, he wrote back, "My dearest, dearest, dearest sweetheart," providing, he explained, a more refined example for her to emulate.[52]

Before she made the trip to India, Anna Arnold Hedgeman, the self-described "New World citizen," had begun to develop a global consciousness that included elements of black nationalism. She had traveled to San Francisco in 1945 to attend the founding of the United Nations, an event that offered black Americans an opportunity to more fully consider their racial identity in an international context.[53] Hedgeman heeded the words of Mary McLeod Bethune, who suggested that "Negro women like all other women must take a part in building this world, and must therefore keep informed on all world-shaping events."[54] As nations on the African continent began to fight for independence, and colonial powers responded with renewed repression, Hedgeman began to think carefully about a transnational role for black Americans, for black women, for herself. She and others began to talk about freedom in global black terms. Her colleagues in the National Council of Negro Women, for example, complained that arguments that Africans were "not ready" for independence sounded an awful lot like defenses of continued segregation at home.

Such consciousness grew as people in the United States gained more knowledge about apartheid, the practice of enforced racial segregation and oppression that became law in South Africa in 1948.[55] In the early 1950s, even before her trip to India, Anna Hedgeman had become executive director of the American Committee on Africa (ACOA), a small coalition of activists whose determination to end apartheid would result in a global movement in the 1970s and 1980s but got little traction at the time. Once again she was at the forefront of a political movement. She traveled around the country with Mburumba Kerira, who would, after his country's independence, become Namibia's first lobbyist at the United Nations; they sought support to pressure the UN into censuring South Africa. The ACOA called for a number of measures, including the immediate recall of the US ambassador to South Africa, an investigation of US economic interests and their effect on apartheid, and the use of the "tremendous prestige" of the US presidency to push for change. Hedgeman promoted the cause at a South Africa Freedom Day in Harlem, where she was invited to "tie the many elements of the program together by relating the South Africa situation to our own here in the United States, New York City, and Harlem."[56]

Anticipating the by now almost rote charges of communism, the ACOA asked Eleanor Roosevelt to send out fundraising letters on its behalf, and she did, providing hearty support to the committee's statements that if people cared about Africa and agreed that American policy had been hijacked by a "tiny, well-financed and vociferous minority" of alleged anticommunists, they could respond by providing support to this organization. "Not every policy offered as an antidote to Communism can be gulped down without question," the committee wrote.[57]

The group paid close attention to African independence efforts over the course of the 1950s and felt the sting of censorship when Hedgeman could not get a piece supporting Ghanaian leader Kwame Nkrumah published in a New York newspaper. She subsequently published a different article, taking her Harlem neighbors to task for their complacency. "Perhaps it is time also," she wrote, "that American Negroes give more attention to world events, with special emphasis on beginning such study with Africa. There was an Africa when there was no United States and no Europe. We are America's major link with that ancient civilization, and we also have the opportunity to serve Africa as she develops continuing relationships with the West."[58]

When Ghana secured its independence in 1957, it was cause for celebration among blacks in the United States. The newly elected president, Kwame Nkrumah, visited Harlem, where throngs of people lined the parade route and ten thousand gathered to hear him speak. Ghana's independence served as a vital symbol to blacks in America and around the world.[59] Dozens of male civil rights leaders eagerly made their way to Ghana to see what black independent leadership would look like, but the new nation drew African American women as well, including Anna Arnold Hedgeman, Maya Angelou, Pauli Murray, and Shirley Graham Du Bois.[60]

When Hedgeman received an invitation to deliver the keynote address at the first Conference of the Women of Africa and of African Descent in the newly independent Ghana, she was overjoyed. The process of decolonization in Ghana highlighted black Americans' feelings of connection to an African past. This was certainly true for Hedgeman, who reflected on her father telling her as a child that "Africa was probably the 'mother' of the world."[61] That belief only intensified as she grew older "The English part of me is well documented," she wrote, "and the French portion is also a matter of record. The African in me has been buried in time, in the machinations of the slave trade, and in the failure of American historians to record my African past." She viewed the conference invitation as an opportunity to explore her relationship "to the remainder of my roots."[62]

Even so, when she exited the plane in Accra, the capital city, Hedgeman found the "Welcome Home" banner that greeted her confusing. She was struck immediately with just how American she was. As she looked at and talked with women who looked, spoke, and acted so differently than she did, she had to wonder: "Is there really any memory which would make me feel of this soil?"[63] The trip would both increase her sense of solidarity with the women, the people, and the countries of Africa and cement her identity as an American—an African American to be sure, but an American. It was an agonizing process, to see oneself so fully and finally identified with such a deeply racist nation. Expatriate Maya Angelou explained her experience in Ghana in similar terms: "Many of us had only begun to realize in Africa that the Stars and Stripes was our flag and our only flag, and that knowledge was almost too painful to bear."[64]

Whatever her realizations about herself, Anna Hedgeman was determined to use her keynote address to celebrate and further the links between black women in the United States and across the African continent. At the very least, they shared a history of oppression and a history of resistance. When she made her way to the podium, on the heels of President Nkrumah and after a ceremonial opening that included prayers, tribal drumming, and dancing, Hedgeman attempted to focus on the links rather than the distances. "It occurs to me," she told her audience of a hundred delegates and a thousand observers, "that a long time ago a bit of me left this coast—a bit of all American women of African descent, left this coast, taking with us the richness of Africa and bringing into a new nation that richness. I cannot report to you that that richness was always appreciated. I can report to you that it was used. I can also report to you that in addition to the fact that it was used, deep in the hearts of those people was always the determination to be free."[65]

If national identity made solidarity difficult, Hedgeman still believed that a shared gender identity held great promise. She had been asked to speak about women in public life, she told the crowd, and immediately refuted the commonly held notion that men lived public lives, women private lives. "It occurs to me," she said, soliciting great applause, "that women have always been in public life, but the men have not always known it." She continued by acknowledging women's multiple roles and their tremendous social value. She had asked a Ghanaian woman how she spent her days, she said, and the woman had told her that she was just a housewife. "What is more important in the world than a housewife?" Hedgeman demanded. "Perhaps," she said, it was the housewife "who carries the major responsibility for what happens to all of us."[66] She spoke of the need for women to work at bettering their worlds, from the grassroots to the global level. The United Nations Commission on the Status of Women was meeting at the same time this group met, she told the audience, to another round of applause. "Africa is in tune with the rest of the world!"[67]

Hedgeman's friend Pauli Murray also addressed the gathering, delivering an equally explicitly feminist speech in these allegedly prefeminist days. Women of all colors and creeds, she told the crowd, shared a history with people of African descent, namely, a history of female enslavement. It was "from these beginnings," she asserted, "that we have moved towards equality." Murray, who would stay in Ghana to help turn the rights she advocated into law, spoke about the importance of legal advances for women, including voting rights, the right to divorce, equal pay for equal work, and the full rights of citizenship within marriage.[68] Like Hedgeman, Murray spoke about the vital role the United Nations could play in unifying nations and ensuring that women could exercise a form of global solidarity.

As she had in India, Hedgeman grew defensive during the Ghana conference when others focused on the role of the United States as an agent of oppression instead of an ally of justice. When a group of women put forward a resolution equating the United States' racial policies with those of South Africa, Anna Hedgeman, Pauli Murray, and most of the other members of the US delegation balked.[69] They identified themselves as representatives of "the largest and most representative organizations of American Negro women," each one of them a leader "in a continuous and militant struggle for freedom in the United States." Claiming global as well as American citizenship, they spoke of carrying on the work of their ancestors as they fought oppression at home, where, they claimed with pride, "we are winning this fight."

For these women, the distinction between their nation and South Africa was fundamental.[70] Unlike South Africa, they believed, the United States was founded on the principle, if not the practice, of equality; they were not simply colonized subjects. The delegates believed their job was not to transform the foundational documents of their country but rather to have the nation live up to them. "We therefore reject and repudiate," they wrote, "any implication that our situation in the United States is comparable to the current situation in South Africa. Moreover, we dissociate ourselves from any American delegate who attempts to commit the American delegates to the support of a resolution or action by this conference which fails to make this vital distinction between the two countries."[71]

After a heated debate, Hedgeman's group was successful, and the resolution passed without mention of the United States. But even at the time, these loyal Americans wondered if they had spoken too defensively. Had they overstated the nation's willingness, never mind its ability, to live up to the promise of equality? Could they not as easily have focused on those documents that restricted liberty as they did on those that promised it? The Africans who introduced the resolution were not naive. Like the rest of the world, they were witnessing media depictions of the violent resistance black Americans encountered as they tried to implement the *Brown v. Board of Education* decision, which six years earlier had outlawed desegregation in the nation's schools. African delegates also had stories to tell about visits to the United States, during which they had to don traditional garb in order not to be treated as less than human.[72] Even at the conference, African delegates watched as several embassies held receptions, but not the US embassy. Was it, they asked, because the US delegates were black?

In what must have seemed an immense role reversal, Africans promised the American delegates support and solidarity. "Africa shall never rest," one delegate announced to the African American women, "until we see you with senators, a full-fledged secretary of state and every other recognition which should come to you. Not because of your color, but because of the legacy of culture behind you and your contribution to American society."[73] When Hedgeman exited the country on a Ghanian airline piloted by a black man, a phenomenon she had yet to encounter in the United States, she had to acknowledge that the sentiment was not as misplaced as it seemed.[74]

Once she arrived back home, where civil rights activism in the South was being met with severe resistance, Hedgeman again had to wonder if she had been too quick to defend her country back in Ghana. A conference on nonviolence at Atlanta University, at which students gave testimony about the ongoing violent resistance to desegregation, disturbed her deeply. "As I listened to the agony expressed by students in the Deep South and recalled all of my own experiences, I wondered seriously whether the Women of Africa and of African Descent who approved that resolution should not have been supported by the twenty of us from the United States who objected."[75]

Over the years, although Anna found it hard to be away from Merritt and from the United States, she felt compelled to take the opportunities to travel that her work and connections offered. In addition to her trips to India and Ghana, she traveled to the Middle East, to East Asia, and to Europe. She continuously sought out what she suggested in her keynote address in Ghana: solidarity among people of color, solidarity among women of color, and justice for all. Longing to be that New World citizen, "part of all soils," Anna Arnold Hedgeman demonstrated, in her life and work, just how tentative and challenging such an identity could be.[76]

9 RUNNING FOR OFFICE

When Anna Arnold Hedgeman returned to the United States from India in the spring of 1953, a significant political shift was underway. Dwight D. Eisenhower had succeeded Harry S. Truman in the White House, and the Republicans held both the presidency and the Congress for the first time in twenty years. In keeping with common practice, most Democratic officeholders in the capital had already submitted their letters of resignation. Hedgeman joined them, asking only that her assistant at what was now the Department of Health, Education, and Welfare be kept on. Trying to take care of those she left behind when she moved on was typical for her, something she would do again and again. In this case she suggested that the woman not only deserved to keep her job but also should get a promotion.

Anna and Merritt had grown to love living in the nation's capital, but after ten years they also looked forward to returning to New York City. They "bravely packed up," as she remembered later, and headed north. It was a bittersweet return. Both her parents and Merritt's had died, there was no longer a house or a family waiting for them in the Bronx, and they felt displaced. Still, for both of them, Harlem beckoned, and as they rode the train north, they took great pleasure in seeing the Manhattan skyline in the distance. Anna, who took pride in her ability to recite poetry, was reminded of a James Weldon Johnson poem, "My City," in which he evokes the sights and sounds and smells of Manhattan. It reminded her that she needed New York, and she hoped desperately that her city would feel the same about her. Even more, she felt inspired to engage again in something big and meaningful, and she embarked from the train ready to challenge New York to embrace something powerful yet undefined, some sort of "genuine 'We The People' movement" through which she could help further democracy and promote justice.[1]

Settling in for what they initially assumed would be a temporary stay at Harlem's Theresa Hotel, Anna and Merritt set about looking for employment and permanent housing. The housing situation proved dismal: the postwar prosperity so much in the news in 1953 seemed to have missed Harlem almost completely. Because of continued racial segregation in housing, real estate operators knew that black tenants had few choices and treated them that way, renting poorly appointed apartments as "furnished" and charging inflated rents. Anna and Merritt decided to stay on at the Theresa, which offered them a suite of rooms at a reasonable rate, a central location, and a bit of celebrity.

When they left New York City for Washington, the stately white terra cotta and brick hotel had only recently opened its doors to black guests, but now a bevy of black entertainers, artists, and socialites called the "Waldorf of Harlem" home. Others stayed at the hotel temporarily while they visited Harlem for a night at the fights or a night at the opera. The tallest building in Harlem, standing on the corner of 125th Street and 7th Avenue, now Adam Clayton Powell Jr. Boulevard, and near Frank's Restaurant, the Apollo Theater, the Harlem Opera House, the African Memorial National Bookstore, and Blumstein's Department Store, the Theresa literally offered a window on Harlem's political, social, and cultural life.

The hotel lobby featured a coffee shop frequented by journalists working on Harlem stories and a bar that was always so crowded, as the *Pittsburgh Courier* described it, that "a man could lose his pants and walk the length of the place without anybody noticing him."[2] The mezzanine level housed a barbershop and a chic women's clothing boutique, and among the businesses on the second floor was the National Black Newspaper Publishing Association. The hotel's elegant two-story dining room hosted formal banquets, fashion shows, and book release parties where intellectuals gathered alongside members of Harlem's high society.[3] Bill Brown, father of future president Bill Clinton's secretary of commerce, Ron Brown, was the manager when the Hedgemans moved in, and future congressman Charles Rangel worked the front desk. Political rallies took place outside, and political intrigue took place inside.[4]

Anna and Merritt would become two of the hotel's high-profile residents, a group that included writer Zora Neale Hurston, socialite Grace Nail Johnson, *Negro Yearbook* editor Florence Murray, and entertainer Bill "Bojangles" Robinson. Both Hedgemans became involved in the life of the Theresa and the surrounding neighborhood. Merritt resumed his New York performing career; when the hotel hosted a party for UN mediator and Nobel Peace Prize–winner Ralph Bunche, he provided the entertainment. The studio for WLIB, the leading black radio station in New York, was in the hotel, and Anna was a frequent on-air guest. In part because of her status and demeanor, in part because the Theresa housed its share of rowdy entertainers, prizefighters, and their fans, Anna was considered one of the hotel's "society ladies."[5] Hotel manager Bill Brown was a ladies' man, with a reputation for slipping into women's rooms, but everyone knew he would not dare try anything like that with Anna Arnold Hedgeman.[6]

Some years later, when Malcolm X left the Nation of Islam and founded the Organization for Afro-American Unity, he set up shop in the Theresa; before it closed in 1967, the hotel saw its last celebrity resident, Jimi Hendrix. But by then Anna and Merritt were long gone, having moved, in 1958, into the brand-new Lenox Terrace, a six-square-block apartment complex filled with professionals and celebrities, dubbed "Harlem's Best Address" by the *New York Times Magazine*.[7]

As exhilarating as life was at the Theresa, Anna Hedgeman sought out experiences at once more simple and more complex than those available at the hotel. She returned to her church, St. Mark's United Methodist, searching for all the things the black church provided: social life, civil rights activity, and spirituality.[8] She joined the national board of the Council of Church Women, the Christian Social Relations Committee of Church Women United, and two National Council of Churches commissions, one on the church and welfare, the other on the church and politics.[9] She also returned to the New York branches of the National Council of Negro Women and the NAACP.

Still, Hedgeman found that Harlem had changed in ways that she had not anticipated, and she had to re-establish herself. Cecelia Cabaniss Saunders had retired from the YWCA, which appeared to have lost both its vitality and its standing in the community. Some of the religious leaders with whom Hedgeman had worked closely, including her mentor John H. Johnson, who had fostered the "Buy Where You Can Work" movement to open up employment on 125th Street to black residents of Harlem, had retired. Many community leaders had moved to Queens or to the Westchester suburbs, and the political scene in New York City seemed lacking to Hedgeman—and contentious.

Soon after Anna and Merritt's arrival, a group of Harlem leaders asked Anna to put her name forward for the position of Manhattan borough president. Robert F. Wagner Jr., the current borough president, was running for mayor and pulling together a Democratic slate, and a good number of people believed she should join the ticket. She initially put them off. Merritt wanted her to rest a bit before taking on too much, but she had also witnessed the fate of other women who had run for elected office. Her close friend Pauli Murray had run as a candidate for city council from Brooklyn in 1949, alongside Herbert Lehman, candidate for the US Senate, and Robert F. Wagner Jr., in his candidacy for Manhattan borough president. The Liberal Party endorsed the entire ticket, but the Democratic Party endorsed only the two men. Wagner and Lehman won in the general election; Murray lost. Ella Baker, head of the New York City branch of the NAACP, ran for the same council seat in 1953, the year Anna's name was brought up for Manhattan borough president, but as a third-party candidate, also on the Liberal Party ticket, Baker had little chance of winning.[10] The Democrats, to the dismay of women in general and African American women in particular, proved reluctant to support women. Hedgeman was reminded of yet another friend, Ruth Bishop, the white woman with whom she had traveled to San Francisco for the founding of the United Nations. She considered Bishop "much more politically astute than many contemporary men in politics," but she watched, exasperated, as her friend was repeatedly relegated to "quiet fund raising" for the party.[11] Pauli Murray would later share her own exasperation with Hedgeman. "I have tended to my knitting," she wrote, facetiously, "while the 'boys' went into electoral politics."[12]

The advocacy group persevered, though, and Hedgeman agreed to let them form the Harlem Citizens Committee for Hedgeman for Borough President, and fundraise and advocate on her behalf.[13] "I grinned to myself," she remembered later, "as I imagined the amazement of the 'political boys,' who were certainly not looking for a woman as part of their team."[14] The committee met the reception she had forecast: the black Democratic Party leader, Hulan Jack, who had benefited from a previous collaboration with Hedgeman when she was at the Department of Health, Education, and Welfare, said, simply, "That's no job for a woman!"[15]

"I am anxious," Anna Hedgeman responded dryly, "to see women join the human race."[16]

It became clear to Hedgeman fairly quickly that Wagner viewed her as an ally but not a potential running mate. Even after the Republicans announced that they would put forward a black candidate for Manhattan borough president, and the Democrats realized they had to do the same, Hedgeman was passed over in favor of Hulan Jack. Wagner and Jack won in the general election, but Jack's office was soon beset by scandal, and he was forced to resign.[17] Anna Hedgeman began to articulate a greater sense of frustration about the discrimination women faced. "From a political standpoint then, I had four strikes against me," she wrote about the experience, "my absenteeism from the city, my being a woman, a Protestant, and a Negro. The woman aspect was the greatest handicap. At that time, it would have been easier to be a Negro, Spanish, and Jewish at the same time than to be a woman in the political life of New York City."[18]

Although she failed to obtain the nomination, the experience whetted Hedgeman's appetite for electoral politics, and over the years she would run for office three times. In the meantime, she signed on as a manager of Robert F. Wagner Jr.'s mayoral campaign. Regardless of her frustration with Wagner, she viewed him as a promising candidate. The son of Senator Robert Wagner, who had led the passage of historic labor legislation, Bob Wagner had been active in housing issues, one of her key concerns, during his tenure as borough president. If she could not succeed him in that position, she could at least help him secure a more powerful office, one that would allow him to bring about positive changes in Harlem and elsewhere.

Hedgeman turned down an appointment as manager of the women's division of the campaign. "Segregation is segregation is segregation," she explained. She objected as much to the actual duties they assigned women, including organizing teas, fashion shows, coffee klatches, and cocktail "sips," as she did to the designation. In much the same way that she had avoided a racial portfolio in the Federal Security Agency, she was determined to resist a gender portfolio now. But in protesting this routine segregation, she offended women as well as men. Some women felt protective of their small corner of power, and took the alleged slight so seriously that Hedgeman had to enlist Evelyn Brand, an active Democrat and Brooklyn attorney, to convince Democratic women that she had not turned against them.

Once she got to work on Wagner's behalf, Hedgeman drew on some of the lessons of the Truman campaign; among other efforts, she targeted the black community by enlisting Eleanor Roosevelt to chair a reception for black donors.[19] She communicated with and looked for ways to support the heads of all the committees, including a housewives' committee, a beauticians' committee, a musicians' committee, a church women's committee, a businessmen's committee, and so on. She readily worked with them, but she resisted being tagged in such narrow ways herself.[20]

Once Wagner won the election and began to put together his cabinet, he again heard from Hedgeman's supporters, this time to let him know that the cabinet seat he had all but promised Harlem rightfully belonged to her. Over the next few days, several names were mentioned in the press, including Hedgeman's, and Wagner finally offered her the position of secretary to the Board of Estimate.

"There it was again—color," she fumed. An African American woman, Ruth Whitehead Whaley, was on her way out, so of course an African American woman would follow her in. The savvy Hedgeman gently tried to shift Wagner's perspective: "Mr. Mayor, it would mean more to you politically if you appoint me to a position not currently held by a Negro."[21] His next suggestion was that she serve as deputy commissioner of welfare, but this too infuriated Hedgeman, who knew that a group of influential Democrats, including her former boss, Oscar Ewing, the former First Lady, Eleanor Roosevelt, and Senator Herbert Lehman, had recommended that Wagner make her the commissioner, not deputy commissioner. She pointed out that a well-qualified woman was already in line for the deputy post and raised the possibility of serving as the mayor's policy assistant. He told her he would think about it.[22]

Wagner alternately resisted and yielded to the pressure he felt from the black community. With only two African Americans in policymaking positions in the city's forty-two departments, and those "only token appointments," according to the *Amsterdam News*, he still did not appoint Hedgeman welfare commissioner. But on the night before the inauguration, following weeks of intrigue, tension, and speculation, Hedgeman received a phone call informing her that she was to be appointed assistant to the mayor of the City of New York.[23] Fearing she might be left out of the inauguration when it actually took place, she did not invite her extended family to the ceremony. She was particularly wary of inviting her two nieces, Carolyn and Julie: "One tries to save youth as long as possible from this 'race business.'"[24]

Hedgeman's initial treatment in the administration seemed to justify her caution. Once she was officially sworn in, with a salary that was roughly half what her white peers received, she was left out of the subsequent "stag" events at which important political maneuvering was taking place. It became clear to her that only one kind of woman was welcome in that environment, a "perfect" woman, one who, as she saw it, "takes orders and never asks questions."[25] Anna Arnold Hedgeman had never been such a woman.

Despite the administration's uncertainty about how to treat her, Hedgeman returned from the swearing-in a celebrity. The Hotel Theresa lobby was crowded with well-wishers, the switchboard flooded with calls. One man brought his five-year-old daughter to meet her and present her with a bouquet of flowers. Veteran reporter James L. Hicks was on hand, celebrating the new mayor's decision as a "master stroke" through which Harlem "planted its foot firmly in the door of big time politics." Hicks delighted in Hedgeman, since what he called her "courage in refusing to take a job from any other colored person," combined with her "daring in 'asking for something big' as Harlemites put it," earned her the loyalty of anyone who had not by now already joined her camp of devotees.[26] The next day, a group of five prominent black women arrived at the Theresa Hotel to escort her to her first day on the job.[27]

But once the festivities ended and she was on her own in City Hall, Anna Hedgeman faced a strange reality: she had no office, no specific assignments, and no designated appointment with the mayor.[28] When her friend—now deputy mayor—Henry Epstein discovered her at a desk she had secured in the hallway, he took her to lunch, where she explained her dilemma. Hedgeman also shared her concerns with her allies in the black press, who immediately drew attention to the injustice. Within a week, the new mayor's assistant had a portfolio, which included welfare, civil service, libraries, museums, air pollution, and the United

Nations. She also had an office, albeit in the basement. The black press, which had been reporting on what they had called the "strange goings-on" at City Hall, was quick to point out that African Americans were no more fond of basements than they were of back doors, but Hedgeman was pleased just to have her own space in what was by all accounts a crowded building.[29]

She began to communicate with multiple city departments, write speeches for the mayor, give talks on her own, and work with Democratic political clubs across the city. As usual, despite the fact that her portfolio was not race-based, she spent a tremendous amount of time working with New York's communities of color. She read and responded to complaints of racial discrimination, including one from a woman who was accosted by police while walking to buy a newspaper, and another from a corrections officer who wanted a change of assignment, but whose requests were repeatedly ignored or denied.[30] She worked closely with the city's many voluntary agencies on a plethora of welfare-related issues, including the needs of the city's youth and aging populations. She wrote frequent newspaper pieces and appeared on numerous radio programs, including that of Mary Margaret McBride, the popular "First Lady of Radio." Hedgeman was widely fêted across the city during these years at testimonial breakfasts and dinners.

Quickly establishing a reputation as a savvy emissary for New York City generally and its black constituents in particular, Anna Hedgeman viewed government as an ally, but a reluctant one, believing that the black community had to make demands of the city and also of its members. Thirty years earlier, while working at the Harlem YWCA, she had learned from her boss, Cecilia Cabaniss Saunders, that people had to literally invest in their communities to feel invested in them. She used that version of black self-help now to harangue her audiences into paying union dues, supporting their churches, and joining civil rights organizations. "If you don't pay for your struggle for freedom, what will you pay for?" she demanded of an audience of postal workers.[31] Hedgeman wanted her neighbors as well as her nation to live up to democratic ideals. She worked hard on legislation that would help the most impoverished New Yorkers, taking a special interest in the housing issues that had plagued her community since the 1920s. She helped pass the Sharkey-Brown-Isaacs Law (1958), the first in the nation prohibiting discrimination in public housing on the basis of race, religion, or nationality; when the legislation made its way to state-level consideration, Hedgeman represented the City of New York at the hearings.[32]

Well aware of the many other women in New York who hoped to gain a foothold in politics, Hedgeman found ways to encourage and help those who had supported her, white as well as black. She organized political workshops for women because, as she saw it, "I knew they had to have a bigger role than they'd ever had."[33] In Harlem, black women outnumbered black men on the voting rolls, and gender was growing as a legitimate political concern.[34] It also became increasingly apparent that having women in office could make a difference in women's lives. Just a year into Anna's service in the mayor's office, fellow Democrat and Theresa Hotel resident Bessie Buchanan won a seat in the New York State Assembly, the first black woman elected to such an office.[35] The first bills Buchanan introduced targeted gender-based discrimination in employment and race-based discrimination in banking, education, and insurance.[36] The following year, Anna Hedgeman was appointed by Governor Averill Harriman to an advisory group to the Woman's Program of the New York State Department of Commerce. Their work was so thorough that it foreshadowed themes that President John Kennedy's Commission on the Status of Women would take on a few years later.[37]

By the mid-1950s, although "'women's lib' was not yet in vogue," as Hedgeman recalled, she was in great demand to talk about the intersections of race, gender, and class.[38] Always frustrated by wasted talent, she grew increasingly committed to the empowerment of black women, who, living those intersections daily, had so much to offer their city.[39] Dubbing them "pioneers," a term she had long appreciated, she penned a column titled "Negro Women Fought Hard for Recognition," explaining that "each of them might well be called 'everywoman.'"[40]

Two things became clearer to Hedgeman as she worked in City Hall: all the problems she cared about, from jobs to housing to education, were linked, and there was far too much calcification in government. And as much as she tried not to be cynical, she felt mistrust when men offered women opportunities, or when whites offered blacks opportunities. The whole political enterprise required a shift in focus, a new level of self-awareness, a new level of commitment. She was an early proponent of what we now call diversity and inclusion, truly believing that a multitude of people, perspectives, and positions would make for a better city. She became determined to educate and inspire the many disparate groups of people with whom she worked, including women, the elderly, schoolchildren, teachers, parents, civic leaders, clergy, and social workers. She gave talks during the workday and on her own time, filling her nights and weekends, urging people to take charge of the city they could all call their own. Despite Merritt's objections, Anna was always on the go. "Negroes sent for me around the country," she explained, "as kind of Exhibit A."[41]

On top of her more local concerns, Hedgeman took on the role of host to New York City's many international visitors. She especially loved taking foreign visitors to Harlem, showing them the community that made her feel both pride and indignation. She served as a liaison to the United Nations, where she took a particular interest in international efforts to improve housing for the world's poor. The bleak housing situation for black New Yorkers must have seemed terribly ironic in that global context. Indeed, she grew more and more vocal about the ways her global consciousness informed her thoughts about race at home. When she was in India, she remembered Mississippi. Now, listening to stories about the struggles of colonized and formerly colonized people around the world, Hedgeman thought of Harlem. She hoped to help eradicate poverty for white Americans as well as for Americans of color, but she could not help but see the links that tied black Americans to black Africans, as well as other marginalized people of color across the globe.

By all accounts, Hedgeman was a powerful speaker who used the podium to promote activist as well as legislative agendas. One night, at a crowded civil rights event at the Waldorf Astoria, she took the stage as the keynote speaker after a long list of powerful orators had delivered sharp demands for racial justice initiatives. "Militancy was the vehicle and action was in the driver's seat," wrote journalist James L. Hicks. "The audience was in no mood for moderation." But, he continued, "let it forever be said that Mrs. Hedgeman rose to the greatness of the honor."[42] During her nearly one-hour address, "she lashed out from her international background as a fighter for full freedom, she drew on her national experience to strike at the defects of her nation's democracy, she rapped New York's schools from her vantage point as the mayor's assistant, and she 'came home' to her audience as a grassroots organizer." Hedgeman drew a standing ovation and brought the audience to tears. As Hicks explained, "Despite the sharpness of Mrs. Hedgeman's criticism, despite the impatience with which she demanded action, and despite the cold and calculating way in which she looked at things, there was still warmth and hope and great inspiration in her plea."[43]

A self-taught historian with a developing expertise in black history, Hedgeman visited innumerable elementary schools, high schools, and colleges, delivering lectures, challenging teachers to prepare more inclusive lesson plans, and sharing some of the many reading lists on black history that she would develop. The children responded enthusiastically to her larger-than-life presence, and she saved many of the endearing thank-you letters they sent her. "Someday I hope you will become the first lady President of the United States," one child wrote, while another told her, "Since you made your speech I have been trying to study and do my work better. As you said that you hope one of us will be in the White House one day, I am hoping I will be one of them."[44] Yet another student explained the impact of her address in some detail:

> I used to be embarrassed when people talked about our ancestors being slaves. Since I heard your speech this feeling was erased from me. You made me feel proud and also very happy. I wish I had the nerve to get up

in front of white people and talk the way you did. I hope that you will go to some of the other schools in this city and speak to them the same way you spoke to us. I think the children in my school gained a lot by your speech. I hope that someday you will be President, and remember when you are eligible my vote is yours.[45]

Hedgeman responded to every letter, encouraging the students to study black history, work hard in school, and go to the library. She gave this last student some additional advice, enlisting her as a civic soldier. "Many people in our community fail to register in order to be able to vote," she instructed the young girl, "and you can help by telling people that they must register and vote as soon as they are old enough."[46]

As much as she served as the voice of a Democratic mayor, Anna Hedgeman remained aware of the vagaries of Democratic support for black New Yorkers and lamented the power the party held over Harlem. She grew increasingly frustrated with the tired approach of white Democratic leaders, who took so little time to actually observe Harlem and tally its needs. Inevitably, they turned to one black voice among the entire chorus of white voices, always a man, to represent black New Yorkers. Such feeble approaches, she observed, generally came to no good. "No one man can have all the answers," she explained, "whether he be Negro or white."[47] She joined the Committee for Political Equality, which encouraged voter registration and participation among Republicans. In a newspaper column after she left City Hall, she laid out her argument: "Harlem is registered 75 percent Democratic and only 20 percent Republican. It is for this reason that 100 percent of Harlem gets bad housing, bad schools, and medical care."[48]

Like many African American women of her generation, Anna Hedgeman saw no conflict between her religious life and her political or civic life. She regularly invoked God or, more often, Jesus, in her public addresses. And as the years went by, she grew more and more certain that the Jesus she believed in was an active god who supported political and civic activism, and she felt a need to share his revolutionary inspiration with others. "We had too often presented him in elegant robes, looking anemic, and showing his wounds," she complained. "There was too little realization of Jesus of Nazareth—the tough guy." The Son of God she lived to emulate did not stand on the banks and urge fishermen to bring in the fish. Instead, he joined right in, pulling in the huge and heavy nets of fish that would feed the poor people of "his world."[49] Hedgeman believed religion transcended race, but she also believed that the black religious community had fostered a quality of faith that black Americans could share, as an invaluable gift to their nation.[50] She felt no compunction about speaking that truth in public, even referencing her faith in the account she gave when she left the City Hall post, explaining that she made the decision "as a Christian, as a citizen and as a Negro."[51]

"To be the first woman, and the first Negro, to serve in the Mayor's Cabinet was a joy," Hedgeman later wrote, but she grew frustrated with her lack of power, disillusioned with politics in general, and enormously frustrated with Mayor Wagner.[52] Unlike his father, whom she viewed as particularly effective on behalf of civil rights, she thought the mayor's approach could be summed up as "don't rock the boat."[53] When he stalled on enacting progressive housing policy, he not only let Hedgeman down on one of her most pressing concerns but, more importantly, as she saw it, also lost one of his most promising opportunities to better the lives of his constituents. When several black appointees were not reappointed during Wagner's second term, she grew even more cynical. In one case, giving in to Cold War paranoia about Republican judge Hubert Delany's civil rights work, the mayor failed to approve his reappointment. Hedgeman knew the family well. She was friendly with Delany's sister, Bessie, a Harlem dentist who took care of so many people in need that Anna teased her about being a social worker rather than a dentist. That the mayor would not stand up for Judge Delany, who had given so enormously to the Harlem community, and who could by no means be considered disloyal to his country, really rankled.[54]

On top of that, Hedgeman's frustration with gender discrimination in local Democratic clubs, in City Hall, and in city and state political offices grew exponentially. Women's participation in New York City government, she believed, provided all New Yorkers the opportunity to realize "that total human wisdom does not repose in a single sex," but few seemed to be listening.[55] She was especially irked about the effect of sexism on life in Harlem, where the assumption that masculinity was a characteristic of able leadership went uncontested. "It was obvious," she observed later, "that women are second-class citizens in politics. Even cigarette smoking does not mean inclusion in the smoke-filled room where policy decisions are made."[56] Hedgeman could easily draw a crowd of five hundred when she gave a speech, but it too often failed to translate into other kinds of power.[57]

Anna Hedgeman believed that neither Congressman Adam Clayton Powell Jr. nor Manhattan borough president Hulan Jack provided Harlem with the leadership the community needed, but Powell's charismatic leadership and Jack's Democratic connections, coupled with their constituencies' automatic support of male political leaders, kept the men securely in office for years. Powell gave her particular pause, as she believed he took credit for the work she and others had undertaken to open 125th Street for black employment. Powell "was there all right," she wrote, "but only after he saw that we were successful."[58] With an incisive insider's view, she wrote a book, *All Shook Up*, about Powell, Jack, and the destructive politics of Harlem. But fearing that its publication would mean the end of her political career, she wrote it in the first person, using the voice of a male political operative. The book got little traction, in part because she published it using an assumed name; political debates are seldom launched anonymously.[59]

Hedgeman began to feel that she might be more effective at influencing City Hall from the outside. "I had had enough of the cynicism of a large city political machine and its worshipers," she wrote later. "I knew that there was strength in many communities of the city and wondered whether these communities could move City Hall."[60] So, even though it antagonized some people in Harlem, she left City Hall less than a year into Mayor Wagner's second term, determined to find a better way to influence the politics of the city. She submitted her letter of resignation on September 25, 1958, wishing the mayor well in his "arduous task."[61] She followed up with a second letter, praising her two secretaries, Anna Paris and Constance Tamalio, requesting that they be treated well following her departure.[62]

Hedgeman issued a public statement, "Why I Left City Hall," in which she proclaimed, "I am coming home to Harlem and the other Negro communities of the City of New York. It is my conviction that the Negro communities of this city and across the country have within them the experience, the ability, the faith, and the potential courage to meet their needs and to give inspiration to America in her moment of world crisis."[63]

Looking for new ways to have an impact on her community and, of course, still needing to earn a living, Hedgeman accepted an offer from S. B. Fuller, the millionaire founder of the cosmetics firm Fuller Products. He hired her, at double her City Hall salary, to run the public relations division of his company and serve as an editor at his newspaper, the *New York Age*. For about a year, she wrote a column in the paper, "One Woman's Opinion," sharing her insights into New York City politics and culture. But her foray into the business world was short-lived; within a year she was planning a run for Congress. In the end, staying true to the "declaration of independence" she and Merritt had signed together more than twenty years earlier outweighed the security of Fuller Products and the salary that came with it.[64]

Just weeks after Anna left City Hall, she and Merritt celebrated their twenty-fifth wedding anniversary. Friends at St. Mark's Methodist Church threw them a party and gave them the symbolic gift of silver service. The Reverend Horatio Hill, who had married them all those years earlier, paid them a tribute, and Merritt gave a speech and sang a rendition of "I Love You Truly." Anna was delighted: to have left City Hall; to celebrate a silver anniversary with the person she still felt close to, in love with, and supported by; and to be marking the occasion among a few close friends, in her church and community, where she felt so much at home.

Some people found Anna and Merritt's relationship hard to understand. They had always been more like partners as we think of them now than as a couple playing out the traditional Cold War–era roles of husband and wife. Even friends who appreciated them and the way they functioned together found it hard to escape the terminology that marked Anna and Merritt as strange or deviant. "Merritt was really like the wife," one friend explained. "He took care of the domestic side of their life. Anna was the hardworking politician and activist. But it worked for them. They were very happy."[65]

It is unlikely that Anna or Merritt would have seen it in exactly those terms. Merritt was, by all accounts, far more private than Anna, uninterested in if not disdainful of party politics, and married to a public person. He supported her work and appreciated her public persona but did all he could to stay out of the limelight himself. And however much Merritt participated in the running of the house, he did not play the role of the traditional wife. He had a successful career as a singer, traveling to performances and pursuing training in Boston as well as New York. Like Anna, he worked irregular hours and devoted a good deal of time to his career. And although Anna had a very active career, she too worried about, and attended to, her spouse's professional concerns as well as his general well-being. They were certainly an anomaly at a time when both "public women" and "private men" caused undue concern, but Anna and Merritt found nothing odd about their relationship. They carved out a way of being married that worked for them, a way that would gain respectability several decades later.

In 1960, the East Bronx Independent Committee for Political Reform, a reform Democratic club, approached the Bronx County boss, Charles Buckley, with a demand: it wanted the Democrats to run black and Puerto Rican candidates for office.[66] The southeastern Bronx district, now considered part of the South Bronx, was roughly 75 percent black and Puerto Rican, but without formal black or Puerto Rican representation the community found little advocacy for the social problems that came with such segregation. Neither the large-scale problems the group identified, including inadequate housing, poor education, and scarce jobs, nor the specific solutions, including more classrooms, housing rehabilitation programs, improved bus service, and an increase in the number of affordable hospital beds, got much traction from white elected officials. Like Hedgeman, the members of this group believed that they had to follow the lead of the Irish, Jewish, and Italian communities that peopled the Bronx before them. The Irish, by moving solidly into the Democratic Party, also made their way into New York City's other institutions, including the courts and the police and fire departments.[67] It was time for blacks and Puerto Ricans to do the same.

Charles Buckley's inflammatory response to the insurgents, that black and Puerto Rican residents of the Bronx were "not ready" to represent themselves, may well have provided the impetus for Hedgeman to run for a congressional seat on a slate of black and Puerto Rican candidates. After all, she had heard something similar when she was told that the Manhattan borough presidency was no place for a woman. This time her race was the deciding factor. She also found appealing the determination of the black and Puerto Rican communities to work together and form one ticket, reminding her of her own efforts in Harlem during the Great Depression. As Sixto Laureano, who shared the ticket with Hedgeman, explained, "Ours is a grassroots movement. Negro and Puerto Rican have tried to go it alone and failed. Now we've found we have common objectives and we are working together."[68]

Anna Hedgeman was certainly qualified. In addition to her years in City Hall, she had lived in the area when she and Merritt lived with his parents, and had served on the board of the Bronx's Forest Houses, the city's first successfully desegregated public housing project.[69] She was also well connected to the Eleanor Roosevelt–Herbert Lehman reform Democrats, who viewed this election year as critical in their attempt to rid New York City politics of Tammany, the infamous Democratic political club that had controlled Democratic nominations for more than a century and had refused to support Anna in the previous election. Photographs of Anna Hedgeman flanked by the former First Lady and Senator Lehman, formerly governor of New York, graced all her flyers. "Feel Neglected?" the flyers asked. "Want a Voice in Washington to Speak for You?"[70]

The reform ticket faced an uphill battle, even with the support of the Roosevelt-Lehman coalition. It lacked sufficient funding, most of its candidates aside from Hedgeman had little name recognition, and the opposition's tactics included attempts to paint them as reverse racists and anti-Semites. Hedgeman scrambled to meet with Jewish leaders and with Senator Lehman, who in the end felt greater pressure to support Jewish candidate Jacob Gilbert than he did to support the reform coalition. She enlisted support from the press, pleading in the *New York Times* for "civic angels" to come forward with funding, and defending the black–Puerto Rican coalition by arguing that racism created rather than defined the slate. Had they not faced discrimination, she argued, these candidates would have been elected to office years earlier.[71] New York newspapers took her candidacy seriously, with one article pointing to a potential "major upset" in the primaries. Another defended her candidacy against the charges of racism, instead vouching for her ability to give all of the neglected people of the district a voice.[72]

Nonetheless, the press found it necessary to focus on her gender and thus, intentionally or not, undermine her candidacy. One profile, "Will She Be 1st Negro Lady in Congress?," acknowledged that Hedgeman tried to avoid questions about cooking and shopping but also described her "lovely cotton and Dacron dress," in which she was "becoming but chic," as well as her apartment, which "fairly sparkled," and a particular chair that "in a shade of rose adds a note of empathic warmth." The article concluded that Hedgeman had the brains and the courage required to become the first African American woman to serve in Congress, but by paying far greater attention to her clothing and decor than her political smarts, the article reduced her to a caricature, that of the happy housewife, which did not apply to her life at all.[73]

The most formidable obstacle to the success of the reform ticket was the Democratic machine's determination to undermine the solidarity blacks and Puerto Ricans had worked toward and truly needed. Worried that the insurgents might prevail in the primaries, party boss Charles Buckley appointed, for the first time, a five-member committee of Puerto Ricans to bring out the Puerto Rican vote for the establishment candidate. He also began to spread the word that blacks, Anna Hedgeman among them, were trying to dominate the coalition. In the end, the insurgents were unable to mount a successful counter assault against the specious claims, and they were defeated at the polls. Hedgeman tried to place their defeat in the most favorable of lights. "I am pleased with the results," she told the press. "We have just begun to fight, because you don't kill corruption in ten minutes."[74]

Hedgeman attributed the loss to three factors. First, people of color were accused of being "racial" the minute they tried to mirror the solidarity that had long been a formidable feature of New York City's white political landscape. Second, white politicians still wanted to exercise significant influence over, if not control of, these ostracized communities. Finally, when blacks and Puerto Ricans worked together to focus on what they shared rather than what set them apart, white politicians who would otherwise be allies balked. Anna Hedgeman would return to these lessons again and again in the coming years, as she tried to move the country forward on its long march toward justice.[75] But in the immediate aftermath of her electoral loss, she had to secure a living, one that would provide not only security but meaning.

10 A "BURR IN THE SADDLE"

ANNA ARNOLD HEDGEMAN, WHITE PROTESTANTS, AND THE MARCH ON WASHINGTON

In January 1963, the United States commemorated the centennial of the Emancipation Proclamation, the country's first deliberate step toward racial justice. But Anna Arnold Hedgeman, temporarily unemployed, was experiencing a crisis of faith about her own prospects as well as the nation's. "I could find no progress," she wrote. "I could find no progress for myself or for any other Negro."[1]

In fact, there was little actually to celebrate as the centennial approached. When it came to implementing the rights of African Americans, the federal government equivocated and state and local governments reneged, even as civil rights workers and citizens across the South continued to face unfathomable acts of violence. In the absence of adequate government response to continued discrimination, other institutions attempted to step up. One such group, made up of more than seven hundred Catholic, Jewish, and Protestant religious leaders, including Hedgeman, convened in Chicago to commemorate the Emancipation Proclamation centennial and decide collectively how to address racism, the nation's "most serious domestic evil."[2]

The National Conference on Religion and Race, the first gathering to address religion and race at the same time, was chaired by Benjamin Mays, president of Morehouse College and mentor to Martin Luther King Jr.[3] "God is the Creator of all mankind or He is the creator of no part of it. He is the Father of all or He is the Father of none," Mays declared, setting the tone. "The life of every person is sacred or the life of no person is sacred. If God cares for the greatest, He cares for the least. Either all or none."[4] King urged conference-goers to push for racial justice in their lives, churches, and communities, since religion "deals not only with the hereafter but also with the here."[5] That sentiment certainly resonated with Anna Hedgeman, whose theological approach also focused on the here and the now.

Hedgeman was there as a leader of Church Women United (CWU), an ecumenical Christian group that had long fought against racism outside its doors and racist practices within. But aside from Mays, King, and herself, few black religious spokespersons were even in attendance, and issues of concern to the "black church," those churches ministering to predominantly African American congregations, were wholly absent from consideration. Hedgeman grew increasingly frustrated during the four-day meeting, and on the last day she took the floor to protest.[6] Who did the talking on matters of religion and race, she asked, and who did the listening? Yes, blacks were by and large Protestant or Catholic, but in a nation blighted by racism, there was little shared religiosity, and *their* church, *her* church, was not represented at the conference.[7] It was the same old story, she lamented: blacks served as "porters" of the conference, providing a means by which to talk about race, but American Christianity, regardless of the Emancipation Proclamation centennial, and regardless of stated principles, continued to re-create itself in its own, unchanged image.[8]

Could these white leaders implement, or even imagine how to implement, the civil rights platform they had so enthusiastically and unanimously adopted during the conference? Did a meeting of this sort really do anything more than expiate white guilt?

Hedgeman had been dealing with these questions for forty years, since her earliest days in the YWCA, when she had tried to convince white Protestant women that segregation contradicted God's law. She found it hard to contain her frustration now, finding herself once again calling on white religious leaders to replace well-meaning gestures with the far more difficult task of Christian practice.[9]

In the coming months, the National Council of Churches (NCC), one of the sponsors of the conference, would tackle these same questions, and in July 1963, the NCC would offer Hedgeman the opportunity she had been preparing for all her life, even if she did not know it: to interpret Christianity as a vehicle for racial justice on a national scale.[10]

The headquarters of the National Council of Churches was in the Interchurch Center, a large square building on the west side of Manhattan. Sometimes called the "God Box" or the "Protestant Vatican," it is across the street from Riverside Church, in a neighborhood that is also home to Union Theological Seminary and the Jewish Theological Seminary.[11] The NCC, an ecumenical agency at the very center of liberal religious power in the United States, represented in the mid-1960s more than thirty Christian denominations. The organization saw itself doing for Christianity what the United Nations did for the world: promoting an international and justice-focused worldview.[12] Hedgeman had a long association with the CWU, an agency at the core of the National Council of Churches that consistently challenged the overwhelmingly male leadership of the larger body.[13] While its most vocal detractors considered the NCC a radical if not communist organization for promoting racial equality, the CWU had the opposite complaint: that the NCC's positions were far too tame.[14]

In the last week of May 1963, following a civil rights campaign in Birmingham, Alabama, that saw police set attack dogs and fire hoses on children, a group of black leaders met with Attorney General Robert Kennedy.[15] After a rancorous meeting, both sides left dissatisfied. The attorney general was taken aback by the hostility the group expressed toward the federal government; the African American leaders were incredulous that Kennedy did not understand that being black meant being enraged much of the time.

It was not just a hundred years since the Emancipation Proclamation; it was already nearly ten years since *Brown v. Board of Education* specifically outlawed segregated schools, but in most of the country, segregation and vastly inferior education for black students continued.[16] "It isn't only what's happening to you," explained novelist James Baldwin, the group's leader, "but it's what's happening all around you all the time, in the face of the most extraordinary and criminal indifference, the indifference and the ignorance of most white people in this country."[17]

Frustrated by their lack of common ground with political leaders, in search of more ready allies, the group met with white Protestant leaders at the Harlem YWCA. Every one of the white religious leaders in attendance, as participant Robert Spike put it, believed they were "clean," that they were without prejudice and on the right side of social justice questions. A few had been on Freedom Rides, many had worked in fellowship with black churches, and most had participated in some kind of civil rights activities. They arrived with their credentials established, they believed. But they had not been invited to the meeting to be lauded; instead, black leaders wanted to know where their churches planned to stand while African Americans continued being denied their most basic rights, and were beaten or killed when they tried to exercise them. During a long night of intense, heated conversation, Spike explained, Baldwin and the others essentially accused the white religious leaders of being "the man."[18]

At the next General Board meeting of the National Council of Churches, Rev. Spike and some of his colleagues demanded that the council act to desegregate church life, push for civil rights legislation, and foment direct community action. Regardless of the unanimity expressed at the national conference months earlier, regardless of the recent publication of Martin Luther King Jr.'s "Letter from Birmingham Jail," petitioning the nation's religious leadership for action, the conference goals had not been implemented.[19] The NCC board responded positively, and the statements that came out of the meeting became "a kind of Bible" for progressive Christians. "Words and declarations are no longer useful in this struggle," the group declared, calling upon white Christians to finally stand up among their peers and share in the experiences black Americans were subjected to on the pathway to racial justice, including personal indignities, alienation, and actual physical suffering. White Christians were pressed to acknowledge and accept that there would be a price to pay "for the tardy obedience of Christ's people" where racial justice was concerned.[20]

The most notable outcome of the meeting was the founding of the National Council of Churches' Commission on Religion and Race (CRR). The commission would move beyond the work of the Department of Racial and Cultural Relations, a largely educational component of the massive NCC bureaucracy that had been founded in 1921, but languishing since behind a series of endless, ineffectual resolutions.[21] Headed by J. Oscar Lee, for years the only black person on the NCC's six-hundred-member professional staff, the Department of Racial and Cultural Relations was best known for its innocuous Race Relations Sunday, an annual event that encouraged white congregations to reflect on and practice some form of racial brotherhood. When Lee attempted to revitalize the department, he met bureaucracy's notorious sidestep—agreement accompanied by inactivity.[22]

To avoid repeating this kind of organizational inertia, the NCC granted the CRR unprecedented operational freedom, the actual power to move its constituent churches to become, alongside the US government and existing civil rights organizations, a "third force" in the civil rights movement.[23] Additionally, and critically, the commission's target audience was not southern racists or recalcitrant political leaders but its own enormous constituency of more than forty million members—almost half of American voters—the "great white middle class" of Protestants who belonged to perhaps the most segregated institution in the land, the church.[24] "Now is the time for action," the NCC declared, inviting Catholic and Jewish leaders to share in the commitment, "even costly action that may jeopardize the organizational goals and institutional structures of the Church and may disrupt any fellowship that is less than fully obedient to the Lord of the Church."[25]

The Commission on Religion and Race brought together a group of young, activist, highly motivated religious leaders whose aim was to invert long-standing church culture. Unlike more conservative Christian leaders, who wanted to be in the world but not of it, these progressives believed Christians had to get out in the world and wanted those at the top to lead their congregations into social justice work, rather than follow them.[26] They decided that rather than wait for their congregants to act, they would both model and demand such Christian practice.[27] The NCC leadership, largely white and exclusively male, began to form the new commission from an impressive interracial group that included the Reverend Martin Luther King Jr., labor leader Victor Reuther, and a number of college presidents, leaders of Christian groups, and heads of civil rights organizations.[28]

Like all NCC projects, the CRR needed big names on top and well-known, hard-working staff members on the ground, people who could not only execute but also step in to influence the commission's policies. The staff was initially small and almost exclusively white and male. But when the Reverend Robert Spike was named executive director, he hired Anna Arnold Hedgeman as coordinator of special projects, a temporary but key appointment. Within a few months, her temporary position became permanent, and she worked for the NCC for the next four and a half years, in positions that included director of special projects, director of ecumenical action, and associate director for racial justice. Over time, four African Americans would be part of the CRR: the Reverend James Breeden, Anna Arnold Hedgeman, J. Oscar Lee, and the Reverend Benjamin Payton. For James Breeden, who was a young minister at the time, Hedgeman seemed to dwarf even director Spike with her experience and erudition.[29]

Anna Hedgeman certainly had a great deal to offer. She had by now served in municipal, state, and federal government, run for political office, worked as a lobbyist and social worker, and organized successful grassroots mobilizations. Her years in Washington, advocating for a permanent FEPC, would help the CRR play a role in implementing civil rights legislation, including President Kennedy's recently introduced comprehensive civil rights bill. She was one of the most respected laypersons with strong ecumenical religious ties active in social justice work in the country. In addition to her links within the NCC, she served on the national board of the National Conference of Christians and Jews (NCCJ); she had had success moving whites and blacks to religious as well as political action; and she had a significant following in Harlem, where she was proudly called "Dr. Hedgeman" since receiving an honorary degree from Hamline University in 1948.[30]

If some of the men on the commission had a problem with her assertiveness, they could not deny her intelligence or judgment.[31] In the CRR, Hedgeman was a black person among mostly white colleagues, a layperson among clergy, and a woman among men. She was, nonetheless, a Christian among Christians, and determined to hold them all to "their commitment as children of God to justice for all men."[32]

Hedgeman was also involved in other organizations that made her an excit-ing if provocative candidate for the CRR. After leaving the Fuller Company in 1960, she spent two years as a consultant to the New York City Board of Home Missions, working to create links between religiously based historically black colleges in the South and African colleges, and between students from all-white and historically black Christian colleges in the United States. Although the Amistad Centers she proposed, campus-based gathering places designed to facil-itate student and faculty exchanges between white and black institutions, never got off the ground, she had built connections with institutions of higher learn-ing, and with young people who sought greater influence over their educational and spiritual lives.[33]

Through Hedgeman, the Commission on Religion and Race would also gain links to powerful New York City labor and political organizations. Two years earlier, A. Philip Randolph had called on her once again, this time to head up his Emergency Committee for Unity on Social and Economic Problems, a spin-off of the Negro American Labor Council. Initially founded to protest housing discrimination and police failure to curtail drug dealing in black communities, under her direction the broad-based coalition successfully supported the hos-pital workers union's efforts to implement the minimum wage for black, white, and Puerto Rican hospital workers in New York City. Hedgeman recruited and worked closely with Malcolm X, then a young minister with the Nation of Islam, whose vehement denunciations of Christianity had the white religious commu-nity, including the NCC, quite nervous.[34] Her skill at reaching across such enor-mous divides would be a great boon to a largely white commission trying to do more than just talk about social change.

Just a few months before she joined the CRR, Hedgeman had also accepted yet another invitation from Randolph, to join a five-member committee to explore—or in her case, revisit—a march on Washington to demand jobs and economic justice. Hedgeman, of course, was immediately brought back two decades to when she assisted Randolph in the original March on Washington Movement. Now, with the support of Bayard Rustin and others, Randolph had begun to seek support from organized labor for a new march.[35] "It is time for the masses of people to move again," he explained at the initial meeting to his care-fully selected group of four men and one woman.[36] Little had changed, he main-tained, and government inaction could be overcome only with serious prodding.

Anna Hedgeman was simultaneously committed to the issues he raised and more than a bit wary about launching a march on the nation's capital. Randolph's longtime base of economic support, the Brotherhood of Sleeping Car Porters, was in decline; the more financially secure NAACP, which favored legisla-tion, seemed unlikely to support a mass action; many of the nation's civil rights leaders were embroiled in the problems of the South; and Hedgeman knew that Randolph often took on more than he could handle. She had recently ended her work on the Emergency Committee for Unity on Social and Economic Problems in much the same way she had ended her work on his National Council for a Permanent FEPC nearly twenty years earlier, frustrated that Randolph's ability to bring people together was not accompanied by ongoing leadership.[37]

Still, there was no debating that too many black Americans continued to live in dire circumstances, and she agreed with Randolph that the solution was decent work with decent wages. The postwar economic boom had bypassed too many urban communities. A number of cities and states had passed the fair employment statutes she and Randolph had worked for, but like the wartime FEPC, they were too weak to make a real difference. New York had implemented fair employment on paper, but industry in general and the building trades in particular practiced outrageous forms of discrimination, automation continued to eat into already scarce job opportunities, organized labor resisted integration, and African American children were still not getting the kind of education that could lead to good jobs and social mobility.

Hedgeman thought that a march might be what people, particularly young people, needed to help them feel empowered to tackle this relentless discrimination. So by the end of that initial meeting, she and the rest of Randolph's advisers agreed to join him in organizing what they called, a hundred years after the Emancipation Proclamation, the Emancipation March for Jobs.[38]

Committee members left the first meeting determined to get support from the major civil rights organizations and, at Hedgeman's insistence, from a variety of women's organizations as well. She proposed that representatives of groups including the National Association of Colored Women's Clubs, the National Council of Negro Women, and various black sororities be added to the administrative committee, both to make the committee more effective and to recognize the contributions African American women had made to the movement for black freedom. The National Council of Negro Women, numbering nearly eight hundred thousand, she pointed out, was no insignificant ally.[39] The men did not listen—or did not care. "As usual," she explained later, "the men must have discussed the matter in my absence and when the first leaflet was printed, I was embarrassed to find that I was still the only woman listed."[40] This kind of sidelining would only grow worse as the weeks wore on and the work ramped up.

The committee soon learned that Martin Luther King Jr.'s Southern Christian Leadership Conference (SCLC) was also considering organizing a march, not to support jobs specifically but to support the passage of civil rights legislation. Hedgeman urged her group to coordinate with the southern movement and combine energies toward one mass action. She arranged a meeting between

King and Randolph at which the two were able to iron out their differences sufficiently to move forward. Planning began for an event scheduled for August 28, 1963, and called the March on Washington for Jobs and Freedom, recognizing a dual emphasis on the end of Jim Crow in the South and improved jobs, housing, wages, and education in the North.[41]

The civil rights leaders heading up the march became known as the Big Six; in addition to Randolph and King, they were Roy Wilkins of the NAACP, James Farmer of the Congress of Racial Equality (CORE), Whitney Young of the National Urban League (NUL), and John Lewis of the Student Nonviolent Coordinating Committee (SNCC). Bayard Rustin served as deputy director of the march, Cleveland Robinson as chair of the administrative committee. The reference to the Emancipation Proclamation was dropped from the march's name, but the group held on to its promise of freedom, and it held on to Hedgeman, who remained on the administrative committee, still the only woman.[42]

In July 1963, the Commission on Religion and Race invited Hedgeman to join its staff as coordinator of special projects. It would be hard to imagine a project more suited to its mission than the March on Washington, and Hedgeman played an enormously important role in two of its specific aims: getting involved in the march's leadership and getting white people, particularly Protestants, to participate. The CRR met resistance when it first tried to involve itself in the march's leadership circle, and with good reason. The major civil rights groups were wary of those they identified as the white religious. They were tired of the white churches' "pious platitudes" and had little interest in relationships that seemed to fail, again and again.[43] Hedgeman shared their cynicism. "I was frankly skeptical," she recalled later, recounting the seemingly endless litany of race-related events she had participated in. "The church had a long history of race relations Sundays, prayer days, brotherhood pronouncements, conferences, seminars, workshops, statements, and resolutions, but action was too often another matter."[44] But her faith and resolve won out, and as someone who had long straddled white and black groups, religious and secular, Hedgeman mediated, successfully, on behalf of the NCC. The success of the march would bring the CRR, and the NCC, far greater credibility within civil rights circles; they owed no small part of that success to Anna Arnold Hedgeman.[45]

When Robert Spike offered her the position, he asked Hedgeman to find thirty thousand white Protestants, along with large numbers of Catholics and Jews, to participate in the march, in the next six weeks. She accepted the challenge and went to work, moving back and forth between the NCC offices on the West Side and the march's administrative office in Harlem. The line between her

CRR work and her administrative work on the march blurred, particularly since she had so little time to make all of this happen.

Under Bayard Rustin and Cleveland Robinson, the administrative committee worked on refining and promoting the purpose of the march, focusing on Randolph's jobs agenda and King's legislative emphasis.[46] Its demands included passage of effective and meaningful civil rights legislation, an end to police brutality against people engaged in peaceful protest, a massive federal works program to provide jobs for the unemployed, a permanent fair employment practices commission, and a national minimum wage that would reach previously uncovered industries and workers. The committee members attempted to keep marchers focused on these issues by authorizing specific wording for the placards people carried: "We Demand" was followed with a number of mandates, including "Decent Housing Now!," "An End to Police Brutality Now!," "Integrated Schools Now!," and "Equal Rights Now!" Similarly, "We March For" was followed by "Jobs for All Now!," "An FEPC Law Now!," and "Full Citizenship Now!" Fundraising was a key aspect of the administrative work. The group ordered buttons to sell and asked for money from each of the organizations it worked with, asking marchers to contribute to pay for one unemployed person to attend the march for every three who paid their own way. If there were no unemployed people where they lived, participating marchers were asked to raise the money anyway and send it directly to the national office.[47]

As the administrative committee wrestled with logistics, it faced dozens of issues. How would hundreds of thousands of people get into and out of the nation's capital? Where would marchers get food? How could they distribute enough water in the August heat? Could marchers be persuaded to leave their children home? Would the District of Columbia police provide adequate support? Could thousands of African Americans, many enormously frustrated with unpunished, ongoing white violence, be relied on to remain peaceful? The committee held meeting after meeting to iron out logistics and get information out to participants.

Building on its existing organizational networks and establishing new ones, the committee coordinated recruitment efforts across the country. Roy Wilkins wrote to every NAACP branch, youth council, and state conference. Others traveled to coordinate trade unionist efforts. With Anna Hedgeman's help, they secured unprecedented cooperation in New York City: the subways would run on a rush-hour schedule after midnight the night before the march, to help get people to the grand caravan of 600 buses leaving the city, 450 of them from Harlem. Bridge and tunnel authorities passed out leaflets with march information at tollbooths, and Hedgeman persuaded Mayor Wagner, her former boss, to designate August 28 a holiday for city workers who wanted to join the march.[48]

At the same time, Hedgeman was working on drawing tens of thousands of white people to the march, a formidable task. Without actually coming out and saying that the presence of so many black people made a peaceful event unlikely, the press played up the potential for violence.[49] The District of Columbia ordered all liquor stores and bars to close, many members of Congress ordered their female staff members to stay home, and some stores packed their merchandise away in warehouses in case of looting. Patrick O'Boyle, archbishop of Washington, DC, wrote a letter instructing nuns in his diocese to stay away from the march, even though he delivered the invocation.[50] As the *Washington Daily News* put it, "The general feeling is that the Vandals are coming to sack Rome."[51]

Hedgeman was not alone in finding the assumptions of violence troubling, nor in noting that, at the same time, white violence against African Americans was vastly underreported.[52] Now, however, such distortions had significant consequences for her work. Many of the white people she was recruiting had never been to the nation's capital, had never spent much time around black people. They hardly needed reasons to be scared off. Determined to overcome the bad publicity and white Americans' unconscious racism, she drew on her long-standing relationships in government and in the religious and women's communities. She worked tirelessly to get the message out to white religious Americans about the hazards of racism—in their lives as well as in the lives of black Americans. Hedgeman spent countless hours on the telephone, asking church leaders to mobilize their members to make the trip, always reminding them that this was an opportunity to act on their Christianity, rather than just preach about it. She targeted, among others, white Christians from the South who "feel concern but have all too little opportunity to express it in their home place." She also persuaded the National Council of Churches to hold a gathering in Washington during the week of the march.[53]

Anna Hedgeman hoped she was building something even larger and more lasting than a one-day mass protest. The March on Washington was a necessity, but to her it was only a beginning. She tried to turn anyone she came in contact with into an active ally in the ongoing fight for racial justice. She orchestrated bell-ringing ceremonies in churches across the country on August 28, so those who remained home would feel part of a nationwide event.[54] She instructed everyone, whether they attended or not, to contact their legislators, laying a foundation for a vast network that would continue after the march. She knew that her next goal would be the president's civil rights legislation, and she contacted clergy and laypeople in Christian, Jewish, and ecumenical groups across the United States with that in mind, urging them on.

Hedgeman helped organize white Christian college students in the North and promoted the CWU's recruitment of white women from the South. She reached out to her FEPC contacts from two decades earlier, reigniting many clergy members' relationship to civil rights. The CRR took the lead in the God Box, but it seemed that the whole of the National Council of Churches wanted to be involved; by early August, reports streamed in suggesting that tens of thousands of white Protestants had made the commitment to march. Lines blurred among the NCC's various agencies, and the staff redoubled its efforts, sending out fact sheets, directions, and entreaties. The last line on the fact sheet identified the song that had by now become the anthem of the civil rights movement, "We Shall Overcome," as the theme song for the day.[55] Even Merritt Hedgeman left the sidelines to join Anna, forming an NCC staff chorus, teaching it freedom songs to sing at work and on the buses to Washington, and producing a printed song sheet for the six hundred bus captains leading delegations from New York City.

Rachelle Horowitz of the Workers Defense League handled the lion's share of transportation arrangements for the march's organizing committee, but Hedgeman did her part as well. Momentum grew, and it began to feel as though there was no stopping people. One man roller-skated from Chicago to DC, an eighty-one-year-old woman got on a plane for the first time, and a group of twenty-one young people (led by the granddaughter of one of Hedgeman's mentors in Brooklyn during the Great Depression) walked from New York City to the nation's capital.[56]

Hedgeman issued press releases with instructions for marchers on what to carry, where to go, how to line up. The administrative committee worked with the public health director of Washington, DC, to ensure that there would be enough first-aid stations. Two thousand police, two thousand National Guard troops, and two hundred park police were on hand, and four thousand members of the army and marines were on alert. Bayard Rustin worked tirelessly to enlist a separate group of two thousand volunteer peacekeepers, many of them from the Guardians, an organization of New York City's black police officers. The committee tried to secure a thousand beds in Washington, in case people did not follow instructions to return home immediately following the march.[57] The details seemed endless, and Hedgeman was exhausted, but her faith that nonviolent mass power could radically change her nation kept her working.[58]

In the final days before the march, fearing some would not find enough to eat, she took responsibility for Operation Sandwich, a mammoth effort. Four hundred interracial, interfaith volunteers recruited from churches and synagogues across New York City, NCC staff, and local businesses gathered at Riverside Church early on the day before the march; working with a catering firm that volunteered its services, Operation Sandwich put together eighty thousand box lunches. Hedgeman and her coworkers used walkie-talkies to coordinate the massive, joyful effort. Just after noon, following a sandwich blessing ceremony, the first in a line of refrigerated trucks left for a warehouse in Washington, where the lunches were stored overnight for the next day's onslaught of hungry demonstrators.[59]

Operation Sandwich was only one of the many minor and major aspects of the march Hedgeman was busy juggling in the final days. Through the CRR, she pushed until the end to get white people from around the country to the nation's capital to demand racial justice. As part of the administrative committee, she attended to myriad last-minute details, clarifying demands, reviewing communications intended for President Kennedy's administration, mobilizing and financing participation of people from the South, mobilizing and financing participation of the unemployed, and finalizing the program, including who would speak and for how long. Many of Hedgeman's concerns in the final days were administrative, or logistical, including health and sanitation issues, the potential for disruptive white supremacists, and celebrities expecting special treatment. But a larger, political concern continued to haunt her as August 28 approached: What role would women play in the March on Washington?

11 THE "DOUBLE HANDICAP OF RACE AND SEX"

AFRICAN AMERICAN WOMEN AND THE MARCH ON WASHINGTON

In 1944, the black press had dubbed Anna Arnold Hedgeman the "young feminist" in A. Philip Randolph's circle, but nearly twenty years later, in 1963, she had made little progress in convincing him of her right, and other women's right, to exercise full leadership in the black freedom movement. Why, she wondered, were men so obstinate? Why did women pose such a threat? "Suffice it to say that the male would be better advised to spend less time mourning the loss of his superiority and more time working in partnership with women," she wrote. "This is all women really want, anyway."[1] From that vantage point, and starting with the first administrative committee meeting in the summer of 1963, Hedgeman tried to impress upon her male colleagues how important it was to include women and women's organizations in their plans for the March on Washington.

For years, Anna Hedgeman had been thinking and talking about the discrimination women faced, delivering lectures and keynote addresses with titles like "Why Women Walk Two Steps behind Their Men," "The Role of the Negro Woman," "Women and the New America," and "Equal-Unequal."[2] She had depended on her network of professional women in government, labor, and religious and civil rights organizations to help her surmount the obstacles she faced trying to realize her personal and professional goals, and knew how much women had accomplished on behalf of civil rights despite being denied significant leadership roles. She was not naive enough to think it would be easy to get men to open the march leadership to women, but she was determined to see it happen.

Hedgeman and her African American female friends and associates had for years been trying to make people think about what

Mary Church Terrell called the "double handicap of race and sex."[3] In so many circumstances—pregnancy and childrearing, inferior employment opportunities segregated by sex as well as race, the exigencies of aging in difficult economic circumstances—black women's experiences differed from black men's experiences. Nevertheless, African American women had formed the backbone of civil rights and church work for much of the twentieth century; as Hedgeman saw it, they had fully earned a voice in national decision-making.[4]

When it came to the march, if there was a single women's organization that deserved a seat at the table, it was the National Council of Negro Women, founded in 1935 by Mary McLeod Bethune. Now headed by Dorothy Height, Hedgeman's friend since they had together worked with New York City's poor during the Depression, the NCNW was the preeminent organization for black women in the United States and among the most significant civil rights organizations of the era. The leaders of the march knew Height, as she served alongside them on the Council for United Civil Rights Leadership (CUCRL), which brokered the March on Washington with the Kennedy administration. Height complained that the men on the council had a limited vision: she often had to convince them that "social" issues such as hunger and children's health were linked to "political" issues like desegregation.[5] Despite Hedgeman's advocacy, Dorothy Height was never granted a formal role in the march. When the Big Six publicly acknowledged that their sponsors had grown to include labor and religious leaders, they began to publicize the names of the Big Ten, which added four white men to the group, but still no women.[6]

To Anna Arnold Hedgeman and Dorothy Height, gender-based slights were petty and routine, but the march was too important an event not to push for at least one woman as speaker. The Big Six, however, had what Height called "a low tolerance" for talk about women and gave them the runaround. Height believed that Hedgeman, the "doyenne of American Negro women," as Pauli Murray called her, should speak, but the men refused. They provided a variety of excuses: the list of speakers was already too long; it would be too difficult to select one woman; if they did choose one, others would be jealous. It never occurred to them that they could have included more than one woman, and the idea that women alone suffered from jealousy would be laughable to the women watching the male leaders jockey for status and recognition. Bayard Rustin argued that singling out a woman to speak was unnecessary, since women were already represented in the labor, religious, and civil rights groups participating in the march. "I've never seen a more immovable force," Height lamented.[7]

The back and forth continued, but the men remained unmoved. Women were featured as singers, recruited as marchers, and relied on as organizers, but they were not granted a speaking voice. A week before the march, Hedgeman again pointed out during a planning meeting that not a single woman was listed as a speaker on the program. A compromise was proposed: A. Philip Randolph would say a few words about African American women's contributions to the struggle, then invite a group of women to stand and take a bow. Hedgeman listened with a deepening sense of frustration. Not even John Lewis, who was considered so young and radical, found this problematic.[8] Clearly, male civil rights leaders, including those who had counted on Hedgeman's skills and hard work over many decades, had great difficulty moving beyond their belief that women were second-class citizens. Historians have too often followed their lead, finding it remarkably easy to leave African American women out of the civil rights histories they helped shape. And historical treatments of the second wave of feminism in the United States continue to give short shrift to these early moves by African American women toward gender equality.[9]

Still frustrated by the meager progress she was making with the administrative committee, Anna Hedgeman reached out to her natural constituency, women. She called a meeting with some trade unionists in Harlem, members of the Negro American Labor Council who had been among the most active fundraisers for the march. These women, too, were disturbed by the slight, and Hedgeman, emboldened, drafted a letter of complaint to Randolph, sending copies to everyone among the Big Six. Then, at the final meeting of the administrative committee, she read it aloud to the group.

It was "incredible," she explained, that no women had been invited to speak at the march. Surely a woman could do at least what they proposed Randolph do—say a few words and introduce the heroines of the movement. She went on to accuse the Big Six civil rights leaders themselves of sexist practices over the years and recommended a few specific women to speak, including Myrlie Evers, the wife of slain civil rights leader Medgar Evers, and Diane Nash Bevel, a leader of the Nashville student movement who could represent both women and youth.[10]

Hedgeman offered to poll black women to find out who they thought should represent them, and she finished the letter by pointing out that she had been on board since the committee's first meeting, and any proposal she put forward should receive "reasonable recognition."[11] The administrative committee agreed, and its "reasonable recognition," a Tribute to Negro Women, resulted in a plan to have one woman stand to make a few remarks then invite several other women to stand and be recognized. Hedgeman felt she had no choice but to accept the compromise. Along with her suggestions of Myrlie Evers and Diane Nash Bevel, the committee added Rosa Parks, who had sparked the Montgomery, Alabama, bus boycott—though it was not general knowledge outside these circles of women until years later that she had done it deliberately; Gloria Richardson, the head of the Cambridge Movement in Maryland, the only major grassroots civil rights campaign outside of the South; Daisy Bates, newspaper publisher, Arkansas NAACP director, and Little Rock Central High School desegregation leader; and Paris Lee, mother of nine and widow of slain voting rights activist Herbert Lee.[12]

Hedgeman was not appeased, but she was quickly caught up in the remaining march details. A few days after the "compromise," though, she, Dorothy Height, and Pauli Murray learned that Randolph was scheduled as the luncheon speaker at the National Press Club, and the others of the Big Ten, all male, had been invited to sit on the platform with him. The National Press Club had only recently opened its doors to black men, and it still refused women membership. Murray, who claimed to have learned her "ABCs" in public relations from Hedgeman, fired off a furious letter to Randolph. "Surely you are aware of the notorious policy of segregation and discrimination against qualified newspaper women practiced by the National Press Club," she wrote. "Not only are women excluded from membership; they are permitted to attend only by sitting in the balcony."[13] Elsie Carper, a *Washington Post* reporter, concurred, calling it "distressing" as well as "ludicrous" that a group fighting for civil rights would choose a segregated venue to promote its cause, pointing out that the balcony was eerily similar to the back of the bus.[14] The women wanted him to cancel, but Randolph said it would be "uncivil," and refused.[15]

The club bent its rules for the day and allowed women to attend as full participants. This left Anna Hedgeman and her colleagues far from satisfied but uncertain about how to proceed. Should they attend the event? Boycott? Protest?

The women understood that the male organizers of the march were once again employing an erroneous formula: if they improved men's lives, women's lives would automatically improve as well.[16] Hedgeman, Height, and Murray, all of whom had long witnessed the greater costs of poverty and racism in women's lives, knew better. But with the march only days away, the issue created a rift among black women activists. Some felt the march was too important to jeopardize, others that discrimination in the fight for liberation was intolerable. Pauli Murray and a few others wanted to picket the National Press Club, but labor leader Maida Springer convinced them they might jeopardize the march.[17] Springer and Murray, who were so close that they later lived in adjoining apartments, never again spoke about the National Press Club incident.[18]

In the end, the men had their way. They not only banned women from speaking but grouped the women to be honored during the march with the wives of the male civil rights leaders, directing them to march together, separately from and behind the men. Coretta Scott King later remembered how unhappy she was at being separated from her husband. "It had been my great wish to march beside him," she wrote, "not from any desire to share the spotlight, but because I wanted the joy of being with him on this special day."[19] Hedgeman did want women to share the spotlight and found these slights a denial of their full humanity. "Negro women, like all women," she wrote about the experience, "must find ways of securing adequate respect for their work, and their potential as fellow members of the human family."[20]

August 28 turned out to be a perfect day for a march, sunny and warm, not too hot or humid.[21] Before the buses began to pass through the Baltimore Harbor Tunnel at the rate of one hundred per hour, masses of volunteers had set up rest areas, a stage, first-aid stations, and food-service areas. March deputy Bayard Rustin, understandably anxious about how the day would go, had arranged to get the best sound system possible. "In my view," he explained, "it was a classic resolution of the problem of how you can keep a crowd from becoming something else. Transform it into an *audience*."[22] The biggest problem was ultimately a good problem for the march to have: the anticipated crowd of a hundred thousand grew to a quarter of a million, and every resource was taxed. People piled off buses and spilled out of trains. They grabbed signs reading "We March for Jobs Now!" or "We Demand an FEPC Law Now!" or "We Demand Equal Rights Now!" and assembled on the National Mall where they listened to the SNCC Freedom Singers, Odetta, Joan Baez, Bob Dylan, and others while they waited to march.[23] More than a thousand reporters were on hand, as were dignitaries of all kinds. Two planes from Hollywood brought such stars as Harry Belafonte, Diahann Carroll, Rita Moreno, Sammy Davis Jr., Charlton Heston, and Marlon Brando to Washington.[24] Another plane, carrying Robert M. Shelton, Imperial Grand Wizard of one of the most notorious factions of the Ku Klux Klan, crashed in South Carolina on its way to the march, tempering the plans of the white supremacist protester.[25]

Marian Anderson was scheduled to sing the national anthem, but she arrived too late because of traffic. Camilla Williams, the first black singer in the New York City Opera, took her place.[26]

The procession was so large that it took three hours to reach the Lincoln Memorial. After "The Star-Spangled Banner" and a religious invocation, A. Philip Randolph opened the three-hour program with a speech in which he proclaimed that the march, rather than an end in itself, was a beginning, "not only for the Negro but for all Americans who thirst for freedom and a better life."[27] Eugene Carson Blake, the first white speaker, chair of the Commission on Religion and Race, spoke after Randolph, urging people to embrace change. "We come, late we come, but we come," he said, talking about white Protestants and indirectly crediting the work Anna Hedgeman had done, recruiting all those white Christians to the march.

John Lewis was scheduled next, but the SNCC leader's speech, even after several reworkings, was still considered too radical for the day. When he agreed to revise it yet again, the march leadership scrambled to find someone to take his slot in the lineup, but they did not invite any of the women to the podium. Instead, they asked the Reverend Fred Shuttlesworth to deliver impromptu remarks. Gloria Richardson, an ally and mentor to Lewis, as well as one of the women being honored, joined Lewis at the back of the Lincoln Memorial to help him craft a speech that would prove acceptable to the leadership but not sacrifice his integrity.[28] Richardson wondered why she was eligible to edit but not deliver any remarks.[29]

In the end, an estimated forty thousand people marched under the National Council of Churches banner, and an estimated fifty to sixty thousand white people attended the march.[30] Anna Arnold Hedgeman was directly responsible for drawing the majority of the whites who attended the March on Washington. In August 1963, one hundred years after the Emancipation Proclamation, she had moved white Americans one step closer to racial justice, one step closer to joining what Randolph called "the advance guard of a massive moral revolution."[31] Her contribution was not recognized publicly, but it was real and profound.

The meager "Tribute to Negro Women Fighters for Freedom" took place after Lewis's revised speech. Daisy Bates stepped to the microphone after an introduction by Randolph, who mistakenly announced she would be giving the women awards. Instead, she announced, "The women of this country, Mr. Randolph, pledge to you, to Martin Luther King, Roy Wilkins and all of you fighting for civil liberties, that we will join hands with you as women of this country." She continued the collective female pledge: "We will kneel-in, we will sit-in, until we can eat in any counter in the United States. We will walk until we are free, until we can walk to any school and take our children to any school in the United States. And we will sit-in and we will kneel-in and we will line-in if necessary until every Negro in America can vote. This we pledge to the women of America."[32]

Randolph stood again and introduced the other women, disregarding the decision that Bates was to do that. He called Myrlie Evers's name, seemingly unaware she was not there. Once corrected, he named the others: Diane Nash Bevel, Gloria Richardson, Paris Lee, and Rosa Parks. A recording of Randolph's faltering speech is telling. "I'm sorry to report to you that sister Evers could not attend our demonstration because of uh, unusual circumstances," he says haltingly. "Uh, who else? Will the . . . [someone behind him says: Rosa Parks] Miss Rosa Parks . . . will they all stand. And Miss, uh [someone behind him says: Gloria Richardson] Gloria Richardson."[33] The women on the stage, of course, recognized the irony of the situation. "We grinned; some of us," Hedgeman remembered, "as we recognized anew that Negro women are second-class citizens in the same way that white women are in our culture."[34] Rosa Parks recalled later on that she had turned to Daisy Bates, assuring her that "our time will someday come."[35]

When Martin Luther King Jr., the "moral leader of the nation," delivered the speech for which the day will always be remembered, Anna Hedgeman, like hundreds of thousands of others, was captivated by his poetic, utopian vision.[36] In a masterful oratory, King invited Americans to share his dream of realizing the freedom the Emancipation Proclamation had promised a century earlier: "We cannot walk alone. We cannot turn back." Hedgeman more than most would have appreciated his hope for Mississippi: "I have a dream that one day even the state of Mississippi, a state sweltering with the heat of injustice, sweltering with the heat of oppression, will be transformed into an oasis of freedom and justice."[37]

As moved as she was by Dr. King's speech, Hedgeman was distressed. She felt that King, with his claim "*I* have a dream," was detaching himself from history—his history, her history, black history. It made her both sad and angry. She cried a bit and scribbled on her program that she wished he had said, "We Have a Dream," acknowledging the collective labor, the collective joy and sadness, the multitude of women and men whose dreams had drawn, led, and summoned so many to the nation's capital that day.[38] Hedgeman included herself in those responsible for making such a hero of Dr. King without teaching him sufficiently. "Only because we didn't properly educate him," she admitted, noting that a complete acknowledgment of black history had to include the ancestors "pulled out of the shores of Africa" as well as the slaves who had "carried the economy" of the growing nation.[39] Importantly, it included women, in the near as well as the ancient past. She wanted Dr. King to deliver a bountiful and inclusive vision of justice, one that recognized the full scope of the black experience.

When the March on Washington for Jobs and Freedom drew to a close, the male leaders made their way to the White House to meet with President Kennedy. They did not include Rosa Parks or "the rest of us who really were responsible for that day," Anna Hedgeman noted indignantly; the women were left to find their way home. The cavalier way Rosa Parks in particular was treated troubled Hedgeman, who considered her the pioneer of this phase of the freedom movement. She was weary of seeing Parks represented as a quiet seamstress, tired from long days at work. Hedgeman knew her as a powerful, savvy civil rights leader who sat down on the bus not because she was tired but because she was sick and tired, fed up with the indignities of daily life in the Jim Crow South, and ready to take her activism to another level.[40] August 28, 1963, Hedgeman felt, might reasonably have been called "Rosa Parks Day."[41]

Despite Bayard Rustin's request that the participants leave town immediately following the march, the National Council of Negro Women scheduled a debriefing in Washington for the following day. Their gathering, called "After the March, What?," began a conversation about the treatment women received both during the march and in the larger black freedom movement. Determined to keep that conversation alive, the NCNW held a second meeting, in November 1963, during which Pauli Murray spoke about the "bitterly humiliating" experiences of the women who had played key roles in civil rights work, only to be given token representation at the march. "The omission," she told the women assembled, "was deliberate."[42] Murray, who would later coin the term "Jane Crow" to describe the ways in which racial and gender discrimination had become entwined, urged her colleagues to action.[43] As she put it, "The Negro woman can no longer postpone or subordinate the fight against discrimination because of sex to the civil rights struggle but must carry on both fights simultaneously."[44]

Even though Murray's talk had little if any impact on male civil rights leaders, it circulated widely and became a consciousness-raising tool for black women, an early feminist document urging them to think about how their limited roles worked against their own dignity and development, and hindered the black freedom movement as a whole. Anna Hedgeman and her colleagues were not alone in giving much while getting little respect in return; after the march they would be joined by African American women of all ages, now ready to listen to a feminist analysis of their civil rights work. Indeed, the histories of civil rights and feminism in this era are entwined.

Septima Clark, who worked for the Southern Christian Leadership Conference, Martin Luther King Jr.'s organization, wrote him a letter complaining about being pushed to the sidelines or ignored; his response was to read the letter aloud to his staff, who laughed.[45] Ella Baker, now widely credited with guiding the Student Nonviolent Coordinating Committee through its coming-of-age process with what Baker's biographer calls her "radical democratic vision," left the SCLC because her potential for leadership in King's circle was so limited. Asked why she did not rise in the organization, Baker was blunt. "First," she said, "I'm a woman."[46]

For some African American women, Anna Hedgeman included, the March on Washington would be remembered as much for raising women's consciousness about gender as it would be for Dr. King's momentous speech. "For many of us," Dorothy Height explained, "the March opened up the dialogue. It made it necessary. We had to talk about it."[47]

There were so many things to talk about. Women involved in the black freedom movement found their prospects for leadership limited, but they had nevertheless accomplished a great deal, in part by making careful choices about when to raise objections. They found ways to exercise leadership that went unnoticed by the men, and they called on each other for support. They did the work of women even when men viewed them only as "ladies."

The postwar idea of a "lady" was a white, married, suburban, apron-clad mother with little social or political consciousness. Few of the women in Hedgeman's cohort fit the bill. Pauli Murray, for example, often dressed like a man, chose male nicknames for herself, and lived in a long-term relationship with another woman; she considered herself transgender before the term even came into use.[48] Hedgeman and Ella Baker were both married, but they traveled a great deal and lived apart from their husbands for significant periods. In an era usually considered prefeminist, Baker never took her husband's name. Anna Arnold Hedgeman used her maiden name, her married name, and both, maintaining that she had three names for a reason: to commemorate herself, her father, and her husband.

Dorothy Height never married and never had children; Anna Hedgeman, Ella Baker, and politician Shirley Chisholm married but did not have children. And these women's relationships with men, when they were married, could hardly be called traditional. Like Merritt Hedgeman, the men in these activist women's lives exercised masculinity in unconventional ways, staying out of the limelight and doing far more than most married men of their generation to maintain their households and support their wives' careers.[49] There was something liberating, in the aftermath of the March on Washington, about getting these kinds of differences, and the challenges that even the most "liberated" of these women still experienced, out in the open.

Still, Hedgeman had to put her concerns about gender on hold, at least for a time. When she and the other members of the CRR returned to New York after the march, they were determined to harness the enormous energy it had ignited. The country seemed electrified by the march in general and by Dr. King's dream in particular. All the talk was of President Kennedy's civil rights bill. Hedgeman's fellow staff members were elated, perhaps too elated, she worried, about the solidarity the march seemed to create. She was savvy enough to know that enormously hard work lay ahead if they were to turn energized white people into long-term warriors for racial justice. Like *New York Times* columnist James Reston, she worried that the march was the "spree," the aftermath the "hangover," and allies for real change perhaps more than a bit fickle.[50] But as the letters and phone calls poured in, with people asking, "What do we do next?" "How do we move?" "Where is the bill?" Anna Hedgeman was more than happy to provide white Christians with guidance and support.[51] As she did so, she grew more hopeful that the spiritual and political power of Christians could be brought to bear in the black freedom movement, and that real racial justice was in the making.

12   THE COMMISSION ON RELIGION AND RACE

The March on Washington was an emotional experience not just for the marchers but also for the millions of Americans who followed the events on radio and TV. That did not mean it was a permanent cure for the racial hatred that riddled the nation, though; it was more like a brief and hopeful interlude. The speakers had done their best to move those who listened not just to agree and empathize but to act, to play a role in bringing change to their own lives and to the living history of their country.

It was clear, the speakers noted as they took the stage, that equal opportunity and racial justice remained aspirations rather than realities. It was a tricky thing, Anna Hedgeman knew, to balance accusations with encouragement, but she believed they succeeded, each in their own way.

Rabbi Joachim Prinz, who had taken the stage after gospel singer Mahalia Jackson and before Martin Luther King Jr., told the crowd that silence and inaction were as dangerous in the United States as they had been in Nazi Germany. The nation had to work together, "for it is not enough to hope together, and it is not enough to pray together."[1]

After King closed his speech with the words of the Negro spiritual, "Free at last! Free at last! Thank God Almighty, we are free at last!" there was no mistaking the intent. The "we" he invoked must include all Americans, and all Americans would benefit, collectively and individually, when freed of the scourge of racism. As unhappy as Anna Hedgeman was about the march's treatment of women, she was nevertheless delighted by its interracial, interfaith character, which she hoped would move a wide swath of people to support her next "special project," the civil rights bill recently put forward by President Kennedy.

In the coming days, her phone ringing constantly, Hedgeman put aside her nagging fear that white people would lack resolve and chose instead to remain hopeful that the march would have a profound effect on Americans' ability to connect racial justice with their commitment to faith.[2] Religious faith had infused the march, and she felt she had reason to count on white religious individuals and church bodies to persevere, rather than return to a state in which they merely gave lip service to racial justice. In reaching out to her so immediately and urgently, white religious leaders made it clear that they looked to the National Council of Churches, the Commission on Religion and Race in particular, for guidance. They too wanted to keep this interfaith effort alive, and they had come to view the CRR as the core ecumenical base for action.

But Hedgeman barely had time to return to ongoing projects, let alone initiate new ones, before tragedy struck in the troubled city of Birmingham, Alabama. On Sunday, September 15, 1963, less than three weeks after the March on Washington, a group of four young girls gathered in the basement of Birmingham's Sixteenth Street Baptist Church. As they discussed the lesson for the day, "The Love That Forgives," an enormous explosion, set by members of the "Invisible Empire," Alabama's vast network of white supremacists, rocked the church. The explosion tore a large hole in the building, buried the basement in rubble, and killed Addie Mae Collins, Cynthia Wesley, Carole Robertson, and Denise McNair.[3] Hedgeman and the other staff members of the CRR, along with civil rights leaders from around the nation, left immediately for Birmingham, where they attended a joint funeral for three of the girls. Delivering the eulogy, Martin Luther King Jr. spoke of love. "We must not lose faith in our white brothers," he told the crowd of eight thousand. "You can bomb our homes, bomb our churches, kill our children, and we are still going to love you."[4] What a contrast to his shared dream of a few weeks earlier, when he looked to a time when "little black boys and black girls will be able to join hands with little white boys and white girls as sisters and brothers."

Photographer Ken Thompson, only twenty years old at the time, had recently joined the commission's staff, and his extraordinary photos reveal the enormity of King's plea and of Hedgeman's personal and professional task: to extend love to people capable of committing or even tolerating such horror.

Anna Hedgeman had, by this point in her life, worked through various stages of loving and hating white people. She had grown up in a family in which race did not determine relationships, in a town where she loved her white neighbors, believing in a God who did not brook disrespect, never mind hatred. Her experiences in Mississippi and Ohio in the 1920s, and New York and Washington, DC, in the 1930s and 1940s, had challenged her ability to love white Americans, whose very whiteness, she came to believe, disallowed their full humanity. The theology that she had begun to develop while at Hamline University four decades earlier had grown more refined and included the study of what we now call "whiteness," the exploration of what it is to be white in the world.[5] In her day, this was highly unusual, as white was the default. But Hedgeman kept at it, and in the aftermath of the Birmingham bombings she maintained that black Americans could provide assistance to their white brethren. In a reversal of the common notion that whites assisted blacks, she wrote, "We must struggle now to help white America free herself of the idolatry of the love of whiteness."[6]

There was a period when Hedgeman had hated white people. She had moved to Harlem in the 1920s specifically to immerse herself in a black community and shift white people to the periphery of her life and consciousness. Over the years, though, she had worked closely with whites and had developed close adult friendships with white women and men. She also increasingly recognized the problematic nature of race as an idea, a label, an identity. After all, she knew that her personal history and genealogy—like that of so many other African Americans—was a multiracial one. Above all, her faith continued to push her toward racial reconciliation rather than rejection. She had by now had some success trying to get black and white people to talk with and not about each other.[7] In Birmingham, however, Anna Hedgeman, like so many others, would be sorely tested.

Ken Thompson's images capture the pain and the dignity of Birmingham's black community. They also show the depth of the mourning, which reverberated far beyond that day and that community. The funeral saw the largest interracial gathering of clergy in the city's history, though it was cold comfort. Although more than eight hundred clergy, black and white, attended the service, not one state or local official was present, and few black Americans had any expectation that justice would prevail.[8] Thompson's camera captured, among other things, the image that Hedgeman believed embodied the event: a stained-glass window of Jesus Christ at the church, the image left intact in the explosion, except for the face of Christ, which had been shattered in the explosion. Hedgeman and her colleagues did not quite know what to make of that, but it seemed to be symbolic.[9]

The CRR staff returned home to New York City, chastened but determined to get to work securing the passage of the civil rights bill then beginning to wend its way through Congress.[10] It was good to have something as concrete as legislation to focus on, and this bill, the most comprehensive civil rights measure to date, would make a significant difference in the lives of African Americans. As controversial as it was overdue, the bill outlawed discrimination in public accommodations, including hotels, restaurants, and amusement parks. Among other provisions, it addressed segregated schools, equal employment opportunity, and obstacles to voting, including literacy tests. Favoring what she called a tri-faith effort, Hedgeman worked to line up Catholic, Protestant, and Jewish leaders to testify on behalf of the legislation.[11] Leaders of the three religious faiths issued an interfaith statement, noting that "the religious conscience of America condemns racism as blasphemy against God" and urging legislators to pass the bill. "We can do no less for God and for our country."[12]

The House Judiciary Committee broadened the civil rights legislation the president put forward, adding a permanent Equal Employment Opportunity Commission, a move that pleased Hedgeman, who had fought long and hard for the FEPC twenty years earlier, and who knew that the jobs component of the March on Washington for Jobs and Freedom was critical to real change in black communities. To many people's surprise, inside and outside Congress, and through a bit of a fluke, the House also adopted an amendment to include the word "sex" in the bill's employment discrimination provision.[13] Democratic representative Howard Smith introduced the amendment under pressure from women but then voted against it in the final House bill. But Hedgeman's friend Pauli Murray wasted no time in drafting enough support to keep sex in the final, Senate legislation, noting both the "historical interrelatedness" of race and gender and the "tragic consequences" of ignoring those relationships. "The rationalizations upon which this sex prejudice rests are often different from those supporting racial discrimination in label only," she argued, later noting that "the two meet in me."[14]

Murray drafted a memo that circulated through Congress and to others who could push for the legislation's passage, including the First Lady, Lady Bird Johnson. "If sex is not included," she explained, "the civil rights bill would be including only one half of the Negroes."[15] Murray's leadership here would have an enormous impact on American women's lives in the coming years and decades: as the depth and consequences of workplace gender discrimination became increasingly apparent, the issue also became actionable in the courts.[16] But here lies another historical chapter that has often been told as a case of "gender," rather than race and gender, although neither can be extricated in the telling.

There was reason to be optimistic that the civil rights bill would pass both houses of Congress. Although southern senators continued to wield a great deal of power, national and international outrage over recent racial violence made it seem likely that senators outside of the South would not give in to their segregationist colleagues as they had in the past.[17] If she successfully saw the bill through passage and implementation, Anna Hedgeman would be fulfilling the commission's mission and mandate, bringing clergy and laypeople together to challenge the racism that was so much a part of American life. Because the administrative committee of the March on Washington still met to talk about next steps, including advocacy for the bill's passage, Hedgeman again played a dual and overlapping role in drawing on and influencing a variety of constituencies.[18]

Determined to leave few things to chance, the CRR developed and advanced a savvy political strategy. Recognizing that lawmakers cared more about registered voters than the rest of their constituents, and that the Midwest could be vital to the bill's passage, they urged white Midwesterners to press their legislators, particularly Republican legislators, to support the bill. Commission member Victor Reuther called it the "Midwest Strategy." Executive director Robert Spike noted the obvious irony that passage of the legislation seemed to lie primarily in the hands of white, largely Protestant Midwesterners, who had little actual experience of the conditions the bill was intended to overcome. But it seemed a promising strategy, and they launched a nine-state legislative-training conference; the trainee-graduates then offered additional training sessions at home and traveled to Washington to meet the key members of Congress.[19]

Hedgeman, who had done significant outreach to the Midwest, both for the FEPC and, more recently, recruiting white Protestants for the march, had a solid network in place. She embarked on a speaking tour of the Midwest and, in one of her most significant political moves, arranged for some of the young, black, seasoned civil rights workers she knew from the Student Nonviolent Coordinating Committee and the Southern Christian Leadership Conference to talk to white Midwestern congregations about their experiences and the importance of the proposed legislation.[20] A minister would open each gathering by talking about the theological basis of civil rights legislation; he would be followed by a black civil rights worker talking from personal experience, a legislative expert reviewing the bill, and finally a local contact person making the connections between the issues and the audience's opportunities for local and national advocacy.[21]

One particular night, in Omaha, Nebraska, Prathia Hall, who had been shot and imprisoned for her civil rights work, took the stage.[22] "I have come tonight not to entertain you," she told her white, Christian audience, "but to trouble you." Hall then described in detail the humiliation and abuse she and so many others suffered. She did the same in five cities, reaching more than seven hundred people.

Several weeks later, when Hall was arrested in Atlanta, the press carried the story, and word spread quickly through those Midwestern congregations. The director of the South Dakota State Council of Churches phoned Hedgeman. "Is it true that Prathia Hall has been arrested?" he asked. "Is she actually in jail? How can we help?"[23] As Hedgeman had hoped, a human connection made all the difference. Those white Midwesterners who knew few if any black people now felt a fellowship with Prathia Hall and began to follow and care about her, feel concern about her safety, and become invested in her legislative needs. If they had such an experience with Prathia Hall, Hedgeman reasoned, perhaps they would begin to care about the black people in their own communities who had been all but invisible to them.

Even though this strategy seemed to be producing results, it was a painful process. As much as Anna Hedgeman appreciated the young activists' willingness to provide this kind of witness, she knew she was taking them away from important work in the South and asking them to shoulder what she considered an additional burden, that of explaining racism to white people who practiced it, however unwittingly.[24] She worried, too, that white Christians would be moved just enough to support the legislation, but then consider themselves absolved of further responsibility. When she spoke with these groups, Hedgeman was always clear that the legislation was a means to justice, not the final step in the journey. She asked people to pray for the bill—and then to organize, to mobilize, to act.[25] She sought not just laborers for this task but converts to the cause and emphasized that the problem was not limited to the South; the entire nation had to change. The civil rights bill would certainly prove effective in the fight against Jim Crow, she explained to a group in Kalamazoo, Michigan, but it would be equally useful to them as they addressed injustice in their own hometowns.

Hedgeman appealed to young people, specifically college students, in additional, targeted ways. Believing that "until America changes its attitudes about color," their educations would fail them, she helped organize a CRR-sponsored student conference in Washington and addressed the 350 Catholic, Jewish, Protestant, and largely white students from eighty college campuses who attended. At the end of the two-day meeting focused on faith and racial justice, the students met with their congressional representatives to push for passage of the bill. Hedgeman's passionate address led to more invitations, and she subsequently spoke at a youth conference at the United Nations Center and trained student groups at Cornell University, Vassar College, Fairleigh Dickinson University, City College of New York, and Queens College.[26] She also urged the CRR to give continued support to young people already involved in the struggle, particularly in SNCC, which she saw as vulnerable to takeover by older and more established civil rights leaders and groups.[27] Like fellow civil rights activist Ella Baker, Hedgeman wanted young people first to gain confidence and then, second, to assume power in the organizations that advocated for racial justice.[28] She knew how powerful an experience it had been to be invited to the Amenia conference, three decades earlier, and to have been identified as a promising civil rights leader.

When she was not traveling to the Midwest to push for passage of the civil rights bill, Hedgeman reached out to another constituency closer to home: women, black and white. She gave a talk to the opening meeting of the Commission on the Status of Negro Women of Greater New York, asking attendees to send telegrams to the White House and, as her host put it, interpreting for them "the job we as Negro women must play" in demanding social change.[29] She recruited support from Church Women United, speaking to the twenty-five hundred delegates assembled at the organization's national conference, focusing again on women's responsibility in getting the measure passed.[30] Church Women United prided itself on its radicalism relative to the National Council of Churches, and Hedgeman did not hold back, sometimes bringing white women in the audience to tears. One night, in Indiana, a woman talked about how insulted she was by Hedgeman's accusations. "You know that isn't the way we are in our church and in our town," she complained about the speaker's characterization of white Americans, but that was precisely the point: racism was endemic, its solution a collective one. After hearing Hedgeman lecture, a white friend asked why she had not shared this anger with her before. Her response was that she had tried, but the friend had not been listening. "Touché," Hedgeman's friend replied, chastened.[31]

All this activity proved effective: letters from women, including leaders of religious organizations, Catholic nuns, and Protestant and Jewish housewives, were prominent among those sent to Congress in support of the bill.[32]

Hedgeman remained attentive to the question of gender in other ways as well. As the CRR enlarged its staff for the legislative effort, she pushed the leadership not to overlook the talented women to be found among Church Women United, whose "extra quality" of experience the CRR "so sorely needed."[33] She also took care to mentor her young, white NCC assistant to move, personally and professionally, toward greater understanding of racial justice.

Carol Anderson had not known a single black person as she grew up working-class in rural Ohio. But while she was attending Ohio's Miami University, a summer job at a resort in New York introduced her to a wider, more complicated world. She met young, African American college students working as waiters, learned that one of her coworkers was gay, something she had never even heard of before, and encountered the civil rights movement. After graduation, her parents approved of her move to New York City because she worked for "the Church," but they had no idea about the politically and socially progressive setting their daughter entered. There, under Anna Hedgeman's tutelage, she thrived.[34] Hedgeman, whom Anderson always addressed as "Dr. Hedgeman," was more supportive than she had ever imagined a boss could be.

Hedgeman gave Anderson an unusual and life-changing degree of autonomy. She invited her to policy meetings in New York and took her to Washington, DC, and to the South, introducing her to Rosa Parks, Andrew Young, James Bevel, and many other civil rights leaders. Anderson worked on whatever Hedgeman was working on, and her boss included her in her busy life, running around Harlem from meeting to meeting, stopping in at Frank's Restaurant on 125th Street, where Anna and Merritt often ate, and where Anna, as Anderson remembered, held court. Anderson saw Hedgeman not just as a mentor but as a living embodiment of the practice of religion, with her simultaneous attention to race and disregard for race, her determination to follow an agenda set by a higher power, and her demand for change in this world rather than the next.[35]

Perhaps because she saw something of herself in the young Midwesterner, or felt the need to challenge all white people on race, or simply because she cared about her, Hedgeman wanted her assistant to learn about race, both its importance and its absurdity. She invited Anderson to take a break from working on the civil rights bill and travel with her to the Southern Christian Leadership Conference's Citizenship Education School in Dorchester, Georgia, where Hedgeman was scheduled to teach at the invitation of her friend Septima Clark.[36] "She brought me along, literally and figuratively," Anderson explained. It was her first trip to the South, and she found it even more profoundly moving than the March on Washington. Participants were risking their lives to learn skills they would use when they returned home to do voter registration work in their own communities, in many cases risking their lives again. Living among black people, and hearing their stories, helped Anderson understand the privilege that came from being white.

When they left Georgia, Hedgeman told Anderson matter-of-factly that she had passed a race test while they were there. Anderson had offered some clothes to a black woman from Louisiana who had lost her suitcase en route; when the woman's suitcase finally arrived, she had taken her clothing back. "All over the South, white women give black women clothes," Hedgeman explained. "But they never take them back. When you took the clothes back, and put them in your suitcase, you didn't know, but you passed a test—that you were indeed a trustworthy human being."[37]

On another occasion, at Lewis Michaux's black nationalist bookstore on 125th Street, Hedgeman introduced Anderson to Malcolm X. She told Anderson she was going to introduce her as a cousin from Dayton, Ohio. Anderson was afraid that Malcolm would call them on the lie and lash into her for being white and entering a black bookstore. "Just watch," Hedgeman said. "He won't blink an eye." He did not; Malcolm said hello, politely, and that was that. He too had white cousins, Hedgeman explained, offering Anderson another way to understand race and racial identity.[38]

Carol Anderson would gladly have worked for Anna Hedgeman for many years, but one day her boss told her, "You'll never get further than this if you stay a secretary. You need to think about next steps." Hedgeman had to push Anderson out the door, but with her boss's encouragement she applied to graduate school. Aware of her financial challenges, Hedgeman kept her on staff part-time while she pursued a master's degree at Columbia University's Teachers College.[39] To this day, Anderson's memories of her boss remain strong and reflect the experience of other women who worked with or for Hedgeman and found her not only warm and encouraging but also decisive, direct, and demanding.[40]

When President John F. Kennedy was assassinated on November 22, 1963, the civil rights community was, like the rest of the nation, terribly shaken. Many had questions about the new president, Lyndon B. Johnson, a Texas Democrat and a southerner. Would he support the pending civil rights legislation or back off? Just five days after the assassination, Johnson made it clear that he was on board.[41] "No memorial oration or eulogy," he told a joint session of Congress and a national television audience, "could more eloquently honor President Kennedy's memory than the earliest possible passage of the civil rights bill for which he fought so long."[42] The "old master of the Senate," who knew Washington as well as anyone on the Hill, refused to compromise on the bill's content and was determined to see the bill through to passage.[43]

But the Commission on Religion and Race could not be sure how things would turn out, and it continued an unremitting campaign, particularly in the Midwest. When the legislation was stuck in the House Rules Committee, Hedgeman arranged for busloads of Midwestern delegates to travel to Washington to urge members of Congress to sign the petition to release the bill. While the bill's opponents warned of impending state socialism if the government gained the ability to legally regulate relationships between the races, the CRR circulated a statement from the *Des Moines Register*, an influential Midwestern newspaper, noting that the "big government" claim was little more than an attempt to cloud the fundamental issue, "civil wrongs based on race discrimination." The *Register* was just one of many Midwestern papers that urged passage. When the House approved the bill in February 1964, almost every representative from the Midwest voted in favor.[44] Anna Arnold Hedgeman's work had had an impact.

When southern senators launched the longest filibuster, or stalling technique, in congressional history, the CRR did not give up on the bill, even though the Senate had never before voted for cloture on a civil rights bill, the only way to end a filibuster and force a vote. Hedgeman and her boss, Robert Spike, sent out a new round of entreaties, soliciting both letters and delegations to Congress. The commission helped organize an interfaith rally at Georgetown University that drew sixty-five hundred people. Archbishop Patrick O'Boyle delivered the opening prayer, as he had at the March on Washington. The press began to take serious note of the power of the church-affiliated groups that, as a *New York*

Times columnist observed, were "throwing their weight" around and posing a real threat to the southern strategy to defeat the bill.[45]

Starting in late April 1964, with the Senate filibuster still in progress, Hedgeman arranged what she described as "daily services of worship and recommitment" at the Lutheran Church of the Reformation, just blocks from Capitol Hill. Every morning at nine, a different group of ministers and lay leaders gathered on a "preaching mission" to lead constituents in an ecumenical service. Volunteer seminary students directed congregants from around the nation to their seats, and afterward to the church basement for daily briefings, at which visitors reported on progress at home and then prepared to stop in on their senators on the Hill. At the same time, a group of Catholic, Jewish, and Protestant seminary students started an around-the-clock vigil near the Lincoln Memorial. The preaching missions remained in place until the bill was released to the Senate for a vote, and the vigils continued until the bill finally passed in June.[46]

Hedgeman worked mainly from New York during this time, orchestrating both the continuous religious services in Washington and the Midwest response, and Carol Anderson stayed on in the capital as her proxy. In the end, more than a thousand people from forty-three states participated in what they called the Church Assembly on Civil Rights, many traveling all night, attending the morning service, then lobbying before they returned home.[47] Many other people wrote letters to their representatives, making direct reference to links between their faith and the pending legislation.[48]

Hedgeman spoke before state legislatures and a variety of audiences in the Northeast as well, and she developed a reputation for being tough and unrelenting. After she accepted an invitation to "tell it like it is" one night in Connecticut, white audience members balked, protesting that they were not the white people she described. She stayed late into the night, talking about race and community and instructing them on what it meant to be white—and how to be responsible. Sometimes complaints about her directness on matters of race got back to the National Council of Churches; there was some talk about just how far they should let her go. In the end, Hedgeman gained more supporters than detractors. She was exceptionally capable of convincing people that action was needed, when there had only been talk and handwringing.[49]

When the Senate finally voted for cloture, several senators and representatives attended the last of these worship services, in recognition of the key role the church movement had played.[50] At the end of that service, Hedgeman talked with Oregon senator Wayne Morse, a supporter of the FEPC bill twenty years earlier. They reminisced about their earlier struggle and rejoiced in where they stood that day, but both were politically astute enough to know their coalition had to remain vigilant until the bill made it through to implementation.

By the time President Johnson signed the Civil Rights Act into law, on July 2, 1964, people from every state in the Union had participated in the religious advocacy effort, visiting representatives and senators, soliciting the support of friends and neighbors, contributing financially, ringing church bells in unison across state lines, and marching in vocal or silent processions.[51] There was no doubt that the churches played a key role in the passage of this critical legislation.[52] Hedgeman was so elated by the experience that she tried to get the daily filibuster-inspired sermons published, but as moving as she found them, sermons are a hard sell. She contented herself with remembering how they provided inspiration as well as solace in such a challenging time.

One practice Anna Hedgeman was through with, though, was leaving women out of the picture. The words of her friend and protégée Pauli Murray, whose post-march NCNW speech had reached publication just weeks before the bill passed, may have been ringing in her ears: "One thing is crystal clear," Murray had written. "The Negro woman can no longer postpone or subordinate the fight against discrimination because of sex to the civil rights struggle but must carry on both fights simultaneously. . . . Clearly, the full participation and leadership of Negro women is necessary to the success of the civil rights revolution."[53] Hedgeman's work had been critical, and she wanted recognition for herself and other women. When President Johnson invited religious leaders to a special event commemorating their role in getting the landmark bill passed, Hedgeman not only attended but also made sure her assistant, Carol Anderson, stood with her in the White House. In accordance with Hedgeman's style of leadership, the two women, black and white, stood together to accept the president's recognition and appreciation.[54]

When the Civil Rights Act of 1964 was implemented, it led directly to the passage the following year of the Voting Rights Act, which would eliminate the final barriers to voting for black Americans. Although Anna Hedgeman did not know it at the time, this was the last time the liberal religious community would work together so effectively, or gain so much ground on racial justice in the United States. In what she well might have considered a supreme irony, their success paved the way for clergy with a very different agenda to launch the religious right and, over the next several decades, push conservative religious values into the mainstream and through state and national legislatures.[55]

At the same time that Hedgeman was working so diligently on the civil rights bill, the CRR extended its reach in another way as well, one she heartily endorsed. The National Council of Churches issued a formal statement, noting that the churches had no right to ask Congress to act for racial justice if they did not expect the same of themselves.[56] The NCC asked its constituent congregations to be open to people of all races, adopt fair employment policies, use multiracial images in their literature, integrate their governing boards, unite to support passage of civil rights legislation, and require that all the companies they contracted with as builders, buyers, or investors practice fair employment. Hedgeman was grateful for the self-reflection and believed that the call came at a good time, bringing new energy to what had become, she felt, a "struggle weary" Commission on Religion and Race.[57] The church group wielded a great deal of economic power, and if white Christians began to see more clearly what economic justice meant within their own church lives, they might enter into the CRR's initiatives with a better sense of the difficulty as well as the rewards of moving closer to racial justice.

Hedgeman embarked on another speaking tour, this time to help church leaders and congregations learn why and how to promote change from within. But despite the NCC's final resolution on desegregating the churches—"Remember always to act in love and without hate or bitterness"—she could not help but feel some bitterness toward the white congregations she met with. Too many seemed reluctant to engage in the hard, long-term work required to eradicate racist beliefs and practices. Some of her listeners wanted her to cut short the talk and simply name one black leader they could follow. Others asked her why African Americans seemed suddenly to be in revolt, or why they were so hostile. Still others pointed to baseball player Jackie Robinson or singer Marian Anderson as evidence of progress. One woman told Hedgeman bluntly that she did not understand what she had to complain about: after all, she was respected, and she had status. The woman was a bit taken aback when Hedgeman told her that her life had been, to some degree, wasted: she had spent so much time discussing the implications of race that she had missed the opportunity to hone any real talents she possessed.[58]

Even though Hedgeman and her colleagues approached this mission with their usual passion and purpose, the CRR had more success in getting national legislation passed than it did getting churches to desegregate their pews or their practices. As many organizations would discover, northern whites were often far more outraged over acts of racism below the Mason-Dixon Line than they were over similar incidents in their own neighborhoods. Hedgeman blamed the failure, in significant part, on the clergy. They had to hone a theology of justice that acknowledged that being Christian meant facing the hard work of racial reconciliation, but many were reluctant to risk controversy by providing their congregants with purposeful direction on matters of racial justice. "Too many white clergymen," she lamented, "still place the peace and unity within their churches above other considerations. They need to do more to 'walk in the way of the Lord.'"

The Commission on Religion and Race was also attempting to figure out its role in the American South, a question that had moved between the background and the foreground of their agenda since their founding in June 1963. Just a few days after the CRR was established, Mississippi civil rights activist Medgar Evers was assassinated in the driveway of his home. The CRR's first official act was to send representatives to Evers's funeral, where local people asked them to live out their mandate by becoming directly involved in the chaos in Mississippi.[59]

As eager to define itself as it was to redefine Christianity, the CRR moved right into direct action—and right into trouble. The commission sent a group of Protestant leaders to Clarksdale, Mississippi, to join a challenge to segregated public accommodations. After three weeks of civil rights leaders there telling them to go home or risk making things worse, the staff members left, dismayed, humbled, and above all worried that they might have further endangered those they left behind. They met in New York to regroup, and a year later the NCC launched the Delta Ministry, a missionary project aimed at Mississippi, which would become one of the NCC's most ambitious and significant programs.[60] Although Anna Hedgeman would not work on the Delta Ministry project directly, she made several trips to the South on behalf of the CRR. Each time she would recall her time teaching in the South, four decades earlier, and was struck not by the contrasts wrought by the passage of time but instead by the devastating continuities of poverty and prejudice that she believed threatened white people's souls nearly as much as they threatened black people's survival.

By the time passage of the Civil Rights Act of 1964 seemed imminent, the CRR, more than a year old, embarked on a second effort in the South. It signed on to the campaign that would become known as Freedom Summer, in which roughly eight hundred predominantly white northern college students traveled to Mississippi to teach in freedom schools, open community centers, and register black citizens to vote.[61] Beleaguered civil rights leaders in Mississippi increasingly felt they were fighting a losing battle, and some believed that placing white college students in what was often literally the line of fire would ensure greater press coverage and, eventually, greater protection for all those seeking to advance racial justice.[62] The sponsoring coalition of civil rights organizations, the Mississippi Council of Federated Organizations (COFO), hoped to capitalize on the energy of the March on Washington and convince white Americans, in an election year, that voting rights were not something to be taken for granted.[63]

Not everyone involved wanted to bring white students to Mississippi, where the COFO staff was largely black, but the coalition's codirector, Bob Moses, did, and he persevered. "The one thing we can do for the country that no one else can do," he argued, "is to be above the race issue."[64] Such a sentiment, not surprisingly, appealed to members of the Commission on Religion and Race. When they realized that COFO lacked the money and time to adequately train the volunteers, the CRR offered to find a training site and fund and oversee the orientation for the students making the journey south for Freedom Summer. The CRR knew that many of the students would be from their churches, and it was eager to play a role in ensuring their personal growth as well as their safety.[65] The CRR also recruited what one historian calls a "heavenly host of ministers, priests and rabbis" who provided counsel but also did everything everyone else did, from mopping floors to teaching to getting spit at and beaten.[66] Finally, the CRR sponsored more than one hundred lawyers who made their way south to provide legal counsel to the volunteers facing arrest and imprisonment.[67]

Recognizing that the African American leaders of the coalition groups, who had long worked in Mississippi, had to provide the leadership for Freedom Summer, the largely white CRR offered to stay behind the scenes, providing money and personnel support and administering the orientation program. Hedgeman and her colleagues invited COFO fieldworkers north for two sessions with educators, psychologists, and community organizers to devise the orientation curriculum. They also began to put out feelers for colleges to host the two week-long orientation sessions. After a few failed attempts, the staff joked that colleges were apparently as conservative as churches, but they eventually secured Western College for Women, in Oxford, Ohio.[68] The CRR also hosted three smaller student orientation sessions: one at LeMoyne College in Memphis, Tennessee; the second at Tougaloo College in Tougaloo, Mississippi; and the third at the First Congregational Church in Washington, DC. In addition, it organized the minister-counselor orientation in Jackson, Mississippi.[69]

In Oxford, Ohio, the two groups of student volunteers, largely white and middle-class, arrived on consecutive Sundays at the brick and ivy-clad two-hundred-acre campus, where SNCC activist Fannie Lou Hamer led them in song before they began their orientation.[70] Hamer spoke with them about love and about God, echoing the imperative that drove the CRR forward: "How can we say we love God, and hate our brothers and sisters? We got to reach them."[71] In the following days the students learned about the geography and culture of Mississippi; about southerners, black and white; and about how to exercise nonviolence and deal with police violence. They faced a tear gas attack and learned how to coach people through the voter registration package, which required copying and interpreting a section of the Mississippi Constitution and defining the duties and obligations of citizenship, all to the satisfaction of the registrar, who could take up to thirty days to inform the candidate of the decision.[72] They learned that Mississippi's teachers had to sign an oath that they would not participate in civil rights activities, that they would teach that slavery had been a happy period in the state's history, and that the Ku Klux Klan had saved the South.[73]

The student volunteers learned necessary security procedures, like locking doors at all times, keeping windows closed, driving five miles below the speed limit, not traveling anywhere alone, and immediately reporting any cars driving by without license plates.[74] They were told never to stand near lighted windows, always to carry a jacket in case they needed it to wrap their heads for protection, how to stun a charging dog, and the importance of knowing all the roads that led in and of town.[75] They learned about the black church and heard lectures on white racism, which the people conducting the orientation openly assumed them to embody. They learned to sing freedom songs and to process the anger projected onto them from the seasoned civil rights workers, who often found the students naive and insufficiently self-reflective. As Hedgeman watched, the northern students grew increasingly silent over the course of the week, as the gravity of the situation became more real for them.

Knowing how difficult it was to communicate with white law enforcement in the South, and witnessing how little progress they had made with white religious leaders, especially in Mississippi, Hedgeman feared the worst.[76] And as the second week-long orientation session got underway, just forty-eight hours after the CRR paused to celebrate the passage of the Civil Rights Act, it learned the worst: three of the members of the initial group, James Chaney, Andrew Goodman, and Michael Schwerner, who had left Ohio just days earlier, had gone missing in Mississippi. As one student described the atmosphere at Western College, "The tension clouded us in until it was all there was to breathe."[77]

By Tuesday, the authorities in Mississippi had located the young men's car; by Wednesday, reporters were swarming the Ohio campus to chronicle the Freedom Summer training program and its participants; by Thursday, they were watching themselves on television.[78] The search for the missing civil rights workers continued long after the training was over and the media spotlight had moved on; it was only after they were missing for forty-five days that an informant's tip led to the discovery of their bodies.[79] Writer Anthony Walton, whose father grew up in Mississippi, captured the stark truth in his brief poem, "Schwerner, Chaney, and Goodman": "Still green silence of the piney hills / Blood red earth, redder still."[80]

Still, Freedom Summer continued. Holly Springs, where Hedgeman had taught four decades earlier, became home to a community center and two freedom schools, makeshift spaces designed to foster political participation among disenfranchised black youth. The college students lived and worked on the Rust College campus, and the description a student provided mirrors that of the young Anna Arnold all those years before. "In the fall of the year when the crop is harvested and the cotton is sold to market," he explained, "the white man gives the Negro what he thinks he needs, without showing the Negro a record of the income the white man has collected for the year. . . . This way of livelihood is not much different from slavery."[81] Volunteers in Holly Springs, one of Freedom Summer's most dynamic projects, received death threats, faced trumped-up police charges, found their tires slashed, and were subject to almost relentless indignities.[82] Yet, all that aside, and even in the face of the economic reprisals against black residents for which the town was well known, the summer volunteers successfully recruited about 150 Holly Springs residents to take the voter registration test.[83]

Like so many others in the summer of 1964, Anna Arnold Hedgeman tried to focus on the victories and on the fact of change, rather than on the inexorably slow pace of it, which she, better than most, understood.

13 MOVING THE JUSTICE FIGHT NORTH

On July 16, 1964, on New York's Upper East Side, an off-duty police officer shot and killed fifteen-year-old James Powell when he and his friends challenged a white building superintendent who had turned a water hose on black students. Police and eyewitness accounts differed significantly on whether or not the boy had brandished a knife before the white officer approached him and then shot him three times. One thing was certain: the officer shot the boy in the back. Six nights of insurrection followed, in Harlem and Brooklyn, resulting in one death, hundreds of injuries, and nearly five hundred arrests.[1]

Anna Arnold Hedgeman, who had been closely monitoring southern acts of violence from her desk at the Interchurch Center across town, was mournfully reminded of the distinction between the North and the South she had noted in 1924, when she moved north from Mississippi: it was the difference between a stiletto and an ax. Racism, she had learned, kills, regardless of the weapon, regardless of the location.[2] It was a lesson many Americans would learn as the civil rights movement began to shift its attention, in the mid-1960s, from the South to the North.

On behalf of the National Council of Churches, Hedgeman met with a group of Harlem residents to respond to the crisis. She left the meeting complaining bitterly about the ways her community was, yet again, so readily condemned as a violent, lawless place where police brutality was justified. She knew it, instead, as a complicated place where simmering summer heat drew out long-standing grievances and frustrations, of black youths in particular, and where police responses were often racist and unforgiving, even deadly.[3]

Over several days of turmoil, the public demanded changes in how the largely white police department and municipal government treated African American residents. In response, the city promised to address police brutality, increase the number of black police officers, and expand the channels of communication between African American communities and City Hall.[4] For Hedgeman, it was a clear case of too little, too late. As she knew all too well, from her days at the YWCA in the 1920s through her years in City Hall in the 1950s, Harlem had been ignored and underdeveloped for far too long, and violence was likely to continue if more fundamental and substantial reforms were not made.[5]

Anna Hedgeman had been making this case for some time. A few years earlier, in 1958, she had engaged in a public spat with *New York Post* journalist Stan Optowsky, who wrote, in a piece titled "Harlem as It Really Is," that "Harlem is a home that nobody loves—Harlem is a cultural center that cultural leaders flee." He wrote of Harlem's "ghastly past" and "inglorious present" and implied that Harlem suffered most principally from the deficits of its residents. In an extended rebuttal published in the *New York Age* and discussed widely in local media, Hedgeman provided Optowsky, and all white New Yorkers, with a history lesson on Harlem's "glorious past," from the Harlem YWCA to the community's struggles for black employment on 125th Street, from its prized black press to its progressive religious thought and action.[6] In explaining that Harlem was simultaneously underdeveloped and a wonderful, inspiring place to live, she made many Harlem residents proud. Only a person with Hedgeman's "yesterdays," her "intelligence, tact, and personality," as one woman explained, could do the topic justice.[7] Now, six years later and in the aftermath of so much violence and destruction, the incredible ease with which people dismissed or disparaged her community, and especially its young people, troubled her deeply.

Because the dire circumstances facing urban blacks crossed state lines, the spark of the Harlem uprising caught in other northern cities, leading to destruction of property, injury, and loss of life during the summer of 1964 in Philadelphia; Chicago; Jersey City and Elizabeth, New Jersey; and Rochester, New York. Hedgeman and her colleagues in the Commission on Religion and Race felt that they had to shift their attention away from Mississippi and toward these clamorous demands for justice so close to home. "Painful readjustment to insistent Negro voices," Robert Spike explained to the National Council of Churches, "will have to occur in the North as well as the South."[8] The staff set out to launch an interfaith, interracial response to the northern urban crisis, one that would emphasize local, grassroots expertise in urban centers in addition to the various resources the commission could marshal from civil rights organizations, university experts, organized labor, and, of course, the churches. The problems differed from the long-standing problems of the South. Transportation, for example, was integrated, but segregation in housing, education, and the workplace cost northern blacks dearly.

Since its founding, the CRR had a mandate to push white religious people toward racial reconciliation, a religious principle as fundamental as it was ignored. It had achieved some notable successes—the March on Washington, the passage of the 1964 Civil Rights Act, and the training of students for Freedom Summer—but when the staff changed its focus from the South to the North, they anticipated being accused of stepping over the line between "responsible witness" and "impulsive activism."[9] Executive director Spike warned, astutely and prophetically: "There will be those who will disapprove of this emphasis of the Commission. Many of them will be the same ones who supported our work when it was in the South."[10]

As the New York City–based staff talked more deliberately about the discrimination African American citizens faced in housing, employment, political organizing, and social services across the North, they realized they had to reach those who found racial justice an admirable goal from afar but might not be so enthusiastic about pursuing it closer to home. The CRR had to find ways to convince its constituency of white Christians a basic theological imperative: racism was, quite simply, a mocking of God that had to be faced and then eliminated.[11]

As a white man and a theologian, Robert Spike understood the complexities of the CRR's challenge. He viewed northern white Protestants as generally good people who tried to exercise fairness and generosity in their lives. Still, he recognized that racism ran deep, and that they were no more accustomed to exploring the discrimination institutionalized in their businesses, banks, political parties, real estate boards, and social and religious agencies than they were at reflecting on the role of racism in their personal lives. Their resistance might be unconscious, but it would be real and it would be strong. But Spike believed the church remained a unique institution with a distinct opportunity to act as a bridge between what he called "the new activism in the ghetto" and people living in "protected suburbs."[12] The CRR had its weapon: Christian theology and a justice-loving Jesus. Eager to play her part in racial reconciliation, particularly when it was paired with racial justice, Hedgeman embarked on yet another speaking tour, giving a series of talks, including one titled "Civil Rights and the Suburbs," to church, women's, and civic groups from Massachusetts to Kentucky, South Carolina to Oregon.

The CRR launched what it called the Northern Cities Project, developing guidelines to approach two pilot cities, Cleveland and Detroit. Both of these cities were feeling the effects of "white flight," the massive migration of whites from urban to suburban areas that resulted in greater segregation in housing and education, and skyrocketing rates of urban decay.[13] In both locations, they worked to ensure that local, grassroots leaders would be central to any social justice efforts, and that the white community would be involved as well.[14] In a move that Hedgeman felt was long in coming, representatives of black churches would be involved from the start, instead of being invited to participate once plans were underway, which had been common practice even within the National Council of Churches.[15]

Hedgeman encouraged the staff to let go of the notion of white Christians aiding or organizing black communities, and think instead of black and white, urban and suburban, wealthy and poor talking with each other and finding mutual solutions to the problems of white flight, joblessness, housing segregation, and inadequate education—problems of the city as a whole. If the idea that these were shared rather than "black problems" had to be sold to the CRR staff, one can imagine how difficult it was to sell to white citizens.[16] Most whites, even those who meant well, were still far more inclined toward "helping" African Americans from afar and patting themselves on the back for it than they were to actually affiliating themselves with them.

The Northern Cities Project provided seed money to strengthen integration efforts in communities in Detroit and Cleveland. It assisted suburban councils interested in developing interracial agendas, supported inner-city organizations furthering local leadership, and assisted with educational programs on the importance of integrated housing.[17] It developed a coalition of interreligious civil rights and social agencies and a program of citizenship education, much like the voter rights programs by now widely in use in the South. It trained young people to become leaders in their communities and challenged local white churches to shift their approach to urban problems from providing food, clothing, and temporary shelter to undertaking advocacy efforts to lessen—or ultimately eliminate—the need for such emergency services. The commission's overall aim was to bring a range of people on board to learn from each other, act in fellowship, and create lasting social change.[18]

As the CRR pushed farther and farther into the North, it met with greater and greater resistance. "The honeymoon is over for the Commission on Religion and Race," Robert Spike announced as early as 1965. "Even our friends show some unease."[19] Part of the problem, as Hedgeman saw it, was that the struggle in the South was "concrete and definitive," whereas unrest in the North proved confounding and elusive: it could not be narrowed down sufficiently to provide a single agenda item for people to rally around, like voting rights or public accommodations.[20] The closer one looked, the more urban problems seemed to multiply, and it was clear that as whites migrated to the suburbs, they hoped to leave nagging problems behind. Their economic prospects improved while the prospects of those left behind worsened, and the farther whites got from the problems geographically, the easier it was to dismiss them. Housing increasingly looked like an issue of property rights rather than of morality. Solidarity was a decidedly hard sell.

On top of that, white Americans who believed themselves to be fair or liberal or progressive did not appreciate being told they were receiving unfair advantages as they fled the cities and entered newly built—but segregated—neighborhoods and schools. The message was particularly fraught at a moment when marks of the good life, including the suburban house with the picket fence, were becoming more available to working-class whites—and increasingly symbolic of success in American life.[21] Many whites, as much as they self-identified as Christian, wanted the commission to back off.

The National Council of Churches had grown accustomed to critiques of its progressive approach to Christian life. Well before the establishment of the CRR, the NCC received complaints, some crackpot and some measured, about its efforts on behalf of racial justice. Some of the NCC's detractors urged southern Protestants not to contribute money to their churches if any of it went to the council. The council was branded, among other things, as a "satanic pseudo-religious organization" that circulated literature by Martin Luther King Jr. and others who favored racial integration.[22] Even early on, the attacks were not all from southerners. Northern critics also lashed out at desegregation efforts, echoing most often the obsession with liaisons between black men and white women that permeated the national consciousness.

One letter writer, assuming his NCC reader to be white and male, suggested that the group's efforts at desegregation would result in his daughter marrying a black man and having his baby. "If you do not want that, stop preparing for it," the man warned. The council staff responded carefully but pointedly to such letters, as Hedgeman had decades earlier when addressing white visitors in Harlem, deftly explaining that black people were far more concerned with jobs than with interracial marriage, an issue so far down their list of concerns that it almost never came up.[23]

Some letter writers used more subtle language, but the fear of miscegenation was a regular undercurrent in the complaints the National Council and then the Commission on Religion and Race received. One woman asked the CRR just how far the church should extend itself in matters of civil rights. Hedgeman, who had long since tired of the question of interracial sexual relationships, and who considered herself black, racially mixed, and quintessentially American, went to the heart of the matter. "From the point of view of some of us," she wrote in response, "the Church should be completely involved in all human issues until they are solved. This, it seems to me, is the commitment a Christian makes as he prays the Lord's Prayer."[24]

When she could, Hedgeman attempted to draw positive attention to the Northern Cities Project. She published an article titled "Toward the New City," outlining the project's efforts with Catholic and Jewish groups, its involvement with local business and political communities, and its attempts to bring black and white citizens together in the interest of planning for what she called the "whole city," an entity in which all people would face opportunities to craft decent lives.[25] She concluded with a religious invitation and admonition, noting that "our faith demands that His will be done, on earth and for all men."[26] But as time went on, the CRR felt its constituent churches shifting away from racial justice concerns and toward what Hedgeman, with regret, called "normal functions."[27] The commission felt the crunch. It had too little money to adequately take on the myriad problems posed by the urban/suburban crisis and had to rely more heavily on volunteers when it desperately needed additional staff. As much as the commission members valued the volunteer laborers and their efforts, they knew from their work in the South that paid staff produced more and better results.[28] Hedgeman wrote to Robert Spike, asking him to do more outreach to fund and staff the CRR, once again noting that women could serve as a vital resource.[29]

The impact of understaffing proved acute: in Cleveland, where the commission hoped to bring sixty thousand new voters to the polls, it succeeded in increasing the voter ranks by only ten to fifteen thousand. In Cleveland and Detroit, bringing blacks and whites together across metropolitan lines required not just the presence but also the cultivation of local interracial teams, an undertaking that required skilled staff. And as anticipated, they encountered northern white liberals in both cities whose enthusiastic leadership seemed to dissipate the closer the epicenter of change got to their own communities.[30] The CRR needed trained staff to persuasively communicate the theological underpinnings of their work, as well as of the work they needed others to take on.[31] As hard as it was to admit, when it came to its work in the North, the Commission on Religion and Race seemed unable to make a significant dent in either the problems facing black citizens or the endemic resistance of white Christians.[32]

As the Northern Cities Project proceeded in fits and starts, Hedgeman developed short-term consultation programs with other urban areas, specifically smaller cities, to share what the staff was learning in Detroit and Cleveland. As hard as they worked, and as committed as Hedgeman was to the CRR's goals, she felt more than a bit skeptical that their approach, which brought people together but left metropolitan political structures largely unchanged, would provide transformation rather than simple respite.[33] In Cleveland, for example, city officials had pushed through the cheap construction of new schools in black neighborhoods not to improve schooling but to forestall school integration.[34] Rather than accept the tired notion that "you can't fight City Hall," the activists the CRR supported and trained needed allies in city government.

Anna Arnold Hedgeman had left the New York City mayor's office in 1958, frustrated with the torpor that seemed to characterize municipal government, and in the midst of the Northern Cities Project she returned to the belief that citizens had to challenge the calcified political structure for meaningful policy changes to occur. As busy as she was at the CRR, she accepted the invitation of Democratic congressman William Fitz Ryan, who was running for mayor of New York, to join his ticket as a candidate for city council president, thus becoming the first woman and first black New Yorker to run for the office. Ryan had opposed the House Un-American Activities Committee, ardently supported civil rights initiatives, and taken a strong stand against war in Southeast Asia. He was a sound candidate, but not the party favorite, and fighting the Democratic establishment was always an uphill battle.

Hedgeman, who had strong support in New York's black communities, particularly in Harlem, gave Ryan's candidacy a stronger foothold. Once he settled on her, a New York paper reported, his ticket "came to life."[35] She took a two-week leave from work in the summer of 1965 and ran a purposeful but ultimately unsuccessful primary campaign. It is unlikely that she expected to win, particularly as an insurgent Democrat, but she was not one to pass up an opportunity to raise consciousness about what a more inclusive democratic process might look like—and result in—in a city like New York.[36]

Hedgeman was promoted as Eleanor Roosevelt's protégée, but the Democratic machine choice, Daniel Patrick Moynihan, tried to make her gender work against her rather than for her. When the Congress of Racial Equality endorsed Hedgeman's ticket rather than his, he attacked CORE as well. "If, for example," he scoffed, in spite of her well-known qualifications, "they prefer Mrs. Hedgeman to a man who has done the kind of things I have in the Kennedy and Johnson administrations, then something's wrong." In the end, regardless of the endorsement of many well-known New Yorkers, including Harry Belafonte, Betty Friedan, Ossie Davis, Diahann Carroll, and Eartha Kitt, and in spite of positive press coverage, the status quo prevailed. Hedgeman was defeated in the primaries, and the Democrats lost the election.[37] She was terribly frustrated with her fellow liberals or, as she couched it, "those who have previously termed themselves liberals," for remaining wedded to the status quo in a party so desperately in need of change.[38]

To make both the city council race and Hedgeman's work at the CRR more complicated, Daniel Patrick Moynihan achieved notoriety that summer when parts of an internal document he wrote while a member of President Johnson's Department of Labor were leaked to the media. The document, which became known as the Moynihan Report, advocated for some policy changes Hedgeman and the Commission on Religion and Race would have supported, including, among other things, jobs programs, an expanded War on Poverty, and family allowances for low-income households. Analyzing urban black life, Moynihan argued that underemployment and the resulting poverty produced few opportunities for black men to support their families, which had grown increasingly dependent on the efforts and earnings of black women. Had the document remained internal, or been through significant prepublication vetting, it might have generated valuable discussion of the need for the federal government to address the complicated issues of inequality.[39] Instead, the report, released immediately after five days of the worst urban rioting of the postwar period, in the Watts district of Los Angeles, appeared to have the stamp of approval of the president—it did not—and to support the idea that urban African American residents were responsible for the urban crisis rather than being its victims.[40] Because the Moynihan Report was filled with ambiguities and internal contradictions, it was then and remains today a significantly contested touchstone for examining racial inequality, particularly in the urban context.[41]

The Moynihan Report, blending "a bureaucratic report, an academic article, and a muckraking magazine feature," provided a muddled and confusing array of arguments and recommendations. It underemphasized policy recommendations and overemphasized sociological analysis, much of it victim blaming and misogynist. Using incendiary language to describe black men's inability to support their families, a problem many African American leaders were already well aware of, Moynihan turned the legacy of racist employment and economic policies into a critique of the black family. It was easy to conclude from this report, particularly the elements that were leaked, that slavery and discrimination had so damaged the black family that only change from within, rather than justice and resources from outside, could save it. The primary way to break the cycle of poverty, the Moynihan Report suggested, was to change black family structure. "After that," Moynihan wrote, "how this group of Americans chooses to run its affairs, take advantage of its opportunities, or fails to do so, is none of the nation's business."[42]

For white Americans who did not want to explore the issues too carefully, this inaccurate and shortsighted understanding of the black family, so different from postwar media representations of white families, made it easy to assign blame for what ailed the nation's urban centers to blacks themselves. It was equally easy to conclude that black women proved the biggest obstacle to black men's success. Centuries of oppression, Moynihan argued, had decimated the black family, creating a "tangle of pathology" and forcing black families into a "matriarchal structure" out of touch with the rest of American society. Black women, rather than lack of opportunity, hindered black men's full employment. "We will not rest," Moynihan wrote in a memo to Lyndon Johnson, "until every able-bodied Negro male is working. Even if we have to displace some females." Some male leaders found this male-breadwinner model compatible with their desires for the black community, but many African American women, including

Anna Hedgeman and Pauli Murray, found it problematic from the start. They well knew that African American women could hardly rely on the family-wage, male-breadwinner system Moynihan blithely and naively advocated.

Instead, many black women applauded the gender equality Moynihan found in African American families and spoke out about the enormous respect they had for black women's work. The report pathologized, or, as Hedgeman complained, presented as "guinea pigs," the women and families she had long worked with, those black women who "washed and ironed, scrubbed and cooked, took endless insults, saved nickels and dimes for tuition because there was not even a grade school in the community," and who themselves knew that the pivotal concern for the black family was economics.[43] Black families were not all alike, of course, contrary to the implications of the Moynihan Report, but if there was one thing they shared it was employment discrimination.

Hedgeman played a significant role in getting the Moynihan Report into the hands of religious and civil rights leaders, starting with one of her protégés, Benjamin Payton, director of the Office of Religion and Race at the Protestant Council, who would go on to launch one of the most scathing attacks on the report. Because Moynihan was one of Hedgeman's opponents in the New York City primary, Payton held off releasing his religiously informed critique of the Moynihan Report until after the primary, which neither candidate won. "I did not want people to say that I was looking for a way to keep Moynihan from getting votes," he explained. "I wrote the paper for much more important reasons."[44] Payton's critique echoed several others already circulating, attempting to shift the discussion from illegitimate births among black women to access to birth control and abortion among white women; from the irreparable damage wrought by slavery to the contemporary problems of inequitable opportunity; and from the malignancy of matriarchy to the black family's enormous coping skills in the face of substandard, often abysmal, housing, employment, and educational opportunities.[45] Over time other leaders, even those who largely supported the male-breadwinner model, spoke up on behalf of black women. As Martin Luther King Jr., explained, "No one in all history had to fight against so many psychological and physical horrors to have a family life."[46] Stokely Carmichael stated it in more colloquial terms: "The reason we are in the bag we are in isn't because of my mama, it's because of what they did to my mama."[47]

In the meantime, the CRR continued its work of documentation and action. As racial violence ravaged northern cities in the mid-1960s, the commission tallied each city's population, percentage of black citizens, injuries and deaths, estimated damage, triggers, police response, and related arrests and convictions.[48] Because they had always aspired to provide more than an emergency response in the wake of rioting, and instead hoped to motivate northern whites to make real changes in politics and in policy, the staff wanted to have data on hand to make their case. A unified attack on what they called "the shame of the cities" required serious consideration of race, poverty, and large-scale economic decision-making by multiple institutions, public and private. As the CRR staff observed the persistent, interconnected patterns of discrimination, they often concluded that racism in the North was so deeply embedded that those Robert Spike called "white men of goodwill" were unable to see it, never mind eradicate it. Hedgeman and her colleagues found it no easy task to educate people about the complexities of the urban crisis: the more complicated the message the CRR staff delivered, the more unwelcome it seemed to be.

Always advocating the Christian view of social justice, the commission tried to bring the life and message of Jesus Christ to bear on the urban crisis, and to return to basic principles: training people for jobs proved no substitute for actual jobs, and urging people to desegregate proved no substitute for building new, desegregated schools, neighborhoods, and hospitals in areas that had been long neglected.[49] As with so many civil rights groups in the last half of the 1960s, economics seemed to them to loom ever larger. The massive problems facing the nation's cities, they concluded, could not be solved locally, or city by city, but instead demanded national political and economic resolve, national political and economic resources. At the same time that the CRR began to articulate more forcefully that a massive influx of federal money was required to address the dire state of the nation's urban communities, the likelihood that it would happen lessened.

The federal government did make massive investments in the 1960s, but not in the cities. One of its growing commitments was the defense industry and the war in Vietnam, which Martin Luther King Jr. would come to call "an enemy of the poor."[50] In July 1965, rather than de-escalate the nation's commitment to war, President Johnson sent an additional fifty thousand troops to Vietnam, signaling his economic priorities.[51] In addition, the federal government provided enormous support for the growth of the suburbs in the form of highway funds, tax incentives, and homeownership subsidies. Despite the founding of some valuable programs like Head Start and the Job Corps, not nearly enough was done for the nation's poor.[52] As New York Times columnist James Reston worded it, President Johnson "overtalked and underfinanced. He declared a war on poverty and financed a skirmish."[53]

Urban riots in 1964 were followed by insurrections in cities across the country in 1965, 1966, and 1967, and with each act of rebellion, white support for the cities waned. Adequately translating black unrest in a way white communities could understand required massive communication skills as well as serious resolve, both of which seemed lacking in the nation's political and religious communities, with the Commission on Religion and Race one of the notable exceptions. The retreat from racial justice seemed rapid, even panicked. As the Vietnam War escalated, white liberals and white Christians shifted their focus, putting their efforts into antiwar activism and further moving civil rights off their agendas. With each instance of urban violence, more whites felt black Americans were pushing too hard for change, and civil rights groups began to experience a decline in donations.[54] Following Malcolm X's assassination, in February 1965, many black people too began to believe that white people should have little if any role in developing black communities. Black resistance to white "help" became more vocal and robust, providing perhaps both a convenient and a sincere reason for whites to abandon the cause of civil rights.

Whatever the impetus, the retreat was palpable. To Anna Hedgeman and her colleagues, it was clear evidence that northern white Protestants, who vilified southern racism and supported Christian efforts to eradicate it, or who felt comfortable providing Christian charity to black neighbors, were unwilling to exercise the introspection and commitment now required of them.

In January 1966, perhaps in part because he recognized that the CRR also needed black leadership, Robert Spike resigned as executive director. He became director of a nascent theology program at the University of Chicago, where he would focus on training students for urban ministries. Several months later, he was found murdered in a guest room on the campus of Ohio State University, where he had helped dedicate a new ecumenical Christian student center the night before. The NCC wanted to investigate, but Jack Pratt, the commission's general counsel, who had played a key role in supporting its civil rights efforts in Mississippi, warned against it: Spike was bisexual and allegedly killed during a sexual liaison with another man. Fearing a scandal, and giving in to their own homophobia, church officials managed to shut down the investigation, and no one was ever charged with Spike's murder.[55]

As forthright and progressive as the CRR was about matters of race, the group shared other prejudices of the time. Even Anna Hedgeman, oddly enough, who had worked closely with Bayard Rustin and had long-standing friendships with Pauli Murray, with writer and social activist Lillian Smith, and with lay theologian William Stringfellow, all of whom were openly gay, at least among their close friends, never mentioned Spike's tragic death in her notes, letters, or remembrances.[56] It is not clear how much of a deliberate decision the CRR made to go along with the cover-up, but the silence remains deafening.

At Hedgeman's urging, Benjamin Payton, a member of the National Baptist Convention, the nation's oldest and largest black religious denomination, and Hedgeman's ally in denouncing the Moynihan Report, was appointed Spike's successor at the Commission on Religion and Race.[57] From the Deep South, and in his early thirties, the Reverend Dr. Payton brought a new and different energy to the CRR. He literally moved up, from his office at the Protestant Council of the City of New York, also in the Interchurch Center, to the commission offices on the next floor. Payton, who considered Hedgeman a valuable mentor, agreed with her that national rather than regional or city-by-city approaches were necessary for real change to occur.[58] He terminated the Detroit pilot project, and soon after that the Cleveland project, and asked the staff to focus on President Johnson's upcoming conference, "To Fulfill These Rights," intended as a means of moving toward the equality promised in the 1964 Civil Rights Act and the 1965 Voting Rights Act.

Hedgeman and her colleagues, who had worked so hard legislatively, particularly on the 1964 Civil Rights Act, and who had grown disillusioned with the Northern Cities Project, were happy to shift their focus.[59] Legal changes, as important as they were, had not ushered in adequate income opportunities, equal housing, or the full rights of citizenship, and as Payton put it, the CRR's programs would fall short if they simply continued to "arouse strong desires without at the same time meeting basic needs."[60] The crisis in housing, he believed, was particularly volatile, but potentially resolvable if the recent legislation was fully implemented. Hedgeman realized that black frustration was both understandable and on the rise, as black Americans were "expected to take on the duties of citizenship without even the privileges of selecting a place to live, which is as much their right as it is the right of the white majority."[61]

When it looked like the White House conference would be taken up with Moynihan's "black family instability" and "problem of the matriarchal black family," rather than with what they considered the real issues, Payton and the CRR staff attempted to shift the focus to what he called "metropolitan stability." A group of about a hundred clergy and laypeople met to challenge the preliminary conference agenda, demanding that the black family be *an* agenda item, not *the* agenda item, and appointing Hedgeman and Payton as delegates through the planning and the actual White House conference.[62]

Despite their efforts, the conference proved an enormous disappointment. "When we reached Washington," Hedgeman explained, "we found that no resolutions were going to be permitted, that they had structured it so that most of the experts were white experts. We were up against a power structure at its best and worst."[63] Of twenty-five hundred invited guests at the June meeting, only 150 represented grassroots organizations, and the business community dominated the discussion. Incensed, Hedgeman complained to the press about the marginalization she and others felt. "I have a feeling I have been taking LSD," she said, intemperately. "This conference is unbelievable. My invitation didn't come until the 23rd of May. I don't know if they thought that Negroes don't have appointment calendars."[64]

Indeed, the speakers list had shifted considerably; instead of hearing from activists planning for the future, attendees heard from businessmen and politicians about past achievements.[65] Even top White House aide Harry McPherson remarked on the incongruity of business leaders "flying in aboard private jets to talk about people whose children ate the paint off windowsills."[66] Although the activists had managed to shift the agenda away from the black family, the conference failed to acknowledge poverty among any other ethnic or racial groups, or that poverty affected millions of white Americans.

The president's desire for consensus at the conclusion of the event dictated that few issues requiring extended deliberation would be discussed meaningfully during the conference, and it became clear that national economic priorities would not be challenged. As *New York Times* reporter John Herbes explained, the planning conference and the White House conference were, in the end, "full of sound and fury but little else."[67] The meeting drew to an end with no serious policy recommendations, and no indication that the Civil Rights Act of 1964 and the Voting Rights Act of 1965 would receive the federal backing they needed to ensure justice for all the nation's citizens. The conference seemed to exemplify one of Benjamin Payton's critical complaints, that white America "has always related well to the poor Negro. It is the intelligent Negro that has been his problem."[68] Hedgeman's frustration was enormous. A liberal Democrat, she believed that a central role of national government was to further democracy, opportunity, and equality, but the White House conference demonstrated a superficiality that seemed endemic and unyielding, illustrating just how poor an ally the federal government could be.

14 BLACK POWER, WOMAN POWER

Four days after the conclusion of the White House conference that had focused on the black family, in problematic ways as far as Anna Hedgeman was concerned, violence struck again in the South. James Meredith, who just a few years earlier had been the first black student to enroll in the segregated University of Mississippi, was shot and wounded. He had embarked on a march, the Meredith March against Fear, from Memphis, Tennessee, to Jackson, Mississippi, to publicize the rights guaranteed by the 1965 Voting Rights Act. Many civil rights leaders joined him, and Stokely Carmichael famously coined the phrase "Black Power" along the route. "We been saying freedom for six years and we ain't got nothin'," Carmichael shouted. "What we gonna start saying now is Black Power!"[1]

How ironic that "Black Power" was born in Mississippi, the poorest state in the nation, where 85 percent of all black families lived below the poverty line and where white citizens believed that "keeping the Negro in his place" was their shared responsibility.[2] The phrase proved almost immediately transformative for young people tired of the glacially slow nature of change. It suggested that black activists could think, plan, and act on their own, without the involvement of white leaders; that blacks had as much right to defend themselves as anyone else; and that blacks did not have to beg for power—like whites, they could assume it.[3] It also provided a clear manifestation of a changing of the guard, from Martin Luther King Jr.'s pleas for nonviolence to younger activists' demands for justice, *now.*

Members of the commission staff were among the few people in the civil rights establishment who did not rush to condemn a phrase that, simply by linking "black" and "power," terrified so many.[4] For Anna Hedgeman, who had long analyzed "whiteness," the terminology held promise, since she believed the real threat to the nation was not black power but the combination of white power and black powerlessness. She remarked, wryly, "There was never such excitement about the dogs, fire hoses, and police officials turned loose on

would-be voters and young students as there was over Stokely's agonized recognition of the need for 'Power.'"[5] In response to what she considered "hysteria," and
to her great delight, Benjamin Payton suggested that the commission develop a
response not by soliciting it from its standard audience, the nation's large white
Protestant denominations, but instead by inviting the major black denominations to come together to give black power serious theological consideration in
advance of any pronouncement about its value or viability.[6]

In what Anna Hedgeman considered one of the most significant civil rights
gatherings of the era, a group of almost fifty black clergy from black as well as
predominantly white denominations gathered in July 1966 to form a new organization, the National Committee of Negro Churchmen (NCNC), which they
envisioned as a link between the churches and the nascent but rapidly growing black power movement. They elected Hedgeman secretary and, in the end,
treated her—the only woman and the only layperson in the group—as a full
member of the activist religious body.

Although her contributions as a religious thinker and advocate have not
been adequately documented or honored, it is almost certain that Hedgeman
helped formulate the theological response to black power the NCNC put forward.[7] In fact, the Reverend James Breeden, who served with Hedgeman on
the Commission on Religion and Race, and who remembers her Christianity
as formative for the commission as a whole, believes she may have initiated
the idea of the NCNC and provided key elements of its theological underpinnings.[8] She had, after all, long considered the ways white power precluded true
Christian practice, and had delivered messages about unchecked white power
to white audiences as far back as her days at the Harlem YWCA. Some listeners
would balk, but others saw her work as critical to advancing white Americans'
consciousness about race. Among her many recent invitations, Hedgeman had
been asked to serve as a planner and facilitator for the first Conference on White
Power for Black People, held in New Jersey. With good reason, Benjamin Payton
continued to look to her for guidance as he promoted the NCNC and entered
the national spotlight. When the group emphasized that its goal was to live out
the Lord's Prayer by working toward heaven on Earth, rather than waiting for it
later, it is hard not to see Anna Arnold Hedgeman's imprint, since this had been
her refrain, in speeches and in written documents, for decades. "Take Jesus to
your community," she would admonish, reminding people that Jesus had been
and continued to be at work in this world, not the next.[9]

Once again, Hedgeman found herself in a strange position. She was, by all
accounts, able to exercise significant influence in the group. Gayraud Wilmore,
its cofounder and later one of the key scholars of black theology, the religious
philosophy that emerged from the work begun by the NCNC, remembered her

well. "She did not wait for the men to offer her a seat at the table," he recalled. "She took it." Wilmore remembered Hedgeman as feisty and outspoken, noting that she had to have a great deal of inner strength to claim a place as a woman among these men. "There she was!" he recalled, still impressed almost fifty years later at how she inserted herself fully and effectively into critical conversations. Each statement the group put forward includes her signature not in a sidebar or footnote as secretary but as a member of the group; each seems to include her imprint as well.[10]

Hedgeman's interest in black power was long-standing. When she moved to Harlem in the late 1920s, she declared herself a black nationalist, realizing her need to live apart from whites in order to experience her full humanity. She had been a member of the original March on Washington Movement, the all-black organization founded to force desegregation of the armed forces and for war-related jobs for black Americans. Even after she abandoned her decision to live and work apart from whites, she continued to work closely with black nationalists. In her "One Woman's Opinion" newspaper column in the 1950s, she counseled blacks to follow the lead of the Irish, Jews, and Italians who had claimed autonomous political and economic power in New York City.[11] She spoke, along with Malcolm X, at a 1962 symposium titled "The Negroes in Our Cities," where she explained that the problem of the inner city was not black nationalism, but white, which distorted white and black people's understandings of each other and themselves.[12] Black power, Hedgeman believed, was a Christian imperative, one that could provide a corrective to abusive and myopic white power. Although the word "empowerment" was not in widespread use then, it captures precisely what she meant when she used the term "black power": the critical empowerment of black Americans.

Nevertheless, Hedgeman was made doubly invisible by the organization's name, the National Committee of Negro Churchmen, since she was neither a minister nor a man, and by the proclamations it put forward, which repeatedly equated black power, theological and otherwise, with black masculinity. In 1968, in keeping with cultural changes in the black community, the group changed its name from the National Committee of Negro Churchmen to the National Committee of Black Churchmen, but even as black women began to challenge the group's gender assumptions, the committee refused to support the ordination of women and resisted adopting a more inclusive name, the National Conference of Black Christians, for more than fifteen years.[13]

The first official act of the NCNC was to publish a statement, "Black Power," in full-page advertisements in the *New York Times* and the *Chicago Tribune*. The controversy over black power, the group noted, was not new, "but the same old problem of power and race which has faced our beloved country since 1619."[14]

They pointed out that whites regularly used power to achieve their goals but that blacks were expected only to appeal to white conscience. "The power of white men is corrupted," they wrote, "because it meets little meaningful resistance from Negroes to temper it and keep white men from aping God."

The NCNC statement included appeals to four groups of people. To political leaders, the clergy noted that the failure to use power appropriately had led to the urban riots, and that black power, like white power, was a critical component of positive change. To white clergy who preached love rather than power, they urged that "what love opposes is precisely the misuse and abuse of power, not power itself." To black citizens, they pleaded for resistance to the idea that calls for black power would erase hard-won civil rights gains: "If those gains are in fact real, they will withstand the claims of our people for power and justice, not just for a few select Negroes here and there, but for the masses of our citizens." Finally, to the mass media, they praised efforts on behalf of justice in the South but reminded them, shrewdly, "so must you operate in New York City, Chicago, and Cleveland."

As Christian leaders, the members of the NCNC urged the nation to put its collective power toward rebuilding the cities. "This is more important," they wrote, "than who gets to the moon first or the war in Vietnam." As for the urban riots, they viewed them in Christian terms, as God's judgment on the nation for "its failure to use its abundant resources to serve the well-being of people, at home and abroad."[15] The organization not only helped translate black power for thousands of black and white Americans but also began the work of formulating a new theological framework, black theology, which redefined "black," redefined "power," and furthered the notion that Christianity is, fundamentally, a radical philosophy and practice of liberation.[16]

The NCNC statement received a mixed response. Some churches ordered reprints by the hundreds, eager to use the statement in study groups organized around understanding the nascent cries for black power. Other churches castigated the NCNC, labeling its member clergy renegades or apostates.[17] But the organization grew, and when it issued its next statement, in anticipation of a white backlash in the November 1966 elections, it accompanied its *New York Times* piece with a media event. Roughly 150 black-robed clerics from twenty states gathered at Trinity Church in lower Manhattan, then walked in a procession to Battery Park and onto a ferry to the Statue of Liberty. "Listen, America!" Benjamin Payton intoned as they stood in front of Lady Liberty. "You have no right to demand of Negro Americans a perfection of morality before you decide that he is worthy of his rights. They're not yours to give! They are the gift of God to the country, and He will take it away from all of us unless all of us share them!"[18]

Because housing issues seemed the likeliest source of white backlash, and white candidates in the upcoming election had started emphasizing the theme of "a man's home is his castle," Payton spoke about open housing. "Nobody denies that," he said of the home-castle analogy. "What we do deny is the right of white Americans to carve out whole sections of this land and to declare that white citizens only may live there." The *New York Times* gave the event ample and respectful coverage. Again, Anna Hedgeman was there, the only woman and only layperson present, robed, and integrated into the day's events.[19]

The National Council of Churches supported the National Committee of Negro Churchmen, providing office space and allowing Hedgeman to work for the group as part of her NCC assignment. She helped draft the NCNC's proposal for a National Economic Development Bank, which would have financed urban renewal, and then solicited support from, among others, New York's Republican governor, Nelson Rockefeller, with whom she had a long working relationship.[20] She served as the only female speaker and the only woman on the organizing committee for a 1968 black power conference sponsored by the New York chapter of the National Conference of Christians and Jews.[21] She organized, attended, or spoke at a number of other black power meetings and conferences and publicly complained about or wrote critical letters to civil rights organizations, including the YWCA, the NAACP, and the Urban League, about their rejection of young people's demands for black power. Hedgeman believed that power was fundamentally American, part of what it meant to be part of a democracy, and a right of black as well as white Americans. She felt inspired by a Jesus who remained, as she put it in 1966, "vigorous, involved, and thank God, controversial."[22]

Perhaps because she was still bothered by the ways in which women were treated at the March on Washington, or in the Moynihan Report, or in her own professional life, or perhaps because she was thinking more and more about black women's history, which would become one of her passions in retirement, Anna Hedgeman took on Martin Luther King Jr.'s interpretation of black power, which she considered negative and incomplete, particularly when it came to women. "It occurs to me to remind you that you are a national and international leader because of Black Power," she wrote to King in 1966, in response to his dubbing the slogan "Black Power" an "unwise choice."[23] Invoking Rosa Parks and the women of the Montgomery Improvement Association, all of whom she believed had been slighted from the first days of the famed bus boycott to the present, she told him, "If the MIA had not been organized for a number of years; if that movement had not developed goals and some procedures and strategies; if the inspiration of it had not caused Rosa Parks to act; there might have been no force to call you from your pulpit to the leadership of the Movement."

"Essentially," she told Dr. King, claiming a place for women as originators of this critical stage of the black freedom movement, "your Nobel Peace Prize came from the same source of 'Black Power.'"[24]

Hedgeman also struggled to make the staff of the Commission on Religion and Race understand the workings of gender. When the National Council of Churches sent a memo to staff alerting them to National Secretaries Day and joking that staff members might offer their secretaries some aspirin to help them deal with life at the Interchurch Center, Hedgeman, the only woman on the commission staff, bristled. She shot off her own memo, equating National Secretaries Day with Brotherhood Week, the patronizing Protestant staple that had white Christians spend one week out of the year making overtures to their black "brothers." Just as black Christians had to determine what kind of brotherhood they wanted, secretaries ought to be the ones to define National Secretaries Day, she wrote. When she asked the secretaries how they would like to observe the event, they told her they wanted the day off. "How do I respond?" she queried her male bosses, prompting at least some consideration of the treatment of women employees in the organization.[25]

Gender issues would become more and more pressing for Anna Hedgeman, prompting her to become a founding member of one of the most influential women's rights organizations of the twentieth century. In 1966, a number of women, including Hedgeman, gathered in Washington, DC, to map out a new organization. Sometimes called the "NAACP for women," and clearly modeled after black freedom efforts, the National Organization for Women (NOW) appealed to a range of activists who had been, some for many decades, laboring to improve the lives of working women.[26] Betty Friedan may be the most prominent of the group, as she served as NOW's first president and wrote what became a vital book for white, middle-class women, *The Feminine Mystique*, but a number of black women were involved in NOW, in instrumental ways, from its founding. It was Pauli Murray who suggested to Friedan that creating a network of women would help move all women into the mainstream of American political life—and who suggested that Friedan include Hedgeman among the founders. "I shall certainly respond favorably," Hedgeman wrote to Murray, "because nobody knows better than I do the need for a militant action organization concerned with the affairs of women."[27]

Anna Hedgeman did become a founding member of NOW, and one of the first five national officers, serving for a time as executive vice president and convening a task force on women and poverty. She pushed the fledgling organization to recognize that the most serious discrimination against women, regardless of race, was at the bottom of the economic ladder.[28] She used her experience in the Commission on Religion and Race to educate other founders of NOW about the costs of poverty, presenting data to show that African Americans earned less but paid more for housing and many consumer goods.[29] Not surprisingly, under her influence the Women in Poverty Task Force advocated for job innovation, equality in education and job training, and, most important, full employment. She also pushed NOW to be more activist and less bureaucratic. When it proposed to undertake a study on the poor women she talked about, she told the board that poor women had been studied enough; it was time to listen to their ideas and opinions.[30]

Hedgeman saw the organization as a way to bring together many of her concerns. She hoped that NOW would represent all women but pay special attention to the challenges faced by poor women and women of color. Recognizing that many of the early NOW leaders were both white and relatively privileged, she asked them to sign on to the initiatives that emerged from her civil rights and antipoverty work in the Commission on Religion and Race. When she knew she would miss an important meeting, she drafted a quick note to Pauli Murray: "I'm counting on you to hold 'Poverty,'" she wrote.[31] Hedgeman also helped draft the NOW statement of purpose, which certainly seems to bear her mark. "We realize that women's problems are linked to many broader questions of social justice; their solution will require concerted action by many groups," the group stated. "Therefore, convinced that human rights for all are indivisible, we expect to give active support to the common cause of equal rights for all those who suffer discrimination and deprivation, and we call upon other organizations committed to such goals to support our efforts toward equality for women."[32]

Although many people believe that the second wave of feminism was populated almost wholly by white women, other black women also played formative roles in the development of NOW.[33] Aileen Hernandez, a former union organizer and then a commissioner in the federal Equal Employment Opportunity Commission, became NOW's second president. Addie Wyatt and Dorothy Robinson, members of the Negro American Labor Council who had joined Hedgeman in protesting the exclusion of women as speakers at the March on Washington, left the council to join NOW.[34] Shirley Chisholm, who would later win a landslide election to the US Congress, founded the first regional NOW chapter, in New York. Hedgeman's friend Septima Clark, widely recognized for having founded citizenship schools throughout the Deep South, soon joined, declaring a bit later, "I'm all for women's liberation," and lamenting how long it took for women to speak up about their needs.[35] And Eleanor Holmes Norton, a SNCC worker who joined the staff of the March on Washington and later became a member of Congress from Washington, DC, found the transition from civil rights to women's rights a natural one.[36] Other women of color joined as well, at Hedgeman's urging. She recruited her close friend Inez Casiano, a Puerto Rican activist from East Harlem, to become a founder; Casiano joined the board and stayed involved in NOW for the rest of her life.[37]

The National Organization for Women provided a space for women like Anna Hedgeman, who had found themselves discriminated against in the same social movements and professions that gave them passion, purpose, and serious political and analytical skills.[38] "There is no civil rights movement to speak for women," the group explained in its statement of purpose, "as there has been for Negroes and other victims of discrimination. The National Organization for Women must therefore begin to speak."[39] The organization's broad agenda, equality for women in public life, provided many opportunities for activism.[40] "Our first order of business," explained founding president Betty Friedan, "was to make clear to Washington, to employers, to unions and to the nation that someone *was* watching, someone *cared* about ending sex discrimination."[41]

One of the first targets of the new organization, in part because of the emphasis of Hedgeman and Murray, was economic discrimination. They pushed to eliminate want ads that specified "Help Wanted Male" or "Help Wanted Female," restricting the most lucrative positions to men and keeping women out of a number of professions. At Hedgeman's urging, NOW supported legislation for women around issues of social security, day care, welfare payments, and tax deductions for working parents.[42] For her, this was one more way of making the demands she and others had been making for decades more inclusive. And, despite another common misconception about the women's movement, several early leaders of NOW purposefully brought their religious convictions to bear on their gendered activism.[43] Still employed by the Commission on Religion and Race when she helped found NOW, Hedgeman saw nothing incompatible about her desire for racial justice, religious justice, and justice for women. They had all been part of the same thing throughout her life, and now they came together in her activism.

But as Hedgeman felt, finally, that she could bring her multiple identities together in her work for social justice, the pendulum was swinging away from civil rights, particularly as proponents, including King, spoke more deliberately about economics. In the end, the retreat of the religious and the resulting demise of the Commission on Religion and Race were rapid.[44] As early as 1965, Robert Spike had warned his staff that their unprecedented activism might not be tolerated for much longer. "What is yet to be decided," he wrote, "is how long such an enterprise can continue. How great is the tolerance of the society of one of its major symbol systems knocking other parts of the system? Is the Commission a fluke, dependent to a large degree upon the uniqueness of the historical situation—the time being ripe—or can there be patterns developed from these experiences that will be useful over a longer period, and for wider purposes of social change?"[45]

Early in 1967, the NCC reabsorbed the Commission on Religion and Race into its massive bureaucracy, eliminating its all-important autonomy and reducing it to little more than a task force. Hedgeman's promotion to associate director for racial justice meant little when race no longer played a prominent role in the NCC's planning. The talk was that Benjamin Payton was too radical. When he left to become president of Benedict College in his native South Carolina, Hedgeman was delighted that he was going to lead a historically black college in the South, but she knew his departure did not bode well for race work in Christian communities.[46]

In the fall of 1967, at a national board meeting in Atlanta, Anna Hedgeman discovered, to her surprise and chagrin, that the organization had announced her retirement in the conference program. Yes, the NCC had a mandatory retirement age, and at sixty-eight, she was beyond it, but no one had spoken with her about this milestone. She saw the anonymous gesture as both inhumane and telling. Back in New York, the director of her division apologized. The personnel department had automatically submitted her papers and he, buried in bureaucracy, had not been aware of it until the board meeting. He raised the possibility of hiring her to do some consulting work, but when he did not follow up, Hedgeman knew not only that she was leaving but that her religion and race projects would fade away with her departure from the NCC.

Anna Hedgeman stayed on the national board of the National Organization for Women until after she retired from the National Council of Churches, playing a strategic role as the organization defined itself. Thanks to her influence, NOW got office space at the Interchurch Center. One of the organization's mandates was to ensure that the federal government's Equal Employment Opportunity Commission, the organization designed to carry out the mandate of the Fair Employment Practices Committee for which she had worked so hard two decades earlier, eliminated gender discrimination in the workplace. Hedgeman made sure her voice was heard, advocating for her friend and fellow board member, Inez Casiano, to be appointed an EEOC commissioner, and for Pauli Murray to be appointed EEOC general counsel. She worked the other side, too, pushing the Commission on Religion and Race and other religious bodies to get on board in support of women's rights.[47]

Hedgeman struggled to figure out her relationship to the growing feminist movement. As much as she advocated for women's rights, she had grown weary of putting energy into organizations that relied for their definition on one element of identity, whether that was race, gender, or religion. On the face of it, race did not play a significant role in her departure from the board of NOW. Perhaps she, like many other women of color, was troubled by the idea, promoted by some feminists, that men as a group were the main culprits in women's oppression. The black men in her life had so little economic or social power they could hardly be called "the oppressors." But Hedgeman was no political neophyte, and she was not in the habit of leaving organizations when she had differences with other members, even on fundamental issues. Pauli Murray resigned before Hedgeman did, over what she considered Betty Friedan's autocratic leadership, the organization's narrow focus, Murray's refusal to identify solely on the basis of gender, and the lack of representation of poor women.[48] Hedgeman too complained about the "leaders," most likely referring to Friedan, but she remained committed to legislative action; regardless of its limitations, she believed NOW could play an important role in mandating equality for women.[49]

In the end, a form of structural discrimination edged Hedgeman out of the National Organization for Women. It expected its board members to support the organization financially, and she did not have the means to do that.[50] As long as she remained employed by the Commission on Religion and Race, she had an employer-supported link to NOW. But once she retired, nearing seventy and with almost no financial cushion, Anna had to regroup and think about herself, her husband, Merritt, and their life together in a new way.[51] She did not fight the NOW rule; instead, she resigned. Hedgeman herself had long chastised African Americans who did not provide financial support to labor unions and civil rights organizations; she herself had done so, loyally, even in times of hardship, and it must have been painful for her to realize she no longer could.

For more than four years, racial justice and, with Hedgeman's urging, gender justice had become visible in American Protestantism, but gender justice never really took hold, and racial justice too quickly lost its centrality in Christian theology and practice. An astute secular spokesperson, Hedgeman could and did articulate the religious imperative of recognizing and righting power imbalances by examining not just the elements of power as they were used against black people (economic power, political power) but also the more hopeful responses (Christian power, black power, the power of women). But the National Council of Churches deemed Hedgeman redundant, and it was time to move on. She began to cancel appointments for 1968, abandoning projects already in place and those in the planning stages, realizing that the heady days of church-based activism on issues of religion and race had, by and large, ended.[52] She accepted the National Council's customary retirement gift, a Bible, but politely refused a party; after all, approaching seventy but still feeling young, Anna Arnold Hedgeman had no intention of retiring from public life as an active, public force for justice.

15 REFUSING RETIREMENT

THE HEDGEMAN CONSULTANT SERVICE

Until Anna Arnold Hedgeman was faced with the reality of her forced retirement, she had not thought of her age as a barrier of any kind; in fact, she had barely thought about it at all. Now, though, as she began to wind down her work at the National Council of Churches, she felt more than a bit of trepidation. For one thing, she could hardly afford to retire. Long ago, she and Merritt had drafted a shared "declaration of independence," but this path, while righteous and rewarding, had not been an easy one. She accepted that her own life choices had kept her struggling financially. "I could have been sitting here rich," she believed, "but I had always to be me."[1] She expected to work for pay for some time to come, and she saw no reason not to. Both Anna and Merritt had experienced some health issues, but they approached their seventies still feeling healthy and strong, and neither of them was ready to retire.

Hedgeman believed she could actually be more effective professionally than ever before. She had by now fused together an unusual array of experiences and had refined an approach to articulating the cause of justice for a range of Americans, old and young, black and white, male and female, religious and secular, activist and establishment.[2]

Having played a key role in the nation's most dynamic racial justice efforts from the 1920s through the 1960s, Hedgeman had achieved a lived understanding of what some historians would come to call the long civil rights movement.[3] She wanted to continue to use that experience to help people, organizations, and legislative bodies move forward. She had worked with people of every political and religious stripe, in and out of government, in and out of the religious community, in and out of her beloved Harlem community. She had learned that the federal government could be an important ally in the fight for racial justice, but that there was nothing automatic, assured, or unproblematic about that support.

She had learned something similar about the church: as much as fairness and equality were inscribed in religious texts, nothing guaranteed their implementation. God was on her side, she had no doubt, but his followers had proved fickle far too often. Hedgeman had also grown in her understanding of racial difference, seeing race simultaneously as artificial and consequential: paradoxically, she wanted white people to forget she was black and yet never to forget she was black. And regardless of ongoing frustrations, her faith, determination, and experience provided her with ample energy to want to continue to engage in the world.

As she packed up her belongings at the Interchurch Center, Anna Hedgeman realized that within days she would have no job title, no employer, no organizational framework, and no income aside from a small Social Security pension. She recognized, grudgingly, that she had entered a whole new category of the disenfranchised: the elderly. It occurred to her that many other women and men must also be "at the peak of their powers," as she put it, also facing a thwarted desire "to give service in the world of work."[4] Hedgeman might not have been alone in feeling angry at being pushed aside because of her age, but she still felt isolated, lacking the language to describe what we now call "ageism" and think of alongside racism and sexism. "I knew," she explained, "that I could not turn off the accumulated comprehensions that had been achieved because of a birthday date."[5] It would take other members of her generation, facing discrimination in employment, insurance, health care, and housing, while still feeling vital and engaged, to found the first advocacy organizations for older people, the Gray Panthers and the American Association of Retired Persons (AARP).[6]

But in 1968, the AARP had not yet been founded, the Gray Panthers was a fledgling and relatively unknown organization, and the Hedgemans were on their own figuring out how to spend their remaining years actively and comfortably, in their own characteristically modest way. Merritt continued to work but did not earn enough to support the two of them by lecturing on Negro spirituals, or with his singing, which he often did accompanied by Anna's sister Olive, a pianist and composer. Had he been white, Merritt surely would have been able to take advantage of far more opportunities, but in the late 1960s and the 1970s there were still innumerable obstacles for black artists trying to get performance dates and recording contracts, even in New York City.[7] Now he faced the additional obstacle of age.

In keeping with their declaration of independence, and wanting to ensure that young black artists would encounter better prospects than he had, Merritt devoted much of his time to serving on the board of the Waltann School for the

Creative Arts in Brooklyn. A founding member, he helped shape the school's philosophy, which maintained that "creativity is not the exclusive possession of genius" but, instead, that "all of us can use it, if we will, to deepen and enrich our lives." Waltann focused on providing young people, particularly those who were likely to be overlooked, with training and evaluation by working artists. The school provided inexpensive classes and career counseling to children referred from foster homes, public schools, and other institutions.[8] Needless to say, Merritt's work with Waltann was unpaid.

In her final days at the National Council of Churches, as Anna Hedgeman made calls to cancel consultations with a variety of people, she discovered that many were reluctant to sever their ties not only with the NCC, which had made no plans to replace her in this work, but also with Hedgeman herself. "We want you," she heard again and again. "How can we be in touch with you?"[9] She suggested to several contacts that she could continue to work with them if they paid a consultancy fee and covered her travel costs, and each of them enthusiastically agreed. She and Merritt felt inspired enough by this to form the Hedgeman Consultant Service, based out of their Lenox Terrace apartment in Harlem.[10]

"In these days of women's liberation," Hedgeman remembered a decade later, "I must pay special attention to my husband who has always studied and planned with me."[11] Now, though, Merritt did more to support Anna's career than at any previous time, devoting much of his energy to getting the business off the ground, then helping to manage Anna's demanding schedule. He organized a portfolio of her work, including speeches, interviews, newspaper pieces, and radio broadcasts, editing her most pressing concerns and promising solutions into succinct form. From there, Anna developed talks for a variety of audiences and occasions and utilized her vast national network of connections to get contracts with white as well as black groups, and with organizations serving children as well as adults.

The Hedgemans decided on an approach to the business that would maximize Anna's consulting opportunities while leaving her time for reading, maintaining connections with civil rights organizations and leaders, and keeping up with current events. She continued some of her community work, including serving as vice president of the Harlem NAACP, but now let go of some of her volunteer efforts and tried to fold others into her consulting practice.[12] She honed her expertise in black history, in legislative history, and in issues like housing and education. Since many white organizations that had been part of the civil rights movement had by now turned their attention to the Vietnam War, she read as much as she could on colonialism, war, and Southeast Asia.

Anna Hedgeman vehemently opposed the Vietnam War. It was not just that it took desperately needed economic resources away from what she and other civil rights leaders considered national priorities; Hedgeman, with her long view of the twentieth century, saw clear and disturbing links between World War II and the war in Vietnam. She knew from her husband's experience, as well as her own work on behalf of wartime and permanent fair employment legislation, that black soldiers during World War II could neither serve to their capacity nor secure the respect they deserved for the military service they did provide. While many things had changed, the same forces of discrimination were at work in Vietnam, where black soldiers were killed at rates well above their representation in the military population.[13]

In 1966, in response to the needs of the war machine and under pressure to create opportunity for low-income youths, President Johnson launched Project 100,000, which relaxed requirements for enlistment in order to recruit more underprivileged Americans into the military. In wartime, of course, this meant these young men went directly into combat. Black soldiers recruited into the program were wildly overrepresented and also sustained casualty rates twice those of men in any other category in the military. Hedgeman felt she had to oppose the war "as definitively as possible."[14] Among other things, in 1968 she served as one of the sponsors of the Jeannette Rankin Brigade, a peaceful march on Washington of ten thousand women in protest against the war.[15]

Consultancy work put Anna Hedgeman in contact with a range of audiences. Sometimes she spoke to all-white audiences, but she refused to address only "black problems," instead turning the audience's attention to the problems of the "whole" society, often to the consternation of her listeners. If they hoped she would help them think through racial issues from a distance, they were mistaken; she always counseled them, in a respectful but firm manner, that the responsibilities of citizenship included a serious and sustained commitment to furthering racial justice.[16] As she had decades earlier at the Harlem YWCA, Hedgeman grew exasperated when whites asked her what it was that black people really wanted, revealing how little they had been listening or learning through the tumult over the years.

"It seemed incredible," she fumed, "that all of the agitation in the South and in northern cities should not have produced a white citizenry not only aware of what Negroes wanted but also embarrassed that Black people should even have had had to ask for it, sit-in for it, stand-in, wade-in, march-in, or even make a request for it."[17] Still, she never gave up. "Don't waste any time being 'ashamed of white people,'" she counseled one white woman who wrote to her. "You and I must help them find maturity. I still believe that it can be done and I trust that you do also."[18]

Hedgeman often found herself serving in the position of referee, negotiating conflicts between young and old, black and white. When she was in mixed black and white audiences, she tried to get the two groups to talk with each other, but she increasingly felt that more preaching and less listening were taking place—on both sides. The late 1960s and the 1970s witnessed a distinct backlash against civil rights, with many white Americans responding to increased tensions by pulling back from rather than leaning in to change, with their votes or with their dollars. The black cultural nationalism then in vogue, elements of which she approved of, frustrated her too, particularly when it seemed to reduce blackness to skin color or hair texture. Hedgeman grew exasperated with young black people who viewed white people as the enemy, who refused to actually listen to her or to anyone else, or who made blanket assertions about black identity, as though there were one black identity. When a young artist copied Leonardo da Vinci's *Last Supper* and painted each disciple a different color, with Judas pictured as the only white apostle, Hedgeman countered that such tokenism was inaccurate and irresponsible. The artist informed her she simply was not black enough to understand.[19]

Hedgeman would often try to get black and white groups to enhance their working relationships by separating them first. She would work with each group, and then at some point she would say to the blacks, "He is learning. Give him a little time. Explain to him. Tell him the truth." Then she would shuttle back across the room, down the hall, or across town to the white group and say, "You are making progress. Go back again. Say these things to the groups you have been working with that you have been saying to me."[20] For those whites who continued to insist that such cooperation would lead to interracial sexual relationships, particularly between black men and white women, she developed a comic but heartfelt response: "If you can't resist us, we do insist upon matrimony. All of the other arrangements have been tried."[21]

She also spent a good deal of time trying to explain young black people to their elders. She had not hesitated to take on Martin Luther King Jr. when he railed against black power, and she took on many far less famous people closer to home. Some older black residents of Harlem, with a deeper historical memory of the freedom movement and how things used to be, still walked through local banks to get a look at black clerks when they were hired. Now many of their children and grandchildren scoffed at opportunities in the business world, focusing instead on the stark reality that despite middle-class educations and jobs, black Harlemites still could not get a cab to or from their homes. Older black Americans had struggled for decades to ensure that their children could attend integrated colleges that had once been segregated institutions, and now a number of young black people were demanding black-only dormitories and social spaces.

As much as integration seemed a project of hope to one generation, it seemed a project of despair to the next. Young people noted with disgust, with anger, and, as Hedgeman pointed out, with good reason, that integration seldom seemed to be a two-way process. People moved from "inferior" black schools or neighborhoods into "superior" white ones; the reverse simply did not happen. Implicitly, such integration efforts suggested that it was not underfunding that hurt schools and neighborhoods but rather the presence of blacks in them. Why should young black people listen to white people who fabricated such nonsense, or to older black people who tolerated it, or who even endorsed it through their aspirations? "Distrust," she lamented, "was the order of the day."[22]

Scholars have pointed to the "bridge" role that black women have so often taken on, mediating differences within and among various communities.[23] Anna Hedgeman, long accustomed to this role, continued it through the 1970s and into the 1980s, as she developed consultancies with schools, colleges, churches, and civic and political groups. One of the ongoing issues she mediated was that of language. What term should Americans of African descent use to name themselves: Negro, Colored, black, Black, Afro-American, African-American, African American? Many older people in the community had long insisted on capitalizing "negro" and, now that it was accepted, considered "Negro" the most dignified term. For them, "black" took that dignity away. "Don't they know," the older generation complained about the younger, "that the white man is glad to offer them lowercase?" And "Black," many felt, even when capitalized, reduced them to a color, something they had soundly rejected when they moved away from "colored."

When some young people adopted "Afro-American" or "African American" as they embraced their cultural heritage, many older people said it was well and good to know more about Africa, but they identified as American, not African. Hedgeman herself came to prefer "African American," without a hyphen, and developed an animosity to "black." She even asked the staff of the Schlesinger Library at Radcliffe College to remove her name from its list of "black women who have achieved against the odds," explaining that she could not be part of the only group in the world to be identified solely on the basis of color.[24] As a consultant, she was less pedantic, trying to get people to listen to each other as they figured out collectively how such a large and diverse community might best identify themselves, with dignity.

Hedgeman worked with a number of colleges determined to either close the educational gap between black and white students or respond to young people's calls for changes in curricula and college life.[25] After Benjamin Payton, with whom she had worked so closely, became president of Benedict College in Columbia, South Carolina, he hired Pauli Murray to join his administration and develop remedial programs in reading and math. Murray invited Hedgeman in as chief consultant on literacy, and together they developed a reading center for underprepared students. Their work had an immediate impact: achievement tests in the first year demonstrated that the program doubled the rate of improvement in reading among first-year students.

Benedict College's success with the reading center may well have helped the college secure grants from the US Department of Education and the Ford Foundation, allowing Hedgeman to design and lead a six-week summer institute for faculty from seven historically black colleges in South Carolina. Following what she described as their "painful discovery" that they themselves knew so little black history, the group took on the demanding curriculum she had designed. "They turned us inside out," one professor noted with admiration—and perhaps more than a bit of exhaustion.[26]

The assassination of Martin Luther King Jr. just months prior to the summer institute, in March 1968, weighed heavily, but Anna Hedgeman, like Pauli Murray, felt the best path forward remained nonviolent social change, of which education formed a critical part.[27] They infused the program with activism; the group examined a widely used American literature textbook and drafted a letter of complaint to the book's editor and publisher. The book "suffers from the same myopia in government, industry, private institutions and dominant attitudes which helped to produce the riots of 1964–1967," they wrote, noting that it failed to include "a single contribution from an American Negro, an American Indian, a Spanish-speaking American, or an American of Oriental origin."[28]

By no means was Hedgeman the first to call for the study of black history or to point to the costs of an educational system that acknowledged the contributions only of white Americans. Some of the people she most admired, including A. Philip Randolph, had been soapbox orators in Harlem in the 1920s and 1930s, providing black history lessons right there on the sidewalks of New York. Arthur Schomburg, who founded what became the Schomburg Center for Research in Black Culture, demonstrated by the gift of his enormous book collection his belief that history could "restore what slavery took away."[29] Ella Baker, Anna Hedgeman's neighbor and friend, started a Negro history club at the Harlem library when she first moved to New York in the 1920s.[30] And Carter G. Woodson, who founded the Association for the Study of Negro Life and History in 1915, to promote the study of black history, had served as an inspiration to both Anna and Merritt, both of whom had been members of the organization's board of directors.[31]

Nevertheless, Anna Arnold Hedgeman played an important role in furthering the study of black history. When she worked in the mayor's office, she gave innumerable talks to elementary school children, speaking not only about the importance of studying and paying attention in school but also about how vital it was to understand one's own history. "You have made us proud of our race by telling us of the good things our race has done to make our world," one child wrote in a letter of thanks. "You told us something different from what we heard here in Harlem."[32] She had also urged black churches to teach black history to young people. When asked why churches should get involved, she turned to scripture. "Jesus said 'Suffer little children to come to me,'" she stated, "and 'I am come that ye might have life and that ye might have it more abundantly.'" No child could have abundant life when he was unsure "that his own life and the group with which he is most related has value."[33]

Hedgeman spent years talking about the need for black history to a vast array of people and groups, some of whom were more likely to listen to her speak colloquially and inclusively about what black history meant to her and her community than they were to venture into a library or listen to the demands of young radicals. She spoke passionately, for example, about her love of New York's St. Patrick's Day parade and her admiration for the way Irish Americans retained their connection to the "old sod." She grew up without an "old sod," she explained, admitting her early reluctance to be associated with the Africa she and so many other Americans had collectively grown up with. Rather than a motherland of music, fables, and old sod, she had imagined a vast, undifferentiated continent of dust, jungle, and poverty.[34] Hedgeman offered her listeners a promise, that just as she had once shared their ignorance they could now share her pride.

Anna Hedgeman felt so much support from her many audiences that she remained inspired to run for political office. She told an audience of churchwomen, cautioning them not to snicker, that she just might run for president. "I have the qualifications," she told them, "you have elected three who have less, furthermore I am a woman and men have made a sorry mess of things, and I am a Negro which means I have some of everybody, a mingling of many nationalities."[35] In 1968, in a final bid for political office, she tried to unseat incumbent Charles Rangel in the New York State Assembly. With her most significant source of support coming from the Club of Independent Democratic Women, she ran her most gender-focused campaign, stressing the need for adoption services, child care services, and improved recreation facilities for young people, all of which were widely cited as women's concerns and none of which were staples of male-driven political policy.[36] Rangel, a popular politician who went on to earn a seat in Congress and become one of its most successful lawmakers, was the most formidable opponent she faced in her bids for office. Hedgeman's concerns barely got an airing, and she was soundly defeated. It was a difficult era for black women in politics, since asserting a female identity was increasingly perceived as an abandonment of racial identity. For all of her accomplishments, which would be recounted in the dozens of awards, citations, and honorary degrees she received in the coming years, Anna Hedgeman, female and African American, and unwilling to play down the significance of either part of her complicated identity, could not win a seat in politics.

With her lifelong facility for moving among institutions, Hedgeman returned from politics to her consultancy business, gaining many short-term contracts as well as several long-term appointments, one of those with Manhattanville College, a Catholic women's college just north of New York City. Hedgeman came on board in 1969, after black alumnae held a five-night campus sit-in and issued a list of demands, including courses in black studies, funding to recruit and support black students from other urban areas in the North, and an imme-diate increase in the number of African American students, faculty, and admin-istrators. They argued that the college called attention to its black students to demonstrate its commitment to diversity but never went beyond using the students as "mere showcase people for the outside world," offering them a voice "only when it was necessary to maintain a false image of peaceful coexistence."[37] Once college administrators, who considered themselves socially progressive, got over their shock, they hired Hedgeman to come to campus to help them face the immediate crisis and engage in some long-term planning.

Like many young people of their day, the Manhattanville students seemed to distrust anyone over forty, and Anna Hedgeman was now seventy years old. Four students arrived in her office before she had even unpacked her things, demand-ing to know who had selected her, what her role on campus would be, and why they had not had the chance to vet her before she came. Finding them intemper-ate but earnest, and not about to let them bully her, Hedgeman informed them she was to take on the issue she believed would make the most difference: diver-sifying the student body, the faculty, and the curriculum. She spent one day a week on campus helping faculty revise their teaching materials and assisting the administration with the outreach necessary to recruit a more diverse faculty. She helped them think about what a black studies program might look like, then served as the program's consultant once it was in place.

This consultancy both led to and followed a host of others, including stints with hospitals, libraries, and public elementary and high schools in and outside of New York City; the New York State Department of Education; a range of colleges in New York, New Jersey, California, and Nevada; and whole school districts, including the Minneapolis public school system. She exam-ined proposals on recruiting students of color, shared the educational materi-als that she amassed or produced, counseled faculty on how to teach content they found uncomfortable to talk about, and encouraged a range of educators to accept that their learning was every bit as important as their students' learn-ing. She tried to explain that teachers, whom she considered key to the entire project, had to work with the community in order to, as she put it, "avoid the feeling that 'we are being experimented on.'"[38] Audiences found her inspiring, demanding, and sometimes vexing, as she alternated between encouraging change and insisting on it.[39]

In the late 1960s and through the 1970s, as white residents and jobs moved out of New York City and drugs and neglect increased in poor neighborhoods, the public schools deteriorated significantly, and Hedgeman was often called in to offer guidance. In 1966, nearly 85 percent of all sixth graders in Harlem read below grade level. That same year, at Benjamin Franklin High School in East Harlem, only 17 of 894 students graduated with academic diplomas that qualified them for college. Functionally illiterate children wrote tragic short essays about the heroin addicts and drug dealers who had taken over their buildings, streets, and neighborhoods. One boy in Harlem, when asked to write a fable, told this tale:

> Once upon a time there was two men who were always fighting so one day a wise man came along and said fighting will neer get you anywhere then they went to church and the preacher said you should not fight and they got mad and knock the preacher out. Can't find no ending[40]

Many white educators and policymakers would have responded with pity or disbelief, but Hedgeman focused on the disparity between the enormous strengths of the city's poorest residents and the dearth of opportunity afforded them. "There is a need for teachers to have more understanding of the community," she explained, "especially the strengths of the people."[41] Hers was a unique and valuable perspective on change.

For three years, from 1970 to 1973, she worked with New York City's District 9 in the Bronx, a predominantly black and Puerto Rican community whose residents had among the lowest incomes and educational levels in all of New York. The task force she was assigned to tried to examine the whole picture, recognizing that children's learning was greatly influenced by family circumstances. It looked to see what jobs existed in the community or nearby, then developed training programs for adults for likely job openings in health care, office and clerical work, and building repair and maintenance.[42] But the task force also focused on the children, trying to improve reading levels and find innovative ways to address behavioral problems in the schools. It viewed underachieving children not simply as disadvantaged but also as individuals who tapped into valuable inner resources in their struggles to learn. The task force discovered that ongoing discrimination increased the likelihood that children would be labeled incapable of learning. Although she did not use the term, Hedgeman encountered cultural racism in testing, an issue that would become a major educational issue and be addressed more fruitfully decades later.

In one commonly used test designed to evaluate self-image, children were asked questions about the cartoon character Charlie Brown. Did he like to be with men, or did he not like to be with men? The test was meant to reveal evidence about the children's father-son or father-daughter relationships, but many of the boys read homosexuality into the question, and both boys and girls read vulnerability. Another question asked whether or not Charlie Brown wanted a lot of material things. The "right" answer was that he did not want a lot of things, and poor children who answered that he did were considered greedy—but in fact all they wanted was what many white children took for granted. They needed "a lot of things" just to pull even, an urge that was hard to resist in a society that glorified the acquisition of goods, despite any explicit messages otherwise.[43] Children in District 9 had learned a lot about survival but almost nothing about negotiating the differences between what society claimed to value and the values it actually conveyed.

Anna Arnold Hedgeman maintained a full schedule through the 1970s and into the 1980s, completing a draft of a book, "Negroes of New York," and turning down full-time jobs teaching at Hobart College in upstate New York and as dean of women at Fisk University in Nashville.[44] She pieced together a range of consultancies and maintained a peripatetic schedule, changing her title to consultant on urban affairs and then adding teaching to her portfolio. She accepted part-time assignments at a number of colleges, including SUNY New Paltz, New York University, and Columbia University. In 1980, the year she turned eighty-one, she commuted between New York and Princeton, New Jersey, to teach a course on women and theology at Princeton Theological Seminary.

Hedgeman published a second memoir, *The Gift of Chaos: Decades of American Discontent*, in 1977, following up on *The Trumpet Sounds: A Memoir of Negro Leadership*, which she had published in 1964. She also set to work on another book, "The African American Woman's Unique Experience: Fragments of the Spirit," believing that black women's stories "had to be told."[45] Had she completed this work, it would have been among the first histories of black American women to reach publication. Sadly, before the 1960s it had not occurred to her that such a book was necessary, and during the 1970s and 1980s Anna was so busy working and eventually attending to Merritt, who was ill, that she could not devote the time needed to complete the project.[46]

In the late 1970s, Merritt began to experience a serious decline: already dealing with diabetes, which had begun to affect his quality of life, he suffered a stroke. From then until his death in 1988, he alternated between living at home and at the Greater Harlem Nursing Home, just a few blocks from their apartment. Anna began to turn down a number of consultancies, favoring those closer to home. She organized her day around her nursing home visits but, remarkably, still responded to an impressive array of invitations, many of them unpaid. These included nominating candidates for the presidency of Columbia University; serving on the state's human rights commission; providing advocacy for Harlem Hospital and for the Schomburg Library; talking with the staff of the Ford Foundation about the needs of the black community; serving on advisory committees on human rights, child welfare, vocational rehabilitation, housing, mental health, alcoholism, and youth violence; and fighting the encroachment of Columbia University into Harlem.

Over the years Hedgeman provided significant service to Harlem Hospital, advocating for the hiring of black nurses and then black doctors, for a new building and improved services, and for new leadership. Things changed, and for the better. The old saying "Hit your momma, you die; go to Harlem Hospital, you die" would no longer be heard on the streets, but the racism that had rendered the hospital lacking for so long was hard to eradicate.[47] When the eighty-year-old Hedgeman took to the podium in 1980, to deliver a talk on black history in the hospital's auditorium, a group of white doctors talked loudly as they waited outside the auditorium for their own meeting to begin. When a black woman in the audience called them on their behavior, one of the doctors replied, "To you time means nothing, but to us . . ."[48]

Hedgeman also continued her work on behalf of women. She served on a committee that recommended the legalization of abortion in New York State, earning a letter of thanks from Governor Rockefeller, who called hers among the finest reports he had ever received.[49] She also maintained a commitment to global women's issues, exploring the links between women of African descent and African women, participating in the UN Decade for Women conference in 1980, and serving on the advisory council for the UN Association of New York.[50] She also tried to keep alive the legacy of Eleanor Roosevelt, who Hedgeman believed presented a model for activism on race, gender, and international justice right up until her death in 1962.[51]

It was not just that Anna Hedgeman demonstrated the fair treatment of women; she also demanded it. Once, on a college consultancy, after she shared a meal at a restaurant with a group of students, she noticed that the students had not left an adequate tip. She sent her host a letter afterward, enclosing the difference to make a 15 percent tip, and asking him to follow up with the waitress and the students.[52] On another occasion, when Harlem leaders proposed a series of statues of black heroes to be placed on 125th Street, she publicly took to task the Reverend Charles Kenyatta, who had served as Malcolm X's confidant and bodyguard, for including no women on the list.[53] When she was asked to weigh in on the proposed national holiday to remember Martin Luther King Jr., she could not help but make a pitch. "The proposed holiday," she noted, "should recall Rosa Parks," who, as she had long maintained, sat on that bus so that Dr. King could stand before the nation."[54]

Hedgeman also fought to maintain the link between the black freedom movement and the burgeoning women's liberation movement. The *Los Angeles Times* reported on her "stealing the show" at a conference on the topic, critiquing young African American women who considered women's liberation simply "another white political fad."[55] She lectured young feminists on the origins of NOW, which she was proud had been interracial, and came to believe more and more acutely that, as she put it, "only women can lead in stopping the holocaust which threatens all life."[56] Still, within feminist organizations, Hedgeman sometimes practiced strategic separatism, calling for meetings of black women only, so as to "share the beauty and the agony of our educational experiences before we call in any of our potential white colleagues."[57]

In spite of his deteriorating health, Merritt did what he could to support Anna, from the nursing home and on his occasional extended visits home. In 1980, on the fiftieth anniversary of his graduation from Fisk University, he gathered the strength to make a trip to his alma mater to accept the prestigious Society of Golden Sons and Daughters Award.[58] He never lost his love for religious folk music and lived by his motto: "Music is heavenly and divine; the universal language of mankind."[59] He too continued to engage in some social protest and service, complaining publicly that the 1980 dedication of the Schomburg Center for Research in Black Culture omitted black spiritual music, which he considered vital to the development and richness of the Harlem community; he also served as president of the nursing home's residents' council for five years.[60]

In the 1980s, before laptop computers or smartphones, Anna spent more and more of each day with Merritt at the nursing home, without access to a telephone. She tried to get some work done on her book on African American women's history but found it impossible to forge through the massive project. She obtained funding from the Rockefeller Foundation and the Phelps Stokes Fund but in the end could not turn her copious notes and outlines into a text. The book gave her a purpose, however, and she was loath to let it go. In 1984, when Pauli Murray let Hedgeman know that she had nominated her for a Spingarn Medal, the prestigious award given annually by the NAACP, Hedgeman asked her to take back the nomination. Her book was critical of the NAACP, she explained, and it would be embarrassing both for her and for the organization if she received the award and then published the book. Hedgeman's continued frustration with the NAACP mirrored what she felt about other civil rights leaders and organizations; she still bristled at their intolerance of youthful cries for change and their rejection of women.[61]

Like other women active in civil rights work, Anna Hedgeman had not been with any one organization long enough to accrue an adequate pension. The declaration of independence she and Merritt made in the 1930s freed them to do what they thought was right, but it also ensured that they would often live paycheck to paycheck. When Merritt's health reached a critical point, they found it hard to make ends meet and sought help from Fred Samuel, a New York City Council member for Manhattan, who took their case to the city's housing authority and requested Section 8 affordable housing for the couple. "There are few New Yorkers," Samuel wrote, "whose contributions to the social, cultural, and political life of our city match those of Mr. and Mrs. Merritt Hedgeman." Ironically, Anna had been a finalist for the post of chair of the City Housing Authority in 1966. Now, with failing health and small fixed incomes, the couple needed that agency's help.[62]

Samuel made several attempts on their behalf, to no avail. Merritt and Anna finally and reluctantly relieved him of the responsibility of fighting any longer on their behalf. "Even during the Emergency Relief Days," Anna explained sadly, "with its rigid relief requirements, we made every effort to assist responsible clients to maintain their customary standard of living."[63] Older people, she now realized, faced significant hardships if they relied primarily on Social Security, a social safety network that, however important, had discriminated against African Americans and against women from the start. In this case the couple's Social Security income, modest as it was, took no account of illness and disqualified them from obtaining additional help to ease the way through their final years.[64]

Friends and family noticed how Hedgeman struggled, and they tried to intervene, but she would have none of it. Following an exchange of letters in which Anna Hedgeman had written to Pauli Murray about Merritt's failing health, Murray sent her an unsolicited check for $2,000, expressing gratitude for the emotional support Anna and Merritt had provided her over the years. She, more than most of Hedgeman's friends, understood the importance of a book on black women's history, and she hoped her contribution would enable Anna to keep writing while attending to Merritt's needs. Murray praised her friend, calling her a "sister-fighter" and "the Doyenne of American Negro women."[65] Hedgeman returned the check along with a note relating some of her fond memories of their early days together in Harlem but also suggesting, brusquely, that they did not actually know each other very well.[66] It may be that Hedgeman took offense at the donation, but it may be that she also took offense at Murray's suggestion that they were opposites. "You warn of the dangers. I insist on speaking of the possibilities," Murray had written, with admiration, but perhaps without thinking how her words might come across.[67] Hedgeman certainly would have resisted being categorized that way.

Murray wrote back, understanding that her friend might have been offended by the offer of money but making it clear she would not be put off by anything Hedgeman might say at this point in their lives. "I could count on the fingers of one hand and have some fingers left over the two or three people in the world to whom I would have made such a gesture," she wrote, admitting that it had taken her some time to recognize that others too had a right to make choices "consistent with individual integrity." Arguing with someone she so admired was good for her, Murray wrote in one of their back and forths. "It gives me practice in sparring with a few other notables."[68]

Anna Hedgeman also resisted the overtures of help from her family. She and her sister Blanche had a serious falling-out over Anna's refusal to accept help after she had a seizure and remained alone in the apartment. "You better than anyone else know that you are not a well woman," Blanche complained. "It grieves me to think of you sick and alone." Blanche concluded that she had to respect her sister's choices, no matter how much it hurt them all. "So I am going to move out of your life," she wrote. "I will no longer call and worry you each Sunday. I admire your courage although I think it foolhardy. I love you dearly and wish I could share your load."[69] Anna was no more accommodating of Blanche's daughter, Wanda, who wrote when Merritt was sick, offering to help Anna prepare her papers for their move to Wilberforce University in Ohio, near Wanda's home in Dayton. Rather than invite Wanda to the apartment to figure out the logistics of the move, Anna offered to meet her niece at LaGuardia Airport and talk things over there.[70]

It may be that Anna did not want anyone to enter the apartment. She and Merritt had long joked about her poor housekeeping skills. She was infamous for eating her meals at Frank's Restaurant and using Frank's, rather than her home, as her office. Without Merritt there to clean, or to motivate her to do the cleaning, Anna may have let the apartment go. She eventually accumulated more than two hundred boxes of personal papers, and at least some of them would have been stored in the apartment. She may have felt closed in.

Anna had cordial but fairly distant relationships with her siblings, and at this point it was hard to let them in. She was closest to her sister Olive, Olive's husband, Julius Adams, managing editor of the *New York Amsterdam News*, and their daughters, Julie and Carolyn, who lived for a time at Lenox Terrace and then nearby in central Harlem, but differing political views always made things tense between the two families. The Adams family, staunch Republicans, thought Anna's philosophy promoted dependence and victimhood; Anna viewed them as reactionary. Nevertheless, Olive and Merritt often performed together, and Anna took great pride in Julie's and Carolyn's distinguished careers as dancers. And Olive, like all of Anna's siblings, was enormously proud of the respect the black community accorded her sister.

As she advanced through her mid-eighties, Anna's health declined, and on July 15, 1986, on her eighty-seventh birthday, she moved into the Greater Harlem Nursing Home, joining Merritt. Anna's sister Olive carried them a full Sunday dinner each week. The staff there, who would normally take offense at the suggestion that their cooking was not good enough, admired Hedgeman enough to turn what might have been a slight into a weekly celebration of a pair of Harlem luminaries.[71] Both Hedgemans remained attentive to the larger world, even as their daily lives became more circumscribed. "I have decided that I want to live to be 120," Anna Hedgeman declared at one point, "to see whether we can in this country produce some people who have sense enough to know that they have the world in their hands." Like many other Americans frustrated by its shortcomings, she was a resolute believer in her nation's potential. She never gave up.

Merritt Hedgeman died at the Greater Harlem Nursing Home on March 4, 1988; Anna, aged ninety, followed him on January 17, 1990.[72]

EPILOGUE

FIGHTING FOR HEAVEN, RIGHT HERE ON EARTH

When Christians recite the Lord's Prayer, they pledge to support God, to live in accordance with his righteous teachings. "Thy kingdom come, thy will be done," they pray, "on earth, as it is in heaven." Anna Arnold Hedgeman always ended the Lord's Prayer after "earth." "I put a period at that point because Protestants many times seem to concentrate on the heaven part of the sentence." She worried that Christians were too often ruled by fear, and she believed that God would disapprove of their reluctance to be fully present in the secular world, with all its wonder and all its complications. This is "the world Jesus was sent to," she explained matter-of-factly.[1]

Hedgeman spent her life trying to know and act out a Christian practice of social justice in the world Jesus actually lived in. She cared deeply for the dignity and welfare of all people, but she acted most passionately on behalf of the dispossessed. So many human actions ran counter to what she had learned at home, at church, and in the Bible, but racial discrimination, which distorted the lives of whites as surely as it did those of people of color, became her most fierce political, religious, and personal adversary. She fought it in her neighborhood, in the church, in politics, and in social action organizations of all kinds. She complained at one point that she had wasted her talents by devoting her professional life to the eradication of racism, but once the fight claimed her, there was no turning back.

Present and influential in a remarkable array of civil rights efforts over the course of her lifetime, Anna Hedgeman exemplified the long duration, diverse approaches, and hard-won successes of the black freedom movement. She fought for workplace dignity in the 1920s, access to civil service jobs in the 1930s, equal opportunity in military-related employment during the Second World War and fair employment after it, desegregation of the nation's capital in the postwar period, a desegregated and activist church in the 1960s, and black economic power in the 1970s. For these efforts, she has garnered some limited recognition: her portrait has hung in the National Portrait Gallery, and her name graces a few schools, streets, institutes, and scholarships. But until now, Anna Arnold Hedgeman has fallen victim to the same kind of invisibility she fought against all her life. In truth, it is too easy not to see her, in part because of the difficulty we have in talking simultaneously about race and about the other critical component of her identity, gender.

When we explore the history of the National Council of Churches, even the Commission on Religion and Race, we are likely to see white rather than black, male rather than female, and religious rather than secular leadership. When we explore the history of the 1963 March on Washington, we see intrepid men delivering moving speeches, and both Hedgeman and her critical work on behalf of racial justice before, during, and after the march are rendered invisible. When we accept the conventional understanding that the National Organization for Women and the nascent feminism it represented were white women's concerns, Hedgeman, an architect of the era's most significant effort to bring real and sustained legislative justice to women, is transformed into an interloper. Similarly, when her name appears on the membership list of the National Committee of Negro Churchmen, it is all too easy to reduce her to the group's secretary, a designation that is at the same time both accurate and wildly misleading.

Yet for all the difficulty we have in viewing the whole of Anna Arnold Hedgeman, in seeing her as black, as female, as a secular but devoted Christian, as a New Yorker, as a civil rights leader, and as an independent, progressive Democrat, those identities came together in her life and in her efforts for justice. She saw no contradiction in being a woman among men, a layperson among clergy, a black American among whites. Regardless of those differences, which she ultimately considered superficial but understood to be consequential, she did not hesitate to dig in and get to work. She found ways to bring people from these various groups and identities together, to talk, to listen, to argue, and most importantly, to act on behalf of justice.

There were, of course, limitations. As a woman and an impatient crusader, Hedgeman was unable to step into or carve out a clear career, and she was denied the security that might have accompanied one. "I have not had a career," she stated once. "I worked at life."

In many ways her career trajectory more closely resembles a work profile from our era than from hers: she moved from job to job, trading up or moving out when she wanted to develop fresh skills, realize new goals, or work with different people. Hedgeman was a networker as well as a worker, and she always found ways to ensure that her professional engagements reflected her personal values. In Merritt Hedgeman, Anna found a partner who shared her outlook, and when they signed their "declaration of independence" and tacked it onto the curtain in their little Harlem apartment, they both felt free to pursue a life and not just a living. They shared fifty-four years of marriage and brought to it respect, commitment, passion, and joy.

Anna Arnold Hedgeman's legacies are numerous. Her work in the National Council of Churches, and more specifically in the Commission on Religion and Race, reminds us of a time when the nation's major religions focused their attention on racial reconciliation and racial justice. Through her work with Protestant religious leaders in the National Council of Churches, as well as with Catholic and Jewish leaders in the National Conference of Christians and Jews, Hedgeman praised people and groups for their ideological support but insisted that the reconciliation they promised and prayed over required justice. She recruited the majority of white people who attended the March on Washington and then turned white support for the march into advocacy on behalf of the groundbreaking Civil Rights Act of 1964. She played a formative role in linking Christianity with activism, albeit a role defined today, by and large, by the religious right rather than the religious left.

Anna Hedgeman showed remarkable foresight on some of the most pressing issues of our day, especially those around diversity and whiteness. She played a role in the formation of black theology, validating black Americans' long and justice-minded relationship to Christianity, and challenging those who listened to white ministers, or prayed to a white Jesus, or imagined God to be white, to expand their consciousness in order to expand their humanity. The feminist theologian Mary Daly wrote, "If God is male, then the male is God."[2] Hedgeman would have agreed and taken the argument a step further: "If God is white," she might have added, "then the white is God."

Another of Hedgeman's significant legacies was that her expansive view of justice was not limited to her identity as either an African American or a woman. Like many other black women of her day and since, she practiced what sociologists call "intersectionality," refusing to claim a single identity but instead demanding that justice address the multiple identities of race, gender, social class, and other elements of life that real people live simultaneously. As a Christian, she believed that all people had a stake in improving the lives of both those like themselves and those most unlike themselves. An early proponent of what we now think of as global consciousness, she also developed an acute awareness of the workings of gender and of colonialism. A political liberal, she believed her nation, if it chose to live in accordance with its stated principles, could be a model for justice in the wider world.

Like her mentor and friend A. Philip Randolph, Anna Hedgeman always kept economic justice in the forefront of her mind and work, recognizing that social change required not just a collective determination but also the funding to make it real. She argued persistently that African American contributions to the nation had been profound and profoundly economic, since slavery had provided the backbone for the nation's development. Economic development in black communities, she maintained, was not only necessary but also earned, a long-deserved means of recognizing black Americans' contributions to their nation.

Hedgeman exhorted Christian churches, especially, to recognize themselves as economic as well as spiritual institutions, and to dedicate their vast resources to justice. And when she helped found the National Organization for Women, she organized a task force on poverty, arguing that if the group cared about women, it could demonstrate it by working to improve the lives of those most in need. In her mind, gender, racial, religious, and economic justice could never be disentangled.

Anna Hedgeman was an early practitioner of black history, and here too she leaves a legacy. She knew that if young African Americans knew not only the ignoble history of black slavery but also the noble history of black nation building, they would see themselves quite differently. Similarly, if white people had the opportunity to worship a Jesus who had darker skin than their own, or to learn that Harlem, regardless of the racism that kept it underdeveloped, was a culturally rich mecca for people of African descent from around the world, they would better be able to undertake the racial reconciliation their world required. In order not to see race, as so many well-meaning people claimed, she understood that they first had to see it, clearly and purposefully.

Finally, Anna Arnold Hedgeman, at once a dignified woman and a scrappy freedom fighter, a devout Christian and a demanding feminist, an accomplished political operative and a savvy grassroots organizer, a proud American citizen and an insistent African American voice, reminds us that our past remains as complicated as the individuals who people it—and that our future is up to us. Enough, now, about me, Anna Arnold Hedgeman would say. Let's get to work.

ACKNOWLEDGMENTS

When I first thought about writing this book, I wondered if I would have the good fortune to meet and speak with anyone who had actually known Anna Arnold Hedgeman. It was, after all, more than one hundred and ten years after her birth and more than twenty years after her death. Good fortune was mine, and my first debt is to the people who graciously shared their documents, photographs, and memories with me. These include Hedgeman's family: her sister Olive Arnold Adams, and Olive's daughters, nieces Julie Adams Strandberg and Carolyn Adams, who invited me to their family home and to Olive's hundredth birthday celebration, in Marcus Garvey Park in Harlem. Olive shared stories of the sisters' childhood years in Minnesota, their young adulthood years in New York City, and their growing old together in Harlem. I had the privilege of interviewing Anna's fellow civil rights colleagues Gloria Richardson, Rachelle Horowitz, the Reverend James Breeden, the Reverend Gayraud Wilmore, and the Reverend James Cone.

I benefited, too, from conversations with Sterling Stuckey, whose mother, poet Elma Stuckey, wrote a moving tribute to Anna Arnold Hedgeman; and with Robert Hardy, who was married to Anna's friend and fellow NOW founding board member Inez Casiano. Anna's secretary at the National Council of Churches, Carol Anderson Holmes, welcomed me into her home and family and shared stories about the boss and friend she respected and loved. Carol named her children, Anna and Meredith, after Anna and Merritt, and it has been my pleasure to get to know them a little bit as well.

The project would not have been possible without the generous financial support of Bowdoin College, the William R. Kenan Foundation, and the American Philosophical Society, all of which supported my sabbatical leave and numerous research trips. Members of the staffs of the Schomburg Center for Research in

Black Culture, the Library of Congress, the Presbyterian Historical Society, the Arthur and Elizabeth Schlesinger Library on the History of Women in America, the Bowdoin College Library, the Hamline University Library, the Municipal Archives of the City of New York, the Anoka County Historical Society (Minnesota), the National Afro-American Museum and Cultural Center, the Kheel Center for Labor Management Documentation and Archives at Cornell University, and the General Board of Global Ministries, United Methodist Church, provided me with the most able assistance as I searched for documents and photographs relevant to the project. Lucia Cowles, a Bowdoin College alum, provided me with on-the-ground research at the Minnesota Historical Society, and friend and fellow researcher Julie Gallagher shared papers with me from the University of Massachusetts, Yale University, and Howard University libraries.

My greatest debt in this regard is to the staff of the National Afro-American Museum and Cultural Center in Wilberforce, Ohio. The NAAMCC's director, Charles Wash, provided me access to the more than two hundred boxes of papers of Anna Arnold Hedgeman. He opened the building early and closed it late every day I was there, allowing me to spend long and careful days sorting through the many tens of thousands of unprocessed papers. He also shared in my joy when, on numerous occasions, I would discover gems among the ephemera. In addition to Chuck Wash, I offer my most sincere thanks to Floyd Thomas, Linda Buckwalter, and Jamita Waller. I also appreciate the friends and family in New York, including Larry Scanlon, Mary-Grace Gannon, Jacqueline Vaida, and Alison Scanlon, who welcomed me into their homes as I passed through town for research, sometimes for a night, other times for a week. Thanks, too, to Lindsay and Charlie Prezzano, who so generously invited my family to Barbados to visit family and take a much-needed break from it all.

At different stages of the project, historians and other scholars read part or all of the manuscript and offered helpful critiques and invaluable suggestions. From the very first stages of the book proposal, I received support and guidance from Bettye Collier-Thomas, Beverly Lowry, Jacqueline Dowd Hall, and Catherine Clinton. Since then a number of people have provided incisive readings, and I offer special thanks to Brian Purnell, Judith Casselberry, Julie Gallagher, William Jones, Jeanne Theoharis, Lucy Barber, Christina Greene, and Howard Mittelmark. Anne Clifford, at Bowdoin College, often reclaimed her former librarian persona as she assisted me in searching for hard-to-find documents and images. Susan Faludi provided companionship in writing, and Frances Gouda kindly organized a "women in politics" biographical session for the book's release. Jeanne Bamforth graciously attended to final details.

It is my great pleasure to work, again, with Nancy Toff, my editor at Oxford University Press, whose wit and jargon-reducing pencils are always sharp.

I am indebted to my family and friends for their generous support of this project and all that I do. Thanks to Larry Scanlon, Laura Cavicchi, Sharon Mertzlufft, Andrea Virgone, Eileen Barry, Terri Straub, Julie Boss, Seven Klein, Marilyn Reizbaum, Judith Casselberry, Susie Dorn, Chuck Dorn, Alida Snow, Karen Parker, Lynne McIntosh, and Poppy Arford. My sabbatical leave and year of intensive work on this project coincided with the last year of my mother's life, and her mark is on the book. The oldest of eight children in an Irish immigrant family living in the Bronx, Mary Barry helped her family survive the Great Depression by working at a five-and-ten in Harlem. Little did she know that while she scraped ice cream for cones inside the store, Anna Arnold Hedgeman stood outside, pushing the owners to employ the people who both lived in the neighborhood and spent their hard-earned dollars there. New York stories, intertwined.

This book is for Michael Arthur, my partner of more than twenty years, with whom I share lasting love, dreams of real racial reconciliation for our nation, and two incredible children, Fynn and Maeve

NOTES

Note on abbreviations: names of archival collections, oral interviews, and most newspapers and periodicals are abbreviated. See the bibliography for full citations.

PROLOGUE

1. Greenberg, *To Ask for an Equal Chance*, 27.
2. Anna Arnold Hedgeman, "Letter to Martin Luther King, Jr.," October 26, 1966, MLK.
3. Hedgeman, *The Trumpet Sounds*, 198.
4. Commission on Religion and Race, "Summary of Activities," June–October 1963, NCC.
5. These exceptions are known also for their excellence. See Theoharis, *The Rebellious Life of Mrs. Rosa Parks*; Collier-Thomas, *Jesus, Jobs, and Justice*; Holsaert et al., *Hands on the Freedom Plow: Personal Accounts by Women in SNCC* (Urbana: University of Illinois Press, 2010); Gore, Theoharis, and Woodard, *Want to Start a Revolution?*; Ransby, *Ella Baker and the Black Freedom Movement*; Collier-Thomas and Franklin, *Sisters in the Struggle*; Olson, *Freedom's Daughters*; Mills, *This Little Light of Mine*.
6. AAH-ED 188.
7. Jordan and Reagon, "Oughta Be a Woman."

CHAPTER I

1. OAA-JS; AAH-ED; Anna Arnold Hedgeman, "Autobiographical Sketch, Untitled," Box 81, AAH-N; Harlan Thurston, *Life in Anoka: 1900* (Anoka, Minnesota: Anoka Historical Society, reprint 1993), AHS. Tracks, *Anoka in 1889* (Anoka, Minnesota: Anoka Historical Society, reprint 1976), AHS.

2. Thurston, *Life in Anoka*.

3. Hedgeman, "Autobiographical Sketch: Untitled."

4. Thurston, *Life in Anoka*.

5. Hedgeman, *The Gift of Chaos*, 7.

6. "Afro-Americans in Minnesota," *Gopher*, Winter 1968–69, AHS. See also Lass, *Minnesota*.

7. On Anokans in the Civil War, see June Anderson, "Anoka County History: Anoka's Role in the Civil War," AHS.

8. "Afro-Americans in Minnesota."

9. AAH-ED, 6–8.

10. AAH-ED, 6–8.

11. James S. Griffin, "Blacks in the St. Paul Police Department: An Eighty-Year Survey," *Minnesota Historical Society Quarterly*, Fall 1975, MHS; David V. Taylor, "John Quincy Adams: St. Paul Editor and Black Leader," *Minnesota History*, Winter 1973, MHS. Frederick Parker, of St. Paul, stated in his autobiography that his father was editor of the *Appeal* and that he was a distant cousin of Anna Arnold. See Frederick L. Parker, *Autobiography*, Box 76, AAH-N.

12. "Afro-Americans in Minnesota."

13. A fierce advocate for racial equality, Crogman claimed that the only remedy for the nation's social troubles, the only one "which God can approve," was "even-handed justice meted out to every man." See Crogman, "Negro Education: Its Helps and Hindrances," Box 120, AAH-N.

14. AAH-RM; AAH-KS, 2–4.

15. OAA-JS.

16. US Census, 1910, AHS; US Census, 1920, AHS.

17. Taylor, "John Quincy Adams," 285–86. In a letter from Anna Arnold Hedgeman to S. B. Fuller, she tells him that she grew up in the newspaper world and that her father published an organ that was well known in chamber of commerce circles in Minnesota, North Dakota, South Dakota, Wisconsin, and Nebraska. November 13, 1958, Box 172, AAH-N. Anna Arnold Hedgeman's sister Olive, twelve years her junior, did not remember her father being involved in the newspaper business. OAA-JS.

18. Hedgeman, *The Gift of Chaos*, 4.

19. Hedgeman, "Autobiographical Sketch, Untitled."

20. AAH-ED, 20.

21. OAA-JS.

22. Anna Arnold Hedgeman, "Letter to Marianna Davis," February 15, 1982, Box 68, AAH-N.

23. Hedgeman, *The Gift of Chaos*, 7.

24. Anna Arnold Hedgeman, "Toward a Whole Education," September 3, 1968, Box 162, AAH-N.

25. Hedgeman, *The Trumpet Sounds*, 7.

26. Hedgeman, "Autobiographical Sketch, Untitled."
27. Hedgeman, "Autobiographical Sketch, Untitled."
28. Hedgeman, "Autobiographical Sketch, Untitled."
29. OAA-JS.
30. AAH-RM; OAA-JS.
31. OAA-JS.
32. OAA-JS.
33. Delton, *Making Minnesota Liberal*, 47–48.
34. Delton, *Making Minnesota Liberal*, 47–48.

CHAPTER 2

1. Hedgeman, *The Gift of Chaos*, 4.
2. Hedgeman, *The Trumpet Sounds*, 8.
3. OAA-JS.
4. Hedgeman, *The Trumpet Sounds*, 8.
5. Anna Arnold Hedgeman, "Autobiographical Sketch, Untitled," Box 129, AAH-N.
6. OAA-JS.
7. Hedgeman, "Autobiographical Sketch, Untitled."
8. OAA-JS.
9. Hedgeman, *The Trumpet Sounds*, 8.
10. Hedgeman, *The Trumpet Sounds*, 9.
11. Hedgeman, *The Trumpet Sounds*, 9.
12. Hedgeman, "Autobiographical Sketch, Untitled."
13. AAH-BL.
14. Hedgeman, "Autobiographical Sketch, Untitled."
15. Anna Arnold Hedgeman, "Speech to National Association of Collegiate Deans and Registrars," 1956, Box 74, AAH-N.
16. Hedgeman, "Autobiographical Sketch, Untitled."
17. Hedgeman, "Autobiographical Sketch, Untitled."
18. Hedgeman, *The Trumpet Sounds*, 10.
19. Grace Ridge Campbell, "Oral History Interview," AHS.
20. Hedgeman, *The Trumpet Sounds*, 10.
21. Hedgeman, *The Trumpet Sounds*, 10.
22. Friendships between black and white children remained contested in the North as well as in the South, and white children somehow seemed to learn that they could not last. Parents might be the ones to break off the friendships, or white children themselves might look for opportunities to "seize upon a disagreement to unexpectedly turn on their black playmates." One black woman recalled, "The white children I knew grew meaner as they got older—more capable of saying things that cut and wound." See Litwack, *Trouble in Mind*, 8.

23. Bryn Poole, "Letter to Anna Arnold Hedgeman," September 9, 1966, Box 142, AAH-N.

24. Olive Arnold Adams, "Letter to Vickie Wendel," 1996, AHS.

25. Hedgeman, *The Trumpet Sounds*, 11, 12.

26. Hedgeman, *The Trumpet Sounds*, 11.

27. Hedgeman, *The Trumpet Sounds*, 11.

28. Hedgeman, *The Trumpet Sounds*, 12–13. On Roy Wilkins, see Wilkins, *Standing Fast*.

29. Delton, *Making Minnesota Liberal*, 65.

30. Harlan Thurston, *Life in Anoka: 1900* (Anoka, Minnesota: Anoka Historical Society, reprint 1993), AHS; Campbell, "Oral History Interview"; OAA-JS.

31. Anna Arnold Hedgeman, "Letter to Dr. Scott Johnston," 1982, HUA.

32. Hamline University, "Hamline History," HUA.

33. Anna Arnold, perhaps unbeknownst to her or her father, was part of a trend following the First World War, in which white colleges in the North would see a large increase in the number of black students in attendance. Poulson and Miller-Bernal, "Two Unique Histories of Coeducation," 41.

34. On the global influenza pandemic, see Bristow, *American Pandemic*, and Barry, *The Great Influenza*. On the flu epidemic in Minnesota, see http://minnesota .publicradio.org/display/web/2009/05/07/1918flu. On the great fire of 1918, see Carroll, *The Fires of Autumn*. On the role of Minnesota in the Great War, see Aby, *North Star State*.

35. Hedgeman, *The Gift of Chaos*, 5.

36. Hamline University, "Hamline History."

37. Johnson, *Hamline University*, 196.

38. Johnson, *Hamline University*, 199–200.

39. Johnson, *Hamline University*, 198–99.

40. Hedgeman, *The Trumpet Sounds*, 14.

41. Hedgeman, *The Trumpet Sounds*, 14, 15.

42. Hedgeman, "Letter to Dr. Scott Johnston."

43. AAH-ED, 22.

44. Hedgeman, "Autobiographical Sketch, Untitled."

45. AAH-BL.

46. Hedgeman, "Letter to Dr. Scott Johnston."

47. Hedgeman, "Letter to Dr. Scott Johnston."

48. Hedgeman, "Letter to Dr. Scott Johnston."

49. Johnson, *Hamline University*, 199.

50. Hedgeman, *The Trumpet Sounds*, 15–16.

51. Hedgeman, *The Trumpet Sounds*, 16.

52. Hedgeman, *The Trumpet Sounds*, 15.

53. Hedgeman, *The Trumpet Sounds*, 16; AAH-BL.

54. Hedgeman, "Letter to Dr. Scott Johnston."

55. Hedgeman, "Letter to Dr. Scott Johnston."

56. AAH-ED.

57. Anna Arnold Hedgeman, "The Small College and Our Modern World," November 1960, HUA.

58. Hedgeman, "Autobiographical Sketch, Untitled."

59. David A. Taylor, "Black Women in Minnesota: Fragments from a Lost Diary," Minneapolis YWCA, 1977, Box 129, AAH-N; Anne B. Webb, "Women Farmers on the Frontier," *Minnesota Historical Society Quarterly*, Winter 1986, MHS.

60. AAH-BL.

61. Hedgeman, *The Trumpet Sounds*, 17.

62. Hedgeman, "Autobiographical Sketch, Untitled."

63. Hedgeman, *The Trumpet Sounds*, 18.

CHAPTER 3

1. Desegregation of public accommodations was hard fought in McComb, Mississippi, a town of nine thousand whites and four thousand blacks that was, in 1964, considered the church-burning capital of the South. See Watson, *Freedom Summer*.

2. Hedgeman, *The Trumpet Sounds*, 18; Hedgeman, *The Gift of Chaos*, 6. On the Great Migration of 1915–70, in which nearly six million American blacks left the South for the North and West, see Marks, *Farewell—We're Good and Gone*; Hunt, *Black and White Justice in Little Dixie*; Anna Arnold Hedgeman, "Letter to Dr. Scott Johnston," HUA; Harlan Thurston, *Life in Anoka: 1900* (Anoka, Minnesota: Anoka Historical Society, reprint 1993), AHS.

3. AAH-ED, 26.

4. According to Anna's sister Olive Adams, there were a couple of black adults who lived in Anoka through the years but never another family with children in the schools. OAA-JS.

5. Anna Arnold Hedgeman, "The Small College and Our Modern World," 1960, Box 102, AAH-N.

6. The Schomburg Center for Research in Black Culture, "In Motion: The African American Migration Experience," http://www.inmotionaame.org/home.cfm, accessed September 22, 2015.

7. White, *Too Heavy a Load*, 72.

8. William H. Crogman, "Negro Education: Its Helps and Hindrances," n.d., Box 120, AAH-N.

9. Crespino, "Mississippi as Metaphor," 100; Watkins-Owens, *Blood Relations*, 121.

10. Euchner, *Nobody Turn Me Around*, 96.

11. On the Jim Crow system and trains, see Neverdon-Morton, *Afro-American Women of the South and the Advancement of the Race*; Barnes, *Journey from Jim Crow*; Creswell, *Rednecks, Redeemers, and Race*; Giddings, *When and*

Where I Enter; Shaw, *What a Woman Ought to Be and to Do*; Litwack, *Trouble in Mind*.

12. Polsgrove, *Divided Minds*, 134.
13. Hedgeman, *The Trumpet Sounds*, 19. On Cairo, Illinois, see Lantz, *A Community in Search of Itself*.
14. Hedgeman, *The Trumpet Sounds*, 19; Anne B. Webb, "Women Farmers on the Frontier," *Minnesota Historical Society Quarterly*, Winter 1986, 10–11, MHS. Historian Leon Litwack catalogs the experiences of a number of prominent black leaders as they were subject to Jim Crow practices on public transportation. Among those he cites are Louis Armstrong, James Weldon Johnson, Ida B. Wells, and Richard Wright. See Litwack, *Trouble in Mind*, 9–10.
15. Hedgeman, *The Trumpet Sounds*.
16. Shaw, *What a Woman Ought to Be and to Do*, 91.
17. Shaw, *What a Woman Ought to Be and to Do*, 22.
18. Shaw, *What a Woman Ought to Be and to Do*, 2.
19. Shaw, *What a Woman Ought to Be and to Do*, 1–2.
20. Paula Giddings discusses the "old and special relationship between black women and public transportation" in *Ida*, 262.
21. Giddings, *Ida*, 262.
22. Hedgeman, *The Trumpet Sounds*, 19.
23. McMillen, *Dark Journey*, 8.
24. Hedgeman, *The Trumpet Sounds*, 20.
25. Hedgeman, *The Trumpet Sounds*, 20.
26. Rogers, *Life and Death in the Delta*, especially chap. 1, "Conditions of Life and Death."
27. Creswell, *Rednecks, Redeemers, and Race*, 62.
28. McMillen, *Dark Journey*, 133.
29. "Afro-Americans in Minnesota," 220–21.
30. Bryn Poole, "Letter to Anna Arnold Hedgeman," September 9, 1966, Box 142, AAH-N.
31. Herbert H. Parish, "Letter to William James Arnold," 1938, courtesy of Olive Arnold Adams, OAA-JS.
32. Lee, *For Freedom's Sake*, 3.
33. Rogers, *Life and Death in the Delta*, 21–23.
34. Hodding Carter quoted in Giddings, *Ida*, 15.
35. *From Cotton Field to Schoolhouse*, 24.
36. Goldring/Woldenberg Institute of Southern Jewish Life, "Holly Springs, Mississippi," http://www.isjl.org.
    On black-Jewish relations, see Webb, *Fight against Fear*; Salzman and West, *Struggles in the Promised Land*; Greenberg, *Troubling the Waters*.
37. Giddings, *Ida*, 32–36.

38. Giddings, *Ida*, 177.
39. Patricia Cohen, "Faulkner Link to Plantation Diary Discovered," *NYT*, Feb. 11, 2010.
40. Payne, Swain, and Spruill, eds., *Mississippi Women*, vol. 2. The Troy Female Seminary in New York State is usually considered the first to offer secondary education for women in the United States. It was actually established three years after Mississippi's Elizabeth Female Academy.
41. Rogers, *Life and Death in the Delta*, 239.
42. Giddings, *Ida*, 28–29.
43. Anna Arnold Hedgeman, "Speech to National Association of Collegiate Deans and Registrars," Box 124, AAH-N.
44. "What You Should Know about Rust College," Box 75, AAH-N.
45. Giddings, *Ida*, 29.
46. Rust College, established in 1866, was chartered as Shaw University (in honor of a donor, the Reverend S. O. Shaw, who made a gift of $10,000). In 1882, the name was changed to Rust University in honor of Richard S. Rust, who stayed in the North and raised funds for the college. In 1915, soon before Anna Arnold's arrival on campus, the name was changed again and for the last time, to Rust College. See also Ishmell Hendrex Edwards, *History of Rust College*.
47. Giddings, *Ida*, 28–29.
48. Rogers, *Life and Death in the Delta*, 98.
49. Span, *From Cotton Field to Schoolhouse*, 178.
50. "What You Should Know about Rust College."
51. Rogers, *Life and Death in the Delta*, 97, 98.
52. Hedgeman, *The Trumpet Sounds*, 22.
53. McMillen, *Dark Journey*, 87.
54. Rogers, *Life and Death in the Delta*, 22.
55. McMillen, *Dark Journey*, 79–85; Rogers, *Life and Death in the Delta*, 97.
56. Span, *From Cotton Field to Schoolhouse*, 31–32.
57. McMillen, *Dark Journey*, 85. The years 1895–1917 were considered a time of starvation for black liberal arts colleges. In addition to the lack of federal funds, they suffered from the disposition of philanthropists, who viewed vocational rather than liberal arts programs as "the fundamental solution to the race problem." See Miller-Bernal and Poulson, "Two Unique Histories of Coeducation," 37.
58. AAH-ED, 36.
59. McMillen, *Dark Journey*, 96.
60. Farmer, *Lay Bare the Heart*, 37.
61. Giddings, *Ida*, 83.
62. Farmer, *Lay Bare the Heart,*
63. Hedgeman, *The Trumpet Sounds,* 21; Tracks, *Anoka in 1889* (Anoka, Minnesota: Anoka Historical Society, reprint 1976), AHS. Ted Ownby describes the

humiliating experiences black consumers had while shopping. He also cites a William Faulkner story in which Lucas Beauchamp has to walk a gauntlet of disapproving white men to get his shopping done.

64. Hedgeman, *The Trumpet Sounds*, 21–23; Hedgeman, *The Gift of Chaos*, 7.

65. David A. Taylor, "Black Women in Minnesota: Fragments from a Lost Diary," Box 143, AAH-N.

66. Hedgeman, *The Trumpet Sounds*, 21–22.

67. Litwack, *Trouble in Mind*.

68. AAH-ED, 35.

69. Hedgeman, *The Trumpet Sounds*, 24.

70. Hedgeman, *The Trumpet Sounds*, 24–25.

71. Hedgeman, *The Trumpet Sounds*, 25.

72. Hedgeman, *The Trumpet Sounds*, 26.

73. Hedgeman, *The Trumpet Sounds*, 26.

74. Hedgeman, *The Trumpet Sounds*, 27.

75. Anna Arnold Hedgeman, "Toward a Whole Education," 1968, Box 162, AAH-N.

76. Delton, *Making Minnesota Liberal*.

77. Delton, *Making Minnesota Liberal*.

78. Farmer, *Lay Bare the Heart*, 35, 34.

79. Hedgeman, *The Trumpet Sounds*, 27.

80. Hedgeman, *The Trumpet Sounds*, 28.

81. McMillen, *Dark Journey*, 1.

82. McMillen, *Dark Journey*, 27.

83. Hedgeman, "Speech to National Association of Collegiate Deans and Registrars."

84. Hedgeman, *The Trumpet Sounds*, 23.

85. McMillen, *Dark Journey*, 72.

86. McMillen, *Dark Journey*, 73.

87. Parish, "Letter to William James Arnold," 84, 69.

88. Several scholars have explored black Americans' armed resistance in and before the modern civil rights movement. On Mississippi specifically, see Umoja, *We Will Shoot Back*; Payne, *I've Got the Light of Freedom*; Dittmer, *Local People*.

89. White, *Too Heavy a Load*, 107.

90. White, *Too Heavy a Load*, 107.

91. Shaw, *What a Woman Ought to Be and to Do*, 57.

92. McMillen, *Dark Journey*, 281.

93. Giddings, *Ida*, 141.

94. Marks, *Farewell—We're Good and Gone*, 28.

95. Woodruff, *American Congo*, 69.

96. Rogers, *Life and Death in the Delta*, 239.

97. Rogers, *Life and Death in the Delta*, 24.

98. Crespino, "Mississippi as Metaphor."

99. McMillen, *Dark Journey*, 73.

100. Rogers, *Life and Death in the Delta*, 97.

101. Hedgeman, "Toward a Whole Education."

102. McMillen, *Dark Journey*, 172.

103. McMillen, *Dark Journey*, 246.

104. Rogers, *Life and Death in the Delta*, 179.

105. Hedgeman, *The Trumpet Sounds*, 28.

106. Hedgeman, *The Trumpet Sounds*, 28.

107. Hedgeman, "Toward a Whole Education."

CHAPTER 4

1. Hedgeman quoted in Ann Geracimos, "Muscling In on the March to D.C.," *NYHT*, August 8, 1963.

2. Hedgeman, *The Trumpet Sounds*, 30, 43.

3. Hedgeman, *The Trumpet Sounds*, 30.

4. Weisenfeld, *African American Women and Christian Activism*, 3, 27.

5. Robertson, *Christian Sisterhood, Race Relations, and the YWCA*, 3.

6. Robertson, *Christian Sisterhood, Race Relations, and the YWCA*, 2.

7. Weisenfeld, *African American Women and Christian Activism*, 32.

8. Weisenfeld, *African American Women and Christian Activism*, 28.

9. AAH-ED, 36.

10. Robertson, *Christian Sisterhood, Race Relations, and the YWCA*, 43.

11. Robertson, *Christian Sisterhood, Race Relations, and the YWCA*, 43.

12. Weisenfeld, *African American Women and Christian Activism*, 38.

13. Weisenfeld, *African American Women and Christian Activism*, 190.

14. Hedgeman, *The Trumpet Sounds*, 30.

15. Hedgeman, *The Trumpet Sounds*, 31.

16. Weisenfeld, *African American Women and Christian Activism*, 197.

17. Giddings, *When and Where I Enter*, 156.

18. Hedgeman, *The Trumpet Sounds*, 33, 32.

19. Robertson, *Christian Sisterhood, Race Relations, and the YWCA*, 126.

20. Robertson, *Christian Sisterhood, Race Relations, and the YWCA*, 94.

21. Hedgeman, *The Trumpet Sounds*, 33.

22. Hedgeman, *The Trumpet Sounds*, 32.

23. AAH-ED, 49.

24. Hedgeman, *The Trumpet Sounds*, 34.

25. Hedgeman, *The Trumpet Sounds*, 34.

26. Hedgeman, *The Trumpet Sounds*, 35.

27. Hedgeman, *The Trumpet Sounds*, 36.

28. Hedgeman, *The Trumpet Sounds*, 36.

29. Shaw, *What a Woman Ought to Be and to Do*, 91.

30. Weisenfeld, *African American Women and Christian Activism*, 32.

31. Hedgeman, *The Trumpet Sounds*, 37.

32. Hedgeman, *The Trumpet Sounds*, 39.

33. Hedgeman, *The Trumpet Sounds*, 39.

34. David Levering Lewis writes of "the translation into brick and asphalt of the New Negro's own special, cartwheeling nationalism—that made the Golden Age possible." See Lewis, *When Harlem Was in Vogue*, 103.

35. Corbould, *Becoming African Americans*, 10.

36. Corbould, *Becoming African Americans*, 95.

37. Corbould, *Becoming African Americans*, 98.

38. Gallagher, *Black Women and Politics in New York City*, 17.

39. Douglas, *Terrible Honesty*, 90. The short story, "City of Refuge," published in the *Atlantic Monthly* in 1925, tells of Gillis, who arrived in Harlem "with the aid of a prayer and an automobile."

40. Hedgeman, *The Trumpet Sounds*, 51.

41. Hedgeman, *The Trumpet Sounds*, 41.

42. AAH-RM, 68.

43. Hedgeman, *The Trumpet Sounds*, 44.

44. Hedgeman, *The Trumpet Sounds*, 44.

45. Osofsky, *Harlem*, 120. Osofsky notes that "practically every major Negro institution moved from its downtown quarters to Harlem by early 1920s"; he includes in his account all the major churches, most of the social service agencies, and many fraternal and civic organizations.

46. Weisenfeld, *African American Women and Christian Activism*, 92–99.

47. Weisenfeld, *African American Women and Christian Activism*, 115; *The Y Level* 3, no. 5 (1930), Box 128, AAH-N; Robertson, *Christian Sisterhood, Race Relations, and the YWCA*, 115.

48. *Y Level*.

49. *Y Level*.

50. *Y Level*.

51. Weisenfeld, *African American Women and Christian Activism*, 169, 70.

52. "Harlem Portraits," *Pittsburgh Courier*, November 11, 1944, Box 1, AAH-SC.

53. Cecelia Cabaniss Saunders, "Branch History, Harlem YWCA," Box 128, AAH-N.

54. Weisenfeld, *African American Women and Christian Activism*, 165.

55. Weisenfeld, *African American Women and Christian Activism*, 163.

56. Cecelia Cabaniss Saunders, "Letter from the Young Women's Christian Association of the City of New York to W. E. B. Du Bois," June 14, 1930, WEBMA.

57. Hedgeman, *The Trumpet Sounds*, 51.

58. Anna Arnold Hedgeman, "Letter to Pauli Murray," January 23, 1984, Box 23, AAH-N.

59. Weisenfeld, *African American Women and Christian Activism*, 188.
60. Weisenfeld, *African American Women and Christian Activism*, 39.
61. Pauli Murray, "Letter to Anna Arnold Hedgeman," Box 3, Folder 3, AAH-SC; Anna, along with the National Urban League's Lester Granger and the NAACP's Thurgood Marshall, provided Pauli Murray with reference letters when she applied to Howard University School of Law. See Pauli Murray, "Letter to Anna Arnold Hedgeman," February 13, 1941, Box 15, Folder 384, PMP.
62. Robertson, *Christian Sisterhood, Race Relations, and the YWCA*, 147.
63. Weisenfeld, *African American Women and Christian Activism*, 163.
64. Hedgeman, *The Trumpet Sounds*, 44.
65. Hedgeman, *The Trumpet Sounds*, 44.
66. Hedgeman, *The Trumpet Sounds*, 45, 165.
67. Hedgeman, *The Trumpet Sounds*, 45.
68. Saunders, "Branch History, Harlem YWCA."
69. Saunders, "Branch History, Harlem YWCA."
70. Judith Weisenfeld quotes from an interview she had with Jean Blackwell Hutson, who remembered the friendships and marriages that developed from meetings in the YWCA lobby. Weisenfeld, *African American Women and Christian Activism*, 163.
71. AAH-ED, 59.
72. AAH-ED, 59–60.
73. Like many other black women, Anna Arnold was well aware of the sexual dangers black women faced. On how sexual violence provided momentum for the civil rights movement, see McGuire, *At the Dark End of the Street*.
74. Hedgeman, *The Trumpet Sounds*, 51.
75. Gill, *Harlem*, 171.
76. Watkins-Owens, *Blood Relations*, 132.
77. Gill, *Harlem*, 300.
78. Watkins-Owens, *Blood Relations*, 134–35.
79. Osofsky, *Harlem*, 134.
80. Lewis, *When Harlem Was in Vogue*, 216.
81. Lewis, *When Harlem Was in Vogue*, 109.
82. Takaki, *A Different Mirror*, 324.
83. Frazier quoted in Takaki, *A Different Mirror*, 325.
84. Douglas, *Terrible Honesty*, 319.
85. Greenberg, *"Or Does It Explode?,"* 32–34.
86. Lewis, *When Harlem Was in Vogue*, 108.
87. Greenberg, *"Or Does It Explode?,"* 14.
88. Greenberg, *"Or Does It Explode?,"* 21.
89. Chapman, *Prove It on Me*, 125.
90. YWCA, "The New Trade School," Box 128, AAH-N.

CHAPTER 5

1. Hedgeman, *The Trumpet Sounds*, 55.
2. Greenberg, *To Ask for an Equal Chance*, 1.
3. Weisenfeld, *African American Women and Christian Activism*, 178; Lewis, *When Harlem Was in Vogue*, 240.
4. *Opportunity*, February 1931.
5. Boyd, *Baldwin's Harlem*, 10.
6. Cecelia Cabaniss Saunders, "Branch History, Harlem YWCA," Box 128, AAH-N.
7. Hedgeman, *The Trumpet Sounds*, 56.
8. Hedgeman, *The Trumpet Sounds*, 57.
9. Hedgeman, *The Trumpet Sounds*, 54, 56.
10. Hedgeman, *The Trumpet Sounds*, 57.
11. Cheryl Greenberg describes housing conditions during the Depression in Pittsburgh and Detroit. In Pittsburgh, almost 60 percent of apartments housing blacks had no toilets. In Detroit, 34 percent of apartments housing blacks needed major repairs, while the rate for apartments housing whites was only 6 percent. See Greenberg, *To Ask for an Equal Chance*, 93.
12. Anna Arnold Hedgeman quoted in Boyd, *Baldwin's Harlem*, 12.
13. Saunders, "Branch History."
14. Gray, *Black Female Domestics during the Depression in New York City*, 38.
15. Greenberg, *To Ask for an Equal Chance*, 27.
16. Gray, *Black Female Domestics during the Depression in New York City*, 39.
17. Saunders, "Branch History."
18. May, *Unprotected Labor*, 126.
19. Weisenfeld, *African American Women and Christian Activism*, 181.
20. Gray, *Black Female Domestics during the Depression in New York City*, 47–48. The YWCA employment agency was the only agency to follow up on the women it placed.
21. Historian Danielle McGuire argues that the history of the civil rights movement is "rooted in African-American women's long struggle against sexual violence." See McGuire, *At the Dark End of the Street*, xix. McGuire focuses largely on the 1940s and later, but Anna Arnold and her colleagues understood the threat of sexual violence that domestic workers faced in the 1920s and 1930s.
22. See Gray, *Black Female Domestics during the Depression in New York City*, 83. Brenda Gray conducted oral interviews with more than one hundred women who lived in New York City and worked as domestics during the Depression. One of the women reported seeking out jobs that let out by early evening. Given the degree to which women on the street corners talked with each other, even chasing away women who were willing to work for too little in wages, we can surmise that other women also took measures to protect themselves from sexual assault.
23. Height, *Open Wide the Freedom Gates*, 81.

24. Saunders, "Branch History."
25. See Boris and Nadasen, "Domestic Workers Organize!," 413–37.
26. May, *Unprotected Labor*, 121, 48, 54.
27. Gray, *Black Female Domestics during the Depression in New York City*, 39.
28. Saunders, "Branch History."
29. Greenberg, *"Or Does It Explode?,"* 80.
30. Ella Baker and Marvel Cooke, "The Bronx Slave Market," *Crisis* 42 (November 1935). On Baker, see Ransby, *Ella Baker and the Black Freedom Movement*; on Marvel Cooke, see Harris, "Marvel Cooke," 91–126.
31. Hedgeman, *The Trumpet Sounds*, 69.
32. Greenberg, *To Ask for an Equal Chance*, 57.
33. Boris, "Domestic Workers Organize!," 419–20.
34. Jones, "Harder Times," 512–15; quotation on p. 512. See also Kessler-Harris, *In Pursuit of Equity*, see especially "Designing Women and Old Fools: Writing Gender into Social Security Law"; and Downey, *The Woman behind the New Deal*.
35. Gray, *Black Female Domestics during the Depression in New York City*, 66, 67. On the role of the federal government in relation to African Americans and racial advancement, see King, *Separate and Unequal*.
36. Greenberg, *"Or Does It Explode?,"* 47.
37. Greenberg, *"Or Does It Explode?,"* 166–67.
38. Greenberg, *"Or Does It Explode?,"* 53–54.
39. Lewis, *When Harlem Was in Vogue*, 306.
40. Gray, *Black Female Domestics during the Depression in New York City*, 46.
41. Osofsky, *Harlem*, 113.
42. Greenberg, *To Ask for an Equal Chance*, 98.
43. Greenberg, *"Or Does It Explode?,"* 60–61.
44. Greenberg, *"Or Does It Explode?,"* 58.
45. Hedgeman, *The Trumpet Sounds*, 50.
46. Watkins-Owens, *Blood Relations*, 111.
47. Hedgeman, *The Trumpet Sounds,* 58.
48. Hedgeman, *The Trumpet Sounds*, 58.
49. Hedgeman, *The Trumpet Sounds*, 60.
50. Miller, *Born along the Color Line*, 19.
51. Hedgeman, *The Trumpet Sounds*, 62.
52. Hedgeman, *The Trumpet Sounds*, 62.
53. Hedgeman, *The Trumpet Sounds*, 58.
54. AAH-ED, 61.
55. AAH-ED, 58.
56. Anna Arnold Hedgeman, "Unpublished notes," Box 14, AAH-N.
57. AAH-ED, 61–62.
58. Hedgeman, *The Trumpet Sounds*, 63.

59. Hedgeman, *The Trumpet Sounds*, dedication.
60. AAH-KS, 1.
61. Hedgeman, "Unpublished notes."
62. Anna Arnold Hedgeman, "Autobiographical Sketch," Box 129, AAH-N.
63. Merritt Hedgeman, "Untitled," Box 144, AAH-N.
64. Hedgeman, "Autobiographical Sketch."
65. Hedgeman, "Unpublished notes."
66. Hedgeman, *The Gift of Chaos*, 5.
67. Hedgeman, *The Trumpet Sounds*, 68.
68. Hedgeman, *The Trumpet Sounds*, 68.
69. Height, *Open Wide the Freedom Gates*, 55. As a girl growing up outside of Pittsburgh, Dorothy Height joined the YWCA. When she and her friends decided to visit the Pittsburgh YWCA so that they could learn to swim, they were told no black girls could use the pool. She later became assistant executive director of the 137th Street YWCA, after Anna Arnold's time there, and then later executive director of the Phillis Wheatley YWCA in Washington, DC. She and Anna Arnold Hedgeman would cross paths many times in their personal and professional lives.
70. Sanchez-Korrol, *From Colonia to Community*, 25, 28.
71. Lorrin, *Puerto Rican Citizen*, 75.
72. Hedgeman, *The Trumpet Sounds*, 71.
73. Hedgeman, *The Trumpet Sounds*, 72.
74. Hedgeman, *The Trumpet Sounds*, 73–74.
75. Hedgeman, *The Trumpet Sounds*, 77–78. Black journalist Marvel Cooke would write about Hedgeman's leadership at the Ashland Place YWCA in Cooke, "Woman of Tremendous Energy Is Behind Guns at Ashland Place," *NYAN*, May 13, 1939.
76. AAH-ED, 62.
77. Musician Eubie Blake would memorize his music so as not to seem to be reading it; that went over better with white audiences, who saw his talent as raw and untutored. See Douglas, *Terrible Honesty*, 431.
78. Lanker, *I Dream a World*.
79. Hedgeman, *The Trumpet Sounds*, 79. See also AAH-RM, 82–83.
80. Beverton, "Fauset, Crystal Bird."
81. Hedgeman, *The Trumpet Sounds*, 79–80. See also "Mrs. Hedgeman Highly Honored at Huge Brooklyn Reception," *NYAN*, January 31, 1942, which noted her efforts on behalf of interracial cooperation in New York City.

CHAPTER 6

1. "Office of Civilian Defense," The Eleanor Roosevelt Papers Project http://www .gwu.edu/~erpapers/teachinger/glossary/office-civilian-defense.cfm.

2. See Goodwin, *No Ordinary Time*, particularly chapter 11, "A Completely Changed World," 270–99.

3. Gallagher, *Black Women and Politics in New York City*, 62; McEnaney, *Civil Defense Begins at Home*, 18.

4. "Office of Civilian Defense."

5. In a tribute to Eleanor Roosevelt, Anna Arnold Hedgeman remembered attending several talks given by Roosevelt before they formally met. Anna would always sit up front, hoping Roosevelt would see her as "a repeat customer." "It was good to see a woman courageously saying things that needed to be said—she would look up and down each row of people before she spoke as though she was trying to fathom each individual." From Anna Arnold Hedgeman, "Tribute to Eleanor Roosevelt," Box 172, AAH-N. Evidence that Eleanor Roosevelt recommended Anna for the position can be found in FBI files, Anna Arnold Hedgeman.

6. Gilmore, *Defying Dixie*, 377.

7. AAH-ED, 87.

8. Hedgeman, *The Trumpet Sounds*, 80.

9. AAH-ED, 87.

10. Hedgeman, "The Role of the Negro Woman," 467.

11. Dalfiume, "The 'Forgotten Years' of the Negro Revolution," 102.

12. Garfinkel, *When Negroes March*, 28.

13. Hedgeman, *The Trumpet Sounds*, 80.

14. On the US military–Red Cross agreement, see Guglielmo, "'Red Cross, Double Cross.'"

15. "American Red Cross History," http://www.redcross.org/about-us/history/red-cross-american-history/contributions-people-of-color; Starr, *Blood*; see also Love, *One Blood*.

16. Hedgeman, *The Trumpet Sounds*, 81.

17. Hedgeman, *The Trumpet Sounds*, 82. On Charles Drew's death, and the rumor that he died because a white hospital in North Carolina would not treat him, see chapter 2 of Love, *One Blood*. Although it was rumor rather than true in the case of Charles Drew, such medical neglect did result in the deaths of other African Americans.

18. Anna Arnold Hedgeman, "Your Part in the Fight for a Permanent FEPC," Box 12, AAH-N.

19. Kesselman, *The Social Politics of FEPC*, 7.

20. Edward Rothstein, "Over There, and Here as Well: 'WWII & NYC' at the New-York Historical Society," *NYT*, October 4, 2012.

21. Garfinkel, *When Negroes March*, 24.

22. See Morehouse, *Fighting in the Jim Crow Army*; Brandt, *Harlem at War*.

23. Merritt Hedgeman, "Untitled," Box 144, AAH-N.

24. Merritt Hedgeman, "Letter to Ersa Posten," January 30, 1974, Box 66, AAH-N.

25. "Sings with First Lady," n.d., Box 66, AAH-N.

26. On the Tuskegee Airmen, see Moye, *Freedom Flyers*.

27. Kersten, *A. Philip Randolph*, 55.

28. AAH-ED, 88.

29. AAH-ED, 88–90.

30. Richards, *Maida Springer*, 81.

31. Richards, *Maida Springer*, 81.

32. "Push Fight on Prejudice in New York Women's Clubs," *CD*, April 3, 1943. See also "New York Women's Federation Accused of Color Bar," *CD*, March 27, 1943; "Midtown Business Women Win Charter in Race Bias Dispute," *NYAN*, May 1, 1943.

33. In fact, when at one point Anna was laid off from the Office of Civilian Defense because of budget cuts, a protest launched on her behalf by Harlem leaders led to her reinstatement. See "Dismissed, Retained in OCD Staff Cut," *NYAN*, July 17, 1943.

34. James Hicks, "Another Angle," *NYV*, June 2, 1979.

35. Williams, *Servants of the People*, 31.

36. Arnesen, *Brotherhoods of Color*, 18.

37. Arnesen, "A. Philip Randolph," 79.

38. Williams, *Servants of the People*, 32.

39. Pfeffer, *A. Philip Randolph*, 45.

40. Sitkoff, "African American Militancy in the World War II South," 70.

41. On the MOWM's origins, see Taylor, *A. Philip Randolph*, 130. Belinda Robnett claims that an unnamed black woman at a Chicago strategy session posed the idea and that Randolph seconded it—and then moved on it. See Robnett, *How Long? How Long?*, 47.

42. Kesselman, *The Social Politics of FEPC*, 3.

43. Bates, *Pullman Porters and the Rise of Protest Politics in Black America*, 155.

44. Sitkoff, "African American Militancy in the World War II South," 70–85.

45. Bynum, *A. Philip Randolph and the Struggle for Civil Rights*, 167.

46. Sitkoff, "African American Militancy in the World War II South," 89–91.

47. Taylor, *A. Philip Randolph*, 165.

48. Taylor, *A. Philip Randolph*, 220.

49. Taylor, *A. Philip Randolph*, 154.

50. Murray, *Pauli Murray*.

51. Shaw, *What a Woman Ought to Be and to Do*, 200.

52. Gilmore, *Defying Dixie*, 365.

53. Gilmore, *Defying Dixie*, 359.

54. Cobble, *The Other Women's Movement*, 14.

55. Reed, *Seedtime for the Modern Civil Rights Movement*, 203.

56. Reed, *Seedtime for the Modern Civil Rights Movement*, 41.

57. Anderson, *A. Philip Randolph*, 266–67. For a description of the "cohort of young black women" who pushed for wartime employment for African American women, see Jones, *The March on Washington*, 45–47.
58. Bates, *Pullman Porters and the Rise of Protest Politics in Black America*, 157.
59. Taylor, *A. Philip Randolph*, 133.
60. Kersten, *A. Philip Randolph*, 59.
61. Bates, *Pullman Porters and the Rise of Protest Politics in Black America*, 159.
62. Bates, *Pullman Porters and the Rise of Protest Politics in Black America*, 165.
63. Taylor, *A. Philip Randolph*, 184.
64. Kersten, *A. Philip Randolph*, 63.
65. Gilmore, *Defying Dixie*, 364.
66. Kersten, *Race, Jobs, and the War*, 138.
67. Hedgeman, "The Role of the Negro Woman."
68. George L. P. Weaver, "Letter to A. Philip Randolph," n.d., Box 12, AAH-N.
69. Kesselman, *The Social Politics of FEPC*, ix.
70. Hedgeman, *The Trumpet Sounds*, 86. On the demise of the MOWM, see Sitkoff, "African American Militancy in the World War II South."

CHAPTER 7

1. See Jones, *The March on Washington*; "To Plan 'Back FEPC' Parley," *PC*, January 1, 1944.
2. Jones, *The March on Washington*, 74.
3. AAH-ED, 91.
4. AAH-ED, 92.
5. Hedgeman, *The Gift of Chaos*, 4.
6. Hedgeman, *The Trumpet Sounds*, 88.
7. Hedgeman, *The Trumpet Sounds*, 88.
8. AAH-ED, 94; Kesselman, *The Social Politics of FEPC*, 46.
9. Pauli Murray, "Letter to Anna Arnold Hedgeman," February 11, 1946, Box 73, Folder 1280, PMP; Anna Arnold Hedgeman, "Telegram to Pauli Murray," February 25, 1946, Box 73, Folder 1280, PMP.
10. Hedgeman, *The Trumpet Sounds*, 88.
11. "Refused Service in Senate Cafe, Women Protest," *CD*, September 16, 1944.
12. National Committee on Segregation in the Nation's Capital, *Segregation in Washington*, 2.
13. National Committee on Segregation in the Nation's Capital, *Segregation in Washington*, 6.
14. National Committee on Segregation in the Nation's Capital, *Segregation in Washington*, 6.
15. Karl E. Meyer, "Washington, USA: A Colonial Portrait," *NL*, March 18, 1963, 17; Ward, *Defending White Democracy*, 71–78.

16. National Committee on Segregation in the Nation's Capital, *Segregation in Washington*, 88.

17. Kesselman, *The Social Politics of FEPC*, 41.

18. Harry McAlpin, "Un-covering Washington," *ADW*, June 23, 1945.

19. Kesselman, *The Social Politics of FEPC*, 40.

20. Anna Arnold Hedgeman, "Your Part in the Fight for a Permanent FEPC," Box 164, AAH-N.

21. Hedgeman, *The Trumpet Sounds*, 91–92.

22. Anna Arnold Hedgeman, "Tribute to A. Philip Randolph on His 87th Birthday," Box 151, AAH-N; "Urge Support of FEPC Here," *PC*, January 27, 1945; "Anna Arnold Hedgeman Heads Fine Staff," *PC*, December 1, 1945; "Anna Hedgeman Begins FEPC Drive Monday," *CC-P*, April 28, 1945; McAlpin, "Un-covering Washington"; "FEPC Rally Set for March 16th at Golden Gate," *NYAN*, March 10, 1945; "Intensity Drive for Permanent Federal FEPC," *NNJG*, September 22, 1945.

23. In a 1983 letter from Hedgeman to Benjamin Payton, she recalled that A. G. Gaston let her use his office, and offered to do some typing for her, decades earlier when she traveled south for the National Council for a Permanent FEPC. See Anna Arnold Hedgeman, "Letter to Benjamin Payton, President of Tuskegee Institute," February 17, 1983, Box 68, AAH-N.

24. Reed, *Seedtime for the Modern Civil Rights Movement*, 162. Louis Kesselman argues that although the churches were "ripe" for civil rights activity, the National Council helped move them forward. See Kesselman, *The Social Politics of FEPC*, 128. See also Chen, *The Fifth Freedom*.

25. Kesselman, *The Social Politics of FEPC*, 46.

26. *BAA*, August 10, 1946; *CD*, August 10, 1946.

27. AAH-ED, 94.

28. Pfeffer, *A. Philip Randolph*, 117.

29. Kesselman, *The Social Politics of FEPC*, 37.

30. Ellen Hoffman, "Rep. William L. Dawson Dies," *WP*, November 10, 1970.

31. Hedgeman, *The Trumpet Sounds*, 89.

32. Both cited in Hamilton and Hamilton, *The Dual Agenda*, 280n89.

33. Pfeffer, *A. Philip Randolph*, 107.

34. Jones, *The March on Washington*, 75–76.

35. Kersten, *A. Philip Randolph*, 63; Kesselman, *The Social Politics of FEPC*, 40–41, 49.

36. Kesselman, *The Social Politics of FEPC*, 174.

37. Chen, *The Fifth Freedom*, 67.

38. Paula Pfeffer argues that Hedgeman was "abrasive" in her treatment of the regional leaders, but she provides no documentation following the argument. See Pfeffer, *A. Philip Randolph*, 100.

39. Ransby, *Ella Baker and the Black Freedom Movement*, 142.
40. Boris Shishkin, "Boris Shishkin to A. Philip Randolph," August 12, 1946, Box 258, FEPC Folder, NAACP.
41. McAlpin, "Un-covering Washington."
42. AAH-ED, 96.
43. Pfeffer, *A. Philip Randolph*, 104.
44. Hedgeman, "Your Part in the Fight for a Permanent FEPC."
45. Hedgeman quoted in Kesselman, *The Social Politics of FEPC*, 46.
46. Kesselman, *The Social Politics of FEPC*, 128–42.
47. Kesselman, *The Social Politics of FEPC*, 201.
48. For this detail, I also consulted a prepublication draft of Jones, *The March on Washington*.
49. Kesselman, *The Social Politics of FEPC*, 71.
50. Kesselman, *The Social Politics of FEPC*, 81.
51. "Anna Arnold Hedgeman Heads Fine Staff."
52. "Seven Volunteer for Free Office Work for FEPC," *ADW*, February 6, 1946.
53. Kesselman, *The Social Politics of FEPC*, 61–63.
54. Anna Arnold Hedgeman quoted in Kesselman, *The Social Politics of FEPC*, 37.
55. Garfinkel, *When Negroes March*, 214n40.
56. Kesselman, *The Social Politics of FEPC*, 40. See also Louis Lutier, "In Nation's Capital," *NYAN*, November 22, 1947; "A. Philip Randolph Blamed for Failure of National FEPC Council," *CC-P*, August 17, 1946.
57. Charley Cherokee, "National Grapevine," *CD*, June 24, 1944.
58. Sidney Wilkinson, "Letter to Rev. Allan Knight Chalmers," May 19, 1947, quoted in Jones, *The March on Washington*, 78.
59. Pfeffer, *A. Philip Randolph*, 302.
60. See Boyle, *The UAW and the Heyday of American Liberalism*.
61. Boyle, *The UAW and the Heyday of American Liberalism*, 109–10.
62. AAH-ED, 85.
63. Hedgeman quoted in Ramona Bowden, "Racial Strife in Continuation of US Revolution," clipping, March 16, 1967, Box 157, AAH-N.
64. See Arnesen, "A. Philip Randolph," 86–87; Hedgeman, "Tribute to A. Philip Randolph on His 87th Birthday." Labor leader Maida Springer had a similar relationship with Randolph. She refused to take on MOWM work until someone told her that Randolph believed in her. "Well, I was dead in the water, then," she recalled later. See Richards, *Maida Springer*, 88–89.
65. AAH-ED, 133.
66. AAH-ED, 99.
67. AAH-ED, 100.
68. White and Maze, *Henry A. Wallace*, 261. White and Maze make no mention either of Hedgeman or of the role African Americans played in the 1948 campaign.

69. Lawson, *Running for Freedom*, 13.
70. Lawson, *Running for Freedom*, 33. See also Gardner, *Harry Truman and Civil Rights*, 589–91.
71. McCullough, *Truman*, 720.
72. McCullough, *Truman*, 587.
73. Henry Lee Moon quoted in Dudziak, *Cold War Civil Rights*, 261n16.
74. Lawson, *Running for Freedom*, 36.
75. Burnes, *Harry S. Truman*, 137.
76. Hedgeman, *The Trumpet Sounds*, 96.
77. Wallace, *The Price of Vision*, 393.
78. McCullough, *Truman*, 645.
79. McCullough, *Truman*, 645.
80. Gardner, *Harry Truman and Civil Rights*, 101.
81. Leuchtenburg, *In the Shadow of FDR*, 23.
82. Gardner, *Harry Truman and Civil Rights*, 120.
83. Gardner, *Harry Truman and Civil Rights*, 112. See also Hedgeman, "The Role of the Negro Woman."
84. Franklin and Collier-Thomas, "For the Race in General and Black Women in Particular," 37; "National Council of Negro Women Lauds Truman at 13th Annual Confab," *ADW*, October 17, 1948.
85. Manning, *William L. Dawson and the Limits of Black Electoral Leadership*, 111; Franklin and Collier-Thomas, "For the Race in General and Black Women in Particular."
86. Manning, *William L. Dawson and the Limits of Black Electoral Leadership*, 111.
87. See Manning, *William L. Dawson and the Limits of Black Electoral Leadership*, 111.
88. Manning, *William L. Dawson and the Limits of Black Electoral Leadership*, 96.
89. Hedgeman, *The Trumpet Sounds*, 95.
90. Manning, *William L. Dawson and the Limits of Black Electoral Leadership*, 111.
91. Manning, *William L. Dawson and the Limits of Black Electoral Leadership*, 111.
92. Hedgeman, *The Gift of Chaos*, 21.
93. Anna Arnold Hedgeman, "Untitled Talk," n.d., Box 150, AAH-N.
94. Anna Arnold Hedgeman, "Letter to Daisy Bates," 1982, Box 68, AAH-N; "Arkansas Leader Donates $1000 to Truman Campaign," *ADW*, July 24, 1948; "Atlanta Leaders Form Local Truman for President Committee," *ADW*, September 14, 1948; "Negroes Step Up Tempo for Truman's Election," *ADW*, September 22, 1948.
95. "Negroes Step Up Tempo for Truman's Election."
96. Gardner, *Harry Truman and Civil Rights*, 122.
97. Gardner, *Harry Truman and Civil Rights*, 137.
98. Harry S. Truman, Harlem Speech, October 29, 1948, quoted in Gardner, *Harry Truman and Civil Rights*, 122.

99. President Truman was granted the Roosevelt Award again in 1952, also in Dorrance Brooks Square. He spoke about the earlier event and the First Lady's experience there. Harry S. Truman, "Address in Harlem, New York, upon Receiving the Franklin Roosevelt Award," October 11, 1952.

100. Gardner, *Harry Truman and Civil Rights*, 145.

101. See Lawson, *Running for Freedom*, 36; Gardner, *Harry Truman and Civil Rights*, 90, 100, 44; Hamby, *Man of the People*, 464–65; Ferrel, *Harry S. Truman*, 282–83; Manning, *William L. Dawson and the Limits of Black Electoral Leadership*, 111–13.

102. On the role of blacks in the election, see Dudziak, *Cold War Civil Rights*, 27.

103. Quoted in Manning, *William L. Dawson and the Limits of Black Electoral Leadership*, 113.

104. Quoted in Manning, *William L. Dawson and the Limits of Black Electoral Leadership*, 112.

105. As noted earlier, the black press was clear about Anna's contributions. Journalist James Hicks described her as a "good gambler" when it came to Truman. "Uses an occasional 'damn' but always in the right places," he wrote, "Likes pretty hats." James Hicks, "Big Town," *CC-P*, September 3, 1949.

106. Ransby, *Ella Baker and the Black Freedom Movement*, 4.

CHAPTER 8

1. On African Americans' relationships to foreign policy in this period, see Plummer, *Window on Freedom*, 464; Hedgeman, "The Role of the Negro Woman."

2. Manning, *William L. Dawson and the Limits of Black Electoral Leadership*, 114. On black patronage in an earlier era, see Masur, "Patronage and Protest in Kate Brown's Washington."

3. Manning, *William L. Dawson and the Limits of Black Electoral Leadership*, 114.

4. Manning, *William L. Dawson and the Limits of Black Electoral Leadership*, 117.

5. Manning, *William L. Dawson and the Limits of Black Electoral Leadership*, 114.

6. Manning, *William L. Dawson and the Limits of Black Electoral Leadership*, 116.

7. "Job Description: Assistant to Administrator, Federal Security Agency," 1948, Box 124, AAH-N.

8. "Anna Arnold Hedgeman: Autobiographical Sketch," Box 129, AAH-N.

9. "Highlights of 1949," *NYAN*, December 31, 1949; "High U.S. Post to Anna Hedgeman," *PC*, February 19, 1949; "The Courier Salutes," *PC*, February 26, 1949.

10. Jones, "An End to the Neglect of the Problems of the Negro Woman!," 119. On Jones, see McDuffie, *Sojourning for Freedom*; Davies, *Left of Karl Marx*. McDuffie argues that although Jones's anticapitalist politics set her apart from women like

Hedgeman, Jones did collaborate with her "more politically mainstream sisters" (10). The fact that Jones specifically noted Hedgeman's radical potential, and its loss to mainstream politics, certainly supports McDuffie's argument.

11. Manning, *William L. Dawson and the Limits of Black Electoral Leadership*, 117. Dawson was speaking at an engagement sponsored by the Dallas Council of Negro Women that drew eight hundred women.

12. Hedgeman, *The Gift of Chaos*, 22.

13. Hedgeman, *The Trumpet Sounds*, 97.

14. Hedgeman, *The Trumpet Sounds*, 97–99.

15. AAH-ED, 119.

16. AAH-ED, 119.

17. AAH-ED, 117; see also Borstelmann, *The Cold War and the Color Line*; Plummer, *In Search of Power*.

18. "Mid-century White House Conference on Children and Youth Draws More than 6,000," *TI*, December 16, 1950.

19. "Mrs. Anna Arnold Hedgeman, Assistant to Federal Security Administration, in Washington's Freeman's Hospital," *TI*, December 16, 1950.

20. Hedgeman, *The Trumpet Sounds*, 106; "Hedgeman Seen as Dark Horse for National Council Post," *WA-A*, November 15, 1949.

21. See Horne, *The End of Empires*.

22. Chester Bowles, "Letter to Jane Hoey," 1952, Box 22, AAH-N.

23. Bowles, "Letter to Jane Hoey."

24. Chester Bowles, "Letter to Secretary of State," 1952, Box 8, AAH-N.

25. In an interview thirty years after the India trip, Hedgeman identified Whitney Young as the National Urban League representative in India. In fact, it was Lester Granger who made the trip and who provided the keynote address titled "Basic Human Needs" at the international conference. Young succeeded Granger as executive director of the Urban League in 1961. See Lester Granger, "Letter to Mrs. Bowles," September 15, 1952, Part III, Series 1, Box 86, Folder 81, CBP.

26. Hedgeman, *The Gift of Chaos*, 26.

27. AAH-ED, 121. On black Americans and the FBI in the Cold War, see Plummer, *Rising Wind*; Dudziak, *Cold War Civil Rights*; Polsgrove, *Divided Minds*; Lieberman, "'Another Side of the Story.'"

28. AAH-FBI, 1949, obtained by author under Freedom of Information Act.

29. AAH-FBI, 1949.

30. AAH-FBI, 1949, 1952, 1963, 1964.

31. AAH-FBI, 1964.

32. Hedgeman, *The Trumpet Sounds*, 100.

33. Anna Arnold Hedgeman, "Letter to John," December 13, 1952, Box 122, AAH-N.

34. Anna Arnold Hedgeman, "Letter to Mrs. Krishnaswami," April 17, 1953, Box 122, AAH-N.

35. Hedgeman, *The Trumpet Sounds*, 100.
36. Anna Arnold Hedgeman, "Letters to Merritt Hedgeman," 1952–53, Box 123, AAH-N.
37. Hedgeman, *The Trumpet Sounds*, 100.
38. Hedgeman, "Letter to John."
39. Anna Arnold Hedgeman, "Untitled Document, India Trip," n.d., Box 122, AAH-N.
40. Hedgeman, "Untitled Document, India Trip."
41. Hedgeman, *The Gift of Chaos*, 31.
42. Hedgeman, "Untitled Document, India Trip."
43. Bowles, *Ambassador's Report*, 31.
44. Hedgeman, *The Gift of Chaos*, 28.
45. "How Not to Make Friends," *Time*, August 25, 1952, Box 111, Folder 496, CBP.
46. Chester Bowles, "Letter to Donald Montgomery," January 22, 1953, Box 89, Folder 137, CBP.
47. Chester Bowles, "Letter to Donald Montgomery," February 27, 1953, Box 89, Folder 137, CBP.
48. Chester Bowles, "Racial Minorities in American Life," February 1953, Box 115, Folder 541, CBP; Schaffer, *Chester Bowles*, 144–45, 74–75, 98.
49. Chester Bowles, "Letter to Walter White," July 9, 1952, Box 92, Folder 212, CBP.
50. Hedgeman, "Letters to Merritt Hedgeman."
51. Anna Arnold Hedgeman, "Letter to Galip Kardam," March 31, 1953, Box 123, AAH-N.
52. Hedgeman, "Letters to Merritt Hedgeman."
53. Von Eschen, *Race against Empire*, 70; see also Anderson, *Eyes off the Prize*; Plummer, *Windows on Freedom*.
54. Plummer, *Rising Wind*, 136.
55. See Gaines, *African Americans in Ghana*; Horne, *Mau Mau in Harlem?*; Borstelmann, *The Cold War and the Color Line*.
56. Jane M. Kerina, "Letter to Anna Arnold Hedgeman," June 22, 1960, Box 12, AAH-N.
57. Eleanor Roosevelt, "Letter, 'Dear Friend,'" n.d., Box 126, AAH-N; American Committee on Africa, "Statement on the US, the UN, and the Congo," n.d., Box 126, AAH-N.
58. Anna Arnold Hedgeman, "One Woman's Opinion," *NYA*, April 25, 1959.
59. Gaines, *African Americans in Ghana*, 2.
60. Polsgrove, *Divided Minds*, 133–37.
61. Hedgeman, *The Gift of Chaos*, 194.
62. Hedgeman, *The Trumpet Sounds*, 135.
63. Hedgeman, *The Trumpet Sounds*, 135.
64. Polsgrove, *Divided Minds*, 190.

65. Anna Arnold Hedgeman, "Women in Public Life: Keynote Address in Ghana," July 18, 1960, Box 127, AAH-N.

66. Hedgeman, "Women in Public Life."

67. Hedgeman, "Women in Public Life."

68. Pauli Murray, "Speech, Conference of Women of Africa and of African Descent," July 18, 1960, Box 40, AAH-N.

69. The resolution called on the women to resolve that "the women of the world be urged by the first Conference of African Women and Women of African Descent to oppose with the utmost vigor segregation, discrimination and oppression in the Congo, Algeria, South Africa and the United States." See Anna Arnold Hedgeman, "Africa and American Racial Practices," June 21, 1961, Box 126, AAH-N.

70. Anna Arnold Hedgeman's resistance to including the United States in a list alongside South Africa was similar to Eleanor Roosevelt's resistance to the Civil Rights Congress's essay "We Charge Genocide," which was submitted to the UN Secretariat in New York City and the General Assembly in Paris in 1951. Roosevelt felt that the document insufficiently distinguished between the "institutionalized murder" of the Nazis and the "institutionalized oppression" of the United States. See Plummer, *Rising Wind*, 202.

71. "Statement to the Conference of African Women and Women of African Descent."

72. Hedgeman, "Africa and American Racial Practices."

73. Hedgeman, "Africa and American Racial Practices."

74. Hedgeman, *The Trumpet Sounds*, 139.

75. Hedgeman, *The Gift of Chaos*, 201.

76. Hedgeman, *The Trumpet Sounds*, 135.

CHAPTER 9

1. Hedgeman, *The Gift of Chaos*, 38; Hedgeman, *The Trumpet Sounds*, 106–7.

2. Wilson, *Meet Me at the Theresa*, 94.

3. Wilson, *Meet Me at the Theresa*, 112.

4. Wilson, *Meet Me at the Theresa*, 153.

5. Wilson, *Meet Me at the Theresa*, 115.

6. Wilson, *Meet Me at the Theresa*, 155.

7. Ernest Dunbar, "The View from Lenox Terrace," *New York Times Magazine*, March 3, 1968.

8. Greenberg, *"Or Does It Explode?,"* 103.

9. Margaret Donaldson, "She Is Assistant to New York's Mayor," *Christian Advocate* 131, no. 6 (February 1956).

10. Gallagher, *Black Women and Politics in New York City*, 100–103.

11. Hedgeman, *The Gift of Chaos*, 39.

12. Pauli Murray, "Letter to Anna Arnold Hedgeman," November 25, 1983, Box 96, Folder 1703, PMP.

13. Harlem Citizens Committee for Hedgeman for Borough President, "Letter to Joseph Pinckney, Victory Democratic Club," July 1953, Box 14, AAH-N.

14. Hedgeman, *The Gift of Chaos*, 39.

15. Anna Arnold Hedgeman, "Untitled." After Harlem congressman Adam Clayton Powell Jr. made derogatory remarks about First Lady Bess Truman's membership in the Daughters of the American Revolution, Powell was unable to secure patronage appointments like the one that provided Hedgeman's entrée into national politics. From her position in the FSA, Hedgeman assisted Hulan Jack in his efforts to achieve a federal patronage appointment from his district. See Hedgeman, *The Trumpet Sounds*, 109; Miller Center of Public Affairs, University of Virginia, "Bess Truman."

16. AAH-BL.

17. Hedgeman, *The Trumpet Sounds*, 111.

18. Hedgeman, *The Gift of Chaos*, 39.

19. Anna Arnold Hedgeman, "Tribute to Eleanor Roosevelt," n.d., Box 172, AAH-N.

20. William Brown, "Letter to Anna Arnold Hedgeman," n.d., Box 1, AAH-N.

21. Hedgeman, *The Trumpet Sounds*, 113.

22. Hedgeman, *The Trumpet Sounds*, 114.

23. Vernon Sinclair, "Anna Hedgeman Appointed Aide to the Mayor," *AN*, January 9, 1954, 1; "Mrs. Hedgeman Named to City Cabinet Post," *AN*, January 30, 1954; *AN*, November 28, 1953.

24. Hedgeman, *The Trumpet Sounds*, 114.

25. Hedgeman, *The Trumpet Sounds*, 116–17, 23.

26. James L. Hicks, "Hulan Jack, Mrs. Hedgeman Get Top Jobs," clipping, n.d., Box 161, AAH-N.

27. Hedgeman, *The Trumpet Sounds*, 116.

28. Within days of Hedgeman's appointment, Edward Lewis, of the New York Urban League, wrote a letter to the new mayor to protest her publicly posted salary. See Edward Lewis, "Letter to Mayor Robert F. Wagner, Jr.," January 4, 1954, Box 76, Folder 1062, RFW.

29. Hedgeman, *The Trumpet Sounds*, 116–17; Gaines, *African Americans in Ghana*, 122.

30. "Mayoral Correspondence," 1954–58, AAH-N.

31. Herschel Richey, "Convention Impressions," *Postal Alliance*, September 1955, Box 4, AAH-N.

32. "Validity of Municipal Law Barring Discrimination in Private Housing," 729.

33. AAH-ED, 154.

34. On black women outnumbering men on voting rolls, see Gallagher, *Black Women and Politics in New York City*, 87–88.

35. Gallagher, *Black Women and Politics in New York City*, 104–5.

36. Gallagher, *Black Women and Politics in New York City*, 105.

37. Gallagher, *Black Women and Politics in New York City*, 109.

38. Hedgeman, *The Gift of Chaos*, 43.

39. On women and wasted talent, see AAH-ED, 153–54.

40. Anna Arnold Hedgeman, "Negro Women Fought Hard for Recognition," *NYA*, September 3, 1955.

41. AAH-ED, 147–48.

42. James L. Hicks, "New 'Black Joe' Is Utility Club Hit," *NYAN*, June 21, 1958, 1, 9.

43. Hicks, "New 'Black Joe' Is Utility Club Hit," 9.

44. "Letters from Students, Mayoral Correspondence," 1958, Box 3, AAH-N.

45. "Letters from Students, Mayoral Correspondence."

46. Anna Arnold Hedgeman, "Letter to Barbara Payne," 1958, Box 3, AAH-N.

47. Anna Arnold Hedgeman, "Why I Left City Hall," *NYA*, October 25, 1958.

48. Anna Arnold Hedgeman, "Draft of "'One Woman's Opinion," October 19, 1959, AAH-N.

49. Hedgeman, *The Gift of Chaos*, 41.

50. Hedgeman, *The Gift of Chaos*, 232.

51. Hedgeman, "Why I Left City Hall."

52. Hedgeman, *The Trumpet Sounds*.

53. Hedgeman, *The Gift of Chaos*, 45.

54. AAH-ED, 160. Bessie and her sister Sally Louise "Sadie" would become famous years later as the Delany Sisters of a best-selling book. Delany, *Having Our Say*.

55. Amos Landman, "Statement by Anna Arnold Hedgeman to National Conference on Government," November 9, 1954, AAH-N.

56. Hedgeman, *The Trumpet Sounds*, 123.

57. "Assistant to New York Mayor Attracts 500 to Statler," *CC-P*, June 1, 1957.

58. Ray, *All Shook Up*, 49.

59. Ray, *All Shook Up*, 49. Evidence of Hedgeman's authorship can be found in Elizabeth McHarry, "Letter to Archibald Ray," Box 32, AAH-N; AAH-ED, 173.

60. Hedgeman, *The Gift of Chaos*, 45.

61. Anna Arnold Hedgeman, "Letter to Mayor Robert F. Wagner, Jr.," September 25, 1958, AAH-N. See also "Aide to Mayor Resigns: Mrs. Hedgeman Will Work for a Cosmetics Firm," *NYT*, clipping, Box 3, AAH-N.

62. Anna Arnold Hedgeman, "Letter to Mayor Robert F. Wagner, Jr.," October 1, 1958, Box 3, AAH-N; AAH-ED, 153.

63. Hedgeman, "Why I Left City Hall."

64. AAH-ED, 154–77; Hedgeman, *The Trumpet Sounds*, 126–28.

65. Wilson, *Meet Me at the Theresa*, 196.

66. Myrna and Harvey Frommer argue that the general practice in New York City politics was to run, for the slots of mayor, comptroller, and president of the city

council, one man from the Bronx, one from Manhattan, and one from Brooklyn, one Irish, one Jewish, and one Italian. Residents of Staten Island and Queens, women, and people from other ethnic or racial groups were decidedly and deliberately left out. See Frommer and Frommer, *It Happened in Manhattan*, 249–50.

67. Anna Arnold Hedgeman, "One Woman's Opinion," *NYA*, January 23, 1960.

68. East Bronx Independent Committee for Political Reform, "Candidate Hedgeman in the News," 1960, Box 158, AAH-N.

69. Gonzalez, *The Bronx*, 114–15.

70. East Bronx Independent Committee for Political Reform, "Feel Neglected? Want a Voice in Washington to Speak for You?," Box 158, AAH-N.

71. East Bronx Independent Committee for Political Reform, "Candidate Hedgeman in the News."

72. "'Neglected' Races Asking Reform," *NYP*, April 22, 1960; "In the Background," *NYP*, March 20, 1960; "Bronx Negroes Seek Gains in Primaries," *NYAN*, June 4, 1960.

73. Rhea Calloway, "Will She Be 1st Negro Lady in Congress?," *CC*, June 4, 1960.

74. "Hedgeman, Hawkins Lose in Bronx," *NYAN*, June 11, 1960.

75. Hedgeman, *The Trumpet Sounds*, 133.

CHAPTER 10

1. Hedgeman, *The Trumpet Sounds*, 166.

2. King, "A Challenge to the Churches and Synagogues," 171. For more about the Emancipation Proclamation centennial and the National Council of Churches, see "Emancipation Proclamation 100th Anniversary," January 1, 1963, RG6, Box 46, Folder 3, NCC.

3. Dr. Martin Luther King Jr. had spoken about the upcoming centennial: "There is but one way to commemorate the Emancipation Proclamation. That is to make its declarations of freedom real; to reach back to the origins of our nation when our message of equality electrified an unfree world, and reaffirm democracy by deeds as bold and daring as the issuance of the Emancipation Proclamation." Martin Luther King Jr., "New York Civil War Centennial Commission Emancipation Proclamation Observance Speech," September 12, 1962, Box 27, AAH-N. On the life of Benjamin Mays, see Jelks, *Benjamin Elijah Mays*.

4. Ahmann, *Race*, 3.

5. King, "A Challenge to the Churches and Synagogues," 157.

6. For more on Church Women United, see Collier-Thomas, *Jesus, Jobs, and Justice*.

7. See Hedgeman, *The Trumpet Sounds*, 175–77.

8. AAH-ED.

9. Anna Arnold Hedgeman, "Handwritten Notes, National Conference on Religion and Race," 1963, Box 33, AAH-N. As Bettye Collier-Thomas puts it, "Like the

ubiquitous interracial meetings of the 1930s, '40s, and '50s, the conference was long on rhetoric and short on proposals for programs of action." Collier-Thomas, *Jesus, Jobs, and Justice*, 420.

10. For histories of the National Council of Churches, see Gill, *Embattled Ecumenism*; Collier-Thomas, *Jesus, Jobs, and Justice*. Gill's focus is on Vietnam, but she nevertheless provides a fairly comprehensive history of the council as a whole and of the CRR, which provided a powerful model for the council's later antiwar work. Collier-Thomas's comprehensive work is the definitive source for the history of black women's involvement in the National Council and in its member organizations.

11. In the first of his trilogy of works on the United States in the years of Martin Luther King Jr., Taylor Branch explores the history of Riverside Church. See Branch, *Parting the Waters*, 38–39.

12. Gill, *Embattled Ecumenism*, 4, 47.

13. Findlay, *Church People in the Struggle*, 49.

14. Gill argues that for its entire life the NCC has lived "in the crosshairs of conservatives eager not only to criticize it but to destroy it and the ecumenical movement it advocates." See Gill, *Embattled Ecumenism*, 7. Both the Hedgeman Papers and the NCC Papers contain newspaper clippings, letters, and flyers accusing the organization of communist leanings. A typical example is "What Do You Really Know about the NCC?" by the Kalamazoo Chapter of Christian Laymen. "This country should be warned," they cautioned, "and should be braced, for a Negro insurrection which is nothing less than a Communist invasion of American cities." See Kalamazoo Chapter of Christian Laymen, "What Do You Really Know about the NCC?," 1964, Box 94, AAH-N. See also Collier-Thomas, *Jesus, Jobs, and Justice*; Gilkes, *If It Wasn't for the Women*.

15. McWhorter, *Carry Me Home*; Branch, *Parting the Waters*; Eskew, *But for Birmingham*.

16. On the *Brown* decision, see Patterson, Brown v. Board of Education; Kluger, *Simple Justice*.

17. James Baldwin quoted in Henry Clark, "Congress, the Church, and the Kairos," September 4, 1963, NCC.

18. Robert Spike, "The Church and Civil Rights: A Contemporary Account of Mission in Action," November 1965, AAH-N.

19. In his letter, King wrote: "If today's church does not recapture the sacrificial spirit of the early church, it will lose its authenticity, forfeit the loyalty of millions, and be dismissed as an irrelevant social club with no meaning for the twentieth century. See King, "Letter from Birmingham Jail."

20. President's Temporary Committee of Six on Race, "A Report of the President's Temporary Committee of Six on Race," June 7, 1963, Box 40, AAH-N.

21. For a comprehensive history of the Commission on Religion and Race, see Findlay, *Church People in the Struggle*. See also President's Temporary Committee of Six on Race, "A Report of the President's Temporary Committee of Six on Race."

22. Findlay, *Church People in the Struggle*, 19. Findlay argues, in fact, that Race Relations Sunday was so popular in part because it demanded so little (*Church People in the Struggle*, 18–19). Lee outlined the history of Race Relations Sunday, and his attempts to improve on it, in J. Oscar Lee, "Race Relations Sunday, Then and Now," February 1954, RG6, Box 46, Folder 15, NCC. See also A. C. Sterling, "Builder of Brotherhood: Dr. J. Oscar Lee of National Council of Churches Devotes His Time to Welding Harmony among Races, Newspaper Reprint," October 20, 1951, RG6, Box 46, Folder 15, NCC.

23. "Description of the Commission on Religion and Race," May 4, 1965, p. 19, Box 22, AAH-N. See also Branch, *Pillar of Fire*, 104–5.

24. Robert Spike, "Report of the Executive Director to the Commission on Religion and Race," September 15, 1964, RG6, Box 2, Folder 14, NCC; Gill, *Embattled Ecumenism*, 4. Later, when the Reverend Benjamin Payton was appointed the first black executive director of the Commission on Religion and Race, he made plain his objections to Race Relations Sunday. Instead of holding an annual " 'Be-Kind-to-Negroes' week," he argued, or any other of the "little aspirins by which we salve our consciences," Christians should develop "a drama which celebrates our life together in metropolis." See Benjamin F. Payton, "Report to General Board," February 23, 1966, RG6, Box 47, Folder 29, NCC.

25. Hedgeman, *The Gift of Chaos*, 76.

26. Findlay, *Church People in the Struggle*, 35, 37.

27. Gill, *Embattled Ecumenism*, 15, 61.

28. See CRR notes, Box 103, AAH-N.

29. JB-JS.

30. Hedgeman was a runner-up for the honorary title of mayor of Harlem in 1964, the only woman to make it that far in the consideration. The honorary degree drew significant notice from the black press. See "Mrs. Hedgeman Made Doctor of Humane Letters," *NNJG*, June 19, 1948; "Mrs. Hedgeman Gets College's First Honorary Degree," *PC*, June 29, 1948; "Women Plan Honor for Anna Hedgeman," *NYAN*, July 3, 1948; "Mrs. Hedgeman Honored by YWCA Group," *NNJG*, July 24, 1948.

31. Jon Regier, an NCC administrator, issued Bob Spike a warning about Anna Arnold Hedgeman. "If you feel that you want Anna Hedgeman, I would strongly urge that you hire her in a spot that is not a line job. Her know how is valuable, but her image among many and her ability to work a line operation aren't too hopeful," he wrote. This is particularly interesting given that it follows a memo a week earlier in which NCC general secretary Edwin Espy admonished that "every possible effort" had to be made to hire nonwhite candidates for NCC openings. See Jon Regier, "Memo to Robert Spike about CORR," July 14, 1963, NCC; R. H. Edwin Espy, "Personnel Policy with Respect to the Racial Inclusiveness of NCC Staff," July 5, 1963, NCC.

32. Hedgeman, *The Trumpet Sounds*, 177.

33. Anna Arnold Hedgeman, "Terminal Resume," December 20, 1962, Box 102, AAH-N; Anna Arnold Hedgeman, "Description of Bringing Students Together," n.d., Box 16, AAH-N. See also AAH-ED, 177–79. The role of religion in the lives of student activists has been significantly understudied, as Robert Cohen points out. See Cohen, "Introduction."

34. Jones, *The March on Washington*, 144–45.

35. Garrow, *Bearing the Cross*, 270.

36. Hedgeman, *The Gift of Chaos*, 64.

37. Hedgeman, *The Trumpet Sounds*, 168.

38. See Hedgeman, *The Trumpet Sounds*, 167–73; Hedgeman, *The Gift of Chaos*, 63–69; Jones, *The March on Washington*, 163. In attendance at the meeting were the Reverend George Lawrence, the Reverend Thomas Kilgore, L. Joseph Overton, Anna Arnold Hedgeman, Cleveland Robinson, and A. Philip Randolph.

39. Jones, *The March on Washington*, xvii.

40. Hedgeman, *The Trumpet Sounds*, 173.

41. Hedgeman, *The Gift of Chaos*, 71; Jones, *The March on Washington*, 167. Historians have long debated the ideological origins of the march and the various demands of its most active participants. For a review of the debates and an analysis that views the demands for economic justice and civil rights as mutually reinforcing, see Jones, "The Unknown Origins of the March on Washington."

42. Much has been written about how some of the male civil rights leaders objected to the appointment of Bayard Rustin, whom they knew to be homosexual, to direct the march. Randolph, who knew Rustin well, would not back down, and Rustin was appointed. It is interesting that the men found ways to put sexual orientation aside at the same time that they were completely intractable when it came to gender. See biographies of Rustin, including D'Emilio, *Lost Prophet*; Levine, *Bayard Rustin and the Civil Rights Movement*; Anderson, *A. Philip Randolph*.

43. Spike, "The Church and Civil Rights"; Robert Spike, "Report to the Commission on Religion and Race," February 21, 1964, Box 150. See also Hedgeman, *The Trumpet Sounds*, 177–78.

44. Hedgeman, *The Gift of Chaos*, 77–78.

45. Robert Spike, "Report of the Executive Director," September 5, 1963, Box 150, AAH-N. See also Anna Arnold Hedgeman, "Memo to Robert W. Spike," January 20, 1963, Box 39, AAH-N.

46. See D'Emilio, *Lost Prophet*, 327–57.

47. March on Washington Committee, "To All Americans," 1963, Box 103, AAH-N.

48. Euchner, *Nobody Turn Me Around*, 72–73; Jones, "The Unknown Origins of the March on Washington," 43; Jones, *The March on Washington*, 181.

49. Only four people, all of them white, were arrested at the March on Washington. See Branch, *Pillar of Fire*, 133. A *New York Times* article titled "Police Precautions and Festive Spirit of Capital Keep Disorders at a Minimum" spoke of the march's

"gentle army" rather the "emotional horde of angry militants that many had feared." The *Pittsburgh Courier* argued that the peaceful march finally put to rest the notion that black crowds were by definition violent. See Jackson, *From Civil Rights to Human Rights*, 183.

50. Euchner, *Nobody Turn Me Around*, 175.
51. Olson, *Freedom's Daughters*, 289; Branch, *Parting the Waters*, 872.
52. AAH-ED, 184.
53. Jones, *The March on Washington*, 170–71.
54. Jones, *The March on Washington*, 185.
55. Thousands of marchers who sang "We Shall Overcome" along with Joan Baez at the march had sung it much of the way to DC. See Stotts, *We Shall Overcome*.
56. AAH-ED, 187; "Who Is Sponsoring the March on Washington for Jobs and Freedom?," Box 103, AAH-N.
57. *Newsweek*, "On the March," September 2, 1963, clipping, Box 103, AAH-N.
58. Commission on Religion and Race, "Press Releases," clipping, 1963, Box 103, AAH-N; *The National Leader* (Philadelphia), "She Worked 22 Years to Make March a Reality," clipping, Box 102, AAH-N.
59. Spike, "Report of the Executive Director to the Commission on Religion and Race." Spike describes the CRR efforts as occurring "largely under Mrs. Hedgeman's dedicated and brilliant leadership." See also CRR, "Press Release," August 26, 1963, Box 103, AAH-N; "Press Release," August 11, 1963, Box 103, AAH-N.

CHAPTER 11

1. "To Plan 'Back FEPC' Parley," *PC*, January 1, 1944; Anna Arnold Hedgeman, "Equal-Unequal?," n.d., Box 155, AAH-N.
2. Anna Arnold Hedgeman, "Why Women Walk Two Steps behind Their Men," April 30, 1959, Box 130, AAH-N; Anna Arnold Hedgeman, "Women and the New America," October 31, 1956, Box 42, AAH-N; Hedgeman, "Equal-Unequal?" See Hedgeman, "The Role of the Negro Woman."
3. Height, *Open Wide the Freedom Gates*, 146. When Mary Church Terrell died, Anna Arnold Hedgeman published a tribute to her. See Anna Arnold Hedgeman, "Memo to God," *NYAN*, August 21, 1954.
4. The exclusion of women from the march usually warrants about a paragraph in the works that do consider it. For example, see D'Emilio, *Lost Prophet*, 351, in which Hedgeman is described as having "dashed off" a memo to Randolph about the exclusion of women, even though the author notes that Hedgeman had raised the issue earlier.
5. Height, *Open Wide the Freedom Gates*, 141.

6. The Big Ten included, in addition to the Big Six (King, Randolph, Young, Lewis, Farmer, and Wilkins), Mathew Ahmann of the National Catholic Conference for Interracial Justice, the Reverend Eugene Carson Blake of the NCC, Rabbi Joachim Prinz of the American Jewish Congress, and Walter Reuther of the United Automobile Workers. See "Final Plans for the March on Washington for Jobs and Freedom," 1963, Box 157, AAH-N.

7. Height, " 'We Wanted the Voice of a Woman to Be Heard,' " 86–88.

8. Hedgeman, *The Trumpet Sounds*, 178. The administrative committee did alter its list of speakers as other issues arose. For example, when it turned out that the majority of blacks attending the march were employed and members of civil rights organizations, the committee dropped the idea of having two unemployed people as speakers. See *From Civil Rights to Human Rights*, 179.

9. See Olson, *Freedom's Daughters*; Houck and Dixon, "Introduction"; Collier-Thomas and Franklin, *Sisters in the Struggle*; Crawford, Rouse, and Woods, eds., *Women in the Civil Rights Movement*.

10. Hedgeman noted that the Big Six had not "given women the quality of participation which they have earned through the years." She had worked on and off with Randolph for a long time and well understood his reliance on and treatment of women. None of the men had good reputations for working with women. As Thomas Jackson explains in his work on Martin Luther King Jr., King's sexism was not simple. He wanted to marry both a strong woman and a woman who would be a wife and homemaker. He adopted the rhetoric, though, of the freedom fighter and gendered that fighter male. See Jackson, *From Civil Rights to Human Rights*, 8–9. See also Bernice Barnett, "Invisible Southern Black Women Leaders of the Civil Rights Movement"; Collier-Thomas and Franklin, *Sisters in the Struggle*; Ransby, *Ella Baker and the Black Freedom Movement*. Ransby points out that racial uplift, a significant component of the mainstream civil rights organizations, included traditional notions of masculinity and femininity. See section titled "Gender Politics and Grassroots Organizing," 291–98.

11. Anna Arnold Hedgeman, "Letter to A. Philip Randolph," August 16, 1963, Box 17, AAH-N. If the men resisted giving Hedgeman the respect she deserved, many women supported her. "Anna Arnold Hedgeman was one of the most unsung, unheralded people of the movement," claimed *Pittsburgh Courier* reporter Evelyn Cunningham. "I don't think she got the notice she deserved. She did her homework. She had great courage and showed great leadership. She was soft spoken when she needed to be, but she could also raise her voice, and shake her finger." See Bass, *Like a Mighty Stream*, 116.

12. On Gloria Richardson, see Dandridge, "The Energy of the People Passing through Me"; Harley, " 'Chronicle of a Death Foretold.' " On Herbert Lee, see Klopfer, Klopfer, and Klopfer, *Where Rebels Roost*. It is fascinating that the group chose two women who were known because their husbands had been assassinated, when

so many women who were leaders in their own right attended and were involved in the march. I had tremendous difficulty even locating Mrs. Herbert Lee's first name, Paris. See Ernest Herndon, "Cotton Gin Maker Cites 1961 Death of Voting Rights Activist Herbert Lee," *Commercial Appeal*, November 29, 2010.

13. Pauli Murray, "Letter to Anna Arnold Hedgeman," February 11, 1946, Box 73, File 1280, PMP; Pauli Murray, "Letter to A. Philip Randolph," August 21, 1963, Box 39, AAH-N.
14. Olson, *Freedom's Daughters*, 288.
15. Olson, *Freedom's Daughters*, 288.
16. In a letter following Pauli Murray's talk, Whitney Young wrote that black women's goals had to be different from white women's goals. "I would think that Negro women leaders . . . should make their primary goal the lifting of the social, economic, and educational status of their men," intimating that what worked for black men would by default work for black women. See Dickerson, *Militant Mediator*, 292.
17. Jones, "The Unknown Origins of the March on Washington," 44.
18. Richards, *Maida Springer*, 264.
19. King, *My Life with Martin Luther King, Jr.*, 237.
20. Hedgeman, *The Gift of Chaos*, 86.
21. For descriptions of the day of the march, see Barber, *Marching on Washington*; Euchner, *Nobody Turn Me Around*; Gentile, *March on Washington*; Bass, *Like a Mighty Stream*; Jones, *Behind the Dream*; Boyd, *We Shall Overcome*; Jackson, *From Civil Rights to Human Rights*.
22. Euchner, *Nobody Turn Me Around*, 9; Branch, *Parting the Waters*, 872–73.
23. Barber, *Marching on Washington*, 164; Jones, *The March on Washington*, 187.
24. Euchner, *Nobody Turn Me Around*, 70, 97; Jones, *Behind the Dream*, 33–36.
25. Euchner, *Nobody Turn Me Around*, 133.
26. Kersten, *A. Philip Randolph*, 102.
27. Kersten, *A. Philip Randolph*, 103.
28. Branch, *Parting the Waters*, 879. The Tribute to Negro Women directly preceded Lewis's remarks, so one of the women already in place for the tribute could have easily been called upon to step in.
29. GR-JS.
30. Commission on Religion and Race, "Summary of Activities," June–October 1963, RG2, Box 2, Folder 15, NCC.
31. Kersten, *A. Philip Randolph*, 102.
32. Bass, *Like a Mighty Stream*, 127.
33. "Audiotape of March on Washington," August 28, 1963, MMC.
34. Hedgeman, *The Trumpet Sounds*, 180.
35. Brinkley, *Rosa Parks*, 185.
36. Barber, *Marching on Washington*, 170.

37. Jones, *Behind the Dream*, 117.

38. AAH-ED, 188.

39. AAH-BL.

40. Hedgeman, *The Gift of Chaos*, 86. For a comprehensive treatment of Rosa Parks's life and role in the civil rights movement, see Theoharis, *The Rebellious Life of Mrs. Rosa Parks*.

41. Hedgeman, *The Gift of Chaos*, 55. Years later, in 1983, when a national discussion was taking place about commemorating Martin Luther King Jr. with a national holiday, Anna Arnold Hedgeman argued that the proposed holiday "should recall Rosa Parks," noting her work in Montgomery, Alabama, and then later in Detroit, Michigan, where she lived—and continued her activism—for many years. See Anna Arnold Hedgeman, "Notes on Martin Luther King Day," January 1983, Box 70, AAH-N. On Rosa Parks's role in the movement, see Theoharis, *The Rebellious Life of Mrs. Rosa Parks*. Two years after the march, Hedgeman organized a tribute to Rosa Parks, enlisting Pauli Murray to deliver the address. See Anna Arnold Hedgeman, "Letter to Pauli Murray," July 22, 1965, Box 104, Folder 1873, PMP.

42. Pauli Murray, "The Negro Woman in the Quest for Equality," *The Acorn*, June 1964, Box 39, AAH-N. See also Height, " 'We Wanted the Voice of a Woman to Be Heard.' "

43. Murray, "The Liberation of Black Women."

44. Murray, "The Negro Woman in the Quest for Equality."

45. Clark, *Ready from Within*, 77–78.

46. Robnett, *How Long? How Long?*, 94. For the definitive biography of Ella Baker, see Ransby, *Ella Baker and the Black Freedom Movement*.

47. Height, " 'We Wanted the Voice of a Woman to Be Heard,' " 91.

48. Gilmore, *Defying Dixie*, 288.

49. Anna Arnold Hedgeman often recognized this about Merritt, and did so with great appreciation. See Box 123, AAH-N; AAH-ED.

50. Hedgeman, *The Gift of Chaos*, 88–89.

51. AAH-ED, 190.

CHAPTER 12

1. Prinz, *Joachim Prinz, Rebellious Rabbi*, 262.

2. Hedgeman, *The Trumpet Sounds*, 194.

3. Lewis, *The Shadows of Youth*, 141; Blum and Harvey, *The Color of Christ*, 1–5; Jensen, *The Heart of Whiteness*; Jacobson, *Whiteness of a Different Color*; Lipsitz, *The Possessive Investment in Whiteness*; Delgado and Stefancic, *Critical White Studies*.

4. Lewis, *The Shadows of Youth*, 142.

5. On whiteness, see Roediger, *Towards the Abolition of Whiteness*.

6. Hedgeman, *The Trumpet Sounds*, 201.

7. In her memoir *The Trumpet Sounds*, Hedgeman describes her most recent attempt: overhearing a black girl at the march talk about how white people were incidental to the event, Hedgeman introduced the girl to some white civil rights workers, also young, whom she knew. She took pride in leaving them deep in conversation. See Hedgeman, *The Trumpet Sounds*, 190–91.

8. Branch, *Parting the Waters*, 892.

9. The meaning of what had happened to the stained-glass Jesus concerned many Christians, and theologian Reinhold Niebuhr and novelist James Baldwin were among those who spoke publicly about what it might mean. The story traveled around the world, and a group of children in Wales raised funds to commission a local artist to replace it. The new Jesus was black. See Blum and Harvey, *The Color of Christ*, 4, 23.

10. "Description of the Commission on Religion and Race," May 4, 1965, Box 22, AAH-N.

11. Anna Arnold Hedgeman, "Memo to Denominational Race Staff and Social Action Executives," n.d., RG6, Box 7, Folder 15, NCC.

12. Hedgeman, *The Gift of Chaos*, 94.

13. See Kessler-Harris, *In Pursuit of Equity*, 239–40.

14. Murray quoted in MacLean, *Freedom Is Not Enough*, 120.

15. Murray quoted in MacLean, *Freedom Is Not Enough*, 121.

16. Murray, *Song in a Weary Throat*, 355–58.

17. Finley, *Delaying the Dream*, 241.

18. Hedgeman, *The Gift of Chaos*, 100.

19. Findlay, *Church People in the Struggle*, 51–53; See also Prinz, *Joachim Prinz, Rebellious Rabbi*.

20. Hedgeman, *The Gift of Chaos*, 98–99.

21. As I mentioned in chapter 10, a great deal more work needs to be done on the religious imperative at work in student activism of the 1960s. See Cohen, "Introduction."

22. Hall, "Freedom-Faith," 172.

23. Hedgeman, *The Gift of Chaos*, 99.

24. Hedgeman, *The Gift of Chaos*, 99.

25. Mary Marlett, "Challenges State Delegates to Join Civil Rights Struggle," *KG*, May 14, 1964.

26. Anna Arnold Hedgeman, "Summary Report," January 9, 1964, Box 102, AAH-N.

27. Hedgeman, "Summary Report."

28. On Ella Baker as a mentor to young people, see Ransby, *Ella Baker and the Black Freedom Movement*, 246–47, 251–53, 256–57, 259, 269–74, 293, 317, 357, 358, 360, 366–67.

29. Gwendolyn Jones, "Letter to Anna Arnold Hedgeman," October 30, 1963, Box 199, AAH-N.

30. Anna Arnold Hedgeman, "Report of the Coordinator of Special Events," January 4, 1965, Box 5, Folder 3, AAH-SC.

31. March, "Interview on Anna Arnold Hedgeman and the YWCA," n.d., Box 129, AAH-N.

32. Findlay, *Church People in the Struggle*, 57–61.

33. Hedgeman, *The Gift of Chaos*, 101–2.

34. CAH-JS.

35. CAH-JS.

36. Septima Clark, "Letter to Anna Arnold Hedgeman," January 21, 1964, Box 23, AAH-N.

37. CAH-JS.

38. CAH-JS.

39. CAH-JS.

40. CAH-JS.

41. Kersten, *A. Philip Randolph*, 105.

42. Jackson, *From Civil Rights to Human Rights*, 187.

43. Finley, *Delaying the Dream*, 255.

44. Hedgeman, *The Gift of Chaos*, 106–7; Findlay, *Church People in the Struggle*, 54. According to Findlay, for the House vote, there was only one no vote from Illinois, Indiana, and Ohio, and eight of twelve from Iowa, Nebraska, and South Dakota voted yes (*Church People in the Struggle*, 54). When the bill finally passed the Senate, Vice President Hubert Humphrey thanked the commission (62).

45. Hedgeman, *The Gift of Chaos*, 105–6. See also Robert Spike and Anna Arnold Hedgeman, "Memo to All National Council of Churches Boards and Affiliated Organizations," February 21, 1964, Box 23, AAH-N.

46. Findlay, *Church People in the Struggle*, 55–57.

47. Robert Spike, "Executive Director's Report," January 16, 1964, Box 102, AAH-N.

48. Findlay, *Church People in the Struggle*, 57.

49. March, "Interview on Anna Arnold Hedgeman and the YWCA."

50. Anna Arnold Hedgeman, "Notes," 1967, RG6, Box 7, Folder 5, NCC.

51. Anna Arnold Hedgeman, "Report of the Coordinator of Special Events," June 29, 1964, RG2, Box 2, Folder 14, NCC; "Reports, Commission on Religion and Race," 1964, Box 32, AAH-N.

52. Anna Arnold Hedgeman, "Notes," 1964, Box 55, AAH-N.

53. Pauli Murray refers to herself as Anna's "protegee," quoting a letter she sent to her boss at the time, Attorney General Robert Kenny: Pauli Murray, "Letter to Anna Arnold Hedgeman," February 11, 1946, Box 73, Folder 1280, AAH-SC; Murray, "The Negro Woman in the Quest for Equality."

54. CAH-JS.

55. Findlay, *Church People in the Struggle*, 64. As Findlay explains, the success of the religious left "served as a precondition" for the emergence of the religious right. Findlay, *Church People in the Struggle*, 63.

56. National Council of Churches, "A Call to the Churches for Action to Meet the Crisis in Race Relations," December 6, 1963, Box 48, AAH-N.

57. Hedgeman, *The Gift of Chaos*, 103.

58. Hedgeman, *The Trumpet Sounds*, 195–99.

59. Findlay, *Church People in the Struggle*, 79; see also Lyon, "'Doing a Little Something to Pave the Way for Others'"; Reiff, "'Born of Conviction.'"

60. According to Hedgeman, the NCC agreed to sponsor the Delta Ministry directly because the commission was too controversial in the South to sponsor such a program. See Hedgeman, *The Gift of Chaos*, 118.

61. There is an extensive body of literature on Freedom Summer, including Belfrage, *Freedom Summer*; Holt, *The Summer That Didn't End*; Lewis, *Walking with the Wind*; Sutherland, *Letters from Mississippi*; Cagin and Dray, *We Are Not Afraid*; King, *Freedom Song*; Halberstam, *The Children*; Walton, *Mississippi*; Payne, *I've Got the Light of Freedom*; McAdam, *Freedom Summer*; Watson, *Freedom Summer*; Hogan, *Many Minds, One Heart*; Rothschild, *A Case of Black and White*; Olson, *Freedom's Daughters*; Branch, *Pillar of Fire*.

62. On the deliberations about inviting white students south, see Lewis, *Walking with the Wind*, 243–47.

63. Council of Federated Organizations, "Prospectus for the Mississippi Freedom Summer."

64. Cagin and Dray, *We Are Not Afraid*, 226.

65. National Council of Churches, "Statement on Mississippi and the Role of the National Council of Churches in the Mississippi Project," 1964, RG6, Box 47, Folder 30, NCC; See also Cagin and Dray, *We Are Not Afraid*; Bruce Hanson, "Letter to Presidents, Deans, and Religious Advisors of College, Universities and Seminaries," April 16, 1964, RG6, Box 46, Folder 32, NCC.

66. Holt, *The Summer That Didn't End*, 85–86. Robert Spike reported that sixty-one ministers served as counselors during Freedom Summer. Robert Spike, "Report of the Executive Director to the Commission on Religion and Race," September 15, 1964, RG2, Box 2, Folder 14, NCC.

67. Robert Spike described the candidate for the counselor-chaplains this way: "This person must have abilities in inter-personal relations, mature judgment, as well as fortitude. He will also assist the attorney assigned to each group in interpreting legal rights and obligations as they relate to strategies." Robert Spike and Anna Arnold Hedgeman, "Memo to All National Council of Churches Boards and Affiliated Organizations," February 21, 1964, Box 23, AAH-N.

68. Bruce Hanson, "Memo to Commission on Religion and Race Staff," April 20, 1964, Box 39, AAH-N; Robert Spike, "The Church and Civil Rights: A Contemporary Account of Mission in Action," November 1965, Box 150, AAH-N; Spike, "Report of the Executive Director to the Commission on Religion and Race"; Robert Spike, "Memo to All National Council of Churches Staff," April 24, 1964, Box 23, AAH-N.

69. Commission on Religion and Race, "Summary Report of the Commission on Religion and Race," December 3–4, 1964, RG6, Box 47, Folder 31, NCC.

70. Olson, *Freedom's Daughters*, 297.

71. Olson, *Freedom's Daughters*, 297.

72. Belfrage, *Freedom Summer*, 84.

73. Holt, *The Summer That Didn't End*, 87.

74. Belfrage, *Freedom Summer*, 3–30.

75. Sutherland, *Letters from Mississippi*, 30–32.

76. Hedgeman, *The Gift of Chaos*, 117.

77. Cagin and Dray, *We Are Not Afraid*, 350.

78. Cagin and Dray, *We Are Not Afraid*, 350.

79. Holt, *The Summer That Didn't End*, 28.

80. Walton, *Mississippi*, 268.

81. Holt, *The Summer That Didn't End*, 322.

82. Watson, *Freedom Summer*, 177; Holt, *The Summer That Didn't End*, 207.

83. Watson, *Freedom Summer*, 177; Payne, *I've Got the Light of Freedom*, 253. On Holly Springs, see also Hogan, *Many Minds, One Heart*, 79.

CHAPTER 13

1. Farmer, *Lay Bare the Heart*. For the first time, significant numbers of black journalists reported on the riots. See Caldwell, "Harlem."

2. Anna Arnold Hedgeman, "Toward a Whole Education," 1968, Box 42, AAH-N.

3. Anna Arnold Hedgeman, "Report to Robert Spike," September 15, 1964, Box 40, AAH-N; Anna Arnold Hedgeman, "Harlem," July 21, 1964, RG6, Box 2, Folder 14, NCC; Anna Arnold Hedgeman, "Draft Statement to Mayor Robert F. Wagner and the Citizens of New York," 1964, Box 150, AAH-N.

4. Office of the Mayor of New York, "Statement from the Mayor's Office," July 20, 1964, Box 38, AAH-N.

5. Anna Arnold Hedgeman, notes scribbled on Office of the Mayor of New York, "Statement from the Mayor's Office."

6. Anna Arnold Hedgeman, "An Open Letter to Mr. Stan Optowsky," March 10, 1958, General Correspondence, Box 196, RFW; "*New York Post* article clipping and letters in response," March 1958, clippings, Box 11, AAH-N.

7. George D. Cannon, "Letter to Anna Arnold Hedgeman," February 16, 1959, Box 2, AAH-N.

8. Robert Spike, "Report of the Executive Director," April 1, 1965, RG6, Box 47, Folder 29, NCC.

9. Robert Spike, "Statement on the Program of the Commission on Religion and Race," February 24, 1965, Box 150, AAH-N.

10. Spike, "Statement on the Program of the Commission on Religion and Race."

11. Robert Spike, "Report of the Commission on Religion and Race," October 17–18, 1963, NCC.

12. Spike, "Statement on the Program of the Commission on Religion and Race."

13. See Sugrue, *The Origins of the Urban Crisis*.

14. Robert Spike, "Statement to the House of Bishops," April 14, 1965, RG6, Box 47, Folder 31, NCC.

15. Commission on Religion and Race, "Minutes," June 11, 1965, RG6, Box 47, Folder 29, NCC.

16. Hedgeman, *The Gift of Chaos*, 148.

17. Commission on Religion and Race, "Progress Report of Detroit Pilot Project," September 24, 1965, Fox 5, Folder 4, AAH-SC.

18. Jay Moore, "A Strategy for Northern Cities," n.d., Box 40, AAH-N; James C. Moore, "Progress Report of Detroit Pilot Project," September 24, 1965, RG6, Box 47, Folder 29, NCC.

19. Robert Spike, "Report of the Executive Director," January 29, 1965, RG6, Box 47, Foler 28, NCC.

20. Hedgeman, *The Gift of Chaos*, 133.

21. Mass consumption became synonymous with the American dream in the postwar period, but by no means was the dream—or were the goods—accessible to all. See Cohen, *A Consumers' Republic*.

22. "Letters to the National Council of Churches," 1957, RG6, Box 45, Folder 15, NCC.

23. J. Oscar Lee, "Letter to Helen M. Christensen," March 11, 1959, RG6, Box 45, Folder 15, NCC. On the ways in which the sexual abuse of black women by white men, not at all the concern of these white Christians, encouraged civil rights advocacy, see McGuire, *At the Dark End of the Street*.

24. Anna Arnold Hedgeman, "Letter to Joan Kalmers," August 15, 1967, Box 26, AAH-N.

25. Hedgeman, *The Gift of Chaos*, 134–35.

26. Anna Arnold Hedgeman, "Toward the New City," Spring 1965, Box 150, AAH-N.

27. Hedgeman, *The Gift of Chaos*, 135.

28. Moore, "Progress Report of Detroit Pilot Project."

29. Anna Arnold Hedgeman, "Memo to Robert Spike," October 21, 1964, Box 39, AAH-N.

30. James P. Breeden, "Progress Report on the Cleveland Project," September 24, 1965, RG6, Box 47, Folder 29, NCC; Robert Spike, "Report of the Executive Director," September 24, 1965, Box 150, AAH-N.

31. Moore, "A Strategy for Northern Cities."

32. David Goldberg explores the tenants' rights movement in Detroit from 1964 to 1969. Although he does not mention the Commission on Religion and Race, he argues that a policy of benign neglect there led black politicians, activists, and

businesspeople "to take the fall for their inability to overcome externally institutionalized racial limitations and obstacles to collective Black economic and political development." See Goldberg, "From Landless to Landlords," 176.

33. Findlay, *Church People in the Struggle*, 178–79.

34. Friedland, *Lift Up Your Voice Like a Trumpet*, 94.

35. Murray Kempton, "The Long Shot," *NYW-TS*, July 28, 1965.

36. Hedgeman, *The Gift of Chaos*, 136–40.

37. Committee of the Arts, "Support for Ryan-Hedgeman-Dubin Team," 1965, Box 20, AAH-N.

38. Anna Arnold Hedgeman, "Report of Political Adventure and Its Significance to the Commission [on Religion and Race]," September 15, 1965, Box 5, AAH-N.

39. Patterson, *Freedom Is Not Enough*, 62–63. For a discussion of how the Moynihan Report was used to construct a national racial order that included Asians as well as blacks, see Wu, *The Color of Success*, 168–74.

40. Patterson, *Freedom Is Not Enough*, xiv.

41. Geary, *Beyond Civil Rights*, 2.

42. Daniel Patrick Moynihan, "The Negro Family: The Case for National Action," March 1965, Box 85, AAH-N.

43. Anna Arnold Hedgeman interviewed by Katherine Shannon in 1967 and quoted in Jackson, *From Civil Rights to Human Rights*, 254; Anna Arnold Hedgeman, "Negro Women Fought Hard for Recognition," *NYA*, September 3, 1955.

44. Payton quoted in Rainwater, *The Moynihan Report and the Politics of Controversy*, 211.

45. Benjamin F. Payton, "The President, the Social Experts, and the Ghetto: An Analysis of an Emerging Strategy in Civil Rights," n.d., RG6, Box 48, Folder 14, NCC.

46. Branch, *At Canaan's Edge*, 372.

47. Carmichael quoted in Geary, *Beyond Civil Rights*, 119. On Carmichael, see also Savage, *Your Spirits Walk beside Us*.

48. Commission on Religion and Race, "Major Riots, Civil-Criminal Disorders," 1967, RG6, Box 48, Folder 3, NCC.

49. Spike, "Statement on the Program of the Commission on Religion and Race."

50. King quoted in Branch, *At Canaan's Edge*, 11. The NCC supported King in his opposition to the war. See Department of Social Justice, National Council of Churches, "Vietnam and National Priorities," May 1967, Box 32, AAH-N.

51. Friedland, *Lift Up Your Voice Like a Trumpet*, 152.

52. O'Connor, "Swimming against the Tide," 95–96, 105.

53. James Reston quoted in National Council of Churches, "Untitled Document," July 16, 1967, AAH-N.

54. Friedland, *Lift Up Your Voice Like a Trumpet*, 141.

55. Findlay, *Church People in the Struggle*, 175–76.

56. On Spike's death, see Branch, *At Canaan's Edge*, 541–42. On Rustin's homosexuality, see D'Emilio, *Lost Prophet*. On Pauli Murray, see Murray, *Pauli Murray*; Anna Arnold Hedgeman, "Letter to Lillian Smith," June 27, 1956, Box 4, AAH-N. On William Stringfellow, see Johnston, "Bombast, Blasphemy, and the Bastard Gospel."

57. AAH-ED, 193–94.

58. James Findlay interviewed Benjamin Payton for his book on the Commission on Religion and Race. See Findlay, *Church People in the Struggle*, 193.

59. Findlay, *Church People in the Struggle*, 179.

60. Benjamin F. Payton, "Report to the Commission on Religion and Race by the Executive Director, Benjamin Payton," April 25, 1966, NCC.

61. Anna Arnold Hedgeman, "Memo to Denominational Race Staff," June 9, 1967, NCC.

62. Transcripts of tapes recorded during the New York planning meeting are in the Anna Arnold Hedgeman Papers, Box 22, AAH-N.

63. Anna Arnold Hedgeman interviewed by Katherine Shannon in 1967 and quoted in Jackson, *From Civil Rights to Human Rights*, 257.

64. Anna Arnold Hedgeman quoted in Carter, *The Music Has Gone Out of the Movement*, 86.

65. Carter, *The Music Has Gone Out of the Movement*, 86.

66. Carter, *The Music Has Gone Out of the Movement*, 85.

67. Carter, *The Music Has Gone Out of the Movement*, 101.

68. Benjamin F. Payton, "Dr. Benjamin F. Payton to Program Board, Division of Christian Life and Mission," October 6, 1966, RG6, Box 48, NCC.

CHAPTER 14

1. Stokely Carmichael quoted in Hall, "The NAACP, Black Power, and the African American Freedom Struggle, 1966–1969," 49.

2. Van Deburg, *New Day in Babylon*, 32; Kasher, *The Civil Rights Movement*, 132–35; Dittmer, *Local People*, 20.

3. Payne, *I've Got the Light of Freedom*, 379.

4. Findlay, *Church People in the Struggle*, 183. See also Hall, "The NAACP, Black Power, and the African American Freedom Struggle, 1966–1969."

5. Hedgeman, *The Gift of Chaos*, 149.

6. Hedgeman, *The Gift of Chaos*, 150.

7. Mark Chapman describes Anna Arnold Hedgeman's theological frame of reference as it is linked to black nationalism in Chapman, *Christianity on Trial*, 138–42.

8. JB-JS.

9. National Committee of Negro Churchmen, "Untitled," July 16, 1967, Box 75, AAH-N; Anna Arnold Hedgeman, "Speech," n.d., Box 94, AAH-N.

10. GW-JS. When Wilmore wrote about the NCNC in 1973, and then reissued his book in 1998, he mentioned Anna Arnold Hedgeman in the text but did not include her name in the index; he referred to her as Payton's "associate" but failed to explore the meaning of her presence in the group. See Wilmore, *Black Religion and Black Radicalism*, 226. He was eager to recognize this, in hindsight, forty years later.

11. Anna Arnold Hedgeman, "One Woman's Opinion," *NYA*, January 23, 1960.

12. "Program: The Negroes in Our Cities," July 26, 1962, Box 20, AAH-N.

13. Chapman, *Christianity on Trial*, 146–47.

14. "Black Power: Statement by National Committee of Negro Churchmen," *NYT*, July 31, 1966.

15. "Black Power."

16. On the NCNC and its role in the development of black theology, see Chapman, *Christianity on Trial*; Wilmore, *Black Religion and Black Radicalism*.

17. Chapman, *Christianity on Trial*, 77–78.

18. Payton quoted in "Words of the Week," *Jet*, December 8, 1966, p. 30, Box 15, AAH-N.

19. "Nation Warned about Backlash," November 4, 1966, *NYT*.

20. Anna Arnold Hedgeman, "Letter to Governor Nelson Rockefeller," September 12, 1967, Box 21, AAH-N.

21. National Conference of Christians and Jews, "Black Power: A Positive Force," March 28, 1968, Box 104, AAH-N; Anna Arnold Hedgeman, "Memo to General Secretariat, National Council of Churches," RG6, Box 7, Folder 5, NCC.

22. Anna Arnold Hedgeman, "Memo to Jon Regier," March 21, 1966, RG6, Box 10, Folder 2, NCC.

23. Martin Luther King Jr., "It Is Not Enough to Condemn Black Power."

24. Anna Arnold Hedgeman, "Letter to Martin Luther King, Jr.," October 26, 1966, http:www.thekingcenter.org/archives/document/letter-anna-hedgeman-mlk.

25. Anna Arnold Hedgeman, "Memo to Dr. Payton," April 25, 1966, RG6, Box 10, Folder 2, NCC.

26. Giddings, *When and Where I Enter*, 304. The founding meeting of NOW was in October 1966. For more on the history of NOW, see Gilmore, *Groundswell*.

27. Olson, *Freedom's Daughters*, 363; Anna Arnold Hedgeman, "Letter to Pauli Murray," October 11, 1966, Box 50, Folder 894, PMP.

28. Betty Friedan, "Letter to NOW Members," March 17, 1967, Box 132, AAH-N.

29. Anna Arnold Hedgeman, "Memo to National Organization for Women," September 13, 1967, Box 132, AAH-N.

30. Hedgeman, "Memo to National Organization for Women."

31. Anna Arnold Hedgeman, "Letter to Pauli Murray," n.d., Box 51, Folder 899, PMP.

32. National Organization for Women, "Letter to Leaders of Organizations," February 8, 1967, Box 132, AAH-N. Hedgeman's papers contain a draft of the document, annotated with Hedgeman's edits, Box 132, AAH-N.

33. On women of color and the second wave of the feminist movement, see Thompson, "Multiracial Feminism"; Hewitt, *No Permanent Waves*; Harris, "From the Kennedy Commission to the Combahee Collective," 280–305.
34. Roediger, "An Interview with Elma Stuckey, Poet Laureate of Slave Life," 72–76.
35. Cobble, *The Other Women's Movement*, 185–201.
36. Olson, *Freedom's Daughters*, 368.
37. RH-JS.
38. Giardina, *Freedom for Women*, 35.
39. National Organization for Women, "Statement of Purpose," October 29, 1966, Box 32, AAH-N.
40. Giardina, *Freedom for Women*, 3–8.
41. Friedan quoted in Harrison, *On Account of Sex*, 201.
42. Betty Friedan, "Letter to Anna Arnold Hedgeman," September 20, 1967, Box 132, AAH-N.
43. Two of the earliest members of NOW, Sister Austin Doherty and Sister Mary Joel Read, were Catholic nuns.
44. More recent scholarship has focused on Dr. King's increasing commitment to racial justice through economic justice. As James Findlay writes, "King himself developed more radical social and economic views by the time of his death, a fact mainstream church people largely ignored." See Findlay, *Church People in the Struggle*, 65.
45. Commission on Religion and Race, "Description of Commission on Religion and Race," May 4, 1965, Box 2, AAH-N.
46. Benjamin Payton, "Report to the Commission on Religion and Race by the Executive Director, Benjamin Payton," April 25, 1966, RG6, Box 47, Folder 29, NCC; Friedland, *Lift Up Your Voice Like a Trumpet*, 190.
47. National Organization for Women, "Letter to President Lyndon B. Johnson," November 11, 1966, Box 130, AAH-N; Anna Arnold Hedgeman, "Letter to Betty Friedan," December 2, 1966, Box 131, AAH-N. In the end, Inez Casiano was appointed executive assistant to the executive director of the EEOC. She then resigned from the National Board of NOW but stayed active locally, wherever she lived, for the rest of her life. IC-LB, July 2004.
48. See Anna Arnold Hedgeman, "Letter to Betty Friedan," March 27, 1967, Box 132, AAH-N.
49. Anna Arnold Hedgeman, "Letter to Linda Bollinger," n.d. [1976/1977], Box 60, AAH-N.
50. Betty Friedan explained the financial commitment in a letter to members about the board: "They've dipped into their wallets for postage, office supplies, phone calls, travel expenses and other necessities." Friedan, "Letter to NOW Members." Benita Roth argues that this policy negatively impacted NOW's attempts overall to recruit women of color and women from poorer communities. See Roth, *Separate Roads to Feminism*, 107.

51. Anna Arnold Hedgeman, "Letter to Thelma Isaacs," April 21, 1968, Box 2, Folder 20, AAH-SC.

52. Helen Kindt, "Memo to Rev. Jon L. Regier," December 17, 1967, RG6, Box 10, Folder 2, NCC; Anna Arnold Hedgeman, "Memo to Jon L. Regier," November 8, 1967, RG6, Box 10, Folder 2, NCC; Anna Arnold Hedgeman, "Letter to Herluf Jensen," January 16, 1968, Box 102, AAH-N.

CHAPTER 15

1. AAH-ED, 179.
2. Hedgeman, *The Gift of Chaos*, 172.
3. For different perspectives on the notion of the long civil rights movement, see Hall, "The Long Civil Rights Movement and the Political Uses of the Past"; Payne, *I've Got the Light of Freedom*; Lawson, *Running for Freedom*; Cha-Jua and Lang, "The 'Long Movement' as Vampire"; Theoharis and Woodard, *Freedom North*; Theoharis and Woodard, *Groundwork*; Joseph, *Waiting 'Til the Midnight Hour*; Rubio, *There's Always Work at the Post Office*.
4. Hedgeman, *The Gift of Chaos*, 172.
5. Hedgeman, *The Gift of Chaos*, 172.
6. New York City's Department for the Aging was founded in 1968, and Anna Arnold Hedgeman was appointed to it in 1976. Abraham D. Beame, "Letter to Anna Arnold Hedgeman," January 19, 1976, Box 151, AAH-N. Not surprisingly, poor black Americans faced even more dire circumstances in old age than did poor white Americans. See National Caucus on the Black Aged, "Report," 1974, Box 78, AAH-N. She also served on the Harlem Interagency Council on Aging in the 1970s, an organization that gave special concern to hunger among the elderly. See Harlem Interagency Council on Aging, "Memo to Commissioner Jack Goldberg," October 19, 1970, Box 61, AAH-N.
7. On black musicians in New York City, see Biondi, *To Stand and Fight*, 94–97.
8. Merritt Hedgeman, "Notes," n.d., Box 144, AAH-N.
9. Hedgeman, *The Gift of Chaos*, 171.
10. Hedgeman, *The Gift of Chaos*, 173.
11. Hedgeman, *The Gift of Chaos*, 173.
12. Hedgeman, *The Gift of Chaos*, 172–93.
13. On racism and the draft, see Hall, *Peace and Freedom*, 10–11.
14. Hedgeman, *The Gift of Chaos*, 174.
15. Jeanette Rankin Brigade, "A Call to American Women," 1968, in author's personal papers.
16. Hedgeman, *The Gift of Chaos*, 175.
17. Hedgeman, *The Gift of Chaos*, 176–77.

18. Anna Arnold Hedgeman, "Letter to Edith S. Heavenrich," June 25, 1969, Box 2, Folder 21, AAH-SC.
19. Hedgeman, *The Gift of Chaos*, 175–78.
20. Anna Arnold Hedgeman, "Speech," n.d., Box 166, AAH-N.
21. Louis Blue, "Advice and Wit Mark Hospital Dinner Address of Mrs. Anna Hedgeman," *TC* (Kansas City), clipping, February 25, 1996, Box 157, AAH-N.
22. Hedgeman, *The Gift of Chaos*, 181, 77, 85, 83.
23. Belinda Robnett writes about the bridge role black women played in civil rights work, connecting grassroots organizers and larger civil rights organizations. See Robnett, *How Long? How Long?* Biographers of Ella Baker and Fannie Lou Hamer explore the critical bridge role these women played. See Ransby, *Ella Baker and the Black Freedom Movement*; Lee, *For Freedom's Sake*. Black feminists would challenge the notion of the bridge and point out its costs. See Moraga and Anzaldúa, *This Bridge Called My Back*.
24. Anna Arnold Hedgeman, "Letter to Dr. Ruth Hill and Dr. Patricia King," n.d., Box 31, AAH-N. Hedgeman corrected people's usage when she responded to their letters. See Anna Arnold Hedgeman, "Letter to Mrs. Kidre," March 9, 1966, Box 2, Folder 20, AAH-SC; Anna Arnold Hedgeman, "Letter to Ted Hallock," February 10, 1968, Box 2, Folder 20, AAH-SC; Anna Arnold Hedgeman, "Letter to Charlotte Mayerson," October 29, 1964, Box 15, Folder 2, AAH-SC.
25. On the black student demand that led to Anna Arnold Hedgeman's consultancies, and to the emergence of black studies, see Biondi, *The Black Revolution on Campus*.
26. Anna Arnold Hedgeman, "Notes on South Carolina Freshman English Curriculum Development Institute," n.d., Box 92, AAH-N; Murray, *Song in a Weary Throat*, 373–79.
27. See Murray, *Song in a Weary Throat*, 377.
28. Pauli Murray, "Letter to Norman Foerster," October 20, 1967, Box 92, AAH-N.
29. Schomburg, "The Negro Digs Up His Past," 231.
30. Ransby, *Ella Baker and the Black Freedom Movement*, 69.
31. Gertrude McBrown, "Letter to Anna and Merritt Hedgeman," February 1, 1959, Box 9, AAH-N.
32. Floyd B. Taylor, "Letter to Anna Arnold Hedgeman," February 19, 1958, Box 3, Folder 8, RFW.
33. Anna Arnold Hedgeman, "One Woman's Opinion," 1959, clipping, Box 162, AAH-N.
34. Hedgeman, "Speech," n.d., Box 166, AAH-N.
35. Ramona Bowden, "Racial Strife in Continuation of US Revolution," March 16, 1967, clipping, Box 157, AAH-N.

36. "Mrs. Hedgeman Seeks Rangel Assembly Seat," *NYAN*, March 16, 1968. See also *NYT*, March 14, 1968; *NYT*, June 30, 1968.

37. Hedgeman, *The Gift of Chaos*, 188. See also "Notes on Manhattanville College," Box 88, AAH-N.

38. Anna Arnold Hedgeman, "Minutes of Directions Committee, CUNY School of Education," 1970, Box 7, Folder 5, AAH-SC.

39. Boxes 87–92 of the Anna Arnold Hedgeman Papers, AAH-N, contain notes, letters of invitation and thanks, proposals, and a host of materials related to her work to diversify faculty and curricula in schools and colleges.

40. Jeremy Larner, "The New York School Crisis," 1966, Box 86, AAH-N. In 1970 there were an estimated thirty-five thousand drug addicts in Harlem, twelve thousand of them children. See "Congressman Rangel Fights International Narcotics Traffic," *Congressional Record*, February 18, 1971, Box 61, AAH-N.

41. Anna Arnold Hedgeman, "Minutes of Directions Committee, CUNY School of Education," n.d., Box 7, Folder 5, AAH-SC.

42. "Proposal for an Adult Career Opportunities Program," 1974, Box 86, AAH-N.

43. "Evaluation of State Urban Education Projects in Community School District 9, 1972–1973," June 1973, Box 86, AAH-N.

44. Anna Arnold Hedgeman, "Negroes of New York," n.d., Box 171, AAH-N.

45. "She Worked 22 Years to Make March a Reality," 1982, *NL* (Philadelphia), clipping, Box 171, AAH-N.

46. Anna Arnold Hedgeman, "Notes for Introduction to Book on Black Women," n.d., Box 135, AAH-N.

47. Charlayne Hunter, "Clipping, New York Times," August 11, 1971, Box 9, AAH-SC.

48. Genna Rae McNeil, "Letter to Anthony Summers," February 5, 1981, Box 72, AAH-N.

49. Nelson Rockefeller, "Letter to Anna Arnold Hedgeman," April 8, 1968, Box 21, AAH-N.

50. Joy Zollner, "Letter to Anna Arnold Hedgeman," April 2, 1973, Box 2, Folder 23, AAH-SC; Hope P. White-Davis, "Letter to Anna Arnold Hedgeman," September 28, 1979, Box 12, Folder 22, AAH-SC; United Nations, "Seminar on Women in Political Participation," October 29–31, 1979, Box 168, AAH-N.

51. Eleanor Roosevelt, "Letter to Anna Arnold Hedgeman," n.d., Box 2, Folder 14, AAH-SC; Anna Arnold Hedgeman, "Notes on the Death of Eleanor Roosevelt," n.d., Box 172, AAH-N.

52. Anna Arnold Hedgeman, "Letter to J. Daniel White," April 13, 1969, Box 2, Folder 21, AAH-SC.

53. "Propose Statues of Black Heroes along 125th Street," *NYAN*, May 25, 1974.

54. Anna Arnold Hedgeman, "Notes on Martin Luther King Birthday," 1983, Box 70, AAH-N.

55. Renee Ferguson, "A White Fad? The Negro and Women's Lib," *LAT*, October 13, 1970.

56. "Notes," n.d., Box 92, AAH-N; Chris Filner, Invitation to "Liberation: Do You Want to Pay the Price?" symposium, July 18, 1973, Box 63, AAH-N; Anna Arnold Hedgeman, "Letter to Jewel Graham," November 22, 1981, Box 129, AAH-N.

57. Anna Arnold Hedgeman, "Letter to Geraldine Rickman, National Association of Black Professional Women in Higher Education," March 29, 1976, Box 60, AAH-N.

58. Fisk University, "Citation for Merritt Hedgeman, Society of Golden Sons and Daughters," 1980, Box 146, AAH-N.

59. "Merritt Hedgeman, Tenor," n.d., Box 172, AAH-N.

60. Merritt Hedgeman, "The Dedication of the Schomburg Center," *NYA*, October 18, 1980; Jesse H. Walker, "Loving Tribute Paid to Hedgemans," *NYAN*, March 31, 1990.

61. Anna Arnold Hedgeman, "Letter to Pauli Murray," January 13, 1984, Box 72, AAH-N. On Roy Wilkins of the NAACP and black studies, see "Wilkins Assails Black Studies," *New York Post*, clipping, May 13, 1969, Box 78, AAH-N. Hedgeman was also opposed to the NAACP's argument that civil rights, not the war in Vietnam, should remain the business of civil rights groups. See Hall, *Peace and Freedom*.

62. Fred Samuel, "Letter to Joseph J. Christian, Chair, New York City Housing Authority," August 2, 1979, Box 64, AAH-N; "Lindsay Offers Jobs to Out-of-Towners," *NYAN*, October 15, 1966.

63. Anna Arnold and Merritt Hedgeman, "Letter to Fred Samuel," November 18, 1979, Box 64, AAH-N.

64. Congresswoman Shirley Chisholm fought to get Social Security extended to agricultural and domestic workers. This made a big difference for black workers. It did not, of course, remedy the cost to black women of sexism within freedom movement organizations. See Biondi, *To Stand and Fight*, 284.

65. Pauli Murray, "Letter to Anna Arnold Hedgeman," December 27, 1983, Box 72, AAH-N.

66. Hedgeman, "Letter to Pauli Murray," January 13, 1984, Box 72, AAH-N.

67. Murray, "Letter to Anna Arnold Hedgeman."

68. Pauli Murray, "Letter to Anna Arnold Hedgeman" January 18, 1984, Box 72, AAH-N.

69. Blanche Parsons, "Letter to Anna Arnold Hedgeman," n.d., Box 142, AAH-N.

70. Wanda Parsons, "Letter to Anna Arnold Hedgeman," September 20, 1982, Box 142, AAH-N.

71. OAA-JS.

72. "In Memoriam: Merritt Hedgeman," *NYAN*, March 19, 1988; Jesse H. Walker, "Anna Hedgeman Made History during Her Time," *NYAN*, February 10, 1990; Jesse H. Walker, "Loving Tribute Paid to Hedgemans," *NYAN*, March 31, 1990.

EPILOGUE

1. Anna Arnold Hedgeman, "Can a Woman Be a Christian in Politics?," n.d., Box 132, AAH-N. See also Anna Arnold Hedgeman, "Letter to Jane Heston," June 16, 1966, Box 13, AAH-N; Anna Arnold Hedgeman, "We Inquire into Unused Human Resources," June 27, 1958, Box 2, AAH-N.
2. Daly, *Beyond God the Father*, 19.

BIBLIOGRAPHY

MANUSCRIPT COLLECTIONS

AAH-FBI   Anna Arnold Hedgeman Investigations, Federal Bureau of Investigation, 1949, 1952, 1963, 1964

AAH-LC   Anna Arnold Hedgeman Papers, Library of Congress, Washington, DC

AAH-N   Anna Arnold Hedgeman Papers, National Afro-American Museum and Cultural Center, Wilberforce, Ohio

AAH-SC   Anna Arnold Hedgeman Papers, Schomburg Center for Research in Black Culture, New York, New York

AHS   Arnold Family File, Anoka Historical Society Archives, Anoka, Minnesota

APR   A. Philip Randolph Papers, Library of Congress, Washington, DC

CBP   Chester Bowles Papers, Manuscripts and Archives, Yale University Library, Yale University, New Haven, Connecticut

HUA   Hamline University Papers, Hamline University Archives, St. Paul, Minnesota

MHS   Minnesota Historical Society, St. Paul, Minnesota

MLK   Martin Luther King Jr. Papers, the King Center, Atlanta, Georgia

MMC   Moses Moon Collective, American Folklife Center, Library of Congress, Washington, DC

NAACP   National Association of Colored People Archives, Library of Congress, Washington, DC

NCC   National Council of Churches Papers, Presbyterian Historical Society, Philadelphia, Pennsylvania

PMP   Pauli Murray Papers, Arthur and Elizabeth Schlesinger Library on the History of Women in America, Radcliffe Institute for Advanced Study, Harvard University, Cambridge, Massachusetts

RFW   Robert F. Wagner Jr. Papers, Municipal Archives of the City of New York, New York, New York

WEBMA   W.E.B. Du Bois Papers, University of Massachusetts, Amherst

INTERVIEWS

AAH-BL   Anna Arnold Hedgeman, interview with Barbara Lewis, 1985, Box 172, Anna Arnold Hedgeman Papers, National Afro-American Museum and Cultural Center

AAH-ED   Anna Arnold Hedgeman, interview with Ellen Craft Dammond, in Black Women Oral History Project Interviews, Schlesinger Library, Radcliffe Institute, Harvard University, 1978; also in Box 162, National Afro-American Museum and Cultural Center, Wilberforce, Ohio

AAH-KS   Anna Arnold Hedgeman, interview with Katherine Shannon, Moorland-Spingarn Research Center, Howard University, Washington, DC

AAH-RM   Anna Arnold Hedgeman, interview with Robert Martin, Moorland-Spingarn Research Center, Howard University, Washington, DC

CAH-JS   Carol Anderson Holmes, interviews with author, 2012, 2013, 2014

GR-JS   Gloria Richardson, interview with author, 2013

GW-JS   Gayraud Wilmore, interview with author, September 24, 2012

IC-LB   Inez Casiano, interview with Lee Ann Banaszak, July 2004, personal archive, Robert Hardy

JB-JS   James Breeden, interview with author, November 25, 2014

OAA-JS   Olive Arnold Adams, interviews with author, August 9, 2012; May 9, 2013

RH-JS   Robert Hardy, widower of Inez Casiano, interview with author, May 2, 2013

NEWSPAPERS AND PERIODICALS

ADW   *Atlanta Daily World*
AN   *Amsterdam News*
BAA   *Baltimore Afro-American*
CC   *Citizen-Call*
CC-P   *Cleveland Call-Post*
CD   *Chicago Defender*
KG   *Kalamazoo Gazette*
LAT   *Los Angeles Times*
NL   *New Leader*
NNJG   *Norfolk New Journal and Guide*
NYA   *New York Age*
NYAN   *New York Amsterdam News*
NYHT   *New York Herald Tribune*
NYP   *New York Post*
NYT   *New York Times*
NYV   *New York Voice*
NYW-TS   *New York World-Telegram and Sun*

PC	*Pittsburgh Courier*
TC	*The Call*
TI	*The Informer*
WA-A	*Washington Afro-American*
WP	*Washington Post*

BOOKS, ARTICLES, DISSERTATIONS, RECORDINGS

Aby, Anne. *North Star State: A Minnesota History Reader.* St. Paul: Minnesota Historical Society Press, 2002.

Ahmann, Matthew. *Race: Challenge to Religion.* Chicago: Regnery, 1963.

Anderson, Carol. *Eyes off the Prize: The United Nations and the African American Struggle for Human Rights, 1944–1955.* Cambridge: Cambridge University Press, 2003.

Anderson, Jervis. *A. Philip Randolph: A Biographical Portrait.* Berkeley: University of California Press, 1986.

Arnesen, Eric. "A. Philip Randolph: Labor and New Black Politics." In *The Human Tradition in the Civil Rights Movement*, edited by Susan M. Glisson, 79–95. Lanham, MD: Rowman and Littlefield, 2006.

———. *Brotherhoods of Color: Black Railroad Workers and the Struggle for Equality.* Cambridge, MA: Harvard University Press, 2001.

Barber, Lucy. *Marching on Washington: The Forging of an American Political Tradition.* Berkeley: University of California Press, 2002.

Barnes, Catherine A. *Journey from Jim Crow: The Desegregation of Southern Transit.* New York: Columbia University Press, 1983.

Barnett, McNair. "Invisible Southern Black Women Leaders of the Civil Rights Movement: The Triple Constraints of Gender, Race, and Class." *Gender and Society* 7, no. 2 (1993): 162–82.

Barry, John M. *The Great Influenza: The Epic Story of the Deadliest Plague in History.* New York: Penguin Books, 2005.

Bass, Patrik H. *Like a Mighty Stream: The March on Washington, August 28, 1963.* Philadelphia: Running Press, 2002.

Bates, Beth T. *Pullman Porters and the Rise of Protest Politics in Black America, 1925–1945.* Chapel Hill: University of North Carolina Press, 2001.

Belfrage, Sally. *Freedom Summer.* New York: Viking Press, 1968.

Biondi, Martha. *The Black Revolution on Campus.* Berkeley: University of California Press, 2012.

———. *To Stand and Fight: The Struggle for Civil Rights in Postwar New York City.* Cambridge, MA: Harvard University Press, 2003.

Blum, Edward J., and Paul Harvey. *The Color of Christ: The Son of God and the Saga of Race in America.* Chapel Hill: University of North Carolina Press, 2012.

Boris, Eileen, and Premilla Nadasen. "Domestic Workers Organize!" *WorkingUSA: The Journal of Labor and Society* 11 (December 2008): 413–37.

Borstelmann, Thomas. *The Cold War and the Color Line: American Race Relations in the Global Arena*. Cambridge, MA: Harvard University Press, 2001.

Bowles, Chester. *Ambassador's Report*. New York: Harper, 1954.

Boyd, Herb. *Baldwin's Harlem: A Bibliography of James Baldwin*. New York: Atria Books, 2008.

———. *We Shall Overcome*. Naperville, IL: Sourcebooks, 2004.

Boyle, Kevin. *The UAW and the Heyday of American Liberalism, 1945–1968*. Ithaca, NY: Cornell University Press, 1995.

Branch, Taylor. *At Canaan's Edge: America in the King Years, 1965–1968*. New York: Simon and Schuster, 2006.

———. *Parting the Waters: America in the King Years, 1954–1963*. New York: Simon and Schuster, 1988.

———. *Pillar of Fire: America in the King Years, 1963–65*. New York: Simon and Schuster, 1998.

Brandt, Nat. *Harlem at War: The Black Experience in World War II*. Syracuse, NY: Syracuse University Press, 1996.

Brinkley, Douglas. *Rosa Parks*. New York: Viking, 2000.

Bristow, Nancy K. *American Pandemic: The Lost Worlds of the 1918 Influenza Epidemic*. Oxford: Oxford University Press, 2012.

Burnes, Brian. *Harry S. Truman: His Life and Times*. Kansas City, MO: Kansas City Star Books, 2003.

Bynum, Cornelius L. *A. Philip Randolph and the Struggle for Civil Rights*. Urbana: University of Illinois Press, 2010.

Cagin, Seth, and Philip Dray. *We Are Not Afraid: The Story of Goodman, Schwerner, and Chaney, and the Civil Rights Campaign for Mississippi*. New York: Nation Books, 2006.

Carroll, Francis M. *The Fires of Autumn: The Cloquet–Moose Lake Disaster of 1918*. St. Paul: Minnesota Historical Society Press, 1990.

Carter, David C. *The Music Has Gone Out of the Movement: Civil Rights and the Johnson Administration, 1965–1968*. Chapel Hill: University of North Carolina Press, 2009.

Carter, Hodding. *A Sword among Lions: Ida B. Wells and the Campaign against Lynching*. New York: Amistad, 2008.

Cha-Jua, Sundiata, and Clarence Lang. "The 'Long Movement' as Vampire: Temporal and Spatial Fallacies in Recent Black Freedom Struggles." *Journal of African American History* 92, no. 2 (April 2007): 265–88.

Chapman, Erin D. *Prove It on Me: New Negroes, Sex, and Popular Culture in the 1920s*. New York: Oxford University Press, 2012.

Chapman, Mark L. *Christianity on Trial: African-American Religious Thought before and after Black Power*. Maryknoll, NY: Orbis Books, 1996.

Chen, Anthony S. *The Fifth Freedom: Jobs, Politics, and Civil Rights in the United States, 1941–1972*. Princeton, NJ: Princeton University Press, 2009.

Clark, Septima P. *Ready from Within: Septima Clark and the Civil Rights Movement.* Navarro, CA: Wild Trees Press, 1986.

Cobble, Dorothy S. *The Other Women's Movement: Workplace Justice and Social Rights in Modern America.* Princeton, NJ: Princeton University Press, 2004.

Cohen, Lizabeth. *A Consumer's Republic: The Politics of Mass Consumption in Postwar America.* New York: Vintage Books, 2003.

Cohen, Robert. "Introduction." In *Rebellion in Black and White: Southern Student Activism in the 1960s,* edited by Robert Cohen and David J. Snyder, 1–42. Baltimore, MD: Johns Hopkins University Press, 2013.

Collier-Thomas, Bettye. *Jesus, Jobs, and Justice: African American Women and Religion.* New York: Knopf, 2010.

Collier-Thomas, Bettye, and V. P. Franklin, eds. *Sisters in the Struggle: African American Women in the Civil Rights–Black Power Movement.* New York: New York University Press, 2001.

Corbould, Clare. *Becoming African Americans: Black Public Life in Harlem, 1919–1939.* Cambridge, MA: Harvard University Press, 2009.

Council of Federated Organizations. "Prospectus for the Mississippi Freedom Summer." In Len Holt, *The Summer That Didn't End,* 197–203. New York: Da Capo Press, 1992.

Crawford, Vicki L., Jacqueline A. Rouse, and Barbara Woods, eds. *Women in the Civil Rights Movement: Trailblazers and Torchbearers, 1941–1965.* Bloomington: Indiana University Press, 1993.

Crespino, Joseph. "Mississippi as a Metaphor: Civil Rights, the South, and the Nation in the Historical Imagination." In *The Myth of Southern Exceptionalism,* edited by Matthew D. Lassiter and Joseph Crespino, 99–120. New York: Oxford University Press, 2010.

Creswell, Stephen. *Rednecks, Redeemers, and Race: Mississippi after Reconstruction, 1877–1917.* Jackson: University Press of Mississippi, 2006.

Dalfiume, Richard. "The 'Forgotten Years' of the Negro Revolution." *Journal of American History* 55, no. 1 (June 1968): 90–106.

Daly, Mary. *Beyond God the Father: Toward a Philosophy of Women's Liberation.* Boston: Beacon Press, 1973.

Dandridge, Gloria R. "The Energy of the People Passing through Me." In *Hands on the Freedom Plow: Personal Accounts by Women in SNCC,* edited by Faith S. Holsaert et al., 273–98. Urbana: University of Illinois Press, 2010.

Davies, Carole B. *Left of Karl Marx: The Political Life of Black Communist Claudia Jones.* Durham, NC: Duke University Press, 2008.

Delany, Sara Louise. *Having Our Say: The Delany Sisters' First 100 Years.* New York: Dell, 1994.

Delgado, Richard, and Jean Stefancic. *Critical White Studies: Looking beyond the Mirror.* Philadelphia: Temple University Press, 1997.

Delton, Jennifer A. *Making Minnesota Liberal: Civil Rights and the Transformation of the Democratic Party.* Minneapolis: University of Minnesota Press, 2002.

D'Emilio, John. *Lost Prophet: The Life and Times of Bayard Rustin.* New York: Free Press, 2003.

Dickerson, Dennis C. *Militant Mediator: Whitney M. Young, Jr.* Lexington: University Press of Kentucky, 1998.

Dittmer, John. *Local People: The Struggle for Civil Rights in Mississippi.* Champaign: University of Illinois Press, 1995.

Dixon, David E., and Davis W. Houck. "Introduction." In *Women and the Civil Rights Movement, 1954–1965*, edited by Davis W. Houck and David E. Dixon, ix–xxvii. Jackson: University Press of Mississippi, 2009.

Douglas, Ann. *Terrible Honesty: Mongrel Manhattan in the 1920s.* New York: Farrar, Straus and Giroux, 1995.

Downey, Kirstin. *The Woman behind the New Deal: The Life of Frances Perkins, FDR's Secretary of Labor and His Moral Conscience.* New York: Anchor, 2009.

Dudziak, Mary L. *Cold War Civil Rights: Race and the Image of American Democracy.* Princeton, NJ: Princeton University Press, 2000.

Dunbar, Ernest. "The View from Lenox Terrace. *New York Times Magazine*, March 3, 1968.

Edwards, Ishmell Hendrex. *History of Rust College.* Jackson: University Press of Mississippi, 1993.

Eskew, Glenn T. *But for Birmingham: The Local and National Movements in the Civil Rights Struggle.* Chapel Hill: University of North Carolina Press, 1997.

Euchner, Charles C. *Nobody Turn Me Around: A People's History of the 1963 March on Washington.* Boston: Beacon Press, 2010.

Farmer, James. *Lay Bare the Heart: An Autobiography of the Civil Rights Movement.* New York: Arbor House, 1985.

Ferrel, Robert H. *Harry S. Truman: A Life.* Columbia: University of Missouri Press, 1994.

Findlay, James F. *Church People in the Struggle: The National Council of Churches and the Black Freedom Movement, 1950–1970.* New York: Oxford University Press, 1993.

Finley, Keith M. *Delaying the Dream: Southern Senators and the Fight against Civil Rights, 1938–1965.* Baton Rouge: Louisiana State University Press, 2008.

Franklin, V. P., and Bettye Collier-Thomas. "For the Race in General and Black Women in Particular: The Civil Rights Activities of African American Women's Organizations, 1915–1950." In *Sisters in the Struggle: African American Women in the Civil Rights–Black Power Movement*, edited by Bettye Collier-Thomas and V. P. Franklin, 21–42. New York: New York University Press, 2001.

Friedland, Michael B. *Lift Up Your Voice Like a Trumpet: White Clergy and the Civil Rights and Antiwar Movements, 1954–1973.* Chapel Hill: University of North Carolina Press, 1998.

Frommer, Myrna K., and Harvey Frommer. *It Happened in Manhattan: An Oral History of Life in the City during the Mid-Twentieth Century*. New York: Berkley Books, 2001.

Gaines, Kevin K. *African Americans in Ghana: Black Expatriates and the Civil Rights Era*. Chapel Hill: University of North Carolina Press, 2006.

Gallagher, Julie A. *Black Women and Politics in New York City*. Urbana: University of Illinois Press, 2012.

Gardner, Michael R. *Harry Truman and Civil Rights: Moral Courage and Political Risks*. Carbondale: Southern Illinois University Press, 2002.

Garfinkel, Herbert. *When Negroes March: The March on Washington Movement in the Organizational Politics for FEPC*. Glencoe, IL: Free Press, 1959.

Garrow, David J. *Bearing the Cross: Martin Luther King, Jr., and the Southern Christian Leadership Conference*. New York: Morrow, 2004.

Geary, Daniel. *Beyond Civil Rights: The Moynihan Report and Its Legacy*. Philadelphia: University of Pennsylvania Press, 2015.

Gentile, Thomas. *March on Washington: August 28, 1963*. Detroit, MI: New Day, 1983.

Giardina, Carol. *Freedom for Women: Forging the Women's Liberation Movement, 1953–1970*. Gainesville: University Press of Florida, 2000.

Giddings, Paula. *A Sword among Lions: Ida B. Wells and the Campaign against Lynching*. New York: Amistad, 2008.

———. *When and Where I Enter: The Impact of Black Women on Race and Sex in America*. New York: Morrow, 1984.

Gilkes, Cheryl. *If It Wasn't for the Women: Black Women's Experience and Womanist Culture in Church and Community*. Maryknoll, NY: Orbis Books, 2001.

Gill, Jill K. *Embattled Ecumenism: The National Council of Churches, the Vietnam War, and the Trials of the Protestant Left*. DeKalb: Northern Illinois University Press, 2011.

Gill, Jonathan. *Harlem: The Four Hundred Year History from Dutch Village to Capital of Black America*. New York: Grove Press, 2011.

Gilmore, Glenda E. *Defying Dixie: The Radical Roots of Civil Rights, 1919–1950*. New York: Norton, 2008.

Gilmore, Stephanie. *Groundswell: Grassroots Feminism in Postwar America*. New York: Routledge, 2013.

Goldberg, David. "From Landless to Landlords: Black Power, Black Capitalism, and the Co-optation of Detroit's Tenants' Rights Movement, 1964–1969." In *The Business of Black Power: Community Development, Capitalism, and Corporate Responsibility in Postwar America*, edited by Laura Warren and Julia R. Hill, 157–83. Rochester, NY: University of Rochester Press, 2012.

Goodwin, Doris Kearns. *No Ordinary Time: Franklin and Eleanor Roosevelt*. New York: Simon & Schuster, 1994.

Gonzalez, Evelyn D. *The Bronx*. New York: Columbia University Press, 2004.

Gore, Dayo F., Jeanne Theoharis, and Komozi Woodard, eds. *Want to Start a Revolution? Radical Women in the Black Freedom Struggle.* New York: New York University Press, 2009.

Gray, Brenda C. *Black Female Domestics during the Depression in New York City, 1930–1940.* New York: Garland, 1993.

Greenberg, Cheryl L. *"Or Does It Explode?": Black Harlem in the Great Depression.* New York: Oxford University Press, 1991.

———. *To Ask for an Equal Chance: African Americans in the Great Depression.* Lanham, MD: Rowman and Littlefield, 2009.

———. *Troubling the Waters: Black-Jewish Relations in the American Century.* Princeton, NJ: Princeton University Press, 2010.

Guglielmo, Thomas. "'Red Cross, Double Cross': Race and America's World War II–Era Blood Donor Service." *Journal of American History* 97, no. 1 (2010): 63–90.

Halberstam, David. *The Children.* New York: Random House, 1998.

Hall, Jacquelyn Dowd. "The Long Civil Rights Movement and the Political Uses of the Past." *Journal of American History* 91, no. 4 (2010): 1233–63.

Hall, Prathia. "Freedom-Faith." In *Hands on the Freedom Plow: Personal Accounts by Women in SNCC,* edited by Faith S. Holsaert et al., 172–80. Urbana: University of Illinois Press, 2010.

Hall, Simon. "The NAACP, Black Power, and the African American Freedom Struggle, 1966–1969." *Historian* 68, no. 1 (Spring 2007): 49.

———. *Peace and Freedom: The Civil Rights and Antiwar Movements in the 1960s.* Philadelphia: University of Pennsylvania Press, 2005.

Hamby, Alonzo. *Man of the People: A Life of Harry S. Truman.* New York: Oxford University Press, 1995.

Hamilton, Dona C., and Charles V. Hamilton. *The Dual Agenda: Race and Social Welfare Policies of Civil Rights Organizations.* New York: Columbia University Press, 1997.

Harley, Sharon. "'Chronicle of a Death Foretold': Gloria Richardson, the Cambridge Movement, and the Radical Black Activist Tradition." In *Sisters in the Struggle: African American Women in the Civil Rights–Black Power Movements,* edited by Bettye Collier-Thomas and V. P. Franklin, 174–96. New York: New York University Press, 2001.

Harris, Duchess. "From the Kennedy Commission to the Combahee Collective: Black Feminist Organizing, 1960–1980." In *Sisters in the Struggle: African American Women,* edited by Bettye Collier-Thomas and V. P. Franklin, 280–305. New York: New York University Press, 2001.

Harris, LaShawn. "Marvel Cooke: Investigative Journalist, Communist, and Black Radical Subject." *Journal for the Study of Radicalism* 6, no. 2 (2012): 91–126.

Harrison, Cynthia. *On Account of Sex: The Politics of Women's Issues, 1945–1968.* Berkeley: University of California Press, 1988.

Hedgeman, Anna A. *The Gift of Chaos: Decades of American Discontent.* New York: Oxford University Press, 1977.

———. "The Role of the Negro Woman." *Journal of Educational Sociology* 17, no. 8 (April 1944): 463–72.

———. *The Trumpet Sounds: A Memoir of Negro Leadership.* New York: Holt, Rinehart, and Winston, 1964.

Height, Dorothy I. *Open Wide the Freedom Gates: A Memoir.* New York: PublicAffairs, 2003.

———. "'We Wanted the Voice of a Woman to Be Heard': Black Women and the 1963 March on Washington." In *Sisters in the Struggle: African American Women in the Civil Rights–Black Power Movement,* edited by Betty Collier-Thomas and V. P. Franklin, 83–92. New York: New York University Press, 2001.

Hewitt, Nancy, ed. *No Permanent Waves: Recasting Histories of U.S. Feminism.* New Brunswick, NJ: Rutgers University Press, 2010.

Hogan, Wesley C. *Many Minds, One Heart: SNCC's Dream for a New America.* Chapel Hill: University of North Carolina Press, 2007.

Holsaert, Faith, et al., eds. *Hands on the Freedom Plow: Personal Accounts by Women in SNCC.* Urbana: University of Illinois Press, 2010.

Holt, Len. *The Summer That Didn't End: The Story of the Mississippi Civil Rights Project of 1964.* New York: Da Capo Press, 1992.

Horne, Gerald. *The End of Empires: African Americans and India.* Philadelphia: Temple University Press, 2008.

———. *Mau Mau in Harlem? The United States and the Liberation of Kenya.* New York: Palgrave, 2009.

Hunt, Douglas. *Black and White Justice in Little Dixie.* CreateSpace Independent Publishing Platform, 2011.

Jackson, Thomas F. *From Civil Rights to Human Rights: Martin Luther King, Jr., and the Struggle for Economic Justice.* Philadelphia: University of Pennsylvania Press, 2007.

Jacobson, Matthew Frye. *Whiteness of a Different Color: European Immigrants and the Alchemy of Race.* Cambridge, MA: Harvard University Press, 1998.

Jelks, Randal M. *Benjamin Elijah Mays: Schoolmaster of the Movement.* Chapel Hill: University of North Carolina Press, 2012.

Jensen, Robert. *The Heart of Whiteness: Confronting Race, Racism, and White Privilege.* San Francisco: City Lights, 2005.

Johnson, David W. *Hamline University: A History, 1854–1994.* St. Paul, MN: Hamline University, 1994.

Johnston, Marshall R. "Bombast, Blasphemy, and the Bastard Gospel: William Stringfellow and American Exceptionalism." PhD diss., Baylor University, 2007.

Jones, Clarence B. *Behind the Dream: The Making of the Speech That Transformed a Nation.* New York: Palgrave Macmillan, 2011.

Jones, Claudia. "An End to the Neglect of the Problems of the Negro Woman!" In *Words of Fire: An Anthology of African-American Feminist Thought*, edited by Beverly Guy-Sheftall, 108–24. New York: New Press, 1994 [1949].

Jones, Jacqueline. "Harder Times: The Depression." In *Labor of Love, Labor of Sorrow: Black Women, Work, and the Family from Slavery to the Present*, 163–94. New York: Basic Books, 1985.

Jones, William P. *The March on Washington: Jobs, Freedom, and the Forgotten History of Civil Rights*. New York: Norton, 2013.

———. "The Unknown Origins of the March on Washington: Civil Rights Policies and the Black Working Class." *Labor: Studies in Working-Class History of the Americas* 7, no. 3 (2010): 33–52.

Jordan, June, and Bernice Johnson Reagon. "Oughta Be a Woman." *Sweet Honey in the Rock Selections, 1976–1988*. Chicago: Flying Fish, 1997. Recording.

Joseph, Peniel E. *Waiting 'Til the Midnight Hour: A Narrative History of Black Power in America*. New York: Henry Holt, 2006.

Kasher, Steven. *The Civil Rights Movement: A Photographic History, 1954–1968*. New York: Abbeville Press, 1996.

Kersten, Andrew E. *A. Philip Randolph: A Life in the Vanguard*. Lanham, MD: Rowman and Littlefield, 2007.

———. *Race, Jobs, and the War: The FEPC in the Midwest, 1941–46*. Urbana: University of Illinois Press, 2000.

Kesselman, Louis C. *The Social Politics of FEPC: A Study in Reform Pressure Movements*. Chapel Hill: University of North Carolina Press, 1948.

Kessler-Harris, Alice. *In Pursuit of Equity: Women, Men, and the Quest for Economic Citizenship in 20th-Century America*. Oxford: Oxford University Press, 2001.

King, Coretta S. *My Life with Martin Luther King, Jr.* New York: Holt, Rinehart, and Winston, 1969.

King, Desmond. *Separate and Unequal: African Americans and the U.S. Federal Government*. New York: Oxford University Press, 2007.

King, Martin L., Jr. "A Challenge to the Churches and Synagogues." In *Race: Challenge to Religion*, edited by Matthew Ahmann, 155–69. Chicago: Regnery, 1963.

———. "Letter from Birmingham Jail." In *Why We Can't Wait*, 85–110. Boston: Beacon Press, 2011.

King, Mary. *Freedom Song: A Personal Story of the 1960s Civil Rights Movement*. New York: Morrow, 1887.

Klopfer, Susan, Fred Klopfer, and Barry Klopfer. *Where Rebels Roost: Mississippi Civil Rights Revisited*. lulu.com, 2005.

Kluger, Richard. *Simple Justice: The History of* Brown v. Board of Education *and Black America's Struggle for Equality*. New York: Vintage, 2004.

Lanker, Brian. *I Dream a World: Portraits of Black Women Who Changed America*. New York: Stewart, Tabori, and Chang, 1989.

Lantz, Herman R. *A Community in Search of Itself; A Case History of Cairo, Illinois*. Carbondale: Southern Illinois University Press, 1972.

Lass, William E. *Minnesota: A History*. New York: Norton, 1998.

Lawson, Steven. *Running for Freedom: Civil Rights and Black Politics in America since 1941*. New York: McGraw-Hill, 1997.

Lee, Chana Kai. *For Freedom's Sake: The Life of Fannie Lou Hamer*. Urbana: University of Illinois Press, 1999.

Leuchtenburg, William E. *In the Shadow of FDR: From Harry Truman to Barack Obama*. Ithaca, NY: Cornell University Press, 2009.

Levine, Daniel. *Bayard Rustin and the Civil Rights Movement*. New Brunswick, NJ: Rutgers University Press, 2000.

Lewis, Andrew B. *The Shadows of Youth: The Remarkable Journey of the Civil Rights Generation*. New York: Hill and Wang, 2009.

Lewis, David Levering. *When Harlem Was in Vogue*. New York: Knopf, 1980.

Lewis, John. *Walking with the Wind: A Memoir of the Movement*. New York: Simon and Schuster, 1998.

Lieberman, Robbie. "'Another Side of the Story': African American Intellectuals Speak Out for Peace and Freedom during the Early Cold War Years." In *Anticommunism and the African American Freedom Movement*, edited by Robbie Lieberman and Clarence Lang, 17–50. New York: Palgrave Macmillan, 2009.

Lipsitz, George. *The Possessive Investment in Whiteness: How White People Profit from Identity Politics*. Philadelphia: Temple University Press, 1998.

Litwack, Leon. *Trouble in Mind: Black Southerners in the Age of Jim Crow*. New York: Knopf, 1998.

Lorrin, Thomas. *Puerto Rican Citizen: History and Political Identity in Twentieth-Century New York*. Chicago: University of Chicago Press, 2010.

Love, Spencie. *One Blood: The Death and Resurrection of Charles R. Drew*. Chapel Hill: University of North Carolina Press, 1996.

Lyon, Carter D. "'Doing a Little Something to Pave the Way for Others': Participants of the Church Visit Campaign to Challenge Jackson's Segregated Sanctuaries." In *The Civil Rights Movement in Mississippi*, edited by Ted Ownby, 138–56. Jackson: University Press of Mississippi, 2013.

MacLean, Nancy. *Freedom Is Not Enough: The Opening of the American Workplace*. Cambridge, MA: Harvard University Press, 2008.

Manning, Christopher. *William L. Dawson and the Limits of Black Electoral Leadership*. DeKalb: Northern Illinois University Press, 2009.

Marks, Carole. *Farewell—We're Good and Gone: The Great Black Migration*. Bloomington: Indiana University Press, 1989.

Masur, Kate. "Patronage and Protest in Kate Brown's Washington." *Journal of American History* 99, no. 4 (March 2013): 1047–71.

May, Vanessa H. *Unprotected Labor: Household Workers, Politics, and Middle-Class Reform in New York, 1870–1930*. Chapel Hill: University of North Carolina Press, 2011.

McAdam, Doug. *Freedom Summer*. New York: Oxford University Press, 1988.

McCullough, David G. *Truman*. New York: Simon and Schuster, 1992.

McDuffie, Erik S. *Sojourning for Freedom: Black Women, American Communism, and the Making of Black Left Feminism.* Durham, NC: Duke University Press, 2011.

McEnaney, Laura. *Civil Defense Begins at Home: Militarization Meets Everyday Life in the Fifties.* Princeton, NJ: Princeton University Press, 2000.

McGuire, Danielle L. *At the Dark End of the Street: Black Women, Rape, and Resistance—A New History of the Civil Rights Movement from Rosa Parks to the Rise of Black Power.* New York: Knopf, 2010.

McMillen, Neil R. *Dark Journey: Black Mississippians in the Age of Jim Crow.* Urbana: University of Illinois Press, 1989.

McWhorter, Diane. *Carry Me Home: Birmingham, Alabama: The Climactic Battle of the Civil Rights Revolution.* New York: Simon and Schuster, 2013.

Miller, Eben. *Born along the Color Line: The 1933 Amenia Conference and the Rise of a National Civil Rights Movement.* New York: Oxford University Press, 2012.

Mills, Kay. *This Little Light of Mine: The Life of Fannie Lou Hamer.* New York: Plume, 1993.

Moraga, Cherríe, and Gloria Anzaldúa, eds. *This Bridge Called My Back: Writings by Radical Women of Color.* Watertown, MA: Persephone Press, 1981.

Morehouse, Maggi M. *Fighting in the Jim Crow Army: Black Men and Women Remember World War II.* Lanham, MD: Rowman and Littlefield, 2006.

Moye, Todd. *Freedom Flyers: The Tuskegee Airmen of World War II.* New York: Oxford University Press, 2010.

Murray, Pauli. "The Liberation of Black Women." In *Words of Fire: An Anthology of African-American Feminist Thought*, edited by Beverly Guy-Sheftall, 186–98. 2nd ed. New York: New Press, 1995.

———. "The Negro Woman and the Quest for Equality." Speech to the National Council of Negro Women, November 14, 1963, reprinted as "A Female Civil Rights Organizer Condemns 'Jane Crow,'" in *The Acorn*, June 1964.

———. *Pauli Murray: The Autobiography of a Black Activist, Feminist, Lawyer, Priest, and Poet.* Knoxville: University of Tennessee Press, 1987.

———. *Song in a Weary Throat: An American Pilgrimage.* New York: Harper and Row, 1987.

National Committee on Segregation in the Nation's Capital. *Segregation in Washington.* Chicago: National Committee on Segregation in the Nation's Capital, 1948.

Neverdon-Morton, Cynthia. *Afro-American Women of the South and the Advancement of the Race, 1895–1925.* Knoxville: University of Tennessee Press, 1989.

O'Connor, Alice. "Swimming against the Tide: A Brief History of Federal Policy in Poor Communities." In *Urban Problems and Community Development*, edited by Ronald F. Ferguson and William T. Dickens, 77–138. Washington, DC: Brookings Institution Press, 1999.

Olson, Lynne. *Freedom's Daughters: The Unsung Heroines of the Civil Rights Movement from 1830 to 1970.* New York: Scribner, 2001.

Osofsky, Gilbert. *Harlem: The Making of a Ghetto: Negro New York, 1890–1930.* New York: Harper and Row, 1968.

Patterson, James T. *Brown v. Board of Education: A Civil Rights Milestone and Its Troubled Legacy.* New York: Oxford University Press, 2002.

———. *Freedom Is Not Enough: The Moynihan Report and America's Struggle over Black Family Life: From LBJ to Obama.* New York: Basic Books, 2010.

Payne, Charles M. *I've Got the Light of Freedom: The Organizing Tradition and the Mississippi Freedom Struggle.* Berkeley: University of California Press, 1995.

Payne, Elizabeth A., Martha H. Swain, and Marjorie Julian Spruill, eds. *Mississippi Women: Their Histories, Their Lives.* Vol. 2. Athens: University of Georgia Press, 2010.

Pfeffer, Paula. *A. Philip Randolph: Pioneer of the Civil Rights Movement.* Baton Rouge: Louisiana State University Press, 1990.

Plummer, Brenda G. *In Search of Power: African Americans in the Era of Decolonization.* New York: Cambridge University Press, 2013.

———. *Rising Wind: Black Americans and U.S. Foreign Affairs, 1935–1960.* Chapel Hill: University of North Carolina Press, 1996.

———, ed. *Window on Freedom: Race, Civil Rights, and Foreign Affairs, 1945–1988.* Chapel Hill: University of North Carolina Press, 2003.

Polsgrove, Carol. *Divided Minds: Intellectuals and the Civil Rights Movement.* New York: Norton, 2001.

Poulson, Susan L., and Leslie Miller-Bernal. "Two Unique Histories of Coeducation: Catholic and Historically Black Institutions." In *Going Coed: Women's Experiences in Formerly Men's Colleges and Universities, 1950–2000,* edited by Susan L. Poulson and Leslie Miller-Bernal, 22–51. Nashville: Vanderbilt University Press, 2004.

Prinz, Joachim. *Joachim Prinz, Rebellious Rabbi: An Autobiography—the German and Early American Years.* Bloomington: Indiana University Press, 2007.

Rainwater, Lee. *The Moynihan Report and the Politics of Controversy: A Trans-action Social Science and Public Policy Report.* Cambridge MA: MIT Press, 1967.

Ransby, Barbara. *Ella Baker and the Black Freedom Movement: A Radical Democratic Vision.* Chapel Hill: University of North Carolina Press, 2003.

Ray, Archibald (as told to). *All Shook Up.* New York: Agape Books, 1958.

Reed, Merl E. *Seedtime for the Modern Civil Rights Movement: The President's Committee on Fair Employment Practice, 1941–1946.* Baton Rouge: Louisiana State University Press, 1991.

Reiff, Joseph T. "'Born of Conviction': White Mississippians Argue Civil Rights in 1963." In *The Civil Rights Movement in Mississippi,* edited by Ted Ownby, 157–79. Jackson: University Press of Mississippi, 2013.

Richards, Yevette. *Maida Springer: Pan-Africanist and International Labor Leader.* Pittsburgh: University of Pittsburgh Press, 2000.

Robertson, Nancy M. *Christian Sisterhood, Race Relations, and the YWCA, 1906–46.* Urbana: University of Illinois Press, 2007.

Robnett, Belinda. *How Long? How Long? African-American Women in the Struggle for Civil Rights.* New York: Oxford University Press, 1997.

Roediger, David R. "An Interview with Elma Stuckey, Poet Laureate of Slave Life." In *History against Misery*, 72–76. Chicago: Charles H. Kerr, 2006.

———. *Towards the Abolition of Whiteness.* London: Verso, 1994.

Rogers, Kim L. *Life and Death in the Delta: African American Narratives of Violence, Resilience, and Social Change.* New York: Palgrave Macmillan, 2006.

Roth, Benita. *Separate Roads to Feminism: Black, Chicana and White Feminist Movements in America's Second Wave.* Cambridge: Cambridge University Press, 2003.

Rothschild, Mary A. *A Case of Black and White: Northern Volunteers and the Southern Freedom Summers, 1964–1965.* Westport, CT: Greenwood Press, 1982.

Rubio, Philip F. *There's Always Work at the Post Office: African American Postal Workers and the Fight for Jobs, Justice, and Equality.* Chapel Hill: University of North Carolina Press, 2010.

Salzman, Jack, and Cornel West. *Struggles in the Promised Land: Towards a History of Black-Jewish Relations in the United States.* New York: Oxford University Press, 1997.

Sanchez-Korrol, Virginia. *From Colonia to Community: The History of Puerto Ricans in New York City.* Berkeley: University of California Press, 1994.

Savage, Barbara. *Your Spirits Walk beside Us: The Politics of Black Religion.* Cambridge, MA: Belknap Press, 2012.

Schaffer, Howard B. *Chester Bowles: New Dealer in the Cold War.* Cambridge, MA: Harvard University Press, 1993.

Schomburg, Arthur A. "The Negro Digs Up His Past." In *The New Negro*, edited by Alain Locke, 231–37. New York: Arno Press, 1968.

Shaw, Stephanie J. *What a Woman Ought to Be and to Do: Black Professional Women Workers during the Jim Crow Era.* Chicago: University of Chicago Press, 1996.

Sitkoff, Harvard. "African American Militancy in the World War II South." In *Remaking Dixie: The Impact of World War II on the American South*, edited by Neil R. McMillen, 60–92. Jackson: University Press of Mississippi, 1997.

Span, Christopher M. *From Cotton Field to Schoolhouse: African American Education in Mississippi, 1862–1875.* Chapel Hill: University of North Carolina Press, 2009.

Starr, Douglas. *Blood: An Epic History of Medicine and Commerce.* New York: Harper Perennial, 2000.

Stotts, Stuart. *We Shall Overcome: A Song That Changed the World.* Boston: Clarion Books, 2010.

Sugrue, Thomas J. *The Origins of the Urban Crisis: Race and Inequality in Postwar Detroit.* Princeton, NJ: Princeton University Press, 2005.

Sutherland, Elizabeth. *Letters from Mississippi.* New York: McGraw-Hill, 1965.

Takaki, Ronald T. *A Different Mirror: A History of Multicultural America.* New York: Back Bay Books, 2008.

Taylor, Cynthia. *A. Philip Randolph: The Religious Journey of an African-American Labor Leader.* New York: New York University Press, 2006.

Theoharis, Jeanne. *The Rebellious Life of Mrs. Rosa Parks.* Boston: Beacon Press, 2013.

Theoharis, Jeanne, and Komozi Woodard. *Freedom North: Black Freedom Struggles outside the South, 1940–1980.* New York: Palgrave Macmillan, 2003.

———. *Groundwork: Local Black Freedom Movements in America.* New York: New York University Press, 2005.

Thompson, Becky. "Multiracial Feminism: Recasting the Chronology of Second Wave Feminism." *Feminist Studies* 28, no. 2 (2002): 336–60.

Truman, Harry S. "Address in Harlem, upon Receiving the Franklin Roosevelt Award." Public Papers of the Presidents: Harry S. Truman, 1945–1953, 923–25. Washington, DC: Government Printing Office, 1964.

Umoja, Akinyele O. *We Will Shoot Back: Armed Resistance in the Mississippi Freedom Movement.* New York: New York University Press, 2013.

"Validity of Municipal Law Barring Discrimination in Private Housing." *Columbia Law Review* 58, no. 5 (May 1958): 728–35.

Van Deburg, William L. *New Day in Babylon: The Black Power Movement and American Culture, 1965–1975.* Chicago: University of Chicago Press, 1992.

Von Eschen, Penny. *Race against Empire: Black Americans and Anticolonialism, 1937–1957.* Ithaca, NY: Cornell University Press, 1997.

Wallace, Henry. *The Price of Vision: The Diary of Henry Wallace, 1942–1946.* Boston: Houghton Mifflin, 1973.

Walton, Anthony. *Mississippi: An American Journey.* New York: Knopf, 1996.

Ward, Jason M. *Defending White Democracy: The Making of a Segregationist Movement and the Remaking of Racial Politics, 1936–1965.* Chapel Hill: University of North Carolina Press, 2011.

Watkins-Owens, Irma. *Blood Relations: Caribbean Immigrants and the Harlem Community, 1900–1930.* Bloomington: Indiana University Press, 1996.

Watson, Bruce. *Freedom Summer: The Savage Season of 1964 That Made Mississippi Burn and Made America a Democracy.* New York: Penguin Books, 2011.

Webb, Clive. *Fight against Fear: Southern Jews and Civil Rights.* Athens: University of Georgia Press, 2003.

Weisenfeld, Judith. *African American Women and Christian Activism: New York's Black YWCA, 1905–1945.* Cambridge, MA: Harvard University Press, 1998.

White, Deborah G. *Too Heavy a Load: Black Women in Defense of Themselves, 1894–1994.* New York: Norton, 1999.

White, Graham, and John Maze. *Henry A. Wallace: His Search for a New World Order.* Chapel Hill: University of North Carolina Press, 1995.

Wilkins, Roy. *Standing Fast: The Autobiography of Roy Wilkins.* Boston: Da Capo Press, 1994.

Williams, Lea E. *Servants of the People: The 1960s Legacy of African American Leadership.* New York: St. Martin's Press, 1996.

Wilmore, Gayraud S. *Black Religion and Black Radicalism: An Interpretation of the Religious History of African Americans.* Maryknoll, NY: Orbis Books, 1998.

Wilson, Sondra K. *Meet Me at the Theresa: The Story of Harlem's Most Famous Hotel.* New York: Atria Books, 2004.

Woodruff, Nan E. *American Congo: The African American Struggle in the Delta.* Cambridge, MA: Harvard University Press, 2003.

Wu, Ellen D. *The Color of Success: Asian Americans and the Origins of the Model Minority.* Princeton, NJ: Princeton University Press, 2014.

ONLINE SOURCES

American Red Cross. "Contributions of People of Color." http://www.redcross.org/about-us/history/red-cross-american-history/contributions-people-of-color.

Beverton, Alys. "Fauset, Crystal Bird." BlackPast.org. http://www.blackpast.org/aah/fauset-crystal-bird-1894-1965.

Caldwell, Earl. "Harlem." Robert C. Maynard Institute for Journalism Education. http://mije.org/historyproject/caldwell_journals/chapter9.

George Washington University. The Eleanor Roosevelt Papers Project. http://www.gwu.edu/~erpapers/teachinger/glossary/office-civilian-defense.cfm.

Goldring/Woldenberg Institute of Southern Jewish Life. "Holly Springs." Encyclopedia of Southern Jewish Communities, 2014. http://www.isjl.org/mississippi-holly-springs-encyclopedia.html.

Hamline University. "Hamline History." http://www.hamline.edu/about/history.html.

Hedgeman, Anna Arnold. "Letter to Martin Luther King, Jr.," October 26, 1966, http://www.thekingcenter.org/archives/document/letter-anna-hedgeman-mlk.

King, Martin Luther. "It Is Not Enough to Condemn Black Power," October 1, 1966, http://www.thekingcenter.org/archive/document/it-not-enough-condemn-black-power

Miller Center of Public Affairs, University of Virginia. "Bess Truman." http://miller-center.org/president/essays/truman-1945-firstlady.

Schomburg Center for Research in Black Culture. "In Motion: The African American Migration Experience." http://www.inmotionaame.org/index.cfm;jsessionid=f83032813014372188404527bhcp=1.

Steil, Mark. "Recalling the 1918 Flu Pandemic." Minnesota Public Radio, May 8, 2009. http://www.mprnews.org/story/2009/05/07/1918flu.

INDEX

on racial discrimination, 201
  resignation of, 211
police, 159, 189–90
Poston, Mary, 20–22
poverty. *See also* economic justice
  in black communities, 195–96
  education and, 39–40
  efforts to eradicate, 143
  in Mississippi, 36–37, 39–40, 203
  NOW's task force on, 232
  race link to, 28, 30
  urban crisis and, 198
Powell, Adam Clayton, Jr.,
  145–46, 261n15
Powell, Adam Clayton, Sr., 72
presidential elections. *See* Eisenhower,
  Dwight D.; Truman, Harry S.
Price, Leontyne, 36
Prinz, Joachim, 173, 268n6
Progressive Party, 111–13
Prohibition, 11, 19
Project 100, 000, 216
Protestants, 11
  African Americans as, 152
  for Civil Rights Bill, 175–76, 182
  in March on Washington, 3, 158
  race relations and, 79–80
  white, leaders, 153
publications and speeches, 97, 146, 163,
  223, 225
public transportation. *See*
    train travel
  Freedom Rides for, 42
  segregation and racial discrimination
    in, 32, 43, 101–2, 242n14
  in World War II, 84
Puerto Rican community, 107
  campaign with African Americans in
    Bronx, 147–49
  empowering, 77–78
  women in NOW from, 209–10

race relations
  education and Christianity with, 156
  NCNW on international, 129
  paradox of, 214
  Protestants and, 79–80
  at Rust College, 41–42
  during World War II, 83, 84–86
  at YWCA, 50
Race Relations Sunday, 154, 158,
  265n22, 265n24
racial discrimination and injustice,
  243n63. *See also* Jim Crow system;
    segregation
  in armed forces, 88–89, 96
  in blood donations, 86–87
  in childhood, 16–18
  Christianity and, 3, 22, 48, 63, 152,
    171, 184
  in education, 20, 22–23, 34–36, 44,
    153, 186, 222–23
  in employment, 53–54, 62, 77, 88,
    197, 229
  in government positions, 117–19
  at Hamline University, 20, 22–23
  in housing, 66–67, 141, 248n11
  international relations and, 102,
    127–28, 132–33
  Jews and, 90
  legislation compared to action for, 178
  legislation outlawing, 175
  as life-long adversary, 229
  in North, 45, 190–91, 198
  at OCD, 90
  parents' reaction to, 55
  in politics, 140, 141,
    200–201, 262n66
  in public transportation, 32, 43,
    101–2, 242n14
  racial integration as solution to, 51–52
  religion and, 3, 4, 10, 22, 48
  in restaurants, 101, 102